Masterly Batting

100 Great Test Centuries

Compiled and Edited by

Patrick Ferriday & Dave Wilson

First published in Great Britain by
VON KRUMM PUBLISHING
21 Sackville Road
Hove BN3 3WA
www.vonkrummpublishing.co.uk

A CIP record of this book is available from the British Library.

Cover and all interior graphic design by Stewart Karl Davies

Printed and Bound in Great Britain
by Berforts Information Press Ltd. Stevenage

ISBN 978-0-9567321-1-8

Acknowledgments

In the beginning we were five and without the efforts of Martin Chandler, Sean Ehlers and Rodney Ulyate the research would never have finished.

Once the list was completed, the first 75 essays needed to be written and thanks are due to all those that threw their knowledge and energy into this task – all credits for these pieces are listed at the back of the book.

Thanks to all those who offered help and encouragement once the writing process had started. John Woodcock cautioned against subtitling the book *100 Greatest Test Centuries*, Peter Willey gave insights into the art of Lara and Gilchrist (amongst others) and numerous others joined in if only to tell us we had the wrong innings.

Rob Smyth has encouraged and engaged throughout, Andy Baynton-Power has proofed like a demon, Stephen Chalke has been himself and James Mettyear was always trenchant.

The final 25 essays are the heart of the book and for all the words and efforts of all the authors involved we are very grateful and regard ourselves as very fortunate to have received so much enthusiastic help and masterly writing.

The brave newish world of the interweb has made much of this possible. Without *Cricinfo, Cricket Archive, Reliance Ratings, UK Newstand* and the *British Newspaper Archive* the task would have been well-nigh impossible. Equally crucial were the endless books and newspapers, particularly the *Times*, the *Daily Telegraph*, the *Sydney Morning Herald*, the *Cricketer* and the *Jamaica Gleaner*. Above all there was *Wisden*. Almost all essays draw on this source and we are indebted to John Wisden & Co. for their permission especially in essay 21.

Introduction

i/Masterly Batting

Better, faster, more intelligent, less able; the comparative adjective litters the linguistic landscape, one of numerous outcrops of the human mind that requires expression. Just as we need nouns to communicate the names of objects or verbs to describe what we are doing, have done or will do, so these adjectives enable us to pursue what appears to be an atavistic need and desire to measure similar, or dissimilar objects, one against one another. Within that comparison a clue to the actual worth may reside.

There is the statement of undeniable fact and there is the statement of belief. Russia is larger than India and a shark can swim faster than a stickleback, empirical evidence tells us these are true. Who can say with certainty however that it is harder to learn Chinese than Swedish or that Clinton was a better president than Kennedy? We may well hold an opinion on these subjects but we must also accept that a marshalling of facts does not mean that a definitive answer can be reached. Then there are the superlative adjectives – the same rules apply; the Pacific is certainly the largest ocean in the world but was Beethoven the best composer?

What we can be certain of is the constant desire to compare, both in fields where a definite answer exists and ones where no such certainty can bring the debate to a crushing and indelible conclusion. And it is precisely these latter cases that are the most stimulating; opinion is reinforced by fact, fact is questioned, opinion reinforced or, where open minds prevail, altered. In collecting, ordering and expressing these opinions we are expressing basic human urges – to compare like for like, simplify complex realities in order to better understand them, possibly learn something new or just blindly flail in a desperate attempt to dominate.

It is this 'like for like' that must lie at the heart of any meaningful, and consequently entertaining and informative, debate. The last months of 1999 were littered with absurd polls on the greatest human being of the twentieth century; like for like in some senses but the boundaries are just too wide. Gorbachev versus Einstein or Mandela versus Curie. By reducing the parameters we can make the subject more manageable. The greatest sportsperson of the century is still impossible but the *most famous* sportsperson might have some legs. It would be hard to look beyond Muhammad Ali and Pele although in India or Argentina, for example, the answer might be different. But at least the superlative adjective most famous allows an introduction of fact and a subject that is sufficiently tethered to prevent it from wandering off into the distance.

The internet is heaving with comparison websites and the narrower the restrictions the more interesting they become. The greatest modern musician? No. The greatest drummer? Still no. The greatest rock drummer? That might be quite fun. At least we can find out what other people think even if there is no definitive answer. As expected it is names attached to hugely successful groups where the drumming is seen as crucial to their 'sound' which dominate – Keith Moon of *The Who* and John Bonham of *Led Zeppelin.* Amazingly enough Ringo Starr rates highly despite John Lennon's famously damning quip. Technical maestros such as Ginger Baker and Danny Carey are frequent choices but by far the most consistently cited name is Neil Peart.....of *Rush.* Successful and of some longevity indeed but it is clearly musical excellence recognised by rock fans and musical experts alike. There is ultimately no concrete basis, and taste and opinion play a major part but, given the status of this band, it is a surprising choice and maybe for that very reason one that has a degree of credibility.

Sport is different. Taste and opinion are still important but it is strewn with facts and figures and at its heart is achievement and competition where players and teams are constantly measured against one another. After this measurement comes the inevitability of comparison as surely as covers follow rain. If we are pitching one player against another then golf and tennis are particularly appealing. Cricket and baseball have attractiveness as team games within which one or two players may dominate – as Rahul Bhattacharya has put it: 'Cricket is only nominally a team sport. It is cumulative rather than collaborative'.

A ramble around the internet supplies any amount of credible comparisons, particularly in the individual sporting arena, and it is interesting to see how some are considerably more aware of their histories and consider the participants of 100 years ago worthy of comparison with their modern counterparts. Tennis is slightly stymied by the presence of outstanding players still at or near their peaks. What is, however, noticeable is the bias to the modern. In the men's game Rod Laver is the earliest significant entry although the women's does go back to the 1920s with Helen Wills Moody. Golf leans towards the modern with Jack Nicklaus and Tiger Woods being dominant but there is room for the serious consideration of pre-war players such as Bobby Jones and Walter Hagen. Heavyweight boxing gives even greater credence to the dim and distant past; Jack Johnson before 1914, Jack Dempsey in the '20s and Joe Louis in the '30s before Muhammad Ali trumps them all. In all these studies it is a given that fitness, professionalism and all the advantages of the modern age would give an overwhelming advantage so a strict comparison is an absurdity – it is dominance over contemporaries and longevity that must form the bedrock of these opinions.

Team sports offer similar disparities. Football slavishly adheres to the second half of the 20th century with Pele, Johan Cruyff and Diego Maradona (in due course they will be joined by Lionel Messi) the three ubiquitous names – Franz Beckenbauer is left on his own to carry the flag for defenders. Gary Imlach has rightly pointed to the influence of World Cup television coverage in this process – 1958 in Sweden was the first. Baseball is very different, showing a passionate devotion to history (if not pitchers) – Babe Ruth (1914-35) reigns supreme while Ty Cobb (1905-28), Hank Aaron (1954-76) and Willie Mays (1951-73) dispute second position. Cricket tends to follow the same path perhaps because, like baseball, it is assisted by the ability to extract individual statistics which allow viable factual comparisons across different eras. And here we start to approach the crux of the matter; can we really compare athletes of different eras even in the simplest discipline? Usain Bolt is the fastest athlete ever to have lived but does this make him the greatest sprinter ever? Many would argue that he is, but not simply because he holds the world record. It is the yawning gap back to the next best that puts him so far above any other 100m runner. Eventually Marita Koch's 1985 record for the 400m will be broken but that will not by any means make the new record holder automatically the greatest ever – let's first see if the new world best can survive intact for a quarter of a century. Of course Serena Williams would beat Helen Wills Moody in an even match but give the latter a few months to acclimatise and it might be a different matter. But could she possibly dominate now as she did in the 1920s? This is almost unthinkable given the depth and level of competition that she would now face. Professionalism has allowed the net to be thrown far wider and tennis players, and golfers, are no longer drawn from an exclusive and privileged club in a handful of countries.

This increase in competition is considerably less extreme in cricket. In fact the increased exposure to other sports such as baseball has undoubtedly contributed to the decline in West Indian cricket since 1990 and the only area of the world that has seen a significant growth over the last 50 years is Asia. The two oldest Test-playing nations have maintained a complex system of league, club, state and county cricket for well over 100 years that has ensured that precious little talent has remained undiscovered. Cricket was already a career to aspire to in 1890 when the alternative might be the danger of a Nottingham coal mine or drudgery of a Sydney post office for considerably less reward.

Comparing individual cricketers across the ages offers a number of very basic and often unfeasible challenges. Bowling has the problem of wildly differing methods so that placing Wasim Akram against Bishan Bedi is rather like hanging a Rembrandt next to a Picasso and trying to produce a valid comparison. Having said that, we do have statistics which can help even such an unlikely search. Wicket-keeping is hard because of the inevitable (and often unpopular) influence of batting ability and this is further complicated by the increase in limited-overs cricket. How far, if at all, would Adam Gilchrist stand above Alan Knott or Bert Oldfield without his great one-day feats? Allrounders should be equally difficult except that Garry Sobers shreds all opposition with the exception of WG Grace although even here there will be voices for Jacques Kallis, Ian Botham and Keith Miller. And as for batting; the arguments against Don Bradman have always had a hollow ring but beyond him the possibilities are endless. If asked to nominate the greatest ever West Indian batsman, an overwhelming majority would plump for Viv Richards yet it is perfectly reasonable to make a cogent case that he is not even one of the best three. The boundaries are just too ill-defined and a statistical comparison between Richards, Brian Lara, George Headley and Sobers is inconclusive. Ray Robinson likened comparing Grace and Victor Trumper with Bradman and Denis Compton as placing the Pyramids next to Selfridges – one could now easily throw in the E-type Jaguar of Graeme Pollock and Greg Chappell with the iPod of Sachin Tendulkar or Ricky Ponting.

In many senses Test cricket has remained wonderfully unchanged over the last 100 years and it is one of the great pleasures to know that Bill O'Reilly or Hedley Verity could step straight out of the 1930s and start taking wickets or that Headley and Stan McCabe would need just an hour or two to accustom themselves to a modern bat before displaying their brilliance. Don Bradman was convinced that 'any champion of any era would have been a champion in any other era. It is just a question of adaptability.' The idea that over the last 130 years cricket has simply moved in favour of batsmen is just not true.

Of course the rules have been tinkered with over the years. Increasing the size of the stumps in 1931 and the 1935 change to the lbw law were advantageous to bowlers while the front-foot rules and pitch covering gave batsmen a helping hand. Batting equipment has improved enormously but this is countered by improvements in the depth of bowling in most teams while fielding nowadays can scarcely be compared with that only 30 years ago. The DRS may prove to be equally important although where the favouritism lies is not yet clear.

The current list of batsmen (July 2013) with over 10,000 Test runs shows 11 men, all but one averaging over 50. The highest average of these is Kumar Sangakkara's but he stands only 11th in the all-time average (minimum 20 innings) list. Of those above him, five played either exclusively or mostly before 1939. Such a figure was unthinkable before 1914 in international cricket (although Stanley Jackson was just under 49) but records since then indicate a fairly level playing field in terms of balance between bat and ball, with certain peaks and troughs, so figures are at the very least useful in guiding us towards the great performers. But can we really ignore a man such as Victor Trumper who managed 11 centuries on the rain-soaked pitches of England in 1902, scored a century before lunch in a Test and averaged 16 more than any team-mate on that tour? Furthermore this brilliance was continued over a period of 13 years and even as Bradman was nearing retirement there were men who had played against both who were quite certain where the greater genius lay. But Trumper was not an accumulator of huge scores. He cared nothing for statistics and averaged a mere 39.04. If proof were needed that statistics alone are not enough in establishing value, then VT Trumper is that proof. This is precisely what Ray Robinson was thinking of when he wrote: 'Statistics are like rat-traps; apt to snap on the wrong paws.'

We should beware nevertheless that on one day Trumper could show his genius and here we can legitimately compare the short moment of one of his bewitching centuries against other wonders of batsmanship; Wally Hammond or Neil Harvey, Pollock or Sunil Gavaskar. But, 'such batting,' wrote CLR James, 'can come only at moments, and until they come the unfortunate artist has the disruptive task of adjusting himself to what he can do in relation to what he knows is possible.'

Now we have a valid and achievable goal – a serious study of the greatest innings. It is reasonable to assume that we narrow the search to international cricket where competition at the highest level will produce performances of the highest class. The axe next falls on the size of the innings. A three-figure score is the obvious starting point even though we then lose, for example, Gavaskar's nomination for the greatest that he saw – Gundappa Viswanath's unbeaten 97 against the West Indians at Chennai in 1975. How many other gems do we lose? Ted Dexter's blistering 70 off Hall and Griffith at Lord's in 1963 has stayed in the mind of all who saw it – Basil Butcher's century in the same match certainly should also be remembered. So should we cut off at 50 – and then lose Jack Hobbs' masterful 49 on a dreadful Melbourne gluepot, the innings he nominated as better than any of his 199 hundreds? No, the century has a special redolence and it is right that the search starts here.

Objectivity has to be central to the entire exercise. The aim is to find the greatest expression of skill and ability displayed in the almost fleeting space of one innings and for this we need to assess the challenge, the pressure, the contribution and even the *negatives*. We do have at our disposal a number of statistics and these play a part in the final analysis but to presume that a purely statistical exercise can shed much light is fanciful. We know which was the biggest (Lara), we know which was the fastest (Richards) and we also know which provided the greatest percentage of the total team score (Charles Bannerman) but even relying on these three certainties would be a subjective exercise because they must be given a weighting to find a total reading and this weighting of relative importance is in the eye of the beholder. So if we are using subjective assessments based on intensive and extensive research and an intimate knowledge of cricket history, then why not go the whole hog and include all the elements that comprise a great innings? The three already noted (size, speed and percentage) are a good starting point; add to these the bowling attack, the batting conditions, the compatibility of these two, the effect of the innings on the match in question and its effect on the series in turn. Stir in the fault factor in terms of chances given and finally include all other factors under the umbrella of 'intangibles' – this will include injuries, particular pressure such as captaincy, contemporary praise or criticism and even negatives such as running out a partner. Now we have 10 categories. Three are almost purely statistical and the others require a mixture of subjective and objective rating.

One other feature must, unfortunately, be dismissed – beauty, grace or elegance. David Frith has written that *great* refers to practical effectiveness as epitomised by Bradman while *Great* relies to some degree on aesthetic appeal. Writing in the 1970s he thought Hammond was the closest to combining the two and of batsmen of that era Greg Chappell was the nearest to the Holy Grail. But what is this aesthetic appeal, this grace, this beauty? Certain elements must be present; time to spare, light footwork, classical orthodoxy with a hint of the buccaneer, a wide range of shots with maybe a bias to the off side and ease of execution – these seem given credentials and yet the beauty remains in the eye of the beholder. Some may say the extravagant back-lift of Sobers or Lara may be a stigma, others would point to the thrill of such extravagance. Greg Chappell and Rahul Dravid were superbly orthodox and balanced – maybe overly so. Is there beauty in the brutal and frightening aggression of a Gilchrist, Gayle or Sehwag? In an area so reliant on opinion there is also the matter of received opinion to consider. The old turkey of the innate beauty of left handers is probably a result of the rarer days for 'cack-handers' when Frank Woolley bestrode the shires on both sides of World War I. After a long gap, his mantle was languidly accepted in England by David Gower. But for every Woolley there was a Mead and for every Gower a Trescothick as if to balance the equation and bury the turkey.

These 10 categories cover the four elements identified above. *Challenge* in the form of conditions, bowling attack and the suitability of one to the other. *Pressure* with series- and match-standing and intangibles. *Contribution* with size, speed, percentage and match impact. *Negatives* with chances and intangibles. With these we can judge as effectively as possible the skill and ability shown in the compilation of one three-figure score. Finally the 10 categories must be weighted in accordance with their perceived relative importance. A great deal of research was necessary to sort through over 2,000 centuries. The number was reduced piece by piece and at each stage a greater degree of double- and cross-checking between researchers was employed to ensure no worthy candidate should slip through the net.

This is not the first study of this kind, the best known appearing in *Wisden* in 2000 with other fascinating attempts made by Steve Ferrier and Derek Lodge amongst others. However it is the lack of manpower that seems to have driven previous work to a statistically-based approach and these statistics tell only part of the story. Duncan

Hamilton faced this conundrum when writing about Harold Larwood; he felt statistics hadn't done justice to his subject even though Larwood did produce some startling figures. His conclusion was that 'if you can't trust statistics you're obliged to rely on anecdotal evidence'. One could hope that what the statistics indicate or imply is then heartily supported by this other evidence – then you know you are on the right track.

But is it really possible to compare? How can we gauge Hashim Amla against WG Grace beyond beard measurements, is it really possible to measure Michael Slater scoring 123 out of 198 with Len Hutton's 364 in a score of 903? Jack Brown's searing series-winning ton against Jessops's legendary deeds in a dead rubber? What about Bradman's triple in a day in 1930 when set against Hanif Mohammad doing what was needed when taking nigh on three days for the same score. Harvey's mastery on a nightmare of spin compared to Kim Hughes on a track built for speed, Headley almost alone and Gordon Greenidge safe in the knowledge that Richards and Clive Lloyd were padded-up as he hammered 214 at Lord's. Saeed Anwar in front of 100,000 and Stephen Fleming in front of scarcely 1,000 – the winning runs of Glenn Turner against the saving runs of Michael Atherton and the ultimately fruitless efforts of Kumar Ranjitsinhji or McCabe.

The permutations are innumerable and each observer will put emphasis in a slightly different place and find a different outcome. This is a valid attempt to quantify what many will consider unquantifiable but it throws up a succession of breathtaking batting performances and in the descriptions, and not the numbers, is the real magic of what these great batsmen achieved.

The Measuring Stick

One – Size Of Innings

Anyone with more than a passing interest in cricket history knows of the triple centurions: Sandham, Bradman, Hammond and Hutton before 1939, Hanif and Sobers in the '50s, Edrich, Simpson and Cowper in the '60s, just Rowe in the next two decades but no fewer than 11 in the following 20 years including Lara's 400. Lately Clarke and Amla in 2012. Twenty-six in all with only Bradman, Lara, Sehwag and Gayle, passing the mark more than once.

The resonance of such a landmark may dwindle with each successive achievement but it will always be the benchmark of a truly mammoth innings, the concentration and sustained skill required still beggars belief whatever the bowling attack. A three-figure score starting with a '3' is guaranteed to deliver a tingle whatever the effect of the innings on the outcome of the match – maybe it is the nature of the solitary marathon that captures the imagination so effectively. Indeed there is plenty of evidence that these triple centuries do not guarantee a crushing victory – in fact just 11 of the 26 resulted in victories of any sort. Not that this should really be a surprise; in most instances these innings were played out on easy wickets and the triple centurion has often merely ensured the safety of his team.

Slightly lower down the size scale it's clear that any player and any team will prefer a score of 180 to 110 or 265 to 205 but it is equally clear that 60 on a difficult wicket in a low-scoring game is worth more than a double century on an absolute featherbed. By the same token, a century against Pakistan in 1995 is likely to be a much greater achievement than an identical score against the same opposition in 1953 or even 2005.

Only one form of adjustment has been made in this category and that concerns innings before 1914. Since 1918, scoring has remained remarkably consistent over a period of nearly 10 decades but before that there was a considerable difference – the average innings between 1900 and 1914 was around 25 per cent lower than this post-World War I level and before 1900 it was 35 per cent lower. It is a perfectly reasonable presumption that men such as Shrewsbury, Hill and Grace were the equals of men playing 100 years later or that the Hobbs or Woolley of pre- and post-Great War were equally talented so these vintage innings have been raised as indicated above to establish a level playing field.

Size does matter here but it is not the crucial element. A very general conclusion might be that size often means security and cricket is not, or shouldn't be, about mere safety although one must accept that swashbuckling adventure is not always a viable option.

Two – Conditions

Here we are faced with the conundrum of how to make an assessment of something that, on the face of it, defies statistical analysis. In trying to apply any kind of grade to a pitch it is astonishing how many elements there are and very often an equal number of slightly differing opinions. As if this weren't enough there is also the simple fact that a 20 metre strip of turf may well, even though covered, change dramatically in behaviour over the course of five days as weather conditions change and the effect of a spiked-boot pounding takes root.

Beginning from the premise that a scorecard will give an indication of the conditions, we meet our first major problem. It is reasonable to assume that a Test where 40 wickets fall for less than 800 runs has been played under some influence that favoured the bowler more than usual. Any glance at average team totals in Tests will surely attest to this. Similarly a Test where 1,500 runs have been scored and only 25 wickets have fallen falls firmly into the category of 'batsman-friendly'. But these are the neat and easy matches where there was little change throughout the course of the match and there are countless exceptions. Take, for example, the first Test of the 1894-95 Ashes series where 1,461 runs were scored for 32 wickets over the first five days before a rainstorm on an uncovered pitch was followed by hot sun and the inevitable sticky wicket – the consequence was a further eight wickets for just 53 runs and a 10-run victory for England. Not that an uncovered pitch is required – a dusty day-one track deteriorates as the cracks widen and the bowlers' foot marks come into play and by day four the spinners are in heaven. Then there is the reverse: a day-one green-top which then calms down after two sessions – not for nothing has the successful captain chosen to spare his reluctant openers.

The scorecard may help make a supposition about the wicket but it remains only that even where conditions remain unchanged. In the 1957 Edgbaston Test against the West Indies, England were spun out for 186 in the first innings largely by Sonny Ramadhin's 7-49 but in the second they totalled 583-4 with the same bowler sending down 98 overs for two wickets. There was no discernible change in conditions, England quite simply batted very poorly first time and very well thereafter. And what of the remarkable Test in 2011 where Australia and South Africa bowled one another out for a combined total of 143 before Amla and Smith put on nearly 200 on the same pitch which suddenly looked remarkably benign?

The two crucial starting figures are the strength of the batting and the strength of the opposing bowling and from these we can extrapolate an average of balls bowled to dismiss a team under 'normal' circumstances. This figure will rise and fall dramatically and the biggest constant influence on these fluctuations is certainly the pitch conditions. Having used a statistical method to achieve a reading we are now in a position to check this figure by studying match reports and the assessment of players and observers. Around 90 per cent of all innings showed a close correlation between these two methods and the remainder were subject to closer analysis to establish where the blip lay before applying a final rating.

So we need to use available statistics concerning runs scored in different eras and the strength of the relative teams for an indication of how the conditions were playing, but we also need contemporary reports and memoirs for further detail and to be sure that it is the conditions, and not exceptional or inept batting or bowling that are the dominant influence on the readings we are using. Through this dual method we arrive at a measurement that is both reliable and takes into account conditions that differ during the course of the match and even the course of the innings being studied.

Three – Bowling Strength

This category takes us right to the heart of the matter – who was bowling when this wonderful innings was compiled?

The method of establishing the bowling strength of the opposition is very straightforward; the difficulty is in the details and the anomalies. Quite simply the bowling is assessed by using date-specific ICC ratings, thus the Ray Lindwall that England faced in 1948 is not rated the same as the older version of 1959. When Neil Harvey played a match-winning innings against South Africa in 1950 his main obstacles on a spinning wicket were 'Tufty' Mann and Hugh Tayfield. The former was rated fifth in the world, the latter only 19th and yet their career records leave Tayfield as South Africa's greatest spinner and Mann largely forgotten. But that is how they were rated in January 1950.

The finest attack of all time according to these ratings is the 1958 England quintet of Trueman, Statham, Bailey, Laker and Lock with a four-man West Indian combination of Holding, Croft, Roberts and Garner not far behind. Ratings of this nature have never been considered infallible but where no better and more objective guide exists it would be foolish not to follow their findings.

So much for the simple bits. Even if one is prepared to accept these ICC ratings, complexity still lurks around every corner. Who hasn't looked at the above attacks and thought, 'But what use is that West Indian attack on a slow wicket?' or, 'Who needs two spinners on a bouncy, seaming track?' Then there is the question of injuries, bad captaincy and, above all, a bowler having a bad day and not performing anywhere near his ICC rating. It would be quick and simple just to adopt the combined rating of the four or five bowlers on that given day and say 'this is what our batsman had to deal with', but it would obviously be a solution that lacked any credibility. Even Spofforth and Steyn or Marshall and Muralitharan had off days despite being clearly the best bowlers of their time in the world. This is where the objective ICC rating can and must be tempered by a subjective assessment of how close the bowling attack performed to the given rating. Match reports are now introduced.

Injuries may be simple if serious and the bowler concerned doesn't even appear but what about the sore shin or blistered finger that reduces the effectiveness but not to the degree that the bowler can't bowl at all? Only contemporary accounts or later memoirs will reveal the full truth. Equally important is the form of the bowler. The figures do not always reflect the quality of the performance and it is necessary to adjust the ICC ratings where match reports (and not just one) tell us that a particular bowler bowled well above or below the form we would normally expect. Only then can we get an accurate picture of what 'our' batsman was truly facing. An upward adjustment is also made for each wicket that falls at the other end – the logic is simple: nothing revitalises and inspires bowlers as much as taking a wicket and nothing is more dispiriting than battering against the rock of a Dravid or a Ponsford. Finally the adjusted ratings of the bowlers are organised into one composite figure according to the percentage of balls bowled by each of the members of that attack.

It is this marriage of strict statistics massaged by thoughtful interpretation of the accounts of those who were there that will get us as near as possible to an accurate assessment. This then needs further reflection as we consider the effects of the conditions and the suitability of the bowling attack to those conditions. This is dealt with under Compatibility.

Four – Percentage Of Team Total

Amazingly enough, the highest percentage of a completed team innings by one batsman scoring a century still remains with Charles Bannerman whose unbeaten 165 in the first ever Test, back in 1877, represents no less than 67.35 per cent of the Australian total. Since then 10 batsmen have managed to complete centuries that represent over 60 per cent of the team total; Michael Slater comes nearest to Bannerman with a figure of 66.85.

On the face of it this should be the simplest category to estimate – a figure is available showing how much more successful one batsman was than his team-mates against the same bowling attack and, in most cases, under almost identical conditions. But it is the nature of those very team-mates that requires pause for thought. Take for example the cases of Slater against England in 1999 and that of Graham Yallop, also against England, in 1979 when he scored 121 out of a total of 198 thus compiling a figure of 61.11. The side Slater dwarfed included Taylor, Langer and both Waughs, whereas Yallop's fellow batsmen were Wood, Hilditch, Hughes, Toohey and Carlson. With due respect to the 1979 vintage, there is little comparison between the two batting line-ups and it would be correct to presume that the achievement of Slater is consequently considerable greater than just the 5.74 per cent difference between the two figures.

A short list of batsmen who were way ahead of their fellow countrymen over a period of many years must include George Headley, Bert Sutcliffe, Glenn Turner, Allan Border and Andy Flower. Five superb batsmen indeed but all relied to some degree for their dominance on the abilities of their compatriots. Even Don Bradman could never reach such a level of dominance as long as he shared a dressing room with McCabe, Ponsford, Woodfull or Morris.

For the percentage to be fully meaningful and representative we need to factor in the 'talent' of other batsmen in the same team and make an adjustment accordingly. Using the ICC date-specific ratings we calculate what percentage of talent is represented by the batsman under consideration. For example, we can look at two fine innings from the 1930s.

George Headley 169* against England at Old Trafford in 1933 out of a team total of 375. This is 45.07 per cent of the team total.
Headley's ICC rating after this match was 788 and that of the first seven batsmen in total was 2302. Thus Headley represents 34.23 per cent of the batting talent.
Using 25 per cent as a reasonable base mark a deduction is made for the 9.23 per cent above this mark that Headley occupies. Thus his percentage of the team total is adjusted from an actual 45.07 to 35.84 by deducting the 9.23 figure obtained above.

Don Bradman 270 against England at Melbourne in 1937 out of a team total of 564. This is 47.87 per cent of the team total.
Bradman's ICC rating after this match was 936 and that of the first seven batsmen in total was 3982. Thus Bradman represents 23.51 per cent of the batting talent.
No deduction is made as he falls under the 25 per cent cut off.

The reality is that few innings require adjustment because the 25 per cent figure has been placed deliberately high in order to minimise invasion while recognising the cases of Headley, Hanif Mohammad and even the latter stages of Brian Lara's career to be worthy of alteration.

The other point requiring intervention was that of uncompleted innings. For example, Gordon Greenidge's memorable 214 not out in the match-winning 344-1 against England at Lord's in 1984 is 62.21 per cent of the team total. Clearly this figure is not the whole picture because only one wicket fell. The deduction applied in such a case is 3 per cent for each wicket that did not fall – here it is 27 per cent so the final figure is 35.21. This 3 per cent was arrived at by trial and error and represents a fair compromise.

The reasoning remains throughout; it is easier to dominate the batting in a weak team but a high percentage score does have relevance and resonance so the system outlined above is designed to level the playing field to some degree without flattening it out completely.

Five – Chances

As in diamonds so in batting, perfection requires flawlessness and nowhere is a batting imperfection more quickly recognised than in the dropped catch. For this reason any innings worthy of consideration deserves to have all its flaws studied to establish whether or not it is the genuine gem or just masquerading as one under the glitter of big hitting or weight of runs.

There is no statistical wand to wave here, just hard work and research: match reports, eye-witnesses and a sensible interpretation of the available evidence. Innings over the last 30 years have, of course, been subjected to much closer analysis than those of their predecessors and TV replays have largely eradicated the disputed 'chance' – only rarely is it now open to question whether a batsman really did receive a let-off in this way. But even reports from 100 years ago show a large degree of unanimity so it is fair to assume that we can assess how near we are to perfection in this regard whether the century belonged to Ponsford, Pollock or Pietersen. But there are anomalies; for example, when Glenn Turner played his epic double century at Kingston in 1972 he gave just one chance – that chance was rated 'easy' by *Wisden* but 'difficult' by Tony Cozier in the *Cricketer*. In the absence of further evidence a compromise is the only sensible solution.

The basic tenet is to mark down the innings containing chances over that free from such aberrations. The extent of this marking down is measured in two ways: firstly to penalise the batsman for a chance given early in an innings more severely than that towards the end and secondly to penalise an easy chance more than a sharp one.

It seems entirely fair to say that a batsman who scores 200 runs after being put down twice has been considerably more lucky than one who adds only adds 10 more runs but one could equally argue that the luck was the same in both cases – in the first example the batsman concerned simply took advantage of his good fortune to a far greater degree. For this reason the deduction is assessed on the score at the time the chance was given and not how many runs were subsequently added. As to the simplicity of the chance, it is generally accepted that the dropping of a sitter is considerably more damaging to the reputation of an innings than a fizzing half-chance so the three grades are 'easy', 'regular' and 'hard'. Some may argue that it is not actually the nature of the chance but the nature of the shot that should be judged here but such a verdict is rarely offered and certainly not often enough to be able to base any kind of comparison on it.

Each innings is judged in three parts. The first 80 per cent of the innings is penalised on a flat rate, the next 10 per cent on a sliding scale and final 10 is excused any penalties. Quite simply a chance given towards the very end of an innings is less damaging than one given earlier; the work was largely complete when the slice of luck was dolled out. In addition, any chance given above 300 is discounted. For clarity it is best to look at three sample innings.

Clem Hill, 119 Australia v England 1902: chances at 74 (hard) and 77 (hard). A calculation is now employed to bring the penalties as deductions from a base of 100 available for a chanceless innings. The score at which the chance was given is deducted from 300 and then divided by 12. This penalises Hill 18.8, (300 - 74) / 12 = 18.83 for the first chance and 18.6 for the second. Now these penalties must be further adjusted according to the level of chance. Both Hill's penalties are reduced by 20 per cent because they were 'hard' chances – new scores 15.1 and 14.9 so the final total is 100 - 15.1 - 14.9 = 70.

Mark Burgess, 119 New Zealand v Pakistan 1969: chances at 25 (regular) and 41 (easy).
Burgess is penalised 22.9 and 21.6 for his two chances – the higher figures here represent the lower scores at the time the chances were given compared to those in Hill's innings. Burgess' first chance was 'regular' so stays unchanged at 22.9 and the second was 'easy' and is therefore increased by 20 per cent to 25.9. The final total for Burgess is 100 - 22.9 - 25.9 = 51.2.

Stan McCabe, 187 Australia v England 1932: chances at 159 (hard) and 177 (hard).
McCabe's first chance falls in the 80-90 period of the innings and thus the penalty is reduced on the sliding scale from 11.8 to 5.9. A further reduction of 20 per cent is now made because the chance was rated 'hard' so 4.7 is the final deduction. The second chance is not punished at all because it falls in the final 10 per cent of the innings. The final measurement is 100 - 4.7 - 0 = 95.3

All results are then calibrated to a 100-scale where the figure 100 represents a chanceless innings.

So, to return to the beginning: the perfect innings is chanceless and the more chances given, the earlier in the innings they occur and the easier they are the more the splendour is clouded.

Six – Speed

On the face of it we are presented here with a purely statistical category; that is, one that can be judged on figures that are, for the most part, easily obtainable. The strike-rate per 100 balls is the accepted method (having replaced the often impenetrable runs per minute) and this varies enormously from the giddy peak of 189.66 (almost two runs per ball) of Viv Richards in 1986 to the turgid low of 29.2 (less than one every three balls) of Herbert Sutcliffe in 1929. It hardly needs saying that the conditions and bowling attack played a huge part in this divergence and these are addressed elsewhere.

We do not have exact figures for every innings until after 1973 and estimates based on time at the crease and overall scoring rate for the whole team have been applied to 10 of the 100 innings. This method was rigorously tested against other innings where the strike-rates were available and the degree of inaccuracy never rose above three per cent.

But does the history of cricket between Charles Bannerman and Virat Kohli offer a level playing field? Certainly the vagaries of early Test wickets (not to mention the rules governing sixes) sometimes made quick scoring more difficult but this is offset in the Conditions category. More of a concern might be the improved equipment of the last 20 years. How would Adam Gilchrist have fared with Victor Trumper's skinny willow? Maybe one could set that off against the vast improvements in fielding brought about by the one-day game but what we really need is an era comparison to tell us if there really has been a huge increase in scoring rates.

By comparing the decades it becomes apparent that there is actually no great increase. The strike-rate of centuries between 1896 and 1922 was 48.50 and that between 1980 and 1999, 47.76. The period between 1923 and 1949 easily beats 1958 and 1971 and the slowest decade of all was the 1950s. Arthur Shrewsbury and Percy McDonnell back in the 19th century were more than a match for Vinoo Mankad and Len Hutton in this respect.

Moving into the current century there is an increase to 53.50 which represents around nine per cent. More than half that figure is covered by games involving Bangladesh (Gilchrist, Virender Sehwag and Chris Gayle probably cover the other half) and on early evidence the second decade of this century will be considerably slower than the first. In other words, the strike-rate has fluctuated during 135 years of Test cricket but it has not shown a tendency to keep rising or falling so no adjustment is required.

Another issue that must be addressed is the *importance* of speed in an innings. It is unarguable that a batsman scoring quickly puts the opposition on the back foot; captains adjust their fields accordingly and even the most level-headed bowlers are driven to distraction as good-length balls are dispatched to the boundary. But it would be foolish to presume that the speed of an innings is as important on the first morning of a five-day Test as it is on the last day amidst a frantic run chase. These may be extremes although even here one can see the advantage of Don Bradman hitting 300 on day one at Headingley in 1930 over Geoff Boycott grinding out 106 on the same ground in 1967. More difficult are the intermediate innings. How, for example, do we judge a batsman who comes in after the opposition has been bowled out for 150 at tea on the first day knowing that he can bat for eight sessions and ensure a draw and probably a victory for his side if he does so? This was the situation facing Zaheer Abbas at Karachi in 1982 – speed was scarcely an issue beyond the standard situation that if he chose only to defend he would allow the bowling side to attack.

There are instances where speed is of lesser or even minimal importance and these can only be judged by 'eye' and timeless Tests figure large here. Adjustments are therefore made where the need for speed was negligible and the batsman's strike-rate was below 60; the slower the innings, the greater the upward adjustment. The maximum adjustment is +15 per cent and this applied to only four innings in this list with a further 21 receiving lesser increases. Intrusion was kept to a minimum to ensure that those big hitters were rewarded for their deeds without the canny operator playing within the game's parameters being discounted.

Seven – Series Impact

The basis of measurement in this category is a complete matrix of Test series and the basis of this matrix is to identify which matches have the greatest impact on the outcome of the series and which series are the most important. For this it is, therefore, necessary, for once, to look only at the game in which the innings under analysis was played and how that game affected the series. It is important to identify the importance of the series as this can be seen to have a direct implication on the importance of the innings and, by definition, the pressure under which it was played.

It seems perfectly reasonable to give the greatest weight to the longest series. South Africa were only offered a five-Test series in Australia and England when they were considered worthy opponents and when the authorities considered that sufficient crowds would allow such a series to be a viable financial option. This link between the duration of a Test series and the money it is likely to generate is a constant throughout the history of the game and has been made more complex over the last three decades by the introduction of the various one-day formats. The constant also remains that a five-Test series (six being a thing of the past) is the ultimate examination of the relative strength of two teams and the current fashion for a quick two-match 'shoot-out' can only harm the standing of Test cricket whatever the short-term financial rewards.

The most important match is the fifth and final Test of a series where the scores are level at the beginning of the game and the highest rating is given to the team (and thus our batsman) that wins this match. The least important is a one-Test series and the lowest rating is given to the team losing this match. The team in the first example scores 100 points and the team in the second scores nothing. All points in between are covered, factoring in the possible series standing before the match and awarding credit according to a combination of that standing and the result of the match in question.

Three-Match Series

Series Standing Before Second Test	Team A	Points
1-0 – Team A leading	wins/draws/loses	60/40/20
0-1 – Team A losing	wins/draws/loses	50/20/0
0-0	wins/draws/loses	60/30/10

This example makes clear that the result of previous matches in the series has an effect on the points awarded and gives an indication of the relative merit given to each possible outcome. A win is clearly going to be the best result in terms of its influence on the series.

Five-Match Series

Series Standing Before Fifth Test	Team A	Points
1-0 or 2-1 – A leading	wins/draws/loses	90/60/10
0-1 or 1-2 – A losing	wins/draws/loses	80/10/0
0-0, 1-1 or 2-2	wins/draws/loses	100/50/0

If the score stands at 1-0 after the fourth of a five-Test series then theoretically a draw is as good as a win in securing that series. However, a 2-0 series win is better than 1-0 and attacking cricket is rewarded so the win in this situation would get 90 points and the draw 60. If, however the standing had been 0-1 then the win would level the series at 1-1 to garner 80 points whereas the draw would leave a 0-1 defeat and merit only 10 points.

There is also the question of a 'dead rubber'. Consideration was given to a fixed lower score here but the general feeling was that no points should be scored here whatever the result. This has not stopped innings played in these games featuring in the top 100 but they have suffered as a result.

It is important to stress here that *subsequent* results in the series do not affect the rating. A team winning the first match of a four-match series collects 50 points irrespective of whether that series is then won 4-0 or lost 1-3 – it is the series standing directly before and after the game being studied that determine the points being awarded.

Standing beside the length of the series there is another factor – the relative abilities of the two teams. To account for this, an adjustment is made to all scores based on the ICC ratings of the two sides. The higher the combined total the higher the upwards adjustment to a maximum of 20 per cent with a commensurate downwards rating for two weak teams. The former would include, for example Australia versus South Africa in 1969-70, the latter features, amongst others, South Africa against New Zealand in 1961-62 and India in England in 1976-77. One other slight upwards adjustment is made for Ashes series and those between India and Pakistan. Although supporters of the other six Test-playing nations may not agree, these contests have a particular resonance.

The weighting given to this category in the final assessment has, as it must, taken into account that a brilliant innings can still be played in a defeat but there remains the fact that cricket is a team sport and the ultimate achievement is to drive one's team to victory even if glory can still exist for the vanquished.

Eight – Match Impact

On first inspection, the idea of 'match impact' appears both central to assessing the merit of an innings and also relatively simple to ascertain. Surely in a team game an innings that contributes nothing to the overall result is largely meaningless? Think New Zealand: John Reid in 1962, Bevan Congdon in 1973 or Nathan Astle in 2002? All three played marvellous innings that at least partly defined their careers and yet all were ultimately worthless with a team facing a thrashing being beaten. Of course their respective efforts will have raised team morale and confidence and maybe helped in subsequent matches and also provided memorable entertainment of differing sorts but, in the end, defeat was all but inevitable (with the possible exception of Congdon) and defeat duly arrived.

The aim here is simple – to calculate how far the batsman concerned contributed to the success or possible success of his side. To establish this, the state of play at the beginning and end of the innings in question are measured and the difference between the two provides the first working figure. The second comes from the individual contribution during his stay at the wicket compared to that of his partners. As ever, examples are the most lucid guide.

Neil Harvey: Australia v South Africa, January 1950, Durban. This was the fourth innings with Australia chasing 336 for victory. The score was 59-3 when Harvey came to the wicket thus 277 runs were still required. Australia won. Fifty-two other Test matches have been found with very similar team requirements to this game. Of those, none resulted in wins, 21 in draws and 31 in losses (W/D/L = 0/21/31). Harvey's share was 151 of 277. The result is that Australia's innings while Harvey was at the crease scores a perfect 100 in terms of state of play and result. This represents the fact that no other team has emerged from such a daunting position to win a Test match. This maximum figure is now decreased by the fact that Harvey did not score all 277 runs himself – just the little matter of 151. The final total is 95.8 on the 100-scale which is achieved by comparison with this category's highest-rated innings (i.e. 100) which belongs to Brian Lara against Australia in 1999.

Aubrey Faulkner: South Africa v Australia, December 1910, Melbourne. This was the second innings with South Africa trailing by 314 with one wicket gone when Faulkner came into bat. Similar Tests resulted in W/D/L records of 3/18/22. Faulkner then scored 204 as a further 368 runs were added giving South Africa a lead of 54 with four second innings wickets left. Thirty-five other Tests resulted in a similar situation, W/D/L = 21/9/5. We can then say that Faulkner helped to increase his team's chance of victory from seven to 60 per cent. This is then decreased as he (like Harvey) did not score all the runs himself, to a score which equates to 62.5 on the 100-scale. The fact that South Africa would go on to lose after being scuttled out for only 80 in the fourth innings is immaterial in our assessment.

Once again, figures are then calibrated to a 100-scale where the top innings in this category is given a 100 mark.

As with the Conditions category it was necessary to cross check this statistical approach with a more human appraisal. This 'second opinion' uses a scale of one to 10 starting at the lowest doldrum – 'defeat almost certain'. It then works upwards through 'defeat likely', 'losing', 'under hand', 'level', 'upper hand', 'winning', 'winning comfortably', 'victory almost certain' to 'won'. How far up the scale a batsman has pushed his team is sometimes surprising – Ian Botham, for example, at Headingley in 1981 shifted England from 'defeat almost certain' to 'defeat likely'. It was Bob Willis who sent the side rushing up the scales to victory although without Botham he'd never have had the chance. In essence the result is immaterial, only the possibilities when Botham began and ended his innings.

Test matches have long since ceased to be about two results so into the mix must go further sub-categories such as 'still in it', 'draw possible', 'draw likely' and 'team safe' otherwise where would we put the epics of Gavaskar, Atherton or Du Plessis?

At times it may seem to be like juggling jelly but in fact a reliable system is in operation, or rather systems, which can be checked against one another to provide consistent and reliable measurements. Where the statistical and empirical approaches threw up differing readings a further analysis was employed and after this none of the innings showed more than a five per cent differential.

Nine – Intangibles

This is the clearing house for any information that doesn't have another home and a wide variety it contains too, largely relating to peculiarities of individual innings. The majority will add merit to the innings but some will detract from its overall standing.

On the positive side there is:

Illness or injury, particularly where it detracts from the mobility of the batsman in terms of footwork and running between the wickets

Injury during the innings at the hands of fast bowling which requires courage to revisit the scene

Personal pressure, for example captaincy, fear of being dropped, debut, recent bereavement or particular support or hostility from the crowd

Batting with the tail and modifying the style of play to retain as much of the strike as possible

A major contribution earlier in the game with either bat or ball (also a long session of wicket-keeping) Remaining not out

On the negative side there is:

Batting with tail and failing to protect it to any real degree

Running out team-mates

Particular good fortune such as persistent playing and missing, edging through the slips or being out off a no ball

Perhaps the most important part of this category is the written or spoken word. When Don Bradman or Richie Benaud says this was the finest innings he saw it would be foolish not to take notice although it would be equally wrong to presume that their judgement is final and there is nothing else to say. We are looking for an overwhelming tide of opinion and preferably from disinterested sources. Players are notoriously circumspect about naming their best innings and are very often swayed by the circumstances and where they were in their lives and careers. But if an astute observer, be it player or writer, proclaims 'this was the best' then it is worth looking at what else he saw and rewarding the innings accordingly. Likewise an innings can be downgraded by criticism although given the quality we are studying it is more likely to be 'faint praise'. To accumulate the opinions requires the sources are simple: books, newspapers and interviews.

So, how to assess all of these elements? They are all worthy of inclusion but there is no chart or statistical rulebook; it has to come down to judgement. Somehow it is necessary to decide whether Sunil Gavaskar's 220 against the West Indies was more meritorious than Graeme Pollock's 209 against Australia in 1966 from the point of view of physical impairment. The Indian played the entire match with chronic toothache while the South African could barely leave the crease due to an injured leg and toe. Apart from wondering at the sheer bravery and fortitude of both men one might argue that Pollock was more inconvenienced in strict batting terms but there wouldn't be much in it. Some of the other factors are slightly easier; who could deny the personal pressure faced by Brian Lara when scoring 213 against Australia in 1999 or the achievement of Saeed Anwar in front of the biggest ever Test crowd in the same year. Then there is the sheer bravery of Stan McCabe and Kim Hughes against pace bowling. As to the written word, no innings has attracted such plaudits as Stan McCabe's 232 against England in 1938 and it has been rewarded accordingly – but like all the other categories, this is just one element that contributes to the overall picture.

Ten – Compatibility

With two of the most important categories it is glaringly obvious that there is a link that needs exploring, namely the compatibility of the bowling attack to the prevalent conditions. How many Indian finger spinners have relished a sprightly Auckland green-top or English seamers the dry and dusty languor of Galle.

Only in extreme cases is an adjustment necessary – some 10 per cent of the top 100 were affected. If the wicket showed clear bias to one particular kind of bowling then the bowling attack was assessed for its suitability to these conditions. On a spinning wicket two specialist finger or wrist spinners is the fulcrum, with teams having either three or one (or worse still, none at all) gaining or losing credit. For example, Kapil Dev was certainly assisted by the fact that the West Indies fielded only one specialist spinner on a turning track at Chennai in 1988 – Viv Richards and Carl Hooper were used to plug this shortfall. On a seaming or fast pitch three specialists is the tipping point. For example, when Roy Fredericks belted Australia around the WACA in 1975 he was mauling four specialist pace bowlers and deserves credit for so doing. This increase or reduction was then applied to the batsman under study.

Weighting

We have 10 categories, but of unequal importance – how then to assess their relative worth? There is no statistical safety net and no hiding place – it is opinion pure and simple and opinion has a habit of being varied. One person may say match impact is by far the most important while another may point to a magical potion achieved by mixing size, speed and percentage.

Democracy has to be the only answer and a broad range of cricket followers had their say – when the results were in, the 10 categories were recognised as below.

Weighting

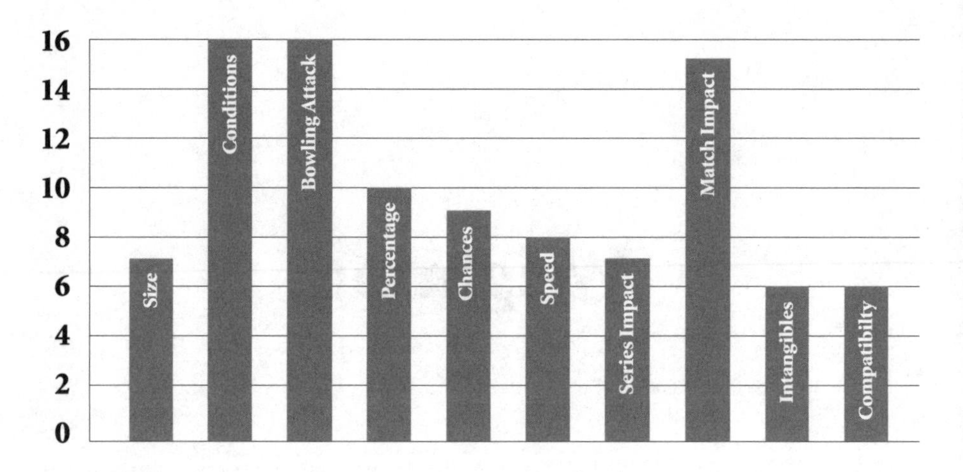

There are a number of dangers inherent in the process of weighting the categories, the most obvious of which is the potential of one to leak into the other and make the whole unbalanced. Is there an inevitability that if an innings is rated highly in one area then it will also receive high marks somewhere else? The clearest potential by far would seem to be the relationship between size and percentage and yet it is the relatively small innings by Charles Bannerman and Michael Slater that lead the percentage ranks while the mammoth efforts of Brian Lara and Garfield Sobers, although dominating the team score, do not come close to matching the peaks of percentage achievements. This fact was relatively easily established. More complex was the desire to be certain that one or two categories were not dominating the final selections. To some degree this pursuit was a misnomer. Of course an innings played on a flat wicket against mainly moderate bowling (arise Hammond 336, Hutton 364 and Hayden 380) would struggle for recognition as it has scored poorly in the two major categories but the essence was to be sure that the final list was not completely dominated by one particular kind of innings. All innings should be capable of recognition whether or not they were played against poor bowling, slowly, on good wickets, with one or two chances or in a dead rubber providing that the other facets were strong enough to outweigh this weakness. And the final 100 does justify this hope. There are great defensive marathons, superb attacking flourishes, winning contributions, innings of brilliance in defeat, dead-rubber epics, huge triples, tiny tons (even one that looks suspiciously like a 99) and even some flat-track bullying – in other words any innings can score poorly in any category and still be resurrected in the nine others.

The importance of the weighting can clearly be seen by comparing the 'raw-data' results with those that are weighted as described above. Don Bradman's innings that finds itself at number 60 would have been number 19 if all categories had been given equal importance, the innings at number 81 would have been number 22 under the same circumstances and number 28 on the list has vaulted up from number 64 due to weighting.

The 10 categories have already been fully explained and many will still dispute the percentages of relative importance applied. What did become increasingly apparent during various testing procedures was the danger of discounting a certain type of innings. For example some might argue that series impact has been overstated, but if that is the case then we have little way of incorporating a negative balance to an innings played in a dead rubber. The aim is to be inclusive not exclusive – raise match impact massively and away go some masterpieces that have been nullified by the failure of team-mates to respond to the example being set. Discount speed and by that disregard the thrilling effect and consequence of an afternoon in the company of Gilbert Jessop or Chris Gayle.

The permutations are endless but these figures seem, after much trying and testing, to be the fairest. Many may disagree but at the very least we can be sure that final list of 100 includes innings that have scored well and poorly in all 10 different categories. It is also worth noting that all eras are well represented in relation to the amount of cricket played – the number of Tests played between 2008 and 2012 was almost the same as that between 1877 and 1951 so for that reason there is an apparent bias to the modern.

Part One
Innings 100–51

Foothills

Sachin Tendulkar – 155*

India v Australia, Chennai 6-10 March 1998

100

With Sachin Tendulkar it's virtually impossible to separate the man from the myth. It was during the series against the touring Australians in 1998, a series billed as pitting the world's champion batsman against the world's champion bowler, that the Tendulkar legend was born as he progressed from the level of boy-genius to fully fledged batting impresario with five centuries against the world champions in just two months. Yet prior to the first Test he was still working on how to counter the threat of Shane Warne coming round the wicket.

Expecting Chennai to be a gift for spin bowlers, Australia decided to pair Warne with debutant off spinner Gavin Robertson. This pair were expected to have plenty of work especially as the depleted opening attack was now Michael Kasprowicz and Paul Reiffel. The rookie immediately endeared himself to his team-mates by scoring a fifty batting at number 10, allowing Australia to build up a 71-run first-innings lead. Tendulkar, felled by Warne for just four in the first innings, came in to bat second time around with India on 115-2, a lead of 44 runs. And here we find the sort of unnecessary embellishment which has built up around the Little Master – reports at the time talk of the match 'hanging by a thread' and that India were in a 'precarious position'; in truth, the game was, at worst, finely poised.

Whatever the state of the match, Tendulkar proceeded to fashion a fabulous innings, exhibiting all of the shots in his considerable repertoire in producing a display described by *Wisden* as 'enthralling'. Steepling sixes, pistol-shot fours and delicate nudges to third-man were executed with equal poise as he treated Australia's attack with utter disdain, to the delight of the massive and vocal crowd. Two century partnerships, first with Rahul Dravid then with Mohammad Azharuddhin, put India firmly in the driver's seat. When Warne finally came round the wicket, pitching the ball unerringly in the leg-side rough, Tendulkar was ready – a six and a four in quick succession convinced Warne this was a bad idea. The man with the best view in the house, umpire George Sharp, considered this to be the finest batting performance he had ever seen.

True, the debutant Robertson often bowled too short, but Tendulkar played every bowler with complete mastery regardless and reserved the harshest treatment for the greatest threat. India eventually declared on 418-4 with a lead of 347, a total Australia were never likely to achieve, and in the end they capitulated for just 168 – victory was India's by 179 runs. Tendulkar's knock had proved to be match winning and he had shown that, in this mood, his batting was definitively the stuff of legend. India repeated the dose the following week in Kolkata and the series was won.

Ricky Ponting – 257

Australia v India, Melbourne 26-30 December 2003

99

This was Ricky Ponting's highest Test score, surpassing his previous best of 242, which he had registered only a fortnight before. He would finish the year 2003 with three double-centuries and a batting average of 100. This one, in the Boxing Day Test match at the MCG, was the most assured of the lot and by far the most valuable. Australia were 1-0 down in the series, having thrown away the second Test, and Ponting had arrived at the crease, batting at number three, in only the seventh over. India's first innings had brought them 366.

Ponting's passage to his hundred was not entirely secure. He struggled to find his balance, especially early on, falling over in the crease as he tried to work to leg. As there was not much swing, however, it caused him far less trouble than it might have done. His off-side game, square and through the covers, was impeccable, and he finished the day unbeaten on 120. The pitch, while variable, was, on balance, a good one – especially against a lethargic Indian attack, hamstrung *inter alia* by Zaheer Khan's gammy hamstring.

The Australians were more cautious on the third day, striving to put the game beyond their opponents who bowled with a great deal more discipline. The bounce was becoming uneven, and batting commensurately more difficult. Steve Waugh, in his final Melbourne Test, sustained a damaging blow to the elbow. Ponting's application, though, had never been better. Where in years gone by he might have been tempted to force the issue, here he was grafting with the best of them. His defence was immaculate and his placement exact. He was, wrote Peter Roebuck, 'so reassuring that he might as well have been smoking a pipe.' His impending accession to the captaincy had never looked more apt.

Approaching 200, Ponting left his crease to Kumble for the first time in the day, hitting him over the top for boundaries in consecutive overs. So unobtrusive had he been all through this innings that Roebuck struggled to recall a stroke of his prior to these two. A push to leg brought up his double-century and he observed the milestone with unwonted exuberance. Recording his second double in successive Tests made him only the second Australian to do so; the identity of the first is pretty obvious.

He became more assertive late in his innings, as the wickets fell around him, farming the strike and refusing easy runs. On 257, he charged again at Anil Kumble, only to proffer an easy stumping. Australia had been 30-1 when Ponting arrived at the crease; he left, some 10 hours later, at 555-9. The *Hindu's* correspondent informed his readers: 'Nothing excites Ponting more than the sight of an Indian bowler.' Ponting's own reaction was priceless. Asked how he felt to have "done a Bradman", he shrugged: "To tell you the truth, I have no idea what you're talking about."

Kumar Sangakkara – 199*

Sri Lanka v Pakistan, Galle 22-25 June 2012

"I had one delivery to get to the 200 and I let the opportunity go...you control your own destiny."

Part philosopher, part pragmatist, Kumar Sangakkara after a scoreboard error denied what he thought was a sparkling double-century in the first Test against Pakistan, becoming just the second Test batsman, after Zimbabwe's Andy Flower, to be stranded on 199 not out. He was left to rue missing out on the chance of a single at the end of that over, tailender Nuwan Pradeep being dismissed before Sangakkara had an opportunity to regain the strike. Despite missing that particular milestone the innings was by no means lacking in records, however, as he became the quickest ever to amass 2,000 runs against a single opponent. In taking only 26 innings to pass that landmark, he thus surpassed Gavaskar, Lara and Bradman – exalted company to be sure.

Although 300 runs were scored on the first day, conditions were not easy – as Pakistani skipper Mohammad Hafeez lamented after stumps on day one: "We were a bit unlucky... there were escapes when we could have got [Sangakkara] out. We have some plans against him and we'll try them tomorrow." So much for that – Sangakkara moved from an overnight 111 to 199 not out in helping Sri Lanka post a sizeable first innings total of 472.

He had earlier been somewhat fortunate to reach even a hundred, as a nervous quick single on 99 necessitated a desperate lunge to beat the throw. That incident was in contrast to his somewhat prudent early start as he found Saeed Ajmal difficult to deal with, an edge past slip being allowed to fall safely. However, once Sangakkara passed fifty he began to open up, taking everything the Pakistanis had to offer in his stride.

Next day, scoring proved even more difficult, 13 wickets falling for 219 runs and the first 11 overs yielding just seven runs. However Sangakkara continued serenely on, though he ran out Rangana Herath when he pushed him for a risky second in order to keep the strike. Finally, with everyone, including Sangakkara, believing he needed a six to reach a double century he duly obliged, removing his helmet in salute only to be immediately brought down to earth again with the news that he still had one run to go. Alas, it was not to be.

Pakistan were unable to match the batting of Sangakkara and were skittled out for just 100, the match result at that point being in little doubt as Sri Lanka ultimately enjoyed a victory by 209 runs. There were no hard feelings on his missed milestone, as he pondered the sagacity of experience; "Now, when you go back and take a breather, you realise there are bigger things than getting out or not out on 199." Not in cricket though, surely?

Dudley Nourse – 231

South Africa v Australia, Johannesburg 24-28 December 1935

97

The young man looked up at the scoreboard from his place in the field: 100-0. The Australian team had already won the first Test comfortably and were now cruising in their first innings of the second match, chasing South Africa's pitiful score of 157. To make matters worse this young man had been bowled for a duck in the first innings by fast bowler Ernie McCormick on a blameless wicket.

Arthur Dudley Nourse was from South African cricketing pedigree. His father Dave Nourse had been a cricket warrior, known as the 'Grand Old Man', who played Test cricket for over 20 years and was to make his final first-class appearance against Australia during this tour. It seems Dave gave his son little practical advice regarding cricket. "I learned to play cricket with a paling off a fence. Now you go and do the same", was all the training he proffered to the young Dudley.

After the fine opening stand of 105, Australia lost regular wickets and ended up with a lead of only 93. Nourse found himself at the wicket on Boxing Day with the score at 90-3 after a sombre festive break. The pitch was now showing signs of wear, especially from the footmarks left by McCormick, and this gift to Clarrie Grimmett and Bill O'Reilly forced Nourse to spend a long time playing himself in and, after taking 20 minutes to open his account, he had crawled to just 13 out of 132-3 at tea. After the break he went on the attack, being especially tough on McCormick whom he repeatedly cut hard to the boundary, with five slips waiting for an edge that did not come. He gave his first chance at 65 when Chuck Fleetwood-Smith dropped a difficult one in the outfield and as stumps approached the home crowd became excited with Nourse approaching his century. Unfortunately they were to be disappointed as he finished the day on 98 of 254-4.

After retiring to bed early, he had a restless night, hearing the clock strike each hour until drifting off at about 3am. He returned to the crease next day determined to bring up his first Test century. The plan thereafter for South Africa was obvious, the other batsmen would try and stay while Nourse went for the bowling with his lovely drives and vicious cuts. His eagerness to attack the spinners almost brought his downfall when a stumping was missed but nothing now appeared able to stop the young man as he mastered the bowling, rushing to his 200 as the other batsmen struggled and rain threatened. Finally, at 231, he was caught in the covers, having registered the highest Test score for a South African batsman.

A combination of rain and a magnificent innings from Stan McCabe in Australia's second dig saw the four-day match peter out into a tame draw – way better, however, than the tame defeat that would have occurred without the sterling efforts of Dudley Nourse.

Stan McCabe – 187*

Australia v England, Sydney 2-7 December 1932

96

In December 1932 Stan McCabe was just 22, but a comparative veteran of 15 Tests, and his record was patchy. His highest international score to date, 90, had been recorded in circumstances that gave a taste of what was to come. In the inaugural Test against the West Indies he went out to bat with Australia rocking at 64-3, Don Bradman already gone and a useful looking score of 296 on the board for the visitors. In the end Australia won the game comfortably but without McCabe's innings, and his fourth-wicket stand of 182 with Alan Kippax, that match may have turned out very differently.

The 1932-33 bodyline series is an enduring piece of cricket history, so much so that the series and its main protagonists, Douglas Jardine, Harold Larwood and Bradman, remain a source of fascination to lovers of the game more than 80 years on. In the first Test of the series, at Sydney, Australia batted first and McCabe came to the crease with Australia, lacking the injured Bradman, precariously placed at 82-3. A few balls later the fourth wicket fell as Larwood produced a spell of three for seven. McCabe went for the leg-theory bowling head on in a pulsating innings. He found support initially from Vic Richardson, grandfather of the Chappells, and this pair added 129 before Richardson succumbed to Bill Voce's bodyline. Bert Oldfield followed soon after but, in Clarrie Grimmett, McCabe found a staunch ally, and by the close he had taken his score to 127. Next morning a refreshed Larwood and Voce ripped out three wickets with only 15 more runs added, leaving McCabe with just Tim Wall for company. Despite the ferocity of the bowling, McCabe marshalled the strike so well that the 10th wicket added 55, of which Wall scored just four, before, for once, failing to protect his partner and allowing Wally Hammond to tease a chance out of the number 11, which Gubby Allen at short-leg gratefully accepted.

The statistics of the innings illustrate what Bodyline involved – only Larwood and Voce were bowling it and of McCabe's 187 more than 100 were taken off the Nottinghamshire pair. Only 18 of his runs came in front of square on the offside, and no less than 19 of his 25 boundaries went to the leg-side fence, 13 of them from full-blooded hooks. In the near rout that was the Australian second innings, McCabe made 32; Australia lost the match by 10 wickets and the series 4-1. Subsequently a number of the England side confirmed that after his sustained assault, dropping the leg-theory tactics was seriously considered.

McCabe's own verdict on his innings was: 'It was really an impulsive senseless innings...a gamble that should not have been made', a view for which all research, unsurprisingly, finds no support. What greater compliment could there be than it was an innings that even Bradman could not have played?

Wally Hammond – 240

England v Australia, Lord's June 24-28 1938

In the first Test of the 1938 Ashes series, Eddie Paynter and Stan McCabe became the first players on opposing sides to score double-centuries in the same match. Bill Brown and Wally Hammond repeated the feat in the very next Test at Lord's. How quickly the once-unprecedented accumulates its precedents. Brown's marvellous 206, carrying his bat, was trumped by Hammond's innings in the first Test covered by television cameras.

It came in trying circumstances. England, batting first, started in atrocious fashion, as Ernie McCormick made merry in humid conditions. The ball swung in sharply to the right handers, and leapt up off a lively surface. Bill Edrich and Len Hutton were quickly removed and when Paynter joined Hammond, after only half an hour, England were 31-3.

Hammond was dominant from the start. His century, reckoned the *Times*, 'might have been marked on the score card from the moment he went in.' He and Paynter negotiated the early strife with equal resolution but things became easier as the wicket lost its moisture, and as McCormick lost his length and speed and run-up. Hammond, not made for mercy, took full toll. His fifty came out of a total of 72 in 68 minutes. His technique was immaculate, but the bowling was ragged. The attack centred on leg stump, with the field placed accordingly, in a bootless attempt to staunch the flow. Bill O'Reilly alone maintained his dignity. 'Fleetwood-Smith,' wrote CB Fry, 'bowled sheer unadulterated muck. I have never seen such rubbish in a Test match before.' Hammond tarred and feathered him, going to his hundred in 146 minutes. His partner, too, began to play with more freedom, and the new ball was quickly made old. Paynter fell for 99, their partnership yielding 222 runs, then a record for England's fourth wicket against Australia. Hammond pushed on imperiously, accompanied now by Les Ames, and met everything with the full face of the bat. A mighty drive split the brave Arthur Chipperfield's groping finger when he had 188, but he gave no more real chances. On reaching his double-century, he pulled a leg muscle, but managed to survive the day unbeaten on 210 with England on 409-5.

The next day saw a record crowd and although less authoritative than the previous day, Hammond was nonetheless able to oblige it with a sequence of Olympian drives in posting another record stand, this time with Ames. At 222, he sustained a nasty blow to the elbow. Then his leg stump was untimely ripped but, with 240 to his name, he had more than done his job. Brian Johnston thought it the greatest innings he ever saw; CLR James said the same. 'Never,' held the *Cricketer*, 'has a finer innings been played.' Australia narrowly avoided the follow-on, thanks almost entirely to Brown, and fought back valiantly to secure an even but dissatisfying draw. If anyone deserved to finish on a winning side, it was Hammond.

Kamran Akmal – 113

Pakistan v India, Karachi 29 January-1 February 2006

94

Depending on your point of view, Kamran Akmal is either a victim or a product of the selectorial demand that a Test wicket-keeper is able to wield the willow with the best of them. One of three brothers to have been capped by Pakistan, his career has been dogged by criticism, undoubtedly justified, of the quality of his 'keeping. At the beginning of his career Akmal's batting was undistinguished, but as his glovework deteriorated his batting came to the fore and this innings was to provide him with his third century in four matches.

Karachi was the venue for what proved to be the decisive match in a three-Test series. The games at Lahore and Faisalabad had, as with so many of the previous Tests between the two countries, proved to be tedious and anodyne draws. Here, however, came the most sensational start in the history of Test cricket as the Indian seamer Irfan Pathan took a hat-trick with the last three deliveries of his first over after Rahul Dravid, noting the moisture in the wicket, had invited Pakistan to bat after winning the toss.

Inevitably the Pakistan innings improved after that, but not much, and Akmal came to the crease in just the 11th over, when their sixth wicket fell at 39. His captain, Inzamam-ul-Haq, had told Akmal to play his natural game, and he proceeded to do just that against a buoyant attack of Pathan, Zaheer Khan and RP Singh until, with 113 to his name from only 148 balls, he was eighth out at 236. The innings closed shortly afterwards for 245. There were two significant partnerships for Akmal, 115 with Abdul Razzaq for the seventh wicket and 82 with Shoaib Akhtar for the eighth. Both Razzaq and Akhtar were dismissed for 45. There was but one blemish in Akmal's innings, his opposite number MS Dhoni missing a straightforward stumping chance when he was on 80, but by then the tone of the day's play had changed. Dileep Premachandran, writing in the *Wisden Cricketer*, summed it up when he wrote that 'Akmal engineered a stunning momentum shift'. A century at not far off a run-a-ball in such a situation was a declaration both of intent and fearlessness. It is clear that the wicket played more easily as the day wore on and the ball aged but it was never comfortable, with considerable seam movement throughout, and when India's batsmen had just over an hour to face at the end of the day they lost four wickets to the pace bowlers.

Next day, India conceded a narrow first-innings deficit of just seven runs. In the final innings they did just a little better, 265, with Yuvraj Singh scoring a fine century that was not dissimilar to Akmal's. The visitors' problem was that in their second innings every man in the Pakistan top order got at least a half-century, and their 599-7 declared meant that victory went to the hosts by the small matter of 341 runs to seal a series win.

Graham Gooch – 135

England v Pakistan, Leeds 23-26 July 1992

93

England and Pakistan went to Headingley for the fourth of a five-Test series, with the tourists 1-0 up following a two-wicket win in a low-scoring thriller at Lord's. For this match the England selectors made a number of changes, Alec Stewart taking over as wicket-keeper while Somerset seamer Neil Mallender came in for his debut. Stewart dropped down to number four and Michael Atherton resumed his place as Graham Gooch's opening partner, a combination that had already yielded some big stands.

Javed Miandad won the toss for Pakistan and chose to bat but, with only Saleem Malik standing firm, the tourists soon subsided to 80-5. Mallender was among the wickets as 'the ball came off sluggishly, occasionally keeping low and always seaming and swinging'. With bad light forcing an early finish, Pakistan closed on 165-8. Next day, Malik continued to marshal the tail but ran out of partners on 82 with the total 197.

One year earlier, on this ground, Gooch had given a masterclass against the feared West Indies attack, carrying his bat and enabling England to record their first home win against those opponents for 22 years. The bowling on this occasion was hardly less formidable, even if they were more likely to target the batsman's toes than his helmet. Wasim Akram and Waqar Younis, left and right arm, swung the ball at express pace, the murky Leeds sky perfect for their style of bowling. They were backed up by Aaqib Javed, an English-style seamer, and the leg-spinner Mushtaq Ahmed, wily beyond his years. All of the quick men had experience with counties, indeed Waqar had taken over a hundred wickets for Surrey in 1991. Wasim, the oldest of the four at 26, was remembered by all from the tour of 1987 and, of course, they'd seen off England in a World Cup final in March.

The opening stand of 168 by Gooch and Atherton was their seventh of over 100, and unusually the junior partner matched his captain run for run, contributing 76 before losing his off stump to Wasim. Gooch had survived two lbw appeals from Waqar in the 40s, but replays showed that in both cases the in-swing would have taken the ball past leg stump. His persistence in playing forward to counter the unreliable bounce was a masterpiece of planning and execution, driving the pace bowlers to distraction as umpires Palmer and Kitchen refused to guess. Once Atherton had been replaced by Robin Smith, Gooch took command, striking Mushtaq over long-on for six and long-off for four.

His seven-hour 135 was put into perspective by the dismal collapse that followed his dismissal to Mushtaq's googly. However, with Mallender taking five second-innings wickets, England were left just 99 to level the series – two weeks later Wasim and Waqar showed that Gooch's defiance was only temporary.

Azhar Mahmood – 132

South Africa v Pakistan, Durban 26 February-2 March 1998

92

Early 1998 and Azhar Mahmood was quite simply the most exciting young prospect in world cricket – just 23 years of age and already an indispensable member of a thrilling Pakistan team. His precision line-and-length fast-medium bowling a perfect foil to the explosive brilliance of Shoaib Akhtar, Waqar Younis and Wasim Akram and lower middle-order batting capable of making Inzamam-ul-Haq or Saeed Anwar look pedestrian.

Pakistan's team of all talents arrived in South Africa with just one, unhappy, previous visit behind them, the 'Inaugural Test' at Johannesburg in 1995 which resulted in a thumping, courtesy of Fanie de Villiers. There was now, however, little to choose between the two sides. What South Africa might have lacked in brilliance they made up for in sheer bloody-minded determination as they had shown in Pakistan the previous year, with a magnificent century by Gary Kirsten in the final match deciding the result. Azhar Mahmood made his mark in the first game of the series with an unbeaten century and half-century on debut.

This return series which followed two months later was always destined to be both close and fiery with neither side exactly over-endowed with shrinking violets. Mahmood made an immediate impression in the first Test by hitting 136 in Pakistan's only innings in a rain-spoilt draw although even this paled in comparison with the efforts of Pat Symcox who became only the third-ever player to score a Test century batting at number 10.

The teams moved next to Durban and South Africa, eschewing all thoughts of spin, duly dropped the heroic Symcox and brought back de Villiers to join Donald, Pollock, Klusener and Kallis in a fearsome pace battery. On a wicket described variously as sluggish and two-paced, Hansie Cronje had little hesitation in inserting and was rewarded with an immediate tumble of wickets as Pakistan sank to 89-5 before Mahmood, two days shy of his 23rd birthday, strode to the wicket. For the following 200 minutes he dominated proceedings with an array of cuts, drives and pulls, bringing his team around as he nursed a fragile tail while moving imperiously to a century. So effective was his placement and manoeuvring of the strike that he was able to add 80 with Akhtar and take 80 per cent of the bowling. The attack remained intense but Mahmood was a match for it all causing one reporter to write that he 'caused many to gasp in wonderment'. Allan Donald confessed, 'I have yet to find his weakness' and that was something only the very best could lay claim to.

The innings closed at 259 with Mahmood last out for 132, bowled by Donald, after hitting 24 boundaries. Most important of all, Pakistan were still alive and kicking and another masterly innings was still to be played. Sadly this was Mahmood's last Test century as his career petered out – a great talent only partially fulfilled.

Greg Chappell – 176

New Zealand v Australia, Christchurch 19-22 March 1982

91

Greg Chappell arrived at Lancaster Park, for the third Test, in the worst form of his cricketing life, having recorded eight international ducks since December 1981. Added pressure was that this three-match series in New Zealand was his first visit to the 'Shaky Isles' since the infamous 'underarm incident'. The series to that point saw the home team one up after two Tests, Chappell having scored 32 and 24 in his two innings.

Things did not appear to be getting any easier for the Australian captain in his bid to find form and to square the series, with Geoff Howarth, the Kiwi captain, choosing to bowl on a fast pitch which provided movement and sharp lift for the bowlers. Chappell came to the crease with the score 57-2 and never looked comfortable on the first day; playing and missing regularly, he was dropped behind on 32 and survived a very confident lbw appeal on the same score, both off the bowling of the superb Richard Hadlee. If Chappell had been dismissed, Australia would have been in a perilous position but as it was they finished the rain-interrupted day at 202-5, with Chappell a scratchy 76.

From stumps to midnight, Chappell consumed 17 cans of beer, but maintains he still managed eight hours sleep. Whether it was the amber fluid or the sleep, it was noted how much more relaxed the Australian captain looked on day two. Seemingly at ease on the still difficult pitch, he pulled or hooked at every opportunity until Howarth put two men out deep. Whether this was a plan or he was trying to compensate for poor bowling is unclear, still the Kiwis kept bowling short and Chappell kept smacking them to the boundary. One such pull for four brought up his 20th Test century from 144 balls. Even Hadlee, who was a class above the rest of the bowlers, seemed intent on pitching short only to see the ball disappear for six. As the visitors in the crowd sang "C'mon Aussie, c'mon", Chappell moved to 176 and an even hundred in the session. Just after this he edged to the 'keeper and without waiting for the umpire's finger an obviously angry Chappell left the field ripping off his gloves as he departed. His 100 on the second morning had taken just 91 balls with 14 fours and two sixes and appropriately Chappell rated it one of his very best.

In the face of Dennis Lillee and Jeff Thomson, on a still unpredictable pitch, New Zealand, chasing 353, just failed to avoid the follow-on and were all out for 149. There was doubt whether Chappell would actually make New Zealand bat again, especially as Lillee would be unable to bowl in the second innings, but, clarifying his thoughts, he said: 'I've always been taught if you've forced the follow-on you bloody well enforce it.' Despite a better effort in the second innings from the home team, led by John Wright's battling century, Australia won the match by eight wickets. Man of the match, GS Chappell.

Frank Worrell – 191*

England v West Indies, Nottingham 4-9 July 1957

90

After disappointment against Australia in the Caribbean in 1955, Frank Worrell played almost no first-class cricket until he took his place in the West Indies squad for their 1957 tour of England. It was not a happy trip. There was disharmony within the party and Worrell, overlooked for the vice-captaincy, was less than happy. Worst of all, despite considerable success against the counties, the Test series was a demoralizing experience for the tourists, as they lost 3-0 and found themselves between a rock and a hard place in the two drawn Tests. England easily avenged the ignominy of 1950. Amidst the general misery there were occasional vintage performances from individuals, and the visitors drew the third Test courtesy of a superb unbeaten 191 from Worrell. He carried his bat, and scored more than half of his side's total. *Wisden* said of him that he 'batted all through Saturday, waging a remorseless battle against some splendid bowling and excellent fielding'.

England had won the toss, batted, and 20 minutes after tea on the second day declared on 619-6. There was no way the West Indies could win the game and, after a crushing innings defeat at Lord's, few expected this outcome to be any different. England skipper Peter May had at his disposal two of England's finest-ever opening bowlers, Fred Trueman and Brian Statham, both at the peak of their powers. The other two members of his attack, Jim Laker and Trevor Bailey, were, at 35 and 33, entering the veteran stage of their careers, but it was only a year since Laker had demolished Australia, and barely a fortnight since Bailey's match haul of 11-98 had been the crucial factor in England's win in the second Test.

The fact that the West Indies had new openers, Worrell and Garry Sobers, who had bowled 21 overs each in England's innings, had the home side smelling blood but the pair battled through and were still there at the close at 59-0. The sun beat down on Trent Bridge next day but the England bowlers gave everything. Early on, Trueman bowled a vicious bouncer at Worrell, drawing from one of the noisy Caribbean contingent in the crowd a cry of "Play the white man, Trueman". The next delivery was a yorker that crashed into Worrell's foot. The concentration in the middle was intense, and he withstood everything that the England bowlers could throw at him, even after a lunchtime shower had freshened up the pitch. At the close West Indies were 295-3, Worrell unbeaten on 145.

There was then a rest day, and plenty of rain in the meantime, and the West Indies almost collapsed in a heap on the fourth morning, until Sonny Ramadhin helped Worrell add 55 for the last wicket before leaving his skipper stranded. The follow-on was duly enforced, but with the ill-starred Collie Smith playing a wonderful hand in the second innings the visitors kept England at bay just long enough to secure the draw.

Chris Gayle – 165*

Australia v West Indies, Adelaide 4-8 December 2009

Neither side was what it had been. Australia had lost three of their last five series; the West Indies, not having triumphed in a Test Match down under since 1997, had lost their previous nine matches there. The hosts, however, were at least a shadow of their former selves. There was little in Chris Gayle's side, ranked ahead only of Bangladesh, even to hint at its lineage. It wasn't only their want of quality, they seemed also to be sorely lacking in commitment. Gayle himself, lured by the lucre of the Indian Premier League, had arrived a mere two days before the start of a recent series against England, declaring that he "would not be so sad" if Test cricket were to perish. The first Test of this series lasted not even three days. That he had retained the captaincy, after all this, was just a tad surprising. "I'm not going anywhere", came his defiant response.

The turnaround at Adelaide commenced with an assertive first innings of 451. It continued, after Australia reached 174 without loss in reply, with some ingenious bowling and some inventive captaincy. The Australians added just 260 more, leaving the West Indies with a small but invaluable lead, their first against Australia in a decade.

The pitch was slowing and spinning when Gayle opened the second innings. He started confidently, closing the third day unbeaten on 12. Ricky Ponting declined to attack on the fourth, and Gayle accepted the singles, going to his fifty in good time, but showing the kind of patience and purpose which tends to surprise those who follow his career only superficially. The Australians gave him nothing and his second fifty required 101 deliveries. The jig he danced in celebration, which thoroughly amused his team-mates, furnished evidence enough to Peter Roebuck 'that he does care about Test cricket'. Gayle continued to commit himself. Struggling with cramp, still he struck the ball sweetly. His timing was immaculate, but he never forced the issue, hitting only one six. The headlines – 'Gayle Force Rocks Ponting's Men' and 'Gayle Blows Away The Critics' – looked sillier than ever.

The Australians lacked penetration, especially after Peter Siddle cried off with a hamstring injury. Ben Hilfenhaus could not play, and rarely had they been so thin on spin. Doug Bollinger bowled with fervour, but for reasons best known to his captain went largely unused. Ponting's neglect of the slip cordon was no less egregious.

The West Indies batted too long on the final day, but did afford their captain the honour of carrying his bat. He finished, after 441 minutes and 285 balls, with 165. The second-highest score was 27. Set 330 to win, Australia looked vulnerable on 139-5 after tea, but a draw was always the likeliest result. Gayle was made man of the match, 'but his greatest achievement', noted Mike Coward, 'was to convince his men that victory was attainable.'

David Boon – 143

Australia v New Zealand, Brisbane 4-7 December 1987

88

David Boon's Test career began when he was 23 with Australian cricket at a low point and, with the rest of his team, he performed only fitfully in the mid-1980s. But then Australia won the 1987 World Cup and the surge of confidence was still evident less than a month later when New Zealand came to the 'Gabba for Australia's first Test match since Mike Gatting's side had won the 1986-87 Ashes series with something to spare.

This was the New Zealand of Richard Hadlee and Martin Crowe that had recently won a series in England for the first time and two years previously had taken their first ever series in Australia. Crowe was at the peak of his powers and Hadlee, despite being 36, was still at the top of his game and indeed in this match was to pass Dennis Lillee's record of 355 Test wickets. Hadlee was also fond of Brisbane, having taken his Test-best there in November 1985, 9-52 and 15 for the match, in an innings victory.

The wicket for this game looked just as inviting as that on which Hadlee had previously prospered, Boon himself describing it as a 'classic, juicy 'Gabba strip', and it was as well for Australia that Allan Border won the toss and invited New Zealand to bat. The Australian seamers proceeded to enjoy themselves and the visitors were all out for a painstaking 186 early on the second morning. As for the Australian reply, the scorecard tells its own story. The wicket was undoubtedly a little easier than on the first day, but only one of the other Australian batsmen got to grips with the bowling. Boon batted outstandingly for almost the full day for his 143. He didn't offer the New Zealand fielders anything and indeed was only dismissed as a result of a rash call by Steve Waugh. At the moment of his dismissal Australia were 219-4, so he had scored more than 65 per cent of the team total. Of the other Australians, only leg-spinner Peter Sleep got out of the 20s and Geoff Marsh's 25 was the second-highest contribution from the specialist batsmen. In fact no player on either side managed to reach even half of Boon's score.

Why was Boon so successful that day? In his own words: 'I made Hadlee bowl to me, rather than trying to bat to him. I felt so comfortable about letting balls go...I forced him to bowl into my pads and it was from balls bowled on this line that I scored plenty of runs'. Hadlee confirmed that 'David had worked out a way of playing me that reduced my effectiveness' and he described the innings as 'magnificent'.

New Zealand did a little better in their second innings, but the mere 94 Australia then needed was managed with ease. It was of course the start of an era of growing baggy-green dominance that endured for almost two decades, but without Boon's 143 the dawning of the new age would have had to wait a little while longer.

Graeme Pollock – 274

South Africa v Australia, Durban 5-9 February 1970

It was to be more than two decades before South Africa played Test cricket again after their 1969-70 home series with Australia but they made sure they went out in style, winning all four Tests against Bill Lawry's side. The victory margins demonstrate the degree of dominance: 170 runs, an innings and 129 runs, 307 runs and 323 runs. When the Australians arrived, their confidence high following a 3-1 series win in India, Lawry declared that Ian Chappell was the finest batsman in world cricket, a comment that can have served only to reinforce the South Africans' determination to win, and to do so convincingly.

The first Test was won comfortably and it speaks volumes for Graeme Pollock's innings in the second match that it has rated higher than that of team-mate Barry Richards. At Durban, Richards almost joined the select band of three to have scored a century before lunch on the opening day of a Test and he certainly would not have looked out of place in the company of Victor Trumper, Charles Macartney and Donald Bradman. As the last over before lunch began with Richards on 94, and the score on 126-1, Ali Bacher was bowled trying to give his partner the strike. As he walked back to the pavilion all talk on the ground was that it was Richards, and not Chappell, who was the best in the world. Perhaps Pollock heard, and that is why his innings was as exhilarating as it was.

After lunch Richards and Pollock added 103 in an hour before Richards went. Pollock carried serenely on. The Australian who eventually dismissed him next day for 274, Keith Stackpole, wrote later, '...here was a hard, relentless cricketer, a master'. The innings brought with it a succession of records. At 210, Pollock beat his own previous highest innings. Twenty-three runs later he went past Dudley Nourse's Test record for South Africa against Australia, and then at 236 the highest score by a South African against Australia in a first-class match. When he reached 245 the record for the highest Test innings in South Africa was taken from Eddie Paynter, and finally at 256 he went past the previous South African record, Jackie McGlew's 255. The only disappointment was that he did not go on to challenge Garry Sobers' Test high of 365. Even with fielders ringing the boundary the Australians were powerless as their tiring attack was mercilessly thrashed by an immensely powerful man wielding a heavy bat – 43 times the ball crossed the rope, Pollock was not a man for running. Eighth out at 575, South Africa went on to 622 before Bacher declared. The demoralised Australians were dismissed for 157 and 336, Chappell nought and 14.

Back in 1964, when he first saw him, Don Bradman had described Pollock as "the most exciting young batsman in the world". In later life he was satisfied that he was the best left-handed batsman the game had seen.

Len Hutton – 169

West Indies v England, Georgetown 24 February-2 March 1954

86

To describe the MCC visit to the West Indies in 1953-54 as a happy tour would be akin to comparing the bodyline series to a jolly knockabout at Downton Abbey. Most things that could go wrong did go wrong and presiding over four months of acrimony was the first ever professional captain, Len Hutton. These were the two best teams in the world – England having regained the Ashes in 1953 after losing at home to the spin-driven West Indies in 1950. This series would decide who was the best.

Introverted and determined, Hutton was a leader by example – man-management and socialising were not for him as an England captain. Yet he could hardly be blamed for most of the problems: Tony Lock's throwing, Fred Trueman's fusillade of bouncers at the grand old man George Headley, threats to umpires and even the political atmosphere which was described as the 'fag end of white supremacy'. As if this wasn't enough, his team were two down with three to play when they arrived in Guyana, a brilliant side containing Denis Compton, Peter May and Tom Graveney struggling to come to terms with the captain's decree of attritional cricket.

Yet somehow the series was turned around and England eventually left with heads not only intact but even held high. The process began with winning the toss in Guyana and the epitome of a captain's innings as Hutton defied the skills and wiles of Sonny Ramadhin and Alf Valentine in compiling an innings of 169. His superb defensive technique on a slow-turning pitch, allied with the rare ability to read Ramadhin was punctuated by searing drives and delicate glances on the rare occasions when line or length were astray as, hour after hour, the game moved away from the West Indians. He held the side together with flawless batting and intense concentration in sapping heat and humidity for almost eight hours, breaking the home side's dominance, in a team total of 435.

Despite a riot shortly before the close on the third day, which was not enough to force Hutton to order his players from the field (he wanted a couple of late wickets), Brian Statham ate into the West Indies batting first time around and then the combined attack gorged on the carcass as they followed on. A nine-wicket victory was the result.

England, once again inspired by Hutton, won the final Test to level the series. The tour was universally agreed to have been a horrid one but Hutton's batting throughout (677 runs at 96.71) was as good as any of the performances of Hobbs or Hammond in Australia. Physically and mentally exhausted by his efforts he played only 15 more Tests scoring a mere 306 runs. Nobody doubted his assertion that this tour had shortened his career by two years at least and many agree that there has never been a finer opening batsman.

Bob Barber – 185

Australia v England, Sydney 7-11 January 1966

85

The 1960s – free love, walls torn down and young men and women casting off shackles and burning bras; a decade of vibrant colour. Not in cricket it wasn't. After the false dawn of the tied-Test series of 1960-61, international cricket sank into a 10-year malaise of slow attritional batting where a first day score of 210-3 was regarded as a solid achievement. There were, of course, the brilliant exceptions: Pollock, Sobers and Kanhai and, briefly, Dexter and Milburn but this was the age of the run-digger Bill Lawry and his acolytes.

Bob Barber played another game. As a young amateur he had been shackled by excessive caution but in a reverse of most careers he became more carefree with age and carefree suited him well. His England record had been patchy but by 1964 he had become a regular; an aggressive, some would say impetuous, left-handed opener and useful leg-break bowler although at the start of the series he was still looking for a maiden Test century.

The first two matches sank in a morass of big and slow scores but at Sydney everything changed for five glorious hours. The pitch was good and the attack only moderate but the manner of Barber's batting was breathtaking. "What I really want to do," he had said earlier on the tour, "is to play one innings as I think the game should be played. And I want to play it at Sydney." The lunch score of 93-0 with Barber on 57 was some indication that he was about to fulfil his desires. Only an hour later he moved effortlessly to his century and when, just before tea, his partner Boycott was out for 83 the pair had put on 234. After the break, John Edrich took the Boycott role, nudging and pushing but most of all enjoying the superb entertainment emanating from the other end. For another hour Barber flayed all-comers before succumbing to weariness, being dismissed for 185 scored off 255 balls. This wasn't how it was done on the first day of a Test and he was given a rousing reception by a 40,000-strong home crowd. English batsmen had performed great deeds in Australia but nothing like this on an opening day since George Gunn in 1907.

The plaudits rolled in – John Woodcock called it 'one of the truly great displays of batting in Test cricket', *Wisden* dubbed it 'the superlative achievement of the whole tour' and Australian opener Lawry was equally effusive.

Despite a middle-order collapse on day two, England posted a big score and, on a crumbling wicket, dismissed Australia twice for an innings victory. Australia were to level the series with a re-modelled team featuring just two specialist bowlers – the Ashes had reverted to hard-nosed grind.

Frank Tyson described the series as 'most engrossing' but 50 years later it looks mighty dull, with one exception – the shining light of Bob Barber's one and only Test century.

Viv Richards – 232

England v West Indies, Nottingham 3-8 June 1976

82=

It was just one word, but when England skipper Tony Greig's ill-advised "grovel" comment was broadcast on the eve of the first Test in Nottingham a proud, young batsman by the name of Vivian Richards felt the sting more keenly than most and at a stroke was handed all the motivation he needed. He would go on to stamp his authority indelibly on what was to prove a long, hot summer for England's cricketers, amassing a Bradmanesque 829 runs in only four matches, giving him a world-record 1,710 runs in the calendar year which was to stand for 30 years.

Richards' confidence, already sky-high as the result of an eye-opening start to the year with four Test centuries already under his belt, was sorely tested after Clive Lloyd chose to bat on a benign-looking Trent Bridge strip; as many as a dozen errant shots could have sent him trudging back to the pavilion. After lunch, however, it was a different story as Richards at last found his groove – Bob Woolmer sent down several short-pitched balls which were pulled contemptuously to the square-leg boundary, and soon every shot was rocketing out of the middle of the bat. Each bowler was treated with the same disdain, his awesome power drawing chants of "Gro-vel, gro-vel" from the ecstatic West Indian fans. At stumps he had reached 143 not out from a total of 274-2.

Richards continued the next day without missing a beat, many of his shots being touched with what Tony Cozier in the *Kingston Gleaner* would proclaim 'The unmistakable stamp of greatness'. Shortly after lunch, he became the first player ever to score a double-century in his first Test against England, as he crowned his thrilling display with an electrifying assault which brought 36 runs from his final 13 shots.

The end came when the urge to loft the ball over Greig couldn't be stifled and his power was finally found wanting. During a stay of seven and a half hours Richards had served up a breathtaking feast of power hitting, smashing four sixes and 31 fours to put the West Indies apparently out of sight on 408-3, though without his magisterial presence they soon folded to 494 all out.

What followed was always going to be an anti-climax, but the way the game petered out was nonetheless a huge disappointment. England replied with 332 due mainly to David Steele's doughty century, and Richards' second-innings 63 allowed Lloyd to declare with England needing 339 in 315 minutes. Fat chance – with no Richards in the England side to make this a realistic target, the match ended with England ambling to 156-2 at the close.

But for a day and a half, cricket lovers were enthralled by a powerhouse who, as Cozier asserted, had England 'groveling at his feet'. It would indeed be a long, hot summer.

Kapil Dev – 109

India v West Indies, Chennai 11-15 January 1988

Kapil Dev's century against the West Indies in January 1988 was the foundation stone on which India's series-saving victory was built during this fourth and final Test. The West Indies were in the middle of 15 years undefeated in Test series and, leading 1-0 after three, seemed on course to extend their dominance before stumbling in the face of two extraordinary performances. On a Chennai pitch which *Wisden* described as 'underprepared' all batsmen would require a degree of luck to last for long and after winning the toss, in his first and only Test match as skipper, Ravi Shastri bravely opted to bat.

The West Indian pace attack of Patrick Patterson, Courtney Walsh and Winston Davis was not perhaps the Caribbean's finest vintage. Still, in Patterson captain Viv Richards had a bone-jarringly hostile pace bowler still capable of roughing up any opposition while Walsh had bowled brilliantly throughout the series and Davis was still capable of the disconcerting slipperiness that had broken Paul Terry's arm at Old Trafford in 1984. Despite a combined total of just 42 Test appearances as the concluding encounter of the rubber got under way, supporters of this trio could point to 42 wickets in the preceding three Tests. Anticipating turn, the West Indies also included Clyde Butts, the off-break bowler, backed up by Richards and Carl Hooper.

On the first morning only Arun Lal had looked remotely at home on a fizzing and variable surface, bristling with confidence during his 69. His dismissal at 156-5, with India teetering on the brink of collapse, paved the way for Kapil to join Ajay Sharma. What followed was the finest and most important of Kapil's three Test centuries against the West Indies. Immediately he set about tilting the balance India's way. During his stay at the crease he struck 109 out of 157, his first fifty coming off just 46 balls, and he hit 18 boundaries in total. Given doughty support from Sharma, the two added 113 for the sixth wicket before Sharma was dismissed for 30. At stumps on the first day India were 308-6, a far cry from what had seemed likely as the 'Haryana Hurricane' made his way to the crease.

Although he added only five more next day, the balance had shifted with India closing on 382. Now it was the turn of their debutant leg spinner, Narendra Hirwani. Richards' team were routed, dismissed for 184 and narrowly avoiding the follow-on, as Hirwani took 8-61 on a deteriorating surface. India closed their second knock on 217-8 and the same bowler set about the hapless West Indians once again. They crumbled to a dismal 160 in under three hours. Their tormentor this time had 8-75, giving him an astonishing tally of 16-136. This may be remembered as Hirwani's match but it was Kapil Dev's first-innings pyrotechnics which had paved the way.

Bruce Edgar – 161

New Zealand v Australia, Auckland 12-16 March 1982

To say that cricket relations between New Zealand and Australia weren't exactly cordial when big brother visited little brother in early 1982 would be an understatement. Years of neglect meant that the 1973-74 series was the first time the two countries had met in a Test since a 1946 mismatch. Inspired by Glenn Turner and Richard Hadlee, New Zealand had soon proved worthy opponents and a certain 'underarm incident' ensured that this time Greg Chappell and his fellow tourists would meet a hostile reception. Australia, as expected, won the one-day series and then the first Test was ruined by rain. Rain again was an ever-present factor at Eden Park for the second match but this time it came in bursts not torrents and despite frequent interruptions the match was played to a thrilling climax.

Geoff Howarth elected to bowl (a tactic that had served him well two years earlier against the West Indies) on a 'slow and unresponsive' wicket, largely to keep his batsmen away from the threat of Lillee, Thomson and Alderman. He could hardly believe his good fortune as Chappell and Allan Border ran themselves out off consecutive balls and Australia slumped to just 210. However, by the close parity had been restored with New Zealand at 35-2. Earlier, Bruce Edgar had been relieved that he wouldn't be batting first, but only seven hours later there he was with a snarling Jeff Thomson informing him he'd "never die of a stroke". Having survived this ordeal, on an equally muggy and damp second day he set himself to occupy the crease and that is exactly what he did. As showers sent the players on and off the field he tucked into the slipstream of Howarth and Jeremy Coney, carefully accumulating and regulating his strokeplay to the conditions until New Zealand closed the day at 241-3. Edgar had batted calmly, even when he lost half a tooth top-edging a sweep (Rod Marsh offered to remove the stump) before surviving a confident appeal for lbw when on 99. His 103 not out had the home side in a good position but with work still to do.

With the pitch now responsive to the spin of Bruce Yardley, wickets fell rapidly on the morning of day three but Bruce Edgar was immune to such irregularities until unaccountably chipping a return catch to the spinner. A lapse in concentration was the verdict of the batsman, his first in 500 minutes at the wicket punctuated by nine rain breaks. The *Cricketer* called it 'magnificent…all courage and concentration' and it had underpinned a first-innings lead of 177. Scenting victory, New Zealand harried, pushed and caught their catches and on day five needed just 104 for victory. Early wickets cast doubt on the outcome but Lance Cairns knocked Yardley out of the attack, overseen by the unflappable Edgar at the other end. Richard Hadlee rounded off the win with a six but Bruce Edgar's third and final Test century was the key that had unlocked Australia.

Michael Clarke – 329*

Australia v India, Sydney 3-6 January 2012

81

When Indian captain MS Dhoni won the toss and elected to bat on a seemingly comfortable pitch but with the prospect of early movement, he might have expected some difficulties but not to be skittled for 191. As Australian captain Michael Clarke sat back to watch his top-order batsman knock off this paltry total he would certainly not have envisaged his rest lasting fewer than nine overs. Zaheer Khan three wickets, Australia 37-3.

After an early cut dangerously close to gully, Clarke was in complete control, signalling his intent in the gloaming with three consecutive boundaries off Umesh Yadav. By the end of the first day, Australia had regained the initiative and on the second they were simply overwhelming, Clarke alone plundering 204 runs. Anything too straight was clipped, whipped or pulled to the leg side. When they overcompensated he unleashed drives through the off using his feet to bow the untiring but ineffective spinners to his will. The scoring wheel of Clarke's innings was symmetrical enough to slot straight onto a wagon. He had always been graceful and elegant but now, in the middle of his career, he had grafted concentration onto his natural talent. One chance was offered, and spurned, when Ishant Sharma shelled a catch off his own bowling; it would be an expensive error.

India's misery continued even after they dismissed Ricky Ponting with the new ball, Mike Hussey entering and setting about the bowling with joyful abandon. It was a reminder of the glory days of Australian cricket; Ponting and Hussey, the old-timers, were destined to retire within the year and Clarke, at 30, was the bridge between their generation and the current crop. He looked every bit the 21st-century cricketer with his earring and plethora of tattoos, but behind the million-dollar looks was a glorious, classical batsman, who had eschewed the riches of T20 to focus on captaining his country in the five-day format.

When Clarke brought up the SCG's first Test-match triple-century, on the afternoon of the third day, the game was only at its halfway mark and he had all of cricket's immortal records in his sights. Instead he declared the innings shut on 659-4, a selfless decision from an inexperienced captain and one vindicated by the prized wickets of Virender Sehwag and Rahul Dravid before stumps.

In the year since inheriting the captaincy, Clarke had been booed by a Brisbane crowd, ridiculed by the media for his lifestyle and led an Australian team reckoned to be the weakest in a generation. Now he basked in the adoration of the SCG and ranked alongside Don Bradman in the record books. India never stood a chance; they battled to 400 but still lost by an innings with more than a day left. Demoralised and outclassed, they would go on to lose all four matches of the series – the Michael Clarke era had begun.

Warwick Armstrong – 159*

South Africa v Australia, Johannesburg 18-21 October 1902

80

The 'Big Ship' is largely remembered as the irascible and giant leader of the 1920-21 nearly all-conquering Australians that flattened England 8-0 over two series shortly after World War I, just as Don Bradman's Invincibles were to do (7-0) after the Second World War. But Warwick Armstrong was also a canny wrist spinner and a very fine batsman and he always maintained that it was the 1902 Australian team in England that was the best. It was this team that, after defeating England, stopped over in South Africa on their way home to engage in a three-match series on the matting wickets of the Cape. The one-month beano would bring the two countries together in a Test match for the first time and provide some lucrative and not-too-demanding work for the intrepid 14 players that had spent the last five months slogging around the rain-soaked shires. At least that was the plan.

The first Test showed that a tired Australia and a spirited South Africa were, in fact, quite closely matched as the visitors escaped with a draw after following on. The home side boasted fine players in Louis Tancred, Charlie Llewellyn, 'Barberton' Halliwell and, above all, the mighty Jimmy Sinclair. In addition the red clay outfield and bouncy coir matting wicket was a far cry from what the Australians had been playing on and adapting was proving difficult. The second match, again at the Old Wanderers, looked even bleaker after four sessions with Sinclair having blasted his side to a 65-run first-innings lead. These arrears were cleared for the loss of two of Australia's finest, Syd Gregory and Victor Trumper. But now the newly-promoted opener came into his own. One chance was all Armstrong needed and that came when he was dropped by Tancred.

Tormented thereafter, the fielder recorded that: 'Never did the sound of ball against bat sound so discordant...The crisp shots went like hammer blows and each run that showed itself on the board looked emblazoned and ineradicable.' The reprieved Armstrong stood firm as Llewellyn tormented his team-mates; the cream of Australian batting fell to his clever left-arm spin but there was no moving the big Victorian whose memories of youthful days on artificial wickets was now put to good use. Even a delay as a swirling, vicious dust storm swept the ground, whipping the red clay into the players' eyes, couldn't staunch his concentration and steady flow of runs. He shepherded his side to a total of 309, never rushed and always calm, having carried out his bat for 159. Jack Saunders and Bill Howell, now with something to bowl at, ripped the South Africans to pieces in 22 overs of mayhem and the match was won, coincidentally, by 159 runs.

Armstrong was presented with the match ball, and no wonder. His batting had saved his side from an ignominious defeat and preserved their formidable reputation.

Daryll Cullinan – 103

South Africa v Sri Lanka, Centurion 27-30 March 1998

In 1905 the largest ever gem-quality diamond was brought to the surface in South Africa. When it had been washed this unique blue-white stone weighed 621g and nothing to rival it has been found since. It was named the Cullinan Diamond.

In 1993 in the final Test of a three-match series in Sri Lanka, South Africa's Daryll Cullinan helped ensure a series-winning draw with a century. The two countries wouldn't meet again for another five years, the 'series' was a mere two matches but for South Africa the main obstacle to success was unchanged: Muttiah Muralitharan. Cullinan's current form was not good; just 53 runs in his previous seven Test innings and dropped for the final two Tests of the preceding series against Pakistan. Meanwhile Muralitharan had picked up 17 wickets in two matches against Zimbabwe.

The first Test, at Cape Town, was closely fought and, largely through the efforts of Cullinan, with a century and a fifty, and the all-round skill of Shaun Pollock, the hosts prevailed by 70 runs. When Sri Lanka won the toss and elected to bat in the second at Centurion Park on a pitch that looked decidedly bowler-friendly, the omens were not good for the hosts. Given the conditions, Sri Lanka's painstaking score of 303 was eminently respectable and was certainly helped by an injury to Pollock. South Africa's reply was a shambles; 11-2 became 137-6 and on the third morning defeat was staring them in the face with Murali finding all the assistance he needed and turning the ball 'enormous distances'. Daryll Cullinan alone found a way to cope with the often unplayable, using all his experience to read the turning ball both in the air and off the pitch, resisting for over five hours and completing an error-free century in a total of just 200 before falling to the left-arm spin of Sanath Jayasuriya. The next highest scorer was Mr Extras with 21.

Inspired by the sheer bloody-mindedness, patience and technical excellence of his team-mate, Allan Donald simply blew away a shocked Sri Lankan top order second time around and the rest followed with barely a whimper leaving South Africa to score 226 to win. But this was 26 more than they had managed in their first attempt and the pitch had not flattened out. After falling to 99-3 it looked as if the efforts of Cullinan, who survived just two balls this time, and Donald might be in vain but then captain Hansie Cronje launched into the attack, scoring 82 off just 63 balls in an astonishing assault to complete an unlikely match and series victory.

Rarely, if ever, had the most prolific bowler in the history of Test cricket, with conditions in his favour, found an opponent so resolute. Without this particular Cullinan diamond, Donald and Cronje would never have had such a chance to shine.

Damien Martyn – 142

Australia v Pakistan, Melbourne 26-29 December 2004

78=

On 8 December 2006, just before the commencement of the third Test of the Ashes, Damien Martyn announced his retirement. It came as a shock, especially as the series was very much alive. Some said he jumped before he was pushed, others claimed it was for reasons that would be disclosed in a 'tell-all book', which was never published. Perhaps it was simply because the modest Martyn, at the age of 35, had decided it was time. He had never been one for the limelight; he left that to bigger personalities in the side like Shane Warne, Glenn McGrath and his lookalike Justin Langer, all three of whom had announced they would retire at the end of the series.

It was in 2004 that Martyn had his best year in Test cricket in terms of aggregate and hundreds. He seemed to always be scoring heavily when his team most needed it, and at the end of the year his silky skills were again needed to rescue the all-conquering Australian team who entered the Boxing Day Test leading Pakistan 1-0 in the three-Test series.

The first Christian captain of Pakistan, Yousuf Youhana, won the toss and elected to bat on a flat deck and it was the captain himself who played a great hand, scoring 111 with four sixes. The visitors were eventually dismissed for 341 on the second day. Australia, in the face of hostile bowling by Shoaib Akhtar which touched 150kph (Langer said it was the fastest he'd ever faced), were quickly 32-2, before Martyn joined Langer at the crease. The new arrival faced only one ball from Shoaib before the bowler took a well-deserved rest and Martyn took advantage of his good fortune to settle in against the scarcely less testing Mohammad Sami and Danish Kaneria. Using his familiar superb footwork he hardly mishit a ball, and although he didn't score at a rapid rate he seemed to be in complete control. When Shoaib returned, his pace reduced, Martyn helped himself to a boundary to bring up his fifty from 72 balls. At the end of day two Australia were still in a precarious position at 203-5 with Martyn 67 not out.

Next day, with the pitch now wearing, Martyn continued to play magnificent but controlled cricket, his cut shot in particular being a thing of beauty. He showed trust in tailender Jason Gillespie, with whom he added 93 runs for the eighth wicket, to give Australia an unlikely lead of six runs before receiving a disputed lbw decision which brought his grand innings to a close. This lead was then extended to 38 by the final pair.

Thanks to the great batting of Martyn, who the *Age* thought had earned the 'right to be regarded as the best batsman in the world', the Australian first-innings lead seemed to deflate the Pakistan team who capitulated in their second innings for only 163 allowing the hosts to cruise to a nine-wicket win.

Gilbert Jessop – 104

England v Australia, The Oval 11-13 August 1902

76=

There have been few big hitters who could match 'The Croucher'. A glance through the pages of *Wisden* will confirm that in terms of speed of scoring he has no peers; in a match against Hampshire in 1909, for example, he scored two hundreds, the first of which constituted 161 out of 199 in 95 minutes. But Neville Cardus would not have it that he was little more than a slogger, writing that 'No cricketer lacking science could maintain Jessop's pace and prodigality.'

Leading up to the fourth Test in Manchester in 1902 much of the talk in the newspapers was on whether or not Jessop or Fred Tate should be selected. It is a matter of cricket lore how that turned out, with the hapless Tate dropping the catch which could have saved the series. Jessop was duly reinstated for the final Test, as was allrounder George Hirst, and even though the rubber was already lost the fact that England had not beaten Australia at home for six years ensured there was no lack of motivation for the home side.

Australia made the most of what started out as a decent wicket to score 324 in their first innings, Hirst taking all of the first five wickets. England, by contrast, slumped to 83-6 on Jessop's dismissal. However, Hirst's 43 out of 57 helped England avoid the follow-on, despite Hugh Trumble's eight-wicket haul. Rain had by now made batting more difficult and Australia were skittled out for 121, highlighting the importance of Hirst's work, as England would undoubtedly have lost if required to bat again immediately.

Nonetheless, with a target of 263 on a difficult pitch, one report noted that the outcome was 'altogether against the batting side', and with five wickets down for 48, the England supporters were reconciled to approaching defeat. In strode Jessop, 'thick-set and fearless', apparently unaware of the severity of the situation; he smote 39 in 20 minutes, reached his half-century in 55 minutes, then proceeded to score at a crazy rate, his last 54 arriving in barely 20 minutes. All told he accounted for 104 of 139 in just 75 minutes of mayhem, dragging England back from certain defeat to give her a fighting chance.

Nevertheless there were still 76 runs left to get, but Hirst, playing with great confidence and a steely nerve, guided England to within 15 of the target when he was joined by last man Wilfred Rhodes. It is widely recorded that Hirst announced to his fellow Yorkshireman, "We'll get 'em in singles", and whether or not this is apocryphal they proceeded to do just that, each single being greeted with lusty cheers.

England had recorded an incredible triumph, made possible by Jessop's amazing performance – as the *Edinburgh Evening News* enthused, 'The one and only Gilbert represents at once the uncertainties and splendid possibilities of cricket.' Splendid indeed.

Colin Milburn – 126*

England v West Indies, Lord's 16-21 June 1966

'From start to finish this game had positive action Every man in it wanted desperately to win and not just avoid defeat.'

This is how I remember Colin Milburn, a batsman for whom no game was ever lost and here recollecting the Lord's Test of 1966, featuring not just one but two of the all-time great centuries. The first was played by Garry Sobers, his 161 not out turning the game on its head, and the second was played by Milburn himself.

He had made his debut in the first Test at Old Trafford, following a duck in the first innings with an impressive 94 in the second, though this merely helped to save face as England slumped to an innings defeat. In between the first and second Tests Milburn confirmed his sparkling form with the season's fastest century, just 82 minutes against Nottinghamshire.

The rain-affected match at Lord's shaped up nicely for England as their first innings closed with a lead of 86. A stunning West Indies' collapse then saw them reeling on 95-5 to put England firmly in the driver's seat. Enter Sobers who, with his cousin David Holford, piled up an unbroken sixth-wicket partnership of 274. West Indies declared on 369-5, setting England to make 284 in four hours. Whatever hopes had been held were soon extinguished as the home side were left floundering on 67-4, Wes Hall having despatched Colin Cowdrey and Jim Parks with successive deliveries.

From almost certain victory the day before, England were now staring defeat in the face. Tom Graveney, nursing a bruised thumb, then joined Milburn in the middle. Barely able to steady the bat, Graveney found he had little need to do so as his partner tore into an attack of Hall, Sobers, Charlie Grifffith and Lance Gibbs with utter relish. From a partnership of 130, the senior man contributed just 30. Milburn was absolutely on fire, first launching Hall then Gibbs for six as he knocked off 126 in less than three hours, saving the match for England and treating a vaunted bowling combination with something approaching disdain. It was a rollicking and rolling exhibition of unalloyed power and fun.

Sobers admitted that Milburn was the player the West Indies most feared and described his innings as "magnificent". Always at his best when batting free from inhibition he had continually to fend off criticism of his weight. After failing in the third Test and picking up an injury in the fourth, he was dropped for the final Test, excess pounds being a decisive factor. Milburn's nose-thumbing response was to smash 203 out of 293 against Essex.

Sadly Milburn would never fulfil his massive potential, a car crash in 1969 robbing him of his left eye and he ended his days in a pub car park, dead of a heart attack at just 48.

Percy Sherwell – 115

England v South Africa, Lord's 1-3 July 1907

When the South African tourists arrived in England in 1907, they came as the first wave of a new cricketing world order – at least that was the hope and this hope was, to a large degree, justified. The first contests between the two countries had been a story of privately organised English jollies on the Cape and return visits from second-rate South African sides attracting little interest and no offer of Test cricket. Assiduous effort and no little expenditure hauled the Springboks towards near parity and having defeated England on the matting wickets of the veld they were offered a three-match series in 1907.

The tourists boasted some good-class batsmen, a frightening quick bowler and an unlikely battering ram of four right-arm wrist spinners. In addition to and complementing this unorthodox attack was the captain, opener and wicket-keeper Percy Sherwell. The tourists performed well in the early stages of the summer, but this counted for little as they lined up against an England side boasting such luminaries as Fry and Hayward for the first Test at Lord's. Their fine early form ensured that the ground was almost full as RE Foster chose to bat on a wicket that had recovered remarkably from having been under water. His decision was amply rewarded as the South African googlymen struggled on the soft wicket and, led by an unusually restrained Gilbert Jessop, England closed the first of three days on 428.

When South Africa struggled to 140 all out, Foster had no hesitation in sending the opposition back in and was rewarded with a quick wicket with England still 287 in front. At this point it looked odds-against the South Africans surviving the final three hours of play and taking the game into the final day, but Sherwell had other ideas and, with silent partner Maitland Hathorn, set about turning the game on its head. Together they added 139 in 100 minutes, completely dominating the fearsome trio of George Hirst, Ted Arnold and Colin Blythe that had been irrepressible earlier in the day. South Africa were only 135 behind when Sherwell made his first mistake and played-on for 115. His innings had shown what was possible; his selective aggression had altered the whole aspect of the game and no further wickets fell before stumps were drawn with only 103 between the sides. One newspaper wrote that Sherwell 'Laid about him with such confidence and success that he might have been playing in an exhibition game rather than a test match' and the great Jessop thought the innings 'As good as any I've seen'.

England were still favourites but a draw was eminently achievable and even a South African victory could be considered if the wicket should deteriorate. Above all, the balance and belief had been altered in less than two hours of scintillating batting. The reality was drearily disappointing as next day rain fell and the game was abandoned as a draw.

Don Bradman – 270

Australia v England, Melbourne 1-7 January 1937

74

Don Bradman commenced this innings under greater pressure, and with more popular uncertainty about his prospects, than ever he had before. Since his last Test series, in England in 1934, his first-born son had died; his health had been poor and his form mediocre; just 133 runs in five innings, including two consecutive ducks. With three Tests to play, Australia were 0-2 down in the series. Bradman had only just assumed the captaincy, but already he faced searching questions; there was even quasi-public dissent from certain of his players. The Melbourne crowd, at 87,798, was the largest he ever played in front of and the largest at that point in the history of the game.

The third-day wicket, on the other hand, was 'the worst I ever saw in my life.' Responding to Australia's first-innings declaration at 200, England had closed on 76-9, despite Bradman's efforts to keep them in 'so that Australia could avoid batting on a sticky wicket that evening.' In a bold move for a captain in his position, he inverted his batting line-up, in a bid to protect the top order, not least of all himself. "Why do you want me to open up?" asked Fleetwood-Smith. "Chuck," replied Bradman, "the only way you can get out on this wicket is to hit the ball. You can't hit it on a good one, so you have no chance on this one."

The ruse paid off. When finally Bradman came to the crease, the wicket had recovered, and a slimy ball and run-up were hampering the bowlers. Australia were 97-5, the match well-poised. Bradman started solidly, despite three awkward rain stoppages, to finish the day unbeaten on 56. His century, just after lunch the following day, was slow by his standards. He was sluggish between the wickets, trammelled by influenza and the field spread accordingly, impelling him to take the bulk of his runs in singles. But the circumstances mandated caution. After his 150, he scored with more of his old freedom, to every corner of the ground, and never took a risk. Hedley Verity was superb, but no-one else retarded his progress. Bradman's second century required only 111 minutes. He had informed Neville Cardus earlier in the tour that it was not his intention to score "any more two-hundreds in Test matches". By stumps on the fourth day, he had 248. His sixth-wicket 346 with Fingleton was a record. Australia were 500-6, and the Test was as good as won.

Bradman went on to make 270. At 458 minutes, it was the longest innings of his career. and in 2001 *Wisden* assessed this innings the greatest ever. He then hit 212 and 169 in the final two Tests as well, batting in all for nearly 19 hours and never once presenting a chance. Seldom has there been such a turnaround in a player's form – or, indeed, in a side's. From trailing 0-2, Australia went on to win 3-2. 'Bradman,' wrote statistician and biographer Irving Rosenwater, 'was Australia's spinal column.'

Sunil Gavaskar – 221

England v India, The Oval 30 August-4 September 1979

India arrived at The Oval for the fourth and final Test having endured a fairly disastrous tour after suffering three straight defeats in the limited-overs Prudential World Cup and losing the first Test by an innings. However, more resolve was shown in the following two rain-affected affairs, and they were now looking to level the series. Sunil Gavaskar's Test form had been solid, with four fifties, but still below his own high standards. He'd arrived in England having scored six centuries in his last seven Tests and his overall tally included 19 three-figure scores in 49 matches – no Indian opener before him had scored more than five. His technique and powers of concentration were exemplary and it was said that if you looked up 'straight bat' in the dictionary, there you'd find a picture of him.

The weather was perfect for all five days and, despite the pitch getting easier, England had the upper hand when Mike Brearley declared, leaving India the record-breaking task of scoring 438 runs to win in four sessions. Gavaskar and his opening partner Chetan Chauhan dug in and saw out the day on 76-0, leaving a last day target of 362 runs to win.

On paper the England attack looked imposing: Willis, Botham, Hendrick, Edmonds and Willey. However, Mike Hendrick injured himself early on having bowled a typically miserly spell and played no further part. Yet safety-first remained the watchword for the openers and they added just 137 runs in the first three hours before Chauhan fell for 80.

With wickets in hand, Gavaskar sensed a win was possible and thus began one of the most enthralling finishes to a Test match ever. He and his new partner, Dilip Vengsarkar, put on 153 runs at quicker than a run a ball. Gavaskar was now in total control and scoring most of the runs without taking risks. He had turned the tables on Brearley who responded by slowing the over-rate and dispersing his men to all corners. At the start of the final 20 overs India needed 110 runs for a previously unimaginable win.

The pair kept up with the rate until Vengsarkar went for 52, with 72 still needed. Big-hitting Kapil Dev, out for a duck, and then Yashpal Sharma were surprisingly promoted in front of the experienced and in-form Gundappa Viswanath. Nevertheless, Gavaskar continued to dominate until, with eight overs remaining and 49 required, Brearley gambled on the golden arm of the previously ineffective Ian Botham; alas for India, it worked. Gavaskar was caught at mid-on for a magnificent 221. Thereafter, India were on the back foot and ended the match with fielders round the bat on 429-8, a tantalising nine runs short.

He had led his side from the front, bettering his own record for an Indian opener and scoring 179 runs in a day, again beating his own best. Sir Leonard Hutton rated it one of the best double-centuries he had seen and *Wisden* called it 'inspiring and technically flawless'.

Seymour Nurse – 258

New Zealand v West Indies, Christchurch 13-17 March 1969

72

Seymour Nurse made his debut at Kingston for the West Indies in 1960 against England but, despite scoring a fine 70 against Fred Trueman and Brian Statham, he was immediately dropped to accommodate Clyde Walcott's emergence from Test retirement. It was five years later, when in his thirties, that he finally sealed his place with a double-century against Australia at Bridgetown, but only the English saw him at his real peak as he hit 501 in the series in England in 1966 followed by 434 in the return two years later.

By the time he arrived in Australia and New Zealand for the 1968-69 tour he seemed aware he was on borrowed time. A slender-but-powerful, elegant batsman, he was one of the many disappointments in an ageing side that was beaten 3-1 by Australia – with more competition for places he would certainly have been dropped before partially redeeming himself with a century in the fifth Test. Despite having eschewed all temptations in a quest for total fitness it seemed that his best days were behind him. However, the lesser bowling of New Zealand would prove more to his liking and he was to depart in a blaze of glory.

The first of the three matches, in Auckland, was a personal triumph – scores of 95 and 168 in a five-wicket win. The second was lost to a superb spell of bowling by Dick Motz and with the life, soul and genius of West Indian cricket, Garfield Sobers, clearly exhausted, the visitors looked ripe for the picking with the score 1-1.

Before the final game began, Nurse announced this would be his last Test and within minutes he found himself at the wicket on a damp and miserable Christchurch morning. On a slow and low wicket he applied himself to a recovery from an early wicket using a largely back-foot method in order to moderate the vagaries of the pitch and, with Joey Carew, saw his team through a series of interruptions to stumps, unbeaten on 122. Next day, some top-notch bowling by Motz ripped out a serious middle-order of Basil Butcher, Clive Lloyd and Sobers but Nurse moved on, totally untroubled, dominating successive partnerships before being eighth man out for a flawless 258, well over half the team total of 417. With only three other players making double figures his dominance was plain for all to see.

By the middle of the third day New Zealand were following on. This being a four-day Test they needed to negotiate four more sessions on a pitch now taking some spin, but showed huge application second time around to save a game that an admittedly tired West Indies should have won on the back of such a monumental batting performance. There was no going back and Seymour Nurse left international cricket with a torrent of runs that his bowlers had failed to capitalise on. No batsman has scored more in his final Test innings.

Jacques Kallis – 109*

South Africa v India, Cape Town 2-6 January 2011

71

On the face of it two evenly-matched sides, but India and South Africa had got into the habit of alternately making one another look very ordinary. A two-Test series in India in 2010 had been shared with both sides winning by an innings and the showdown later the same year began in much the same vein. South Africa demolished the visitors at Centurion and then the Indians gained revenge at Durban which left everything open at Cape Town.

After three days of the decider nothing had been decided. Jacques Kallis and Sachin Tendulkar (in an epic clash with Dale Steyn) had dominated the early stages and at the close on day three South Africa led by 50 with eight wickets standing. Within four overs the balance had swayed dramatically as Harbhajan Singh snared Alviro Petersen and Hashim Amla. When AB de Villiers fell before lunch the lead was just 96. Advantage India.

Kallis had batted virtually all morning for just 33 but he had an excuse. Having severely strained his side during his epic first innings he was unable to field and only came in to bat after a series of pain-killing and anti-inflammatory injections. This was the man who, according to inherited wisdom, played for himself and not his team.

His shot play was slightly stunted but his judgement was as sharp as ever despite the medical intervention. With Harbhajan spitting the ball out of the rough and a clustered leg-side field, Kallis chose to reverse sweep into the vacant off side. But the emphasis was to stick and stick he did, through the afternoon with Ashwell Prince and Mark Boucher and then through the evening with Steyn and Morne Morkel on a pitch offering plenty of encouragement for all the Indian bowlers, even if Harbhajan was the only one to really help himself. Occasional moments of aggression punctured the hours of watchful defence and the odd lie-down on the pitch as he came to terms with new waves of excruciating pain.

By the long day's end, Kallis was left stranded, unbeaten, on 109, but with his side leading by 339 there was now only one winner. On the final day the resilience of Gautam Gambhir and Rahul Dravid coupled with the lack of a top-class spinner (and the heavy ball of Kallis) meant that the game petered out into a draw, but there was no contest when the awards were dished out. Player of the match and series – Jacques Kallis.

The man himself quietly reflected that: "Given the situation of the game the second-innings hundred is up there with the best." Boucher was slightly more effusive, informing all and sundry that the pain was the equivalent to that of a broken rib and that, "We have one of the greatest cricketers who ever lived in our own country." A rueful Harbhajan had spent a day trying to break the rock but was scarcely less impressed: "He's got runs on a difficult wicket. He has taken on the responsibility and he has the technique."

Greg Chappell – 182*

Australia v West Indies, Sydney 3-7 January 1976

70

Some players when burdened with the captaincy experience a dramatic drop-off in form, Ian Botham for example. Greg Chappell not only had the pressure of assuming what has been described as the second most important job in Australia, he was also following in his brother's footsteps, Ian Chappell having been ranked by many as Australia's best ever captain. Greg could hardly have had a harder task than his first assignment as captain, an unofficial contest for the best Test team in the world against the West Indies. By the time the two sides came to the SCG for the fourth match, Australia were leading 2-1 in the six-Test series. Any concerns about the hegemony role affecting him had already been dismissed with his average to that point being 84 in the series.

He won the toss and chose to bowl on a pitch that was the same colour as the outfield but, despite the verdant green, some were still surprised by his decision as the best bowler in the world, Dennis Lillee, had been a late withdrawal with pleurisy. With no Lillee to partner an initially wayward Jeff Thomson, the West Indies batted until after lunch on the second day and finished with a competitive total of 355.

When the last of the recognised batsman, Gary Cosier, in only his second Test, joined Greg, who was yet to score, Australia had been reduced to 103-4 by a rampant pace attack. Another wicket would have been disastrous and the West Indies had their chance when Andy Roberts drew the edge from Chappell's bat when on 11; the ball travelled low and quick to the right of Keith Boyce at third slip, who put it down. This chance was the only one Greg Chappell would give until well past his hundred, with *Wisden* recording: 'If ever a missed catch will go down in history as having lost a series this was it.' By stumps on day two, Australia were still a precarious 164-4 with Chappell 38 and Cosier 19.

On day three, Chappell was in complete control while all other batsman struggled against the pace of Roberts and the young tyro Michael Holding, and after bringing up his fifty with a brutal hook off the former he went to lunch on 94. Following the break the visitors took the new ball and Chappell really went for his shots, hooking the first two balls from Roberts to the boundary to bring up his century. He continued on a rampage which was only slowed after he deflected a Holding delivery into his mouth, requiring regular trips to the edge of the pitch to spit blood. Undeterred, Chappell destroyed the bowling, finishing 182 not out in a total of 405. The *Sydney Morning Herald* stated: 'Chappell displayed all the artistry of a master craftsman. Surely, he is the world's finest batsman. It was awe-inspiring, like the skills of an artist.' A dejected and disheartened West Indies crumbled in their second innings, and Australia cruised to a seven-wicket victory.

Glenn Turner – 110*

New Zealand v Australia, Christchurch 8-13 March 1974

In his early years Glenn Turner eschewed all risk. While his skill was such that he could always keep the scoreboard moving by clever placement of the ball, no one would claim that he was a pleasure to watch. His determination was best illustrated by his first Test match against England when, with Derek Underwood at his lethal best on a spiteful Lord's wicket, he carried his bat for 43 in New Zealand's innings of 131.

His greatest contribution to his country's cause came in the 1973-74 home Tests against Australia. At this point in their history, New Zealand were still the Cinderella side of world cricket and Australian confidence was high, particularly as Ian Chappell's men had just completed a 2-0 win in the home leg of a six-match series. The first Test, at Wellington, was a high-scoring draw but conditions at Christchurch were very different.

Australia batted first and, after struggling against an accurate attack, were eventually bowled out for a modest 223. The second-highest scorer in New Zealand's reply was wicket-keeper Ken Wadsworth with 24. A first innings lead of 32 was secured due to the 101 that Turner contributed, an innings that was testament to his guts and determination though he did not bat at all well. It was tough going against fine bowling and spectators lost count of how many times he played and missed. *Wisden* described Max Walker as having 'bowled magnificently on a pitch which allowed him to seam the ball regularly' and Geoff Dymock as being 'almost his equal'. Australia found batting no easier in their second innings and left New Zealand needing 228 for a historic victory.

Turner's batting was as circumspect as in the first innings but this time he was untroubled by the bowling and batted superbly. Richard Hadlee later compared the two innings: 'This was a very different Turner – a master batsman, completely in control.' After a sound start, three quick wickets went down before, with Brian Hastings, Turner put together the fourth-wicket partnership of 115 that won the match. They ran sharp singles judiciously and both drove powerfully when the opportunity arose, neither giving a chance until, right at the end of the fourth day, Hastings fell.

Next day Turner carried on his way, shepherding Jeremy Coney through a partnership of 29 during which he went to his second century with a sweetly struck square drive to the boundary. After that, Turner left centre stage to Wadsworth who struck Greg Chappell through cover to score the winning runs. Altogether he had batted for just shy of 12 hours and, apart from 70 minutes at the end of the first innings, had been on the field throughout the match. There was no doubting the hero – Turner had steered his side to victory and in the process became the first New Zealander to score two hundreds in a Test.

Brian Lara – 196

West Indies v South Africa, Port of Spain 8-12 April 2005

68

It has been said that the truly great don't need to practice and it certainly seems that this was the case with Brian Lara. Prior to the second Test against South Africa at his home ground he had not played a first-class innings in eight months having missed, along with several others, the first Test following a sponsorship dispute. Stripped of the captaincy, Lara's uncertain future had *Associated Newspapers'* Wayne Veysey asking, 'Is this the beginning of the end for one of the greatest batsmen cricket has known?'

In the first Test of the series, at Georgetown, both Wavell Hinds and Shrivnarine Chanderpaul notched double-hundreds as the West Indies forced South Africa to follow on, before the match ended in a draw. But, with the exiled players back in the fold, the West Indies' hopes were high for the second Test.

However, within half an hour they were reeling at 13-2; cue Lara, striding out to a tremendous ovation from his home fans and looking every inch like he had never been away. On a surface described by *Wisden* as 'impishly unpredictable', Lara played an innings which Tony Becca of the *Gleaner* would describe as 'brilliant, truly brilliant', with 'a parade of strokes that matched his best ever in his long and illustrious career'. Twenty of those strokes found the fence on the first day as Lara crafted a sublime 159 not out from the West Indies' stumps total of 281-6. The first-Test double-centurions were reduced to supporting roles, content to provide solid innings of 35 and 32 respectively. Only once did Lara offer a chance, an edge off Jacques Kallis being missed by a diving Mark Boucher when on 77.

During that evening's press conference, Lara expressed his desire to bestow upon his home fans the gift of a double-century, noting that "within the first 15 minutes I thought this could be something big". This century, his 27th, had moved him ahead of Garry Sobers as the leading Caribbean player on the all-time list.

Next day, although the surface gradually became more bowler-friendly, he was determined to honour his pledge. Circumspect while Daren Powell was knocking up 15 in a stand of 19, he changed tack when last man Reon King joined him. At that stage he was on 176 and, refusing singles in order to retain the strike, he advanced to within one boundary of his promised target. Sadly, Andre Nel had no intention of joining the party and, bowling round the wicket, he got one past Lara which took off his off-stump bail. He had racked up 196 of 347 on a tricky surface, no other batsman managing more than 35. With South Africa going on to record an eight-wicket victory, Lara had produced, in a losing cause, what broadcaster Paul Allott described as "one of the very, very best you will ever see".

The end of Brian Lara? Not a bit of it.

Saeed Anwar – 118

South Africa v Pakistan, Durban 26 February-2 March 1998

Saeed Anwar currently resides on a shortlist of two contesting the position of 'greatest batsman to begin his Test career with a pair', his rival for this esteemed honour being Graham Gooch. Having faced just eight balls against the West Indies at Faisalabad in 1990, he disappeared from the international scene for nearly four years but soon after began to make up for lost time. His elegance through the off-side, despite a lack of footwork, became a joy for Pakistan supporters over the next decade although there was often the feeling that with the eye and talent at his disposal he could have scored more heavily.

Arriving in South Africa in early 1998, he was in poor form – just 136 runs in the previous six matches and only 40 in five innings in the three-Test series at home to South Africa the previous year. Added to this were questions about his conversion rate; 14 fifties but only four centuries. This series started poorly for Anwar, with just two in his only innings in the first match, but at Durban he began to find his form again with 43 in a first innings rescued by Azhar Mahmood. The team total of 259 had left the game in the balance and when a burst of terrifying pace from Shoaib Akhtar on day two sent South Africa reeling, the visitors had a lead of 28 on first innings.

Pakistan built steadily on this lead despite the aggression and fire of a five-man pace battery and Anwar dominated partnerships of 101 with Aamer Sohail and then 58 with Ijaz Ahmed. Undoubtedly assisted by the silencing of South Africa's biggest gun, Allan Donald, leaving the field with a muscle strain, Anwar marched on to his century as Shaun Pollock ripped the middle order to shreds. Having been 159-1 they were suddenly all out for 226, setting South Africa a target of 255 to win on a pitch that was helping all bowlers, but it was one that could be scored on as Mahmood and Anwar had shown. Saeed Anwar had laboured for 210 minutes and with over half the team total to his name he had given an imposing Pakistan attack something to bowl at. The supremely gifted timer of the ball had proved that he could also tough it out and play the innings demanded by the conditions.

The key to the denouement was not the pace of Akhtar or Waqar Younis but the aggressive and pushy leg-spin of Mushtaq Ahmed. With a cushion of sorts provided by Saeed Anwar he wheeled through 37 overs and, bit by bit, chipped through the South Africans, finally finishing them off early on the fifth day just 29 short of their target.

It had been a truly wonderful example of Test cricket featuring brilliant bowling from Pollock, Akhtar and Ahmed and astonishing centuries from Mahmood and Saeed Anwar. Test cricket could be proud of itself, as could both teams. South Africa redeemed themselves the following week with a crushing win that tied the series.

Herschelle Gibbs – 196

South Africa v India, Port Elizabeth 16-20 November 2001

It has been an incidental joy of researching and compiling this book that its subjects, quite apart from their common facility with the willow, tend also to be interesting characters. Herschelle Gibbs ranks among the most interesting of them all – or better said, the most salient and controversial. The controversy in this match did not originate with him; it served, for a change, rather to obscure his efforts. They go unmentioned even in his unmentionable autobiography. It is just as well that the exigencies of space do not permit us to detail the Denness affair. For too long it has overshadowed one of the finest displays of aggressive batting ever seen on South African soil.

Gibbs went into the Test in very good nick, his indiscretions in India and the Caribbean apparently behind him. In Zimbabwe earlier in the summer, it had 'seemed almost too easy' according to his biographer Colin Bryden. He had registered a stylish century in the first Test of the present series, his fourth in Test cricket and (this Bryden found 'difficult to accept') his first in South Africa.

When India opted to bowl first, on a green wicket beneath a sunless sky, "we knew," Gibbs said later, that "it wasn't going to be easy." But he was soon surprised: "There wasn't a lot of pace or steep bounce, and not as much sideways movement as we'd expected; also not much for the spinners." In this he spoke for himself; the wickets tumbled regularly at the other end. Javagal Srinath, he noted, "hardly bowled a bad ball all day".

At times it looked as if Gibbs was playing a different game. Botha Dippenaar scored just 29 out of 105 and Jacques Kallis 24 out of 70 in their partnerships with him. His shot selection, especially through the off side, was superb, his cover drives sumptuous even by his standards, and his cutting most unkind. He went to his third century in five innings, and his second in consecutive Tests, off 167 balls, and by the end of the day was unbeaten on 155 out of a total of 237-5. Apart from a strong appeal on 129, he gave no chances. 'Seldom,' wrote Bryden, 'has a day been dominated so much by one man.'

The pitch quickened on day two, but Gibbs preferred the ball coming on. After the early dismissal of Shaun Pollock, he found a willing companion in Mark Boucher who threw the bat at everything in a partnership of 80. Gibbs had 194 when Tendulkar trotted in for his first over. With a double-century apparently assured, he proceeded first to pull a short ball perilously close to mid-on, and then to slice a long hop straight into the hands of backward-point. One moment Elysian, farcical the next – Gibbs's career in microcosm. But he had been at the crease for more than seven hours, and no-one else apart from Boucher managed 30. It was, sadly, a magnificent effort in vain, as the rain came to save India.

Graham Gooch – 123

England v West Indies, Lord's 19-24 June 1980

In an interview for this book, England Test cricketer and umpire Peter Willey was asked which batsman he thought was the most difficult to bowl to. His response was that it lay between Viv Richards and Graham Gooch, with the somewhat surprising qualification that the latter "...was such a good player of spin." Surprising because so many of Gooch's great performances were made in the face of often frightening pace, usually provided by a Caribbean contingent.

However, in his initial Test outing in 1975 he was anything but competent, becoming only the third England player to be dismissed for a pair on Test debut, after Fred Grace and Jim Smith, hardly household names when compared to the player who would go on to pass the great Jack Hobbs as cricket's all-time run-scorer. Nonetheless, it was not until five years after that ignominious start and in his 36th Test innings that he would pass the magical century mark, so the fact that he would achieve it against such a high-quality West Indian pace attack, and at Lord's to boot, is remarkable.

West Indies had won the first Test at Nottingham by two wickets, Gooch having been unlucky to be run out when batting well. In the second Test, at Lord's, the first day started cloudy and cool, necessitating a break for bad light and that, plus the loss of Geoff Boycott, was not the ideal start. Gooch however lost no time in getting into his stride, reaching 52 off 78 balls with some aplomb, as anything short or full was despatched to the boundary. Acting as if a pace quartet featuring Michael Holding, Andy Roberts, Colin Croft and Joel Garner was there for the taking, he sailed to 100 out of 139 as if it was his 100th hundred, not his first, and when he was finally out on 123 it was made from 165 for two. After his departure, Garner and Holding tore England to pieces and just 104 runs were added for the remaining eight wickets with only Chris Tavaré breaking the 20 mark.

Wisden considered his performance as having 'an authority and power seldom seen from an Englishman in the last fifteen years or so' and he received a standing ovation from the enthralled spectators, applause which the West Indies players echoed. That he was later upstaged by man of the match Richards says more about the Antiguan's brilliance than about Gooch; Richards did not have to contend with the West Indies attack. Peter Willey thus had the pleasure of watching Gooch before the pain of being punished by Richards.

Sadly the only winner on this occasion, as so often at Lord's during the previous decade, was the weather, enough time being lost over the final two days for England to save the match. Indeed, all of the remaining three matches were drawn, leaving the West Indies victorious 1-0. England would not get that close to them again for a long, long time.

Allan Steel – 148

England v Australia, Lord's 21-23 July 1884

In Victorian England, 'professional' was a dirty word. Training for sport was considered almost heresy with a true champion expected to be born with a natural ability. In cricket, like no other sport, the professional player was maligned by the establishment, a hero to the masses he was considered nothing more than a servant to the amateur. He had separate changing rooms, ate with the public instead of in the dining room and had to call the amateur 'Sir' or 'Mr', while he in turn would be referred to only by his surname.

Allan Gibson Steel was an amateur through and through. He attended Marlborough and Cambridge, where he gained blues for cricket, rugby and racquets. At his peak he was considered an allrounder second only to WG Grace but unfortunately his employment as a barrister severely limited his cricket. During the 1880s Steel was a first-choice selection for England and he featured in the first three-Test series played in the 'Old Dart' in 1884. Australia had been in a strong position in the first Test of the summer but the loss of the first day (Tests being only three days' duration in England) resulted in a draw. Both teams were greeted by unsettled weather for the second match – the inaugural Test at Lord's.

Australia, batting first, collapsed to 93-6, but 'Tup' Scott's 75 led Australia to a competitive 229. Scott may have felt particularly aggrieved as it was his own captain, Billy Murdoch, acting as substitute for Grace, who took the catch to dismiss him. The injury did not prevent the good doctor opening the innings and by the end of day one England had reached 90-3. Steel joined the not out batsman, George Ulyett, at the commencement of day two in what appeared to be an evenly poised game, although Australia possessed the trump card in the form of the greatest bowler of the period, Fred 'the Demon' Spofforth.

The delicate balance was quickly disturbed by Steel who was so severe on Spofforth that 'he sank at once into a second rate bowler'. The Australian attack was played by Steel with 'ease and confidence' in a display of 'magnificent batting'. He gave one difficult chance at 48, off Spofforth, and on such things games of cricket can be decided. If the 'Demon' had claimed Steel at this juncture, with his confidence up the great bowler may well have won the match for his country. As it was Steel did not offer another chance until well past his hundred and was not dismissed until he had reached 148 in under four hours.

Faced with a deficit of 150, Australia, through the big-hitting Percy McDonnell, started the second innings with aggressive intent. However it was AG Steel's day; he took the ball and bowled the dangerous McDonnell. With this, Australia collapsed for 145 and were beaten by an innings. The third Test ended in a draw and so England, with the strength of Steel, had won the Ashes.

Steve Waugh – 200

West Indies v Australia, Kingston 29 April-3 May 1995

The 1995 West Indies-Australia series proved to be the marking point at which the power balance within world cricket shifted from the long, pace-fuelled era of Caribbean hegemony to a decade of Australian dominance. The visitors had arrived ranked only fourth by the ICC but by Christmas they would be top, having neatly reversed positions with the hosts.

The series began at Bridgetown with Mark Taylor's upstarts, though shorn of their first -choice attack, taking Richie Richardson's side by surprise and winning in three days, a young Glenn McGrath, bowling second change, taking 8-114 in the match. The fractious tone for a charged series was set on that first afternoon when Steve Waugh juggled a cut shot by Lara as it bobbled beneath him. Replays indicated the ball had hit the ground but Lara was given out. "If I had doubts I would not have claimed it", Waugh said later. It's fair to say that both the opposition and their supporters remained unconvinced.

The rain-affected second Test was drawn but the third, at Port of Spain, appeared to restore the old order, a smarting Curtly Ambrose and Courtney Walsh sharing 15 wickets between them and bowling their side to a nine-wicket victory. Waugh's defiant first innings 63 out of 128 hallmarked the batting template – treating each ball on its merits, wearing the unplayable ones if need be and pouncing on the bad ones. This approach would not just bring him 429 runs at an average of 107 in a low-scoring series, but the bloody-minded reputation as the batsman most cricket followers would put their metaphorical mortgages on for the next 10 years. Peppered by Ambrose, Waugh's four-letter response was not just emblematic of his legendary cussedness but a broadsword piercing of the psychological body-armour of the West Indian war machine. "It's Test cricket," the unrepentant Waugh said afterwards. "If you want an easy game, go play netball."

In the final Test, with the four-match series in the balance at 1-1, Steve joined his brother Mark with his side tottering at 73-3 facing a moderate West Indian total of 265 on a good wicket. The twins would add 231 runs in 57 overs and, at times, stun the Sabina Park crowd into silence as they flayed an increasingly demoralised attack to all parts; they 'visibly wilted' noted Steve with some relish. Junior fell for 137 but his older twin – arms, chest and ribs reddened by a barrage of 150 bouncers – batted on in a state later described as 'trance-like' before being last out for exactly 200. He was at the crease for close on 10 hours, faced 425 balls, hit 17 fours and one six and after Paul Reiffel then destroyed the West Indian top order, he had not only consigned the West Indies to their first series defeat in 15 years but wrested from them the mantle of Test team supremacy. Reiffel later described the innings as 'one of the greatest batting feats I ever witnessed'.

Hashim Amla – 311*

England v South Africa, The Oval 19-23 July 2012

Cricket's lumbering scheduling may never allow for a world Test championship but at least 2012 matched the two best teams for three matches. The first Test, at The Oval, with Lord's being the temporary home of Olympic archery, carried the tantalising prospect of a tussle between England's destructive bowlers and South Africa's immovable batsmen.

An Alastair Cook century ensured steady if unspectacular progress for England on the first day but this would prove to be their apex in the series, with a collapse to 385 on day two. Given the conditions only respectable but, given the bowling, there were grounds for optimism and home hopes were raised when Alviro Petersen was out for a duck. This brought in Hashim Amla to join his captain. With two hours left to play under cloudy skies and occasional showers this was a series-deciding session – a few wickets and South Africa would be facing an uphill struggle. Graeme Smith and Amla calmly weathered the storm and with a close-of-play score of 86-1 the omens for England were now ominous.

Day three brought sunshine and a bounty of runs for Smith and Amla, a study in contrasts. South Africa's lumbering, left-handed captain scored almost three-quarters of his runs on the leg side, brute force his greatest ally, whereas Amla dismantled England's bowling with timing, soft hands and balance. The broadsword and the scimitar. Smith's dismissal for 131 merely brought more punishment for England's bowlers. His replacement, Jacques Kallis, effortlessly accumulated runs whilst Amla marched elegantly onwards, peppering the off side, sometimes toying with England by stroking the ball to recently vacated areas.

Amla's batting felt like an extension of his personality, an aura of calm concentration enveloping him at the crease. There were no raucous celebrations when reaching milestones; he simply acknowledged the crowd's warmth and proceeded serenely onwards, adrenaline his enemy. Beneath this composure was the steely core evident throughout his career; it allowed him to overcome a rocky start in international cricket and ignore the carping that he had been chosen on colour rather than ability. At The Oval that personality and marvellous touch and eye enabled him to remorselessly decimate England's tiring bowlers.

The pair accelerated on the fourth day. Never hoicking or slogging, Amla simply readjusted his internal algorithms, caressing balls to areas previously ignored. By the time Smith called a halt, Amla's 311 was the highest score by any South African in a Test.

England's batsmen then folded to the pace of Dale Steyn. Losing the match by an innings they never came close to matching South Africa throughout the series. This contest between the two leading teams determined the primacy of one and confirmed that Amla was South Africa's greatest batsmen since another Durban High School *alumnus*, Barry Richards.

Kevin Pietersen – 202*

England v India, Lord's 21-25 July 2011

61

Still on the crest of their winter Ashes triumph and with momentum sustained by an early-summer win against Sri Lanka, England began the 2011 home series against India with their gaze set firmly on the number one Test spot. To secure the mace for the first time would be a tall order, requiring victory by two clear wins against a side who had sat atop the table since December 2009, had beaten the hosts home and away in the previous two series and had rested several of their senior players for the visit to the Caribbean which immediately preceded this tour.

At Lord's, weather typical of a blighted summer delayed the start of the series and when MS Dhoni eventually won the toss under skies pregnant with the promise of swing, he had no hesitation in electing to bowl. His decision appeared vindicated after the early departure of the openers and with Zaheer Khan and Praveen Kumar moving the ball prodigiously through the leaden air, survival remained the sole objective of Trott and Pietersen as they took England to 127-2 at the close of a rain-interrupted day. Pietersen took a lead from his compatriot and, with studied self-discipline, grafted his way through the heavy gloom to just 22 off 73 balls. His later contention that circumstances were as tough as any he had faced, though a not unfamiliar refrain when he has found scoring a conundrum, was endorsed by his less hyperbolic captain, Strauss, as having been at least "very difficult".

On the second day the clouds lifted. With the attack depleted by the absence of a hamstrung Zaheer, Pietersen, though still watchful, particularly against the probing of Kumar, began to move through the gears. His first hundred for three years, in front of a home crowd grown tetchy with the wait, was his slowest but now he exacted full return on his earlier diligence. He toyed with the previously in-form Sharma before driving him repeatedly between the stumps and mid-on and neutered the threat of Harbhajan to such an extent that an exasperated Dhoni took off his pads and grabbed the ball himself.

Save for a claimed catch at leg-slip when on 49, turned down on review, and a hot-spot reprieve from the ignominy of falling caught behind to the Indian skipper, it was a chanceless innings. Respectful of his team's needs, his duty to his talent and the swing of the persevering Kumar, he paced with restraint until, when pushing for the declaration, he double-declutched thrillingly and with all his old brutal bravura took just 25 balls to score the last 50 of an undefeated 202. In all he hit 21 fours and a six and, as he basked later in the love of his dressing room and his public, would muse that he had "never worked harder". His skipper, reflecting on its role in forming the platform from which the England seamers would win the game, thought it one of the great innings he'd ever seen.

Don Bradman – 334

England v Australia, Leeds 11-15 July 1930

'He will always be in the category of the brilliant, if unsound, ones.'

This was Percy Fender, writing on Bradman prior to the start of the 1930 tour. Poor Percy has been unfairly maligned because of this ill-judged comment but, in fairness, he also said in the same book that, 'he may well become a very great player'. In *The Tests of 1930* which, along with his other Ashes books, is as insightful as any written, he now wrote glowingly of 'The Don' who had, after all, played the two finest innings of the English summer. The first had been 254 in the second Test, an innings in which Bradman said every ball went exactly where he wanted, even the ball from which he was dismissed, Percy Chapman, the English captain, taking one of the best catches ever witnessed at Lord's to end Bradman's stay.

Despite the quality of his Lord's innings it was the unique triple-century he scored in the third Test at Headingley that will be best remembered – Fender thought this innings 'truly magnificent'. The teams entered the match at one Test each and, with a four-day limit, fast scoring was imperative in order to force a win.

Bill Woodfull, the Australian captain, won the toss and had no hesitation in batting. Fender wrote that the pitch was so flat that barely a ball rose above stump height throughout the day even though England could boast a first-rate attack of Larwood, Tate, Geary, Tyldesley and Hammond. Woodfull took the ill-fated Archie Jackson with him to the wicket but within 15 minutes the young Don Bradman was at the crease with the score at 2-1. The burden of scoring quickly would fall on the shoulders of Bradman as his captain was known as the 'worm killer' for his almost non-existent bat lift and often sedentary progress.

Fast scoring hardly describes Bradman's innings as by lunch he had become just the third, and to date the last, Australian to score a hundred in the first session on the first day of a Test match, his score being 105 out of 136. 'Worm killer' Woodfull, whose job was simply to feed the young genius the strike, was just 29 not out. Fender believed the bowlers looked Test class against the other batsmen but not Bradman who continued on his merry way and by tea had scored another hundred in a session – 220 out of 305-2. One myth is that Bradman scored a third hundred between tea and stumps but in reality he managed a mere 89 to finish the day on 309.

He was finally dismissed, early on the second day, for 334 but, with the help of rain, England managed to salvage a draw. Australia went on to win the fifth Test and claim the Ashes, Bradman finishing the series with 974 runs. This tally and his effort of scoring 309 in a single day of a Test remain records.

Brian Lara – 132

Australia v West Indies, Perth 1-3 February 1997

To say that this series was an unhappy one for Brian Lara is to gravely understate. After 26 and 44 in the first Test he had failed to reach double figures in five consecutive innings prior to hitting 78 in the second innings at Adelaide, by which time the West Indies were already beaten. Bad batting was one thing, a bad attitude quite another – after being adjudged caught behind by Ian Healy he had later stormed into the Australian dressing room to remonstrate, despite Clive Lloyd's earlier promise to keep relations civil.

Coming into the fifth Test with the rubber already lost, a Perth pitch having what Matthew Engel, in the *Guardian*, described as 'ferocious pace' and in temperatures reaching 43C, Lara figured to do no better than he had in the previous four Tests.

After Curtly Ambrose had bowled Australia out for 243, Lara strode to the crease at 43-2 – he was to be next out, but by then he had carried the West Indies to an eight-run lead with the score at 251-3. In that time, he had crafted a century which was fashioned from what Tony Cozier described as 'an exhilarating exhibition of strokes', the best of which he saved for Warne, a cover drive to bring up his 100. Indeed, after a slow start it seemed, according to *Wisden*, that 'for him, the cracks closed up and the bounce evened out'. His second 50 came in half the time of the first and he climaxed with 26 in just 14 deliveries off Shane Warne, before the Australian maestro finally had him caught behind. Lara had batted for a shade under four hours and his 132 was scored off 183 balls with 22 fours and a six. He had been ably supported by Robert Samuels, who scored a fine 76 in the slipstream in what would be his last Test.

So much for great batting – at that evening's press conference the acrimony returned as Lara accused the Australians of having subjected Samuels to an unacceptable degree of sledging. Australian captain Mark Taylor countered by claiming that Lara's sledging had itself been unacceptable, calling Lara "an antagonist". Whatever the truth, next day found Lara in hot water with umpires Peter Willey and Darrell Hair; Steve Waugh objected to Lara acting as a runner for Courtney Walsh, the ensuing argument necessitating an on-field lecture from the officials. Back to the cricket, and the tourists ended their first innings with a lead of 141, so that when Australia succumbed to Walsh for 194, the West Indies' openers had merely to knock off the 55 runs required for a 10-wicket victory.

Lara would go on to reach further heights but unfortunately for the West Indies, having been beaten both home and away by the heirs-apparent, they were forced to hand over the crown they had worn for 15 years to an Australian team just beginning to blossom into one of the all-time greats.

Mohammad Ashraful – 158*

Bangladesh v India, Chittagong 17-20 December 2004

58

If it is rare that Man of the Match awards are doled out to players on losing teams, it's practically unheard of for such an award to be made to a player on a team which has been vanquished by an innings. Such was the case with Mohammad Ashraful's rousing unbeaten 158 in the second Test against India at Chittagong in 2004, a performance which signalled a self-belief that would ripple through the side and lift the minnows of Bangladesh to undreamt of heights. The following year they would go on to win their first Test after more than five years as a member of the ICC top ten, albeit against a somewhat depleted Zimbabwe side, but much, much more significantly they would get the better of a world-leading and full-strength Australia to win their first ODI in 107 attempts.

Ashraful had announced himself to the cricket world in his first Test when, aged just 17, he became the youngest batsman to score a Test match hundred, causing then-coach Trevor Chappell to comment; "The manner he concentrates on his batting made me believe that the lad is destined to have a long cricketing journey."

There was no thought of Bangladeshi fireworks during the first two days at Chittagong as India built up a massive first-innings total of 526. When Ashraful walked to the crease Bangladesh had just lost two wickets in four balls. Surely this was destined to be another bad five days at the office for Test cricket's newest recruits. But the 20-year-old proceeded to unveil an innings which had everything – pulls and hooks off the fast men, great footwork against the spinners, stylish cover drives, reverse sweeps, and dances down the wicket as he wore out the bowling and conquered it. His century was reached in a spritely 124 balls and his innings in total was fashioned off 194 balls, including 24 fours and three sixes.

Rarely to that point had Bangladesh avoided the follow-on against top-ranked teams, but Ashraful's innings brought them to within seven runs of avoiding their usual fate. Sadly, he ran out of partners ("I had forgotten to remind Nazmul [Hossain] to go for the run") and in the second innings it was business as usual for Bangladesh as they finished the day on 118-9. On the plus side, they had scored no fewer than 397 runs in a single day.

Despite the magnitude of India's win, as a result of which the series ended 2-0, uppermost on everyone's lips was Ashraful's thrilling innings. No lesser an authority than Sunil Gavaskar considered this knock to be one of the finest Test centuries he had ever seen. Ashraful would later admit that a tip from Tendulkar had inspired him: "Sachin suggested that I should not curb my natural game and always play positive." Mission accomplished and with it questions as to Bangladesh's status as a worthy Test-playing nation were put on hold.

Sanath Jayasuriya – 253

Pakistan v Sri Lanka, Faisalabad 20-24 October 2004

Early in 1996, Sanath Jayasuriya was selected for the Sri Lankan Test team after a 15-month absence, this time opening the batting. Up to this point he'd had a moderate Test career as an allrounder with a batting average of 30 but he hit 48 and 112 to cement his position in the side. Two months later the whole cricketing world knew of this quiet, gentlemanly left hander. He had helped Sri Lanka win the one-day World Cup, claiming the tournament's Most Valuable Player title as he spearheaded the hitherto scarcely tried, but henceforth common practice, tactic of attacking the bowling from the very start of an innings.

Blessed with excellent hand-eye co-ordination which allowed his natural attacking flair to flourish, there were still those who questioned whether, as a big-hitter, Jayasuriya would thrive in the five-day format. Well, he stayed another 12 years and this staying power is affirmed by a Test high of 340 and two double-centuries, the second of which, struck in the twilight of his career, was a particular classic.

In the opener of a two-match series Sri Lanka batted first, but the Pakistani quick bowlers, Shoaib Akhtar and Mohammad Sami reduced them to 147-6 before Thilan Samaraweera, with a determined 100, took the score to 243 all out. In reply, the hosts posted 264 for a lead of 21. Sri Lanka's second innings began badly when Marvan Atapattu bagged a pair. Soon after came perhaps the pivotal moment of the match when Jayasuriya, on nine, was caught behind… but Shoaib had overstepped. Reprieved, Jayasuriya and partner Kumar Sangakkara sped along at over four an over, seeing off some typically hot-blooded bowling from Shoaib, and when the latter departed for 59, Mahela Jayawardene continued in his stead scoring 57. Jayasuriya was content to play second fiddle in these partnerships, but did bring up his hundred with a six over long-on off the spinner Danish Kaneria, and by the end of the third day had scored 131 from a total of 285-3.

Next morning, Sri Lanka unaccountably collapsed from 309-3 to 337-8, just 316 ahead, hardly an unassailable lead on a pitch that had become quite lifeless. Dilhara Fernando then joined Jayasuriya in a 17-over, record-breaking, 101-run partnership. Jayasuriya bullied the Pakistani attack and farmed the bowling to such an extent that his partner faced only 23 balls and scored just one run. With a dazzling shot off Shoaib he became the first Test player to bring up both his 100 and 200 with sixes. Soon after Fernando's dismissal, Jayasuriya himself fell for an outstanding, authoritative 253 in 348 balls that included 33 fours and four sixes. He had hit 122 of the 153 runs scored since the start of the day. Deflated by Jayasuriya's dominance, Pakistan were never in the hunt and Sri Lanka, after a blistering six-over spell of 4-9 by Fernando had decimated the top order, won by 201 runs.

Graham Gooch – 153

West Indies v England, Kingston 10-15 April 1981

56

Lord's in June 1980 against Clive Lloyd's West Indians was the scene of a 25-year-old Ian Botham's second Test as England captain. He won the toss, chose to bat and saw his team manage a draw. Without the intervention of the weather it would have been a defeat, and without Graham Gooch, playing a lone hand for 123 in England's first innings, it would probably have been a crushing defeat long before the heavens opened.

Less than nine months later, in Barbados, a similar knock from Gooch, 116 out of 224, could not prevent England losing by 298 runs. This defeat left England, on the tour that was so marred by the sudden death of assistant manager Kenny Barrington, 2-0 down with two to play. Gooch contributed 33 and 83 as the fourth Test was drawn, and his 153 in the fifth, scored out of an England total of 285, paved the way for a rearguard action by David Gower, ably assisted by Peter Willey, that secured another draw.

Pre-match speculation was that the Sabina Park pitch would be a grassy one, tailored to the West Indian pacemen. In the event it turned out to be relatively benign with just some uneven bounce to worry Gooch and Geoffrey Boycott as they went out to bat on the first morning, after Lloyd had invited England to make first use of the wicket. At lunch they had made 93 without undue alarm – Gooch was on 46.

In the afternoon session he was at his majestic best, moving on to 124 by tea. There was no watchful defence here, Gooch taking on the quick men whenever there was a scoring opportunity. Colin Croft, who is often overlooked when the Caribbean pace pack of the time is remembered, went into the match with 21 wickets at 13.48 in the series. His first four overs cost 33, and the next four 23, with Gooch lifting one short delivery, quite deliberately, over the slips and third-man for six. Along with Marshall, Holding and Garner he was treated with something approaching disdain.

After tea, Gooch was finally dismissed for 153. With his team-mates and extras contributing just 132, England's 285 was not enough and their second innings began 157 runs in arrears. There was a flurry of wickets before Gower and Willey anchored the innings.

Botham had lost back-to-back series against West Indies and he lost his job after defeat in the first Test against Kim Hughes' 1981 Australians. Unlike Botham, Gooch, whose heroics had done so much to keep those margins of defeat as modest as they were, had come back from the Caribbean with his reputation very much in the ascendant. However, as proof positive that cricket is at least as funny an old game as football, by the end of August 1981 Botham was once again the greatest sportsman in the land, and Gooch had been dropped for the final Test after averaging just 13.90 in the first five. But he would be back.

Mark Butcher – 116

England v South Africa, Leeds 6-10 August 1998

55

There were some who genuinely feared for the health of Test cricket in England in 1998. No major series had been won since the 1985 Ashes and an expectation of mediocrity was sapping the patience of the paying public. That year's tourists were South Africa, as ever difficult to beat at the best of times, let alone the worst.

England looked competitive enough in drawing the first Test, but then lost the second heavily before being all but beaten by an innings in the third, a defiant rearguard action from Alec Stewart being the saviour. A rejuvenated side then powered to victory in the fourth, the route beginning in that famous clash between Allan Donald and Michael Atherton. Then at Headingley one of the epic Tests was, largely by virtue of Mark Butcher's first Test century, won to clinch the series. It was the first time in more than 40 years that England had triumphed in a deciding Test at home.

The match was Mark Butcher's 13th cap. His average at that stage was just over 25, with only four half-centuries to show for it, and, despite a couple of fifties earlier in the series, his place was certainly not secure. If that were not enough to dent a young man's confidence, the prospect of what he had to face as he walked out to the middle with Atherton must have been daunting. This was Headingley, a happy hunting ground for seam bowlers for years, and he was up against an immensely strong pace attack. The irrepressible Donald was not alone; he was supported by Shaun Pollock, who was rapidly becoming a byword for skill and consistency, the raw but rapid Makhaya Ntini and the far from negligible bowling talents of the two all-rounders, Jacques Kallis and Brian McMillan.

The wicket was difficult, *Wisden* describing it as 'slow and two-paced, and the bounce grew ever less predictable'. By the time Butcher left, deep into the evening session at 196-5, he had scored 116, including 18 boundaries. He was a left-hander, not an elegant one in the manner of a Gower, but a purposeful batsman who, once he was established, could hit the slightly wayward delivery as well as anyone. The difference in this game was that he seemed at last to have worked out when to play at the ball, and when not to. It was a perfect mix of judicious caution and studied aggression. His innings was chanceless and without it England, whose next highest contributor was Dominic Cork with 24, would have been out of the game before it got going.

On Butcher's dismissal, the last five wickets added just 34. South Africa secured a slender first-innings lead but, after a fine 94 from Nasser Hussain, the victory target was 219. The visitors slumped to 27-5 before Jonty Rhodes, supported by McMillan and Pollock, fought back. Ultimately, however, they fell 23 runs short giving England a dramatic series victory.

Roy Fredericks – 169

Australia v West Indies, Perth 12-16 December 1975

54

The name of Roy Fredericks tends to have faded into the shadows of his illustrious contemporaries but in Australia when his name is mentioned, his innings against Dennis Lillee and Jeff Thomson on a fiery Perth pitch is recalled. He was a genuine opening batsman and his record of 4,334 runs at an average of 42.49 is impressive for his era when, unlike today, Test teams seemingly did not have at least two players averaging over 50.

The 1975-76 series was Fredericks' third against Australia but he had yet to register a century against them. In the first, at Brisbane, of six Tests he managed 46 and seven, the first innings being a whirlwind scored from just 30 balls. The West Indies were comfortably defeated by eight wickets and were criticised for the cavalier attitude which saw them throw their wickets away – in a series that was being billed as the battle for the unofficial world champion Test nation, they were being labelled as the 'Happy Hookers'.

The second Test, at Perth, was expected to suit the fast bowlers from both sides so it was a little surprising when Greg Chappell won the toss and elected to bat, a decision he may have regretted when Australia were 0-1 and then 37-2. Ian Chappell then played one of his finest innings, his 156 guiding Australia to a respectable 329, the next best score being just 45. The Australian innings finished early on the second morning leaving Fredericks to take strike to Lillee. After starting with a 'sighter', he attempted to hook the next delivery but slightly misjudged it and top-edged the ball. Such was the aggression of the swing, the ball flew over the mid-wicket boundary for six.

That one violent shot set the scene for the innings and was the only false stroke the little opener was to play for the rest of his scintillating stay. The first West Indies 50 was up in just 5.3 eight-ball overs. 'Thommo', the fastest bowler in the world, was taken off after just three overs with figures of 0-33, as Fredericks just kept cutting and slashing at anything remotely outside the off stump, often with both feet off the ground at the moment of impact, bringing up his 50 off only 33 balls. At lunch the visitors had flown to 130-1 from 14 overs with Fredericks on 81 not out. Between lunch and tea he continued to attack the bowling, peeling off another 88 runs but alas for the crowd, although happily for the Australian bowlers, after the resumption Fredericks failed to add to his score and was dismissed by Lillee, caught at the wicket. His astonishing runs were made from just 145 balls with one six and 27 fours.

The West Indies finished with 585 and went on to win the match by an innings and 87 runs. This was to be their only win in the series which they eventually lost five Tests to one but Ian Chappell, for one, has never forgotten that day.

Virender Sehwag – 319

India v South Africa, Chennai 26-30 March 2008

Breathtaking, magical, buccaneering, explosive, creative, audacious – just a small sample of the adjectives which observing scribes used in an attempt to do justice to Virender Sehwag's second triple-century, achieved against South Africa on a Chennai shirt-front in 2008. In a match which *Wisden* determined was 'destined to be a draw before a ball was bowled', Sehwag breathed some much-needed life into it with the fastest Test 300 ever.

That South Africa themselves amassed 540 meant that, prior to his batting pyrotechnics, Sehwag had been in the field for two days in sweltering heat. It mattered not; as Sehwag rocketed along from the off, his opening partner Wasim Jaffer contributed just 73 to an opening stand of 213. Sehwag's century arrived from 116 balls and in fine style, as he hoisted Jacques Kallis straight back for a six. After losing Jaffer, Rahul Dravid took over as straight man, but Sehwag was just getting started; his 200 came up in 178 balls, the third-fastest ever and his triple in 278 balls, the quickest on record. In the meantime, Dravid applied more conventional methods to reach his fifty in a sluggish 151 balls – he would later enthuse: "Standing at the other end it was almost like watching a highlights package. I just had to control my own ego and enjoy it."

Records continued to tumble as Sehwag took India to a deficit of just 72 with nine wickets remaining at the end of the third day, an astonishing riposte which he had totally dominated, though he succumbed early the next day for a peerless 319 made from a total of 481-2. At that point there was only one team with a hope of winning, however with Sehwag gone the impetus was lost and with India eventually all out for 627, South Africa were able to see the match to a close on 331-5.

That this performance occurred only a few Tests after Sehwag had been dropped from the side only serves to enhance its magnitude, and indeed chairman of selectors Dilip Vengsarkar called it a "really special knock". His dominance over a high-quality South African attack was absolute – Morne Morkel, the most successful against Sehwag, conceded a strike-rate of over 86; as Kevin Mitchell of the *Observer* noted, South Africa's feted attack had been reduced to the 'poor sods serving up the boundary fodder'.

It was Sehwag's 10th successive century over 150, also a record, as were the consecutive double-century partnerships for the first and second wickets, a feat unique in Test cricket. Adding to his 309 in Multan in 2004 he joined Don Bradman and Brian Lara as the only batsmen to score two Test triples. Unlike those two immortals of the game, Sehwag hit more than his fair share of sixes; his first included six of them, this innings had five along with 42 fours. As Sourav Ganguly later opined, "That's how he thinks, in fours and sixes."

Ian Redpath – 159*

New Zealand v Australia, Auckland 22-24 March 1974

52

Ian Redpath's finest Test century came during the final match of a three-Test series in New Zealand in early 1974. Following a series of equal length in Australia just weeks earlier in which Redpath did not appear, the first encounter between the two countries since the inaugural Test in New Zealand in 1946, Ian Chappell's team crossed the Tasman Sea to face Bevan Congdon's men on their turf full of confidence after a 2-0 home victory. The first match, in Wellington, had been drawn and, with the Kiwis recording a historic five-wicket win in Christchurch a week later, Australia now needed a win to level the series – a situation they had hardly envisaged a month earlier.

In its report, *Wisden* described the standard of pitches for the series as; 'rather like the three bears' porridge, chairs and beds: but the just right one was at Christchurch, and the strip at Eden Park Auckland was as harshly criticised for its vices as was the Wellington one for being over-virtuous.' In a contest completed in three days, 18 wickets fell on the first day alone. Australia, batting first, were indebted to a superb, unbeaten, 104 from Doug Walters and in reply New Zealand were shot out for 112 by Gary Gilmour and Ashley Mallett. Two completed innings in under 77 eight-ball overs; the problems facing the batsmen were not those created by a speedy surface, but rather by a wet one that had been watered too late in its preparation prior to the Test.

In the Australian second innings, Keith Stackpole fell for a duck with the score at two but from then on Redpath went on the counter-attack. Forty-five runs came in the first six overs as he was accompanied by first Ian and then Greg Chappell. With occasionally wayward bowling from the Hadlee brothers early in the piece, Redpath led the charge in helping Australia post their century in 70 minutes. Accurate bowling from Congdon and a miserly Hedley Howarth, the slow left-armer, still had to be surmounted though, and the dampness and lack of pace made strokeplay uncommonly difficult.

It was Redpath's skill in counter-attacking in such conditions that swung the match for Australia. By turns watchful and aggressive, he hit 20 fours from 310 deliveries and gave not one chance in almost six hours. In a historic series suffused with national pride, tensions inevitably rose to the surface. Redpath, according to Glenn Turner, had batted like 'an English pro' as he became only the seventh Australian to carry his bat through a completed Test innings – his unbeaten 159 was more than the New Zealanders managed in either of their innings. On a surface where the ball was still, according to *Wisden*, 'moving about, jumping or keeping down from the many divots taken from the pitch', the bowling was too much for all bar Turner and Australia levelled the series and handsomely saved face.

Younis Khan – 267

India v Pakistan, Bangalore 24-28 March 2005

51

He was the modern embodiment of Pakistan's finest cricketing traditions synthesising the Pathan leadership spirit of Imran Khan, the indefatigability of Hanif Mohammad and the combativeness of Javed Miandad. Younis Khan came into the final Test of the series in fine form having scored 147 in the previous match but put that effort into the shade with this match-winning and series-saving triumph of endurance. A 'behemoth' was one verdict.

When Inzamam-ul-Haq opted to bat on the first morning, it was in the hope of posting a total sufficient to push for the win that would level the series but that ambition looked in jeopardy as he arrived at the crease to accompany Younis with the score at 7-2. The rest of the day belonged to this pair. With the captain taking the lead in his 100th Test they piled on the runs on a surface offering little encouragement to either Harbhajan Singh or Anil Kumble. Shots all round the wicket pierced the field as the normally penetrative spin twins were ground into the dust on a sweltering day. The new ball did nothing to alter the balance and at the close India could reflect on a miserable day and a scoreboard showing 323-2.

Resuming next morning with his score on 127, Younis quickly lost Inzamam but thereafter he assumed control, offering only one chance with his score on 177. But both before and after this error his play, particularly on the off side, was sublime as landmarks fell and the game was taken further and further away from India. By lunch he had added 50 to his score and a further 48 followed in the next session before an acceleration in pursuit of a declaration brought a first sign of recklessness and final dismissal. In all, Younis' 267 contained 32 fours and one six. It was a monument to fitness, patience, endurance and skill. Towards its end he was still running twos and threes hard in the baking afternoon heat. Particularly impressive was his mastery of Harbhajan on the second day, as a pitch much more conducive to spin than on the first offered prodigious turn to the off spinner, who delivered a marathon and exacting spell of bowling, rewarded with a return of 6-152.

India set about their reply with Virender Sehwag, in typically ebullient mood, the mainstay of his side's 449. Pakistan went for quick runs, declaring on 261-2, Younis this time unbeaten on 84. Requiring 383 to win, India looked resolute on the final afternoon as they reached 108-1. The collapse that followed was indicative of Pakistan's reversal of fortune as they bundled out their hosts for 214. Incredibly, an enthralling contest had ended with Pakistan victorious by 168 runs. They shared the spoils of a series in which they had often been second best, the foundations of the unlikely victory here being laid on the opening two days by Younis Khan who was, fittingly, man of the match with this his eighth Test century and the highest score by a visiting batsman in India.

Part Two
Innings 50–26

Ascent

Ian Botham – 149*

England v Australia, Leeds 16-21 July 1981

50

In 1981 England were looking to retain the Ashes. However, thanks to the split in the game that occurred in 1977 between the cricket authorities, on the one hand, and Kerry Packer and his World Series Cricket, on the other, the game's greatest contest was in a state of some confusion. In the 1977 contest England had, following the shock of meeting Dennis Lillee and Jeff Thomson two years earlier, regrouped under Mike Brearley and comfortably overcome an Australian side that lacked Ian Chappell, Ross Edwards and Lillee.

In 1978-79 when the time came for Brearley to defend the Ashes, his side proceeded to decisively beat what was, at best, an Australian second eleven and as a result the famous old urn was retained for the next full series. Frustratingly, however, by the time 1981 arrived that was fairly meaningless, as a three-Test series to celebrate peace returning to the administration of the game, having been hurriedly arranged in 1979-80, saw a proper Australian side brush Brearley's England aside with ease. It had, however, been agreed beforehand that three Tests did not constitute an Ashes series, thus England's hold on the urn was purely technical.

By 1981, Brearley was no longer England captain having handed the baton on to the talismanic Ian Botham, passing on what seemed to be a poisoned chalice – and so it proved. Back-to-back defeats at the hands of Clive Lloyd's West Indies had temporarily tarnished Botham's aura and, after Australia won the first Test in 1981 followed by his recording a pair in a lacklustre draw in the second, the selectors reacted in the way that selectors do and demoted Botham to the rank and file, Brearley being brought back as captain for Headingley. Initially it seemed to have been a fruitless move as Aussie skipper Kim Hughes won the toss and declared on 401-9. England could manage only 174 and, following on 227 behind, found themselves on the fourth afternoon 135-7, still 92 short of making Australia bat again. There were two momentous acts to come: Act I, enter stage left Ian Botham with bat. Act II, enter stage right Bob Willis with ball. The story of how England went on to wrest victory from the jaws of defeat is one of the best known in the game.

The bare bones of the innings are 149 runs, unbeaten, in 219 minutes with 27 fours and a single six. Richie Benaud's description of that straight drive off Terry Alderman as "into the confectionery stall and out again" is English cricket's "They think it's all over" moment. The innings started as a quick thrash by Botham, who encouraged Graham Dilley to do the same, simply to try and restore some pride. In any event it was not a good wicket, Australia's manager describing it as a "disgrace", so there was no point in hanging around. England were, after all, rated 500-1 outsiders by the normally sane Ladbrokes' odds-makers.

Denis Lillee, for one, always called the innings for what it was, an extraordinary fluke. He described Botham's innings as "bloody lucky" and therefore no fault of the Australian bowlers. This is certainly partly correct – Botham threw the proverbial kitchen sink at the ball, there were plenty of edges and much playing and missing but where Lillee is wrong though is his assertion that "we dropped him countless times". That simply wasn't true. Early on in his innings Botham did slash one through the gully area that Ray Bright put down – it should however be borne in mind when judging Bright, that Botham was striking the ball with such power that at one point an attempted hook which he timed so badly that it struck his bat somewhere near the splice still bounced only once before crossing the mid-on boundary. The only other possible chance was when Botham was on 109, Marsh getting fingertips to a top edge. As matters turned out it wasn't a chance at all although, when the incident was replayed, it looked as if Marsh might have increased the possibility of making the catch had he gone for it with one hand rather than both. In any event neither the bowling, fielding or wicket-keeping could be criticised.

The harum scarum nature of the innings is well illustrated by the statistics of Botham's second fifty which took just forty minutes; of the 64 runs he scored between 39 and 103, no less than 62 came in boundaries. Geoff Lawson was bowling at Botham when he was on 95 and a couple of deliveries sum up the innings; the first was a sumptuous cover drive which Walter Hammond would have been proud to call his own, then the century came up with a thick outside edge. The fourth-evening crowd celebrated wildly and Botham's face was lit up by the biggest smile of all. The television cameras cut to the England balcony, showing an animated, not to say frantic, Brearley manically gesturing towards his batsman, just in case they hadn't realised that the impossible was now the merely improbable, and that more runs were needed.

England were 124 ahead at the close of that remarkable fourth day, but had just one wicket to fall and, with Willis dismissed next morning with just five more added, it was surely Australia's game. Graeme Wood started with two fours from a couple of Botham looseners, but then the miracle worker got him at 13, and those watching wondered whether he might produce heroics with the ball as well. He didn't of course, and for a while Australia looked as if they would win comfortably, until the game changed at 56-1. Willis, demonic of appearance and throwing everything he had at the task, had just switched to the Kirkstall Lane End and he produced from nowhere an absolute pig of a delivery to remove Trevor Chappell; with that the mood of the game changed in an instant. Ninety minutes later he had 8-43, and he and Botham, with a little help from their team-mates, had produced what David Frith later dubbed the 'Miracle at Leeds'. The mood of the nation changed, just in time for the match at St Paul's Cathedral a week later, the wedding of Prince Charles and Lady Diana Spencer.

Don Bradman – 103

England v Australia, Leeds 22-25 July 1938

49

Following a complete wash-out at Old Trafford, only the second in the history of Test cricket, the series was deadlocked at 0-0 as the sides crossed the Pennines for the fourth Test at Headingley. The holders, Australia, needed only to win one of the remaining Tests to retain the Ashes. Yorkshire folk knew all about Don Bradman after his 334 and 304 on two previous visits, but it was clear that there would be no triple-century this time. This was a series played under storm clouds, real and metaphorical – the weather continued to threaten, while events in Europe were being followed with much trepidation by those who remembered 'The War to End All Wars' just a generation before. Spectators at the Tests of 1938 must have watched the matches with mixed feelings, glad that the Australians were in England again, but aware of a very real possibility that they would not be back in 1942.

On the tour too, there was conflict. Bradman had asked that his wife Jessie be allowed to join him for the closing weeks of the trip, a request that had been denied by the Board. Australia's master batsman took umbrage and threatened to retire from Test cricket after the tour. Once the row became public knowledge, Australian supporters and media sided with Bradman, and the Board, predictably, capitulated – but the affair left a shadow on what had otherwise been a most successful visit. Most of the counties had been dispatched by an innings, with Nottinghamshire, in the previous game, beaten by the little matter of 412 runs, while Bradman had put together 11 three-figure scores, including his customary double-hundred at Worcester and a five-hour 278 against the MCC, whose attack included England spearhead Ken Farnes. The strength of the visitor's batting was shown in Bradman batting just once in each of Australia's first seven first-class matches.

Joining Farnes in the England attack for this crucial Test would be Bill Bowes and Hedley Verity, playing on their home ground, and Kent's Doug Wright, with fizzing leg breaks off a long, hopping run – the nearest England possessed to Australia's Bill O'Reilly, albeit lacking his accuracy and a temperament akin to a fast bowler. To these could be added England's new captain, Walter Hammond, if he could rouse himself to bowl. All were having good seasons (Farnes took 107 wickets at 18 that year) and these would clearly be conditions more to the bowlers' liking than the batsmen's. England were weakened mainly by having their first-choice wicket-keeper Les Ames sidelined by injury – Fred Price of Middlesex came in for his first cap. South Australia's Mervyn Waite was the other debutant.

On the first morning, Hammond won the toss and elected to bat. Len Hutton, the newcomer from Yorkshire who had been one of four England centurions at Trent Bridge, was missing with a broken finger so Charles Barnett and Bill Edrich opened, however both they and Joe Hardstaff had gone by lunch as O'Reilly began to cut through the England batting – only Hammond, with 76, stood firm. Chuck Fleetwood-Smith took a couple of late wickets as England were all out for 223. Australian opener Bill Brown went for a quick 22 so Ben Barnett was pushed up to partner Jack Fingleton until close of play.

The next day belonged to Bradman. In light that was poor throughout, with the bowlers always in with a shout, he hit a chanceless 103. There was little in the way of support; the nightwatchman Barnett, playing in what would be his only series, stayed more than two hours to record his only half-century for his country, but afterwards only Lindsay Hassett reached double figures, adding a round 50 with his skipper. The debutant Waite had a part to play though, making only three but staying firm while the score advanced by 37 – a crucial contribution in a low-scoring match. This was Bradman's third hundred of the series and his sixth in consecutive Tests, all against England. His innings was ended by a superb delivery from Bowes that removed his middle stump – the Yorkshireman had memorably also bowled him first ball to record his only wicket of the bodyline series. Australia's innings ended shortly afterwards on 242, a lead of 19.

Edrich and Barnett made a good start for England, taking them to 49 without loss on the Saturday evening, but there was little to come after them. O'Reilly was once again the destroyer-in-chief and the killer blow came when he had Hammond caught at short-leg by Brown, first ball. England's most successful bowlers had been Farnes and Bowes, the fast men – this, it seemed, was a pitch that helped both pace and spin in equal measure. Eddie Paynter stayed an hour for 21 and watched the last seven wickets go down, all but one to the spinners. Australia needed just 105 to retain the Ashes, and all the time in the world to make the runs. The openers and Bradman fell cheaply but Hassett, in his third Test, struck a near run-a-ball 33 to settle the issue; nothing that England could do at The Oval would now make any difference.

The *Times* correspondent, writing on Saturday's play, felt that England had done well to restrict Bradman to just over a hundred: 'Such prodigious scores are expected of him, and he has given such trouble before on the Headingley ground, in particular, that a mere century can be regarded as a comparative failure.' England, of course, had still been in the match on Saturday night, 30 ahead with all second-innings wickets in hand but Bradman's innings had proved the difference between the sides – even O'Reilly, who claimed 10 in the match, would have had to agree. One of The Don's smallest Test hundreds was also undeniably one of his best – an innings that won a match and settled a series. Our man from the *Times* again: 'All Bradman's innings are great, but this one perhaps will be remembered longer than some others, for he received little support.'

Bradman's tour was to end in anti-climax at The Oval when he was injured while bowling, having seen his record Ashes score surpassed. But he had achieved his main objective.

Herbert Sutcliffe – 135

Australia v England, Melbourne 29 December-5 January 1928-29

48

Herbert Sutcliffe belonged to a new breed of professional cricketer that came to the fore after the Great War. He bought his suits from Savile Row, was always well manicured, his well-oiled jet black hair never seemed out of place and, unlike so many previous pros, he didn't piss his money up a wall; he, like opening partner Jack Hobbs, invested it in founding a successful sports store.

On the field he generated a regal aura, never seemed rushed and treated all bowlers with disdain. It was this attitude that made Sutcliffe less than popular with the Australian players. On one occasion in a Test match against the old enemy he played a ball hard into his stumps only for the bails to jump up and land back in position. The Aussies gasped like Janet Leigh in her *Psycho* shower. Sutcliffe simply took strike again, as if by divine right, failing to even acknowledge the incredulous fielders or the crestfallen bowler.

Perhaps part of the Sutcliffe self-confidence was derived from his late entry to Test cricket; due to the Great War he was almost 30 years old when he made his debut, against South Africa, in 1924. In his first Test Sutcliffe joined Hobbs in what became, arguably, the greatest of all opening partnerships, appropriately enough beginning with a century stand. Sutcliffe was always considered the inferior batsman despite having the better Test average (60.73 against 56.95), no doubt due in part to his methods. His scoring strokes were predominantly the hook, pull and off drive, plus a shovel shot down to fine-leg. He was the ultimate in playing to his limitations, a self-made batsman who relied on tremendous concentration and an unshakeable belief in his own ability. It was these qualities that would allow him to score one of the great hundreds on a true 'sticky dog' of a wicket at Melbourne in 1929 when most critics gave England a 100-1 chance of victory.

England had arrived for the third Test in Melbourne 2-0 up, needing a win to secure the Ashes. It was as well the matches in this series were played to a finish, as the first Test lasted five days, the second six and the third was destined to end on the seventh. One reason for these protracted battles was the batting strength on both sides. Apart from their openers, England featured Patsy Hendren and Walter Hammond who boasted a final Test average of 58.46, while Australia were endowed with the skills of Bill Woodfull, Alan Kippax and a 20-year-old rookie, name of Don Bradman.

Jack Ryder won the toss and apart from some steep bounce and swing for Harold Larwood in the first session which reduced Australia to 57-3, the conditions boded well for the hosts. After lunch, on a flat wicket, Larwood was attacked by both Ryder and Kippax as Australia, with a cameo 79 by Bradman, spent the best part of two days scoring a laborious 397.

The Australian opening bowlers Ted a'Beckett and Stork Hendry were perhaps the slowest trundlers to ever take a new ball so it was a shock when Hobbs was dismissed for just 20. Sutcliffe, against this popgun attack (save for the great Clarrie Grimmett), would also have been disappointed to fall for a snail-paced 58, but thanks to Hammond who registered his second double-hundred in consecutive Tests, England took a narrow 20-run lead.

Australia did not commence their second innings until mid-afternoon on the fourth day and would not complete it until day six. However, at the end of the fifth day, the score had reached 347-8, with centuries to Woodfull and Bradman, the first of 19 he eventually amassed against England. Writing in the *Australasian*, Jack Worrall believed Australia would need a lead of at least 400 runs to feel safe.

The required lead changed suddenly with thunderstorms in Melbourne during the night which caused pessimistic Percy Fender to write: 'Listening to it, while in bed, as I did, was like listening to the nails being driven into England's coffin.' Worrall wrote that the pitch played into England's hands as Australia did not have a quality wet-wicket bowler but both *Wisden* and Fender thought the pitch was all in favour of the bowlers, with *Wisden* recording 'the ball was turning and at other times getting up almost straight'.

The pitch looked in such poor condition when play finally began, not long before lunch on the sixth day, that most in the press believed England would fail to even make a hundred. Some were also surprised Australia did not declare at eight down in order to bowl at England while the pitch was at its worst; as it was the last two wickets added only four runs, leaving the visitors the unlikely challenge of making 332 for victory.

Hobbs and Sutcliffe successfully negotiated the last two overs before lunch. By tea the pair were still together having added 78 on a brute of a pitch, with the ball leaping head high on average three times an over off a good length. Fender thought the wicket 'behaved as badly as it possibly could'. The batsmen gave a masterclass on a sticky dog, eschewing the drive and cut, chiefly scoring by the pull and hook strokes.

After tea the pitch had started to dry out and although still sticky it lost a little bit of its menace. Even so, playwrite Ben Travers saw the hardening pitch as a 'ghastly petrified corrugation'. Hobbs was out for 49, after a superlative opening partnership of 105; so much for the conjecture as to whether the whole team could manage 100. Towards the end of play the pitch had improved enough to allow the Yorkshireman to play a couple of off drives. By stumps he had scored 89 and England finished day six on 117-1, 161 from victory.

With the immediate danger past, the final day should have been simple but the Australian bowling, roundly criticised the previous day, was much more incisive now. Sutcliffe, first with Douglas Jardine and then with Hammond, moved painstakingly to 135 before falling lbw to Grimmett, but with England only 14 runs from victory he had shepherded his side through the storm and the Ashes were won.

Kumar Sangakkara – 156*

New Zealand v Sri Lanka, Wellington December 15-18, 2006

46=

It is not overstating to say that Kumar Sangakkara is a titan of Sri Lankan, and world, cricket. His statistics speak for themselves: over 10,000 Test runs with an average in the mid-fifties and over 10,000 ODI runs, many of both totals scored while playing as a wicket-keeper. Furthermore, he has been a role model for Sri Lankans everywhere and a fine ambassador for his country. In 2011 he became the first active Test cricketer to deliver the prestigious MCC Spirit of Cricket Cowdrey Lecture. He spoke eloquently on the importance of cricket in Sri Lanka's turbulent recent history and culture and its role in helping to bring together different strands of society there. And he did not hold back with his criticism of the political power struggles that blight the sport in his home country. A standing ovation and widespread acclaim ensued.

On the field he has been a tough, aggressive cricketer and not averse to sledging, albeit with good humour and without abuse, a choice example is a *YouTube* favourite – his welcoming to the crease of Shaun Pollock.

Kumar Sangakkara has hit many fine centuries and arguably his best was played in New Zealand in late 2006. The hosts won the first Test of a two-match series but not without controversy. With nine wickets down in the Sri Lankan second innings and a lead of 117 in a low-scoring match, Sangakkara ran an easy single to bring up an excellent century. His partner Muttiah Muralitharan completed the single and then wandered back to congratulate him with some of the New Zealand fielders joining in. Meanwhile, Chris Martin returned the ball from the deep to 'keeper Brendon McCullum who broke the stumps. When New Zealand claimed the dismissal, the umpire had no choice and they went on to win by five wickets. Sri Lankan captain Mahela Jayawardene accepted the run-out as technically correct but against the spirit of the game. Kiwi skipper Stephen Fleming, no doubt irritated that the incident had overshadowed the victory, tried to use this to motivate his team ahead of the second Test and added salt to the wound by suggesting that Sangakkara had been selfish in taking that single on the first ball of the over and leaving the tailender painfully exposed. Should he perhaps have kept his own counsel?

It didn't look like it when Sri Lanka won the toss, batted and lost their first wicket without a run on the board. But then in came Sangakkara who proceeded to give Fleming plenty to ponder with an even better and more crucial century than his previous one. Fast bowlers Martin and Shane Bond were causing the other batsmen all sorts of problems with pace, bounce and movement yet he remained in complete control and brought up his 50 in just 54 balls. When the fourth wicket fell at 81, he was on 62. Next in was Chamara Silva, fresh from a pair in his debut Test, who appeared to take his cue from his senior partner and joined him in dismantling the 'motivated' attack. Sangakkara's stroke play was both varied and exemplary. There were bent-knee drives, punches through point and a huge pulled six off Martin. The *New Zealand Herald* said of the left-handed batsman afterwards that 'his driving through the off-side, whether on the front or back foot, was Gower-like.' Yet this was not risky hitting; he seemed to know exactly which balls to hit and, equally importantly, which balls to leave. And his partner Silva was no mere spectator as the two of them compiled a century partnership in under 20 overs, during which Sangakkara played a beautifully-placed sweep to bring up his hundred in 113 balls and pass 5,000 Test runs. The pair continued to play their shots until, with the score on 202, Silva was caught at first slip by Fleming for an aggressive, cavalier 61.

This brought in wicket-keeper Prasanna Jayawardene, no relation, who had joined the first XI in Sri Lanka's previous series because Sangakkara and the selectors felt that he was overburdened by keeping wicket and batting first-wicket down. His recent scores prior to this decision didn't really reflect this as he had made 185 and three fifties in his previous nine innings, but it reaped immediate rewards when he hit 287 in his first innings after handing over the 'keeping job. And all but two of those runs were his contribution to the highest-ever partnership in first-class cricket of 624 with Mahela Jayawardene in a win against South Africa. His overall statistics endorse the decision: an average of around 40 when behind the stumps and, astonishingly, approaching 70 when not.

Back to the action: Prasanna hit a chancy 25 before getting out to the last ball before tea. Thereafter, Sangakkara managed to add another 25 runs while his last four partners, who amassed four runs in 18 balls between them, were being skittled out by Bond and spinner Daniel Vettori. There were five ducks in the innings and Sri Lanka finished on 268 with Sangakkara on 156 not out. He'd hit 21 fours and a six in 192 balls, and accounted for over 58 per cent of the team's total. It had been virtually error-free bar a very difficult chance when he was on 143 and running out of partners.

It was typical of Sangakkara to write afterwards that 'the highlight of that first innings was not my hundred, although it grabbed the headlines, but the mental character displayed by Chamara Silva after his pair in the first Test.' And referring to the pre-match hullabaloo he explained that 'the statements that then flowed from a disgruntled New Zealand camp only served to provide us fuel going into Wellington, intensifying our focus and determination to raise our game to a higher level.'

By the end of the day, New Zealand had crumpled to 66-4 with Fleming out for a duck. Sri Lanka went on to win the Test by 217; the brilliance of Sangakkara's innings being complemented by a fine 152 from Silva in the second innings and 10 wickets in the match for that man Muralitharan.

Bruce Edgar – 127

New Zealand v West Indies, Auckland 29 February-5 March 1980

The commencement of the 1980s saw everything in the garden of West Indian cricket rosy and peachy. The big names were back in the fold after their sojourn with Kerry Packer and they were in the process of administering a long-awaited thumping of Australia in their own backyard. Viv Richards was in his pomp surrounded by virtuoso cavaliers and the speed machine was cranked up to the max. Clive Lloyd had the man he craved in fitness coach Dennis Waight and a new sense of professional application had been added to the traditional but brittle Caribbean flair. What could possibly go wrong during one month in New Zealand?

Cricket, being the funny old game it is, threw a curve-ball and everything that could go wrong did go wrong over the course of three famous tests. The absence of an injured Richards would dent any team but surely Greenidge, Haynes, Rowe and Kallicharran would be more than a match for Richard Hadlee and his callow side-kicks?

A home victory in the single one-day international sounded only mild alarm bells as the two sides went due south to Dunedin but cracks in the West Indian armoury soon began to appear and tiredness turned to protest and farce before petulance and then aggression took over. The main issue was the umpiring, particularly the work of Fred Goodall, an official of limited experience and a somewhat officious nature – a dangerous combination. His inclination to give lbw decisions in favour of Hadlee was understandable on a wicket where the ball was moving off the seam and generally keeping low and where the bowler was inclined to go straight and full. Less forgivable was a series of generous decisions favouring New Zealand batsmen adjudged not to have edged balls to the wicket-keeper. Hadlee's 11 wickets had left the home side with just 104 to win on the last afternoon, a target that was reached off the last ball by the last pair, a frantic leg-bye and a missed run-out being the difference between the two teams. Yet this remarkable finish has always been overshadowed by the photograph of Michael Holding kicking the stumps to kingdom-come on being denied a clear deflection to Deryck Murray.

Foolishly the authorities retained Goodall for the next match and matters deteriorated further and were considerably less photogenic. By day three the West Indians were apoplectic at the work of the umpire, particularly his failing to detect a clear gloved catch to dismiss Geoff Howarth. They first refused to take the field and then spent the remainder of the day playing at 50 per cent capacity. With the game slipping towards a draw, Colin Croft entered the fray. Firstly he flicked off a bail when walking back to his mark after being no-balled but what came next was just daft: Croft has always denied barging the umpire deliberately in his delivery stride but the video evidence is fairly damning; it looked ugly and the bowler was absurdly lucky not to receive an extensive ban. A dreary but explosive game meandered to a draw, so the visitors now had only the match at Eden Park to set matters right.

With the offending umpire banished and a pitch described as 'well grassed and watered' the omens were good for the West Indian pace attack. But the toss was won by Geoff Howarth who chose discretion over valour and was rewarded by his bowlers. Hadlee and Gary Troup made hay in the rare moments of sunshine and the West Indies were gone on the evening of a second truncated day for just 220; New Zealand moved comfortably enough to 43-0 by the close. The next day was washed out but, in a move of *rapprochement*, it was agreed that the scheduled rest day would be used instead. So, with three days left, the West Indies desperately needed to make early ground to have a chance of sharing the series. That they failed was largely the work of one man – Bruce Edgar.

The cliché is obvious – qualified chartered accountant more concerned with accumulation than entertainment, the mind of the mathematician not the artist, dull and worthy, solid rather than spectacular. Cliché or not, it is not an unfair assessment of his methods but this was just his kind of day. A combination of unflagging concentration, physical bravery and no little technical know-how saw him dominate an opening partnership of 75 with John Wright before adding a further 96 with his captain. Clive Lloyd chopped and changed, turned from Andy Roberts to Holding, then to Croft and Joel Garner before going back, but it was to little avail. Chanceless and with barely a false shot, Edgar batted the day right through and with it placed New Zealand in a position of security – 19 runs ahead with six wickets in hand. True, the bowlers had been on the road for a long time but they had given it one last shot to save the series and the obdurate opener from Wellington was a match for the best of them. This was no place for a flash-harry and Edgar's 11 boundaries and seven-hour occupation of the crease was just the ticket.

His resistance the following day was brief, bowled by Roberts for 127 priceless runs. Even though the last five wickets clattered for just 28 to Garner, the New Zealand lead was 85 at lunch on day four. With five sessions remaining the West Indians needed a quick 300 in order to declare at lunch on the following day. But the whirlwind Greenidge and his team-mates were hamstrung by tight bowling from Hadlee, Troup and Lance Cairns on a pitch still confining free stroke play and Greenidge crawled to 74 in five hours. The game was up and New Zealand comfortably negotiated 36 overs to secure a draw and a series win; it was somehow fitting that Bruce Edgar should be unbeaten at the end, for it was his batting in the face of a great attack that had secured the unlikely result.

It would be another 15 years and 29 series before any side lowered the West Indian colours again.

Kim Hughes – 100*

Australia v West Indies, Melbourne 26-30 December 1981

45

How do you create a batsman's nightmare? Take the world's fastest bowler, add two of the world's meanest bowlers and throw in the world's tallest bowler. Stir with a pitch which offers uneven bounce and is sprinkled with green patches. Finally serve with the best catching team on earth. This recipe will give you the problem facing Australia for the Boxing Day Test 1981 and the MCG pitch which was designated to be dug up over the next two years. Its reputation for uneven bounce had seen it criticised to the point where it was close to being labelled unfit for play, one of its harshest critics being the Australian captain Greg Chappell. It would be hard to imagine that things could be any worse for a batsman, though it well may have been had Malcolm Marshall been fit to play. Not that Marshall was overly missed, as Michael 'Whispering Death' Holding and Andy Roberts quickly reduced Australia to 8-3. Holding had bowled a vicious bouncer at Chappell, which he tamely snicked behind, this being his fourth international duck in a row.

Out walked Kimberley John Hughes in front of 38,755 fans. He started streakily, playing and missing regularly, which resulted in a few early bruises as the West Indies' bowlers zeroed in on the body. This rusty beginning may be attributed to not having picked up a bat for a week, as his good friend and father-in-law was gravely ill in a Perth hospital. The score soon became 26-4 when Holding had Allan Border caught behind for just eight. The movement and bounce from the pitch may be gauged by the fact that this was wicket-keeper David Murray's fourth victim. Hughes made it to 29 before he started to look comfortable, at least as comfortable as a batsman can be when he is unsure whether the 90mph ball is going to stay low or jump at his throat. He was batting in a helmet but with no face guard and was to say later that his greatest fear was being hit in the face rather than losing his wicket. But there is no mention in any match reports of him taking a backward step. Ian Chappell, 'no coward soul' himself, stated it was the bravest innings he ever saw.

At 59-5 Hughes found an ally in Rodney Marsh. The nuggetty wicket-keeper stayed while Hughes brought up his 50, and took Australia to 111-5, with a streaky inside edge over the top of the stumps from the bowling of an unimpressed Holding. He stood with his arms folded like a petulant child, his mood not improved after his previous ball had been ferociously square cut to the boundary. Commentator Richie Benaud described the half-century as one being made with "guts and determination".

Hughes kept hooking, cutting and riding his luck, with two difficult chances going down, but the West Indies continued to claim wickets at the other end, eventually reducing Australia to 155-9. On 71 he looked destined to fail in his quest to reach his seventh Test century, especially when the last man to join him was a genuine rabbit in Terry Alderman. He wished Alderman luck and was told to start going for the bowling as the bunny did not expect to last long in the headlights. Alderman stoically played defensively and, as all good tailenders should, blocked the straight ones. He also showed courage after being struck on the back of the head by a bouncer from the 6' 8" Joel Garner. He was right behind the next delivery.

Hughes took the advice of Alderman and started to play his shots, which included charging down the pitch to Garner and pulling him for four. By the time he reached 84, with another savage cut off the same bowler, Alderman was still on nought but he eventually broke the shackles with a couple of off drives from the bowling of Colin Croft. Finally, and appropriately, Hughes cut a Garner delivery to the boundary to bring up his hundred, an achievement which Benaud described as "possibly the finest century I have seen". Hughes put both hands in the air holding the bat in one and gave a double-fist pump, before a few shirtless spectators, in the pre-fine days, ran out on to the field to congratulate him.

Perhaps relaxing now he had seen Hughes to his ton, Alderman snicked Croft to the 'keeper and Australia were all out for 198 with the superb Holding claiming 5-45. Hughes' exact 100 was over 50 per cent of his team's score, made from 200 deliveries with 11 boundaries. As he left the field, perhaps the meanest of all fast bowlers and certainly not one given to praise lightly, Colin Croft, shook Hughes' hand and congratulated him on his terrific innings. Later Hughes dedicated the century to his father-in-law who would pass away within the week.

The crowd, who had certainly had their money's worth watching Hughes, were in for more excitement as the West Indies openers took strike in the late afternoon. One hundred and ninety-eight was a competitive score but the visitors, even without the injured Gordon Greenidge, still had the best batting line-up in the world. Despite this they finished the day on 10-4, a testament to the conditions and bowling. Alderman struck first, and then Dennis Lillee, needing just five wickets to become the world-record wicket taker, took over by removing Desmond Haynes, nightwatchman Croft and then, off the last ball of the day, Viv Richards. The crowd by this stage were at fever pitch alternating the chants of "Lillee, Lillee" with "kill, kill, kill".

Lillee duly claimed the record on day two when he dismissed Larry Gomes, eventually claiming 7-83. This fine performance could not, however, stop the West Indies from taking a narrow three-run lead. Hughes only managed eight in the Australian second innings before he was bowled by Holding. Still, with more of a team effort Australia managed 222, Holding again the destroyer claiming 6-62. The West Indies in reply fell for just 161, with Lillee's three wickets giving him 10 for the match and Australia victory by 58 runs.

Despite the great bowling of Lillee and Holding there could only be one man of the match. With everything favouring the bowlers, only one batsman had found the wherewithal to strike back – Kim Hughes.

Jack Brown – 140

Australia v England, Melbourne 1-6 March 1895

The tour of Australia by an England side captained by Andrew Stoddart in 1894-95 was something of a landmark event. For the first time reports on the matches were cabled straight back to England so the public could keep up with events as they unfolded. Fortunately for those who provided the investment that made this possible, the series was one of the most exciting ever played, and littered with outstanding personal performances. England won the first two Tests, without much to spare, before two thumping Australian victories squared the rubber and set up the final Test beautifully. No wonder then that David Frith has dubbed it, in his book, *The First Great Test Series.*

One of the ironies of the series is, therefore, that had the full strength of England been available to Stoddart the tour may well have been much less successful. Any of Stanley Jackson, Arthur Shrewsbury, William Gunn or Bobby Abel would have strengthened the batting of the 13-strong party. Abel accepted an invitation, before withdrawing late in the day and only then was Yorkshireman Jack Brown called up. He was not an established 'name', but in 1894, his second full season, he had made the third-highest aggregate of runs, and amongst Stoddart's men only William Brockwell of Surrey had bettered his average.

Before the series began, one of the tour organisers, Major Ben Wardill, secretary of the Melbourne Cricket Club, had cheerfully said of Brown: "He won't get ten runs in five months, and had better go home." As Brown scored a century in the initial first-class engagement of the tour it proved a rash comment to say the least, and it must have been a source of great satisfaction for Brown to play his greatest innings in front of Wardill.

At home in Yorkshire, Brown was an opener and enjoyed a long and fruitful partnership with John Tunnicliffe, but he batted in the middle-order against Australia. As to the manner of his batting, *Wisden's* 1895 edition said: 'Always possessed of considerable powers of defence Brown overcame...the disadvantages under which he laboured through lack of height, and...the manner in which he scored on the leg side off short-pitched balls invested his cricket with a brightness which is wanting in the play of others of equal fame.'

Australian skipper George Giffen won what, in a timeless Test, was considered a crucial toss and, given the conditions, made the inevitable decision to have first use of the wicket. Batting wasn't always easy due to the tenacious bowling and fielding, but by the close of day one Australia were 282-4. Next morning England claimed two early wickets but there were no rabbits in this Australian side, and their innings did not close until they reached 414.

England's reply was at 110-2 when Brown arrived at the crease. He lost the surviving opener, Albert Ward, almost straight away but after that batted confidently with Archie

MacLaren until, when looking well set, he was bowled by Albert Trott for 30 at 166. On the third day MacLaren went on to record an important century and England eventually conceded a modest deficit, just 29, and were in a much better position than they must have anticipated when Brown returned to the pavilion.

There was a change in the weather as Australia resumed their second innings on the fourth morning at 69-1 with the wind getting up and making conditions difficult all day. The all-out total they eventually posted of 267 was respectable, with only Albert Trott failing to reach double figures, but with England needing 297 for victory the game was hanging in the balance. At the close they had, for the loss of Brockwell, made the first 28 and the next day promised much with the Ashes whispering sweet-nothings to both captains.

There was rain on the fifth morning, and it looked like an impossible sticky dog might extinguish England's chances but happily for the batting side it turned out to be just a shower. Stoddart was out before England had added to their overnight total, and his captain's dismissal brought Brown to the wicket. He might have gone first ball, an outside edge that a more athletic man might have reached eluding Giffen and getting Brown off the mark. England were clearly worried about the possibility of more rain and a deteriorating pitch, and Brown's instruction was no doubt to get on with the task in hand while the going was good. Taking his instructions to heart he got to his fifty just 28 minutes later. Ward, the sheet anchor, added just five to his score in the meantime.

After reaching his half-century, Brown did slow down a little, and conversely there was an increase in the tempo of Ward's batting, the safe haven of lunch being reached with England on 145-2, Brown 80 and Ward 41. After the break, Brown snicked another one through Giffen on 84, but was in no way unsettled as he then took three fours (one all run) in quick succession from Harry Trott to bring up his century in a record 95 minutes.

Brown had another life on 125 before finally, at 140, falling to a slip catch by Giffen, but it had been a true match-winning effort. He and Ward had added 210 in just 145 minutes and in so doing had set a new Test record for the highest partnership. England still needed 59 to win, but lost only one more wicket on their way to their target, that of Ward who was eventually out seven short of what would have been a well-deserved century.

For Ward, although he was only 29, the Melbourne game proved to be the last of his seven caps. The situation was little different for Brown, four years his junior, who won just three more, two in 1896 and one in 1899. It wasn't as if Brown did not do well at county level, and indeed over the years he scored two triple-centuries in an all-conquering Yorkshire side around the turn of the century. His weakness seems to have been his temperament, his county captain Lord Hawke suggesting that his success in Australia had 'turned his head' and that 'perhaps he had more of an eye to his figures than the rest of us'. Sadly, ill health curtailed his career and within 10 years of his great day in Melbourne he was dead.

Gordon Greenidge – 100

West Indies v Pakistan, Kingston 15-20 April 1977

Gordon Greenidge's career was still in its early days. He had begun promisingly against India in Bangalore in 1974-75, hitting 93 and 107 on a rain-affected wicket. The rest of that series was less successful and it was followed, in 1975-76, by a dream-haunting encounter with Australian fast bowling – 'Really the first time I had failed so miserably,' he later recalled. 'It made me realise that batting in Test cricket was more than just crashing a ball about. I knew from that point I had to tighten my game.' This he did well and promptly, scoring three successive hundreds in the 1976 rubber in England (where famously it was Tony Greig who did the grovelling), to be named a *Wisden* Cricketer of the Year.

He was still in good form when Pakistan arrived on the Caribbean shores in 1976-77. He took 536 runs from the five Tests, 182 of which came in this crucial finale. The series was locked at 1-1 but the momentum was with the visitors. After triumphing in the fourth Test by 266 runs, they had just eased to a six-wicket win over Jamaica. They were well adjusted, then, to the look and feel of Sabina Park when a few days later Clive Lloyd won the toss and the West Indies, for the only time in the series, batted first.

The captains were rightly a tad concerned about the wicket as there was a slight ridge, already a few cracks and at the northern end a damp patch on a good line and length. Imran Khan opened the bowling with pace and aggression and hit that patch consistently. Roy Fredericks was caught and bowled with the last delivery of his first over. The rest of the surface was quick, seaming and bouncy in an uneven sort of way and Greenidge was struck a very painful blow when he had only four. On top of all this, like a bamboo branch in a hurricane, the ball was swinging prodigiously. Viv Richards edged one such prodigy through to the wicket-keeper, leaving the West Indies 22-2. Lloyd came in to supply the ballast. He had hit five boundaries, and was promising many more, when the rampant Imran unveiled another marvel. The catch went to third slip; the score was 56-3.

Greenidge, at the other end, looked altogether unperturbed as a marvellous contest between bat and ball ensued. He was still smarting from the blow, and limping noticeably between wickets, but his stroke play withal was uninhibited. He responded to the early setback aggressively but judiciously. Ten fours and two sixes took him to lunch unbeaten with all but eight of his 60 runs coming in boundaries. The square cut was especially violent, displaying to full effect his heavy biceps and forearms. Here he was revealing a great advance, since the Australian ordeal, in his shot selection. He was especially hard on Sikander Bakht, a medium pacer playing in his second Test match, who had to be taken off after three of his overs bled 29 runs. It was much tougher going against the wily and experienced Sarfraz Nawaz.

Greenidge's fourth-wicket stand with Alvin Kallicharran added 90. The latter, cagier than his partner, still registered several boundaries in his 34. He fell to Imran with the score on 146 but Greenidge pushed on, at once bold and careful, forceful and yet guarded: the only constant in all the changes of personnel. With Imran continuing to find pace and bounce, Greenidge's task was now twofold and, as Imran recalls, he accomplished both: 'Not only did he shield the other batsmen from me, but he took me apart with some magnificent shots...[he] played one of the greatest Test innings of my time.' Oddly enough, Greenidge himself recalls giving an easy chance to Asif Iqbal when in the late 70s but in this he upsets the unanimity of opinion. He offered 'no chance', according to the *Cricketer*, in what the *Guardian* agrees was 'a superb chanceless century'. *Wisden* (the ultimate arbiter in these things) says he 'batted flawlessly'.

Debased or not by good fortune, he found himself on 96 not out with 20 minutes left of the afternoon session. He had fallen twice in the 90s in the third Test, but this time there was no mistake. A fulgid cut off the hapless Sikander took him to his first Test century in the Caribbean. The innings was inscribed with 18 boundaries (including three sixes), which accounted for 78 per cent of his runs. From a frankly parlous position, he had taken his side, in trying physical and terrestrial circumstances, to what could at least be described as a stable one. The very next ball he buttered through to Wasim Bari, who took a fine diving catch. The West Indies were 200-5 and Greenidge had scored exactly half their runs.

The last five wickets imparted only 80 more, making this the West Indies' lowest total at Sabina Park since 1971. Given the conditions and the nature of the attack, Greenidge takes on the aspect of a hero. Pakistan mustered just 198 in response and, by the close of the second day, the West Indian openers were at the crease again (Greenidge unbeaten on 51), having extended the lead to 200. Conditions on day three were more amenable to the degree that even Imran was neutered. Both openers, after a gilded passage of stroke play, were dismissed shortly before lunch, within five minutes of each other. Their first-wicket partnership was a West Indian record against Pakistan. Greenidge contributed 82; the total was 182 and the lead 264.

Subsequently, the visitors were set a target of 442 in two days. Romantic whimsies were swiftly quashed as in the 68 balls they faced before lunch on day four, Colin Croft dispatched their top three for just 32; Greenidge held onto the last of them, Sadiq Mohammad, on the third attempt. They rallied with a brave century from Asif and with Wasim Raja playing an admirable supporting role, but were all out early on the final day. The West Indies won by 140 runs, completing their third successive Test-series victory. Awards for man of the match were not then much in vogue, but no-one could realistically doubt the identity of the outstanding performer here.

Garry Sobers – 163*

England v West Indies, Lord's 16-21 June 1966

In 2010 Richard Sydenham produced *In a League of their Own,* in which 100 cricket legends were asked to select their all-time World XI. Despite the fact that many of those contributing refused to select any players they had not seen play, and that the book was published almost 50 years after he retired from Test cricket, the player most nominated was Sir Garfield Sobers.

The man who Ray Robinson described as 'evolution's ultimate specimen in cricketers' was at the peak of his considerable powers when the West Indies toured England in 1966. Sobers was by now captain, preferring to lead by example rather than to inspire as his predecessor, Frank Worrell, had done. And what an example – in this series he would record 722 runs at 103.14, pocket 10 catches and bag 20 wickets, only one shy of Lance Gibbs. However, when the team arrived in the UK most of the newspapers' back-page headlines surrounded Sobers' team-mate Charlie Griffith, labelled by some, most notably Bobby Simpson, as a 'chucker'. That storm weathered, it was the weather which would next grab the headlines, outdoor practices and early matches being severely curtailed by seemingly incessant rain.

On to the first Test, where the West Indies completely overwhelmed England, who lost inside three days for the first time since 1938. Sobers' 161 not out was described by *Wisden* as 'devastating', though he had been somewhat fortunate in having been let off no fewer than four times, but in bowling three different styles and holding five catches he had played a true captain's part. The one-sided defeat meant that MJK Smith was replaced as England captain by Colin Cowdrey, though it was another England selection which would garner more headlines and prove to be far more significant in the long run. Basil D'Oliveira made his Test debut at Lord's, the first 'coloured' cricketer to represent England since the 1930s.

The strip prepared for the second Test had not been used for 11 years, when South African skipper Jack Cheetham had his arm broken, and this fact, coupled with the anticipated overcast skies aiding swing, was expected to make it very much a bowlers' haven. Lord's was indeed wet and miserable at the outset, some five hours being lost in total, including much of the first day. The West Indies succumbed for 269 to an England attack led by Ken Higgs, Sobers contributing 46 before falling lbw to Barry Knight in rather disappointing fashion, not offering a stroke. England replied with 355, to lead by 86, as Tom Graveney, returning after an absence of three years, and Jim Parks both scored 90s.

The pitch sweated under the covers during the rest day and on the following morning the West Indies were left reeling as the first three wickets fell with just 25 on the board. When Seymour Nurse then returned to the pavilion to be replaced by Sobers, he was followed just four runs later by Kanhai – five second-innings wickets down and only nine runs to the good. Sobers himself takes up the story: 'We were really in trouble and there was a lot of nervous chatter in the dressing room when I walked down the steps…I had decided even before I walked out that my policy was to be to go on the attack.'

Kanhai's dismissal meant that Sobers was joined by his cousin and fellow Bajan David Holford, playing in just his second Test. In true captain's style, Sobers walked down the pitch to Holford and told him to relax: 'I told him if he was batting at Kennington Oval… no one would get him out.' Despite the difficulty of the situation, Sobers made no attempt to farm the strike: 'I believe that if you have faith in your partner…he must trust himself.'

In the same year that Barbados achieved independence from Britain, these two now applied themselves to the task of reversing the subjugation of their batsmen by England's bowlers. All day long they batted, then on into the next day as their partnership lasted five and a half hours and realised 274 runs – a 'cricketing Dunkirk' almost unparalleled in the history of Test cricket, giving Sobers the luxury of declaring on 369-5 after Holford had made his hundred. Cowdrey's tactic of crowding Holford with fielders while putting his men out for Sobers was criticised by many, particularly Keith Miller in the *Daily Express*, but nonetheless the pair had taken the West Indies from almost certain defeat to within sight of an astonishing victory.

England were left with a target of 284 in 240 minutes and at first seemed interested, however after Wes Hall and Charlie Griffith sent back four of their batsmen for 67 runs, the tables had turned and now hopes of a West Indian victory were uppermost, though an hour's rain delay tempered that somewhat. At that point, Graveney joined the swashbuckling Colin Milburn, and the presence of the experienced Worcestershire man enabled the big-hitting opener to smash 126 not out as England forced a draw.

'The beauty of my innings for me was that it was all planned and everything I wanted to do came off' said Sobers of a contribution which Neville Cardus described as the most 'impressive assertion of his quality'. He gave just one chance, when Barry Knight missed a flier in the 90s. Holford too had played his part, being lifted shoulder high by exuberant fans celebrating his coming-out party, but sadly he would be denied the opportunity to fulfil his obvious potential, struck down by pleurisy just two years later.

A sparkling 209 not out from Basil Butcher in the third Test gave West Indies an unassailable 2-0 lead. Sobers was back to acting as lodestar in the fourth Test, his 174, made out of just 265 in partnership with Seymour Nurse, included a century between lunch and tea. He then helped himself to eight wickets as the West Indies took the rubber. In all he made three centuries, all over 150, along with two fifties, in just eight innings during the series. Rarely, if ever, has a better captain's example been set.

Sir Garfield Sobers – truly in a league of his own.

Lance Klusener – 118*

Sri Lanka v South Africa, Kandy 30 July-2 August 2000

41

The start of the Sri Lanka versus South Africa series in July 2000 found the tourists in a state of some cognitive dissonance. On the one hand, ranked the number two Test team in the world following successive 2-0 series victories at home to England and away to India, their self-belief was on the up and had been given a further fillip by a 2-1 one-day home -series victory over Australia in April. This win at least served to blur the wince-inducing image from 13 months previously of Allan Donald frozen at the non-striker's end as Lance Klusener hurtled towards him in search of the eminently gettable run which would have propelled them, rather than their gleeful Aussie opponents, into the World Cup final. On the other hand, the relatively lowly Test status of both England and India and the global insignificance of the one-off Challenge Series against the World Cup winners meant that only the innocent could be deluded into thinking such wins sufficient to exorcise the spectre of Edgbaston. And this was a team who, in the three months before embarking for Sri Lanka, had seen their innocence well and truly shredded as the full extent of Hanse Cronje's corruption and betrayal over match-fixing emerged.

It was unsurprising then that, with their formerly revered captain ignominiously banished and with five of the touring party having been called on to testify at the inquiry which damned him, the collective psyche was hardly bristling with confidence at the start of the tour. As Neil Manthorp noted: 'Their former captain was everywhere and nowhere, his ghost haunting the senior players and confusing the new faces in the squad.'

And sure enough, in the triangular one-day series which preceded the Tests, South African self-doubt resurfaced. They beat co-visitors Pakistan easily enough but in the absence of their disgraced former captain, by some distance their best player of spin, they were bamboozled by Muralitharan and lost all three games to the hosts, including the final.

The first Test, at Colombo, saw the Sri Lankan skipper Sanath Jayasuriya elect to bat and then summarily brutalise the visitor's attack, hitting 148 off 156 balls before unleashing Murali to weave his mesmeric web. The spinner took 13 wickets for 171 in a match which the hosts won inside four days, by an innings and 15 runs.

Unsurprisingly, the pitch for the second Test at Kandy had been prepared as a dry turner but heavy rain meant that it had sweated under covers for two days and when Jayasuriya again won the toss he had little hesitation in inserting under cloudy skies. Things started badly for the tourists when, in the first over, Gary Kirsten appeared to be given out caught behind off his pads by the home umpire Gamini Silva, standing in his first Test. Silva later attested that he had given Kirsten lbw but whatever the mode of dismissal it opened the floodgates for the Sri Lankan attack as first the vibrant Vaas and lively Zoysa and then the spinners Murali and Dharmasena drained the life-blood from the South African top order, removing McKenzie, Kallis, Cullinan and Rhodes to leave the visitors at 34-5.

With his team on the verge of complete and abject breakdown, Lance Klusener, the man who had, according to Cronje's testimony, immediately rebuffed him when he had made "faint attempts" to inveigle him into his scam, was perhaps scripted to release the tourists from their paralysis. Brought up by a Zulu nanny with her sons as his childhood companions, fluent in the language that gave him his nickname, the solitary and taciturn 'Zulu' had always had the ability to lift himself clear of the group context. This country boy's singularity and insistence that cricket was only a game did not always sit well with his team-mates. Certainly, his dressing-room observation in the immediate aftermath of the 1999 World Cup semi-final that "nobody died" was ill-timed and, after his team suffered another tied-match debacle in the subsequent tournament four years later, his jarring comment, "At least I'll have two extra weeks for fishing" did little to lift the mood.

Now though, with his side floundering and in thrall to the dominant Sri Lankan spinners, it was this sense of perspective that perhaps gave him the wherewithal to rise above 'group-think' and bring the game back from the brink. Batting with the combative Mark Boucher, the pair blended controlled aggression with watchful defence with Klusener in particular taking the attack to the spinners, hitting Murali straight for six and pulling him hard against the spin on the rare occasion he dropped short. Clouds were lifting.

But then, in the 51st over with the score at 158, 'Zulu' called his vice-skipper for an ill-judged single after playing the ball wide of Muralitharan whose swift throw left his partner well short of his ground. Undaunted (after all, nobody died), the player who had begun his international career as a tearaway fast bowler and number-10 slogger defied any lurking demons and husbanded the tail through a further 34 overs, adding another half-century to his own total and 80 runs to the team's tally from the last two wickets. He finished undefeated for a chanceless 118 from 219 balls in 243 minutes at a carefully measured strike-rate of just over 50. He hit 13 fours and two sixes and took his shell-shocked side from the edge of the psychic abyss to a final total of 253 all out just before the end of play on the first day.

It would prove a score sufficient for the South Africans to squeeze out the narrowest of victories, by just seven runs, early on the fourth day. In a low-scoring game, Klusener's medium pace off cutters, delivered off just five paces, brought two wickets from 24 parsimonious overs but it was his first-innings century, in his view his best, which helped restore his team's faith in themselves. He showed them that Murali was human after all and with a further unbeaten 95 in the final Test, helped his side finish this most testing of tours with honours even and heads held high.

Kevin Pietersen – 142

England v Sri Lanka, Birmingham 25-28 May 2006

40

On the evening of day two of the second Test at Edgbaston between England and Sri Lanka in the summer of 2006, a fan approached Graeme Hick, retired England Test cricketer, and asked if he could have played "that shot" – "It wouldn't even have crossed my mind", was Hick's candid response.

The shot in question was a reverse sweep/switch hit for six off Muttiah Muralitharan, an invocation of such sauce and sorcery that his captain, Andrew Flintoff, was left open-mouthed in amazement along with the enthralled thousands watching in the stands and on television. Neither would it have been considered by any other batsman for that matter, even the great Viv Richards if Angus Fraser is to be believed.

Ironically, Pietersen would lose his wicket just two balls later, the highs and lows of those three balls reflecting the path that many onlookers felt his career had taken since he burst into the Test cricket arena during the 2005 Ashes series. In that Sri Lanka match the following summer, he became the first player since Graham Gooch in 1990 to fashion centuries in three consecutive matches on home soil, a group of luminaries which also includes Herbert Sutcliffe, Denis Compton, Ken Barrington and Allan Lamb. That Pietersen belongs in that class, there can be no doubt.

Pietersen came along at absolutely the right time, as victory in the 'greatest-ever series' brought Test cricket back into the hearts and hearths of the nation, and he featured most prominently at The Oval party with a sparkling 158 that ensured he would lead both the averages and aggregates in his first-ever Ashes contest.

Fast-forward to 11 May 2006 and the earliest ever start to a Test match in England, despite which batting conditions were ideal. Duncan Fletcher had challenged his batsmen to go out and score a double-ton and Pietersen did his utmost, eventually falling on exactly the same score as his Oval triumph, an innings of 158 which he felt was superior to the Ashes knock. Watchful for 45 minutes possibly in deference to his coach, it seemed he had worked out how to play the mystical Murali – 'To me, regularly playing for the ball that turns away from the right-hander, the doosra, gave me a 99 per cent chance of hitting every Murali delivery.' He also went on to add '[To sweep him] is a hazardous business, so I vowed I wouldn't be doing much of that.' Indeed.

Led by Andrew Flintoff, England racked up 551-6 declared and, having skittled the tourists out for 192 must have had high hopes of an opening victory. However, in the greatest escape since Squadron Leader Bartlett led Colin Blythe and company through the tunnel, Sri Lanka batted out almost 200 overs to force a draw which had newspapers up and down the country dissecting Flintoff's captaincy style.

In the second Test, Sri Lanka elected to bat first in bright sunshine. However, the ball moved sufficiently that they were reduced to 65-6 by lunch, eventually succumbing for 141. After the dismissal of England's openers, Pietersen eased himself into it before opening up a Pandora's Box of dazzling gems, including paddle shots from outside the off to pierce a sparsely-populated on-side field, deft cuts, massive sixes and of course, the exclamation point to an innings laden with superlatives, the switch-hit sweep for six.

The victim, Murali, was not pleased to be treated with such disdain; Geoffrey Boycott announced from the broadcasting booth that Pietersen was: "Taking the mickey out of one of the greatest spinners in the world…a reverse 'thump', not a sweep", and Pietersen admitted that Murali had informed him that if he ever tried that again he'd beam him! Mark Nicholas meanwhile opined, "I do hope people don't ever take Kevin Pietersen for granted, and I just wonder how many people realise quite how special he is."

Certainly the gentlemen of Fleet Street appreciated him: 'Sweep Smell of Success' quipped the *Daily Mirror,* while proclaiming him 'Pieter the Great'. Angus Fraser, writing in the *Daily Telegraph*, called the switch hit 'without doubt, one of the most amazing shots recent Test cricket has seen' and David Lloyd pointed out in the *Evening Standard* that, astonishingly, Pietersen's first year in Test cricket still had two months to run.

His 142 was made off just 157 balls as the England score advanced by 221. After losing nightwatchman Matthew Hoggard, he dominated partnerships first with Paul Collingwood and then Flintoff, the latter reduced to contributing just nine off 48 balls as Pietersen left all in his wake. Only once did he seem not to be in control, when a Flintoff straight drive knocked him on his backside, as if to remind his ostentatious partner that he too could hit them a bit. Pietersen recovered to sail from 65 to 100 off just 31 balls.

Once Pietersen's wicket was lost, England collapsed like the proverbial house of cards, four wickets going down for the addition of just five more runs. His innings stood out like an orchid in a field of turnips; no one else managed more than 30. Despite the limp capitulation, this time England were able to press home the advantage and secure a six-wicket victory. But as the song goes, you can't keep a good man down. Murali had been bested in the second Test but he worked his magic in the third – eight second-innings wickets sent England tumbling to a 134-run defeat as Sri Lanka squared the series.

Later that year, in an autobiography wholly unnecessary for a callow 25-year-old, Pietersen gave some insight into why he had played the switch hit. Having come down the pitch three times in succession to Murali, the field had been moved back to remove any options to make big shots: "I needed to hit boundaries and I needed to hit big shots. As he was running up I decided to do it." In other words, we're expected to believe it was his only option. Surely only KP could even suggest such a thing?

Colin McDonald – 170

Australia v England, Adelaide 30 January-5 February 1959

The 1958-59 Ashes series is now chiefly remembered for all the wrong reasons, most notably the accusations of 'chucking' against several bowlers on both teams. However, amidst all the rancour there was at least one reassuring incidence of fair play which was to prove significant to the protagonist, as Colin McDonald threw away his wicket when in sight of a first Test match double-century.

The England team which flew into Australia with the famous urn were strong favourites and, on paper, one of the strongest ever to travel. For Australia, the selection of Richie Benaud as captain came as a surprise considering he had yet to lead even his state side. Despite the high hopes in the England camp, the first Test was what EM 'Lyn' Wellings described as 'the dullest and most depressing' he had ever seen. The might of England could not muster even 200 in either innings, falling to an eight-wicket defeat as Colin McDonald top-scored in Australia's first innings with 42. England's already dwindling confidence can be measured by opener Arthur Milton's recollections: 'I think we knew we were going to lose after the first Test. Trevor Bailey took seven and a half hours to score 68; I remember someone said "Get him out, for Christ's sake!"' Grumblings had already started about Ian Meckiff's action, but no formal complaint was forthcoming at this stage.

The good news for the England team in the second Test was that in the first innings they managed to pass 200 – the bad news was that, after collapsing to 87 in the second, they fell to a second consecutive eight-wicket defeat as Neil Harvey's 167 took its rightful place in Ashes folklore. Thus, after only two matches the best team in Test cricket was already staring series defeat squarely in the face.

The third Test was drawn, though there was an interesting precursor to the fourth Test when Peter May asked McDonald, who was having knee problems, if he wanted to retire. It was his captain, Benaud, who insisted that McDonald bat on with a runner and he was out next ball, but May's sporting gesture was significant. After three Tests, McDonald had now been dismissed three times in the 40s and was still to make a significant score.

That was all about to change at Adelaide. Australia were now dormie-two and a win would regain the Ashes for the first time since 1950-51. The controversial Meckiff was injured and replaced by Gordon Rorke; talk about like-for-like – Rorke's action proved to be just as contentious as Meckiff's. When May won the toss but elected to bowl on a brown, dry wicket, a disbelieving Richie Benaud exclaimed: "Thank you, you have given us the game." McDonald and Jim Burke opened for Australia and there was plenty of playing and missing in the morning but, as the day progressed, McDonald, in particular, grew in confidence. A frustrated English attack switched the line of attack to leg stump only to find him even stronger in that area. He played better than ever before on a good wicket, comfortably outscoring his partner and taking the game, and the Ashes, steadily further away from England. On 94 he survived a close run-out chance and then found himself stalled on 98 for fully 25 minutes before receiving a rousing reception when he at last reached his century. The partnership was finally broken when Burke was out for a circumspect 66, having struck just two fours. McDonald was then joined by Harvey and these two saw things through to stumps with Australia on 200-1, McDonald having scored 112, his first century against England and of enormous value given the state of the series.

The next day was played in sweltering conditions but the pair were undeterred, carrying their partnership to 97 before McDonald retired hurt on 149. As in the previous Test, May allowed him the option of retiring, whereas insisting on a runner in the extreme conditions might have been the more combative option. Mackay then sportingly walked to leave Australia on 294-4, something of a collapse from 268-1. A stand of 75 between Benaud and Norman O'Neill helped the score to 407-7, at which point McDonald returned with Burke as his runner, only slightly restored after a rest day and some much-needed treatment. When he had reached 164 he should have been run out, however umpire Mel McInnes had positioned himself so that he could not see Burke running behind him. Fred Trueman flattened the stumps but he couldn't be given out – those with an unimpeded view agreed that Burke was fully three yards short.

It was then that McDonald showed what a sporting player he was by throwing his bat at everything – 'I threw my innings away but had fun doing it.' Leaving his stumps wide open, he was soon bowled by Trueman for 170. He had batted for 427 minutes in crafting the highest individual score of the series, and this against an attack which featured the great England trio of fast bowlers Trueman, Frank Tyson and Brian Statham, who were playing together for the first and only time. Australia were eventually all out for 476 and with the temperature dropping and a breeze now blowing, the Australian pacemen were able to find some swing, England being bowled out 37 runs short of avoiding the follow-on.

Don Bradman advised the novice captain that the only way Australia could now lose was if he enforced the follow-on. Benaud thanked him politely and promptly did just that. Even though Alan Davidson was injured and unable to bowl, England could only muster 270 for a paltry lead of 34. With McDonald still injured, local boy Les Favell opened and hit the winning runs for a ten-wicket victory, Australia thus taking the series and the Ashes.

McDonald went on to score another ton in the dead-rubber match to give him 519 runs at 64.87, topping both the aggregates and averages. However the 170 he scored at Adelaide would remain his highest Test score and this series the peak of his career. Never again would he get so close to notching a Test double-hundred.

Steve Waugh – 108

England v Australia, Manchester 3-7 July 1997

38

The Ashes weren't much of a contest through the 1990s but, briefly, in 1997 it appeared as if Australia might have a fight on their hands. England had won the first Test after a remarkable initial session in which they took eight Australian wickets, and while the gulf between the two sides looked to be as wide as ever in the second Test, rain salvaged a draw for the hosts. The third match was to be played at Old Trafford. When the two sides had met there in 1993, what had been a difficult pitch to begin with had eventually played into Shane Warne's hands as the game wore on, so although all the signs suggested that the captain who won the toss should elect to field first, Mark Taylor chose to bat.

It was a cold, overcast Manchester morning and the wicket, which had a fair amount of grass on it to begin with, had greened up considerably because of the moisture in the air. England's seam attack consisted of Darren Gough, Andrew Caddick, debutant Dean Headley and Mark Ealham. Headley's promising career was to be cut short by injury, but he was a fine bowler, as were Gough and Caddick as their records would eventually show. Ealham was a bits and pieces cricketer, in truth just short of Test class, but in these helpful conditions he could be a dangerous seamer.

Once the game began, Taylor did not last long as he became Headley's first Test wicket with just nine on the board. Greg Blewett and Mark Waugh were also gone by the time the match was an hour old and Steve Waugh, who had been out for a duck in his only innings at Lord's, was faced with rebuilding the innings with opener Matt Elliott. The ball was swinging and seaming but Waugh got off the mark from his very first delivery, and that helped him settle although he then survived a very confident appeal for lbw, from Caddick, and was beaten several times. If helpful conditions were not enough, all the batsmen had an additional problem with Caddick because the sightscreen was not tall enough to cover the full height of his arm.

Waugh and Elliott got through to lunch without further loss, but the afternoon session was another good one for England. After the opener got what replays suggested was a rough decision to fall to a catch at the wicket, Michael Bevan, Ian Healy and Shane Warne were all dismissed the same way to reduce Australia to 160-7. Waugh was defiant in the face of this, the one man who looked comfortable and, whenever the bowlers deviated from the right line, capable of scoring runs.

Despite the wickets they took, England's bowlers did not, as the day wore on, bowl very well at Waugh. Encouraged by the bounce and their success against the other batsmen, there was a tendency to overdo the short-pitched delivery in the belief that here lay the weakness. This did not unduly trouble him even though the jarring on his right hand, brought about by the number of times the ball hit his bat up around the splice, was such that he had to put it in ice as soon as he got back to the dressing room. There were also too many swing-seeking deliveries well up to him. Even if the textbook half-volleys were in short supply, England seemed to forget that Waugh was a master of hitting the ball on the up and they gave him far too many opportunities to score runs.

The crucial phase of the innings now came with the partnership between Waugh and Paul Reiffel. Had Reiffel gone early, as he was wont to do, then Australia would almost certainly have been dismissed for under 200. Unfortunately for England if he could get over his initial uncertainties he was a capable batsman. He gave a chance, but 'keeper Alec Stewart failed to cling onto a steepling top edge off Headley, and Reiffel settled.

At no point during the day did conditions improve and three times in the last session the batsmen were offered the light. With runs coming readily enough, Waugh was keen to stay on but on the third occasion the skies were so grey that all five lights on the scoreboard meter were illuminated. Waugh was now in two minds as there were just three overs left but, having obtained the assurance from Michael Atherton that those overs would be delivered by Ealham and off spinner Robert Croft, he and Reiffel decided once again to remain. They duly survived, and Croft was kind enough to present Waugh with a short delivery that he cracked through cover-point off the back foot to go to his century. He ended the day on 102, and Australia on 224-7, having shown the application and technical mastery to conquer a real heavy-atmosphere greentop. A great student of the game, Steve Waugh rated this his finest century to that point of his career.

Next morning the remaining three wickets fell for the addition of just 11 more runs, but it was to prove an ample total as England slumped to 161-8 by the close, the heart of their batting, after a decent enough start, being ripped out by Warne. They added just a single on the third morning and Australia then set about building a match-winning lead. By taking three early wickets the England bowlers kept their supporters interested, but then the brothers Waugh added 92 to put the game out of reach. By the end of the day Steve was unbeaten on 82, a courageous and all the more creditable innings because towards the end his right hand was sufficiently damaged to, at times, force him to effectively bat one-handed. Next day the swelling was much reduced, and he did enough to join Warren Bardsley and Arthur Morris as the third Australian to score a century in each innings of an Ashes Test. He eventually went for 116 and Taylor finally declared at 395-8. The lead of 468 was, of course, plenty and well before lunch on the final day Australia had completed a comprehensive 268-run victory and levelled the series. There were further substantial victories in the fourth and fifth matches before England narrowly won the dead-rubber match to make the final score 3-2.

Clive Lloyd – 161*

India v West Indies, Kolkata 10-14 December 1983

Clive Lloyd still looms large in my finest cricketing memory. It was *that* Gillette Cup semi-final at Old Trafford in 1971; David Hughes' fusillade of boundaries in the dark was marvellous theatre but nothing to match the earlier clash of titans. Mike Proctor, blond hair bouncing, tearing in at full pelt only to have 'Big Cat' plant a long right leg down the pitch and smash a good-length ball through the covers. The rest of the world caught up four years later when he hammered 102 in the inaugural World Cup final at Lord's.

The story of how a shell-shocked Lloyd and his team slunk back home after the 1975-76 series in Australia, determined to unearth fast men to trade blows with Lillee and Thomson, has been told in *Fire In Babylon* and within two years he had the players he needed. After a short Packer interlude the West Indies began a period of dominance that would last 15 years; unbeaten in no fewer than 29 Test series.

India and the West Indies would see plenty of one another during 1983 in both the long and short forms of the game and there was already plenty of 'history' after an acrimonious series in the Caribbean in 1975-76 where the fast bowling had reduced the Indians to a team of walking wounded in the Test at Sabina Park. Sunil Gavaskar accused Lloyd of being 'desperate' and said that his deployment of bouncer-happy pace bowlers 'was not great captaincy, it was barbarism.'

A total of 11 Tests had been arranged for 1983, five in the Caribbean before a return series later in the year. The pace of Malcolm Marshall and Andy Roberts proved decisive in a 2-0 victory in the first leg but the win was, again, not without bad feeling. The gap between the two series was spent in England where India surged to an unexpected and famous victory in the World Cup, beating none other than the West Indies in the final. To say that the West Indians were shocked would be an understatement – Lloyd announced he was giving up the captaincy after such a 'dreadful' performance but the Board convinced him to reconsider. They had been knocked from their perch by an inferior side, with the help of a smidgeon of over-confidence, and now those upstarts would have to pay. Payment was indeed another invigorating factor as, arriving in India, they became aware of just what rewards had been garlanded about the necks of the victorious.

The six-Test marathon in India would present one of the sternest obstacles to overcome for a team built on and for speed. They had been beaten there on their previous visit but that was a side hamstrung by Packer defections and at least the Indian pitches were no longer universally predictable as the slow, dreary turners of yesteryear – India now had speed of her own in the form of the prodigious Kapil Dev. But, alone, even he was no match for the combined might of Marshall, Roberts and Holding, so much so that figures of 9-83 in the second innings of the third Test of the series were not enough to avert defeat.

By the time the two sides had arrived in Kolkata for the fifth Test, the West Indies were leading 2-0 and ready to close out the series. But that was not the Caribbean way; Lloyd wanted victory with style, total dominance and maybe just a touch of revenge. In deference to a pitch apparently bare, slow and harking back to the old days, the selectors opted to give spinner Roger Harper his debut *and* retain a four-man pace attack. This was hardly playing for a draw. Even on this unpromising surface, the Indians were blitzkrieged by Marshall, Roberts and Holding, the pitch proving to be more unpredictable than dead. After choosing to bat, the Indians had reeled to 63-6 before Syed Kirmani and Dev effected some repairs and steered the side to a total of 241. Dev then switched seamlessly to high-class pace bowling and on day two the West Indies stood tottering on 88-5, tail exposed and ripe for a chopping. Its only protection was the ability to swish and the presence of the captain, Clive Lloyd. Swish it did – Marshall and Roberts both made half-centuries as Shivlal Yadav and Maninder Singh span in tandem, with the pace of Dev the prime danger. Watching over it all was the looming presence of Clive Lloyd – no longer the belligerent thrasher of his youth, now, at 39, he was the seasoned and level-headed winner of matches. Hour after hour he coaxed his team-mates and with infinite patience, gradually wrested the initiative away from India and then carried on until his team was in a winning position. After over eight hours of restraint and perseverance, in which he hit only 12 boundaries, the innings closed at 373 with Lloyd undefeated on 161. It was a captain's innings *par excellence* which *Wisden* chose to describe as 'dour'. Others were scarcely more generous. The *Daily Telegraph* reported that it would 'not rate among his more spectacular efforts' while Dicky Rutnagur could only praise his 'technique, concentration and stamina'. A 12-year-old, Dwivedula Venkat Srikanth, captures the essence better: 'A magnificent, superlative and spectacular 161. As he walked back to the pavilion, the entire stadium stood and applauded this old man for his stunning batting feat.' He had played precisely the innings his team required and as the man at least partly responsible for the team selection, he took his responsibilities and shepherded the tail. Lloyd once claimed, 'I used to embarrass the young players into doing well' – whether or not that was quite true there can be little doubt that this innings in Kolkata was the epitome of the captain's flair and diligence that combined the inspiration of Frank Worrell with the example of Garry Sobers.

The Indians had missed their chance – instead of facing a large deficit the West Indies now led by 132 and, after some disheartened and foolhardy batting, that was enough to secure an easy victory. India all out for 90, Marshall 6-37. The home side, so recently mobbed by ecstatic supporters after winning in England, had their bus stoned. The series was won 3-0 and Lloyd topped the averages at 82.66 – 30 clear of Gavaskar, Viv Richards and the rest.

Saeed Anwar – 188*

India v Pakistan, Kolkata 16-20 February 1999

36

So what do you want from a Test match? Closely fought, evenly matched cricket, liberally laced with individual brilliance played by two teams of the highest class both absolutely determined to win? In February 1999 you could throw in the facts that the teams were the world's biggest rivals, that the game was a ground-breaking attempt to start a series of world championships, that it was played in front of the biggest crowd ever, that it had enormous political ramifications and that play was twice suspended due to riots. This gives an inkling as to the contents of the Kolkata Test between India and Pakistan.

These two countries had been kept apart for 10 years before a three-match series was arranged for 1998-99 only for it to be truncated as the third and final match was hijacked to become the curtain-raiser for the first ever Asian Test Championship, a four-match tournament that would also include Sri Lanka. Each side would play each other once and a system including bonus points would decide who would contest the final in neutral Dhaka. This in itself was hugely symbolic as international cricket had last been seen there in 1969, when Bangladesh was still part of East Pakistan, and a neutral ground hadn't been used for a Test since Trent Bridge hosted Australia and South Africa in 1912.

With Sri Lanka lacking Muttiah Muralitharan and Sanath Jayasuriya, it was clear from the outset that the opening fixture at Eden Gardens, India against Pakistan, would be crucial to the final outcome – equally clear was the fact that the sides were evenly balanced based on the 1-1 draw in the two preceding matches although the Indians would start favourites after Anil Kumble's famous 10-74 ensured a big win in the second game. Little wonder then that the five fiery and memorable days attracted an estimated 500,000 spectators.

The prospect of a seaming pitch gave Pakistan's captain, Wasim Akram, some pause for thought on winning the toss and within an hour he held his head in his hands as his team were reduced to 26-6 by an inspired opening attack of Javagal Srinath and Venkatesh Prasad. Any way back was hard to envisage even after Saleem Malik and Moin Khan had raised the score to 110. A final total of 185 was good considering the dreadful early passage but represented only half of what had been envisaged six hours earlier. If the heaving throng in attendance had been ecstatic on day one, its mood can only have shifted to calm benevolence by mid-afternoon on day two as India eased to within 38 of the Pakistan total with just two wickets down. Then came Shoaib Akhtar's vicious in-swinging yorker twice in two balls to dismiss Rahul Dravid for 24 and, horror of horrors, Sachin Tendulkar for a golden duck. Having been 38 runs behind with eight wickets in hand, India were dismissed just 38 runs ahead and Pakistan were batting again on day two and still the ultimately most significant incident had yet to take place. This time it was the turn of India's captain, Mohammad Azharuddin, to place his head in his hands as he dropped Saeed Anwar at first slip for two – his only consolation being he knew not what he had done.

If Srinath's 5-46 on day one had been outstanding, then his work on day three was the stuff of legend. Tirelessly he probed, darting the ball off the seam and leaving the Pakistan batsmen all but helpless. Nightwatchman Saqlain Mushtaq hung around for 21 and Yousuf Youhana managed an intrepid half-century but, with one exception, the remainder wilted in the face of Srinath's 8-86. But what an exception. Riding his good fortune of the previous evening, Saeed Anwar unfurled the innings of a lifetime. Cautious against the continued excellence of Srinath he unleashed sumptuous drives, cuts and flicks off his legs as wicket after wicket fell at the other end. Displaying timing that Barry Richards described as amongst the best he'd ever seen, he continued to bisect a field laid to stifle with boundary after boundary, powerful front-foot pulls mixed with the deftest of late cuts. With Kumble and Prasad keeping the pressure on there was no respite but, seemingly unperturbed by the huge and largely hostile crowd and the significance of what he was achieving, he moved with a straight six past 50 and onto his century – but, with the total on 151, still not enough to give his colleagues something to bowl at. As the shadows lengthened and the smog of rush-hour Kolkata pervaded the ground, he carried on and on until he was left stranded, unbeaten on 188 having hit 23 fours and a six from a total of 316, leaving India to get a difficult, but not impossible, 279 to win.

In a game of high drama it seemed that the denouement might be relatively quiet as openers Ramesh and Laxman carefully accumulated 100 – surely India were gliding to victory? But, with two quick wickets, Saqlain had started to find some spin and balanced the scales; then came the tipping point. On a stage made for Tendulkar, the hero of all India was run out after colliding with the anti-hero, Shoaib Akhtar, in mid-pitch. The subsequent riot was all but inevitable given the highly-charged atmosphere but, to their eternal credit, Tendulkar and his side stayed calmer than their supporters and peace was restored and play resumed. A collapse ensued and at 231-9 the game was again halted by burning newspapers and a hail of projectiles before the stadium was cleared and the final rites were enacted in an eerie silence completely at odds with the cacophony of the previous four days.

It could have been so much worse. Injuries were negligible and diplomacy asserted, no-one sought to make political capital and the jack was forced back in the box. Fortunately these five days could, and should, be remembered for scintillating, spine-tingling cricket and, despite the 13 wickets of Srinath, it was the calm and assured brilliance of Saeed Anwar that won the day.

The rest of the tournament was a huge anti-climax. Pakistan beat Sri Lanka in a one-sided final but everyone already knew that the finale had been reached in Act I.

Ian Smith – 173

New Zealand v India, Auckland 22-26 February 1990

35

When Matthew Hayden eclipsed the world record Test score with 380 against Zimbabwe, there were those who sought to devalue his achievement, coming as it did against a cricket team in growing disarray. Even so, as aggrieved as Brian Lara may have felt, Ian David Stockley Smith had every right to feel more so, as he was deprived of his hold on the record for the fastest-ever Test 150 in even more lopsided circumstances.

Though he had flattered to deceive in one-day cricket with a strike-rate of almost 100, it's safe to say that Stockley's performance in Auckland arrived pretty much out of the blue, being surrounded by an 11, 9, 2, 1, 0 and four DNBs. His one previous century in 71 Test innings had come six years before, during New Zealand's first-ever Test-series victory against England, though that was under no real pressure as he came in at 302-6 with New Zealand only needing a draw.

In the two previous Tests of this series, Smith had batted just once, New Zealand enjoying a ten-wicket victory in the first, being helped in no small part by his six catches. The second match was ruined by rain; however, some drama was added to that tepid draw by a piece which appeared in the *New Zealand Herald*, in which DJ Cameron accused the Black Caps' fielders of 'cricketing grubbiness'. Bemoaning 'the modern cricketer's naked ambition to take wickets by whatever means are within their reach' he concluded: 'Who would want to play under that cricketing creed?' though he did point out that Smith, normally one of the most enthusiastic appealers, had remained mute while his team-mates cavorted.

Nonetheless, Cameron's barbs had spurred Smith, who thought the criticism may have had a negative impact on impressionable youth, into wanting to 'pull a big one' in the final Test, at Auckland. But when John Wright sprinted off the pitch towards the bathroom, Smith knew from that 'tell' that he had lost the toss. Indian seamers Kapil Dev and Manoj Prabhakar took full advantage of the humidity and a green pitch to move the ball about alarmingly, so that shortly after lunch six New Zealand batsmen were back in the pavilion with just 85 runs on the board.

At that point Richard Hadlee joined debutant Shane Thomson, the two of them stemming the tide a little with a 46-run partnership. At 131-7, Smith walked out to face an attack for which Atul Wassan was doing some considerable damage with 4-40. Smith was at first content to play straight man to 'Paddles', who was 'taking the long handle' to the Indians. Smith had asked Hadlee how he was going to play it: "As I see it, Stockley, as I see it. If he pitches it up, it's gonna go!" Inspired by his swashbuckling partner, Smith took out his bat with enough success that by tea the pair had put on 77 in 68 minutes, being greeted by a much-improved dressing-room atmosphere.

One ball after the hundred partnership was reached, Hadlee was bowled for 87. Though New Zealand were, at 234-8, in a much happier position than at lunch, Smith now felt some pressure at the loss of Hadlee, telling himself: "Show some balls, son." Joined by Matthew Snedden, the tail-enders set themselves bite-sized targets, 250, 260, 270, so that by the time Smith next glanced at the scoreboard he was shocked to find he was in the 90s. Nail-bitingly sat on 98 while Sneds blocked out a maiden at the other end, after jabbing nervously at five balls, he tickled one down the leg side and ran the requisite two for his hundred, his first in 55 Test innings.

When the Indians took the new ball, a mid-pitch conference with Snedden determined that each ball should be played on its merits, or lack thereof. Having already taken 17 off one of Wassan's overs, Smith now grabbed 12 off the first four balls of another. A further conference resulted in the entreaty not to do anything stupid – his response was to smash two sixes off the final two balls to give him a record 24 off a single Test over.

During a further conference they noticed Wright pointing at his watch, Sneds proffered, "Maybe he wants us to still be in at stumps?" "Either that," replied Smith, "or he's off to the betting shop and he wants us to stay in until he gets back!" When Snedden was out shortly after, the pair had added a record 136 for the ninth wicket. Smith had been suffering from arm cramps, though the broadcasters teasingly pointed out that the cramps were in the 'wrong' arm. Smith ended the day on 169 not out from just 128 balls, with New Zealand at 387-9 in an immeasurably stronger position than they had been at the start of his innings.

Three hundred and nine runs had been scored in the last two sessions alone and Smith had scored at a phenomenal rate – circumspect while Hadlee made hay, he had reached his first 50 in 56 balls, the second in 39 and the third in a crazy 23 balls, reaching his 150 off a record 118 deliveries. Of the 153 scored between Hadlee's dismissal and stumps, Smith had hit all but 22.

He was trapped lbw to Prabhakar early the next day as New Zealand finished on 391, the bruised Wassan finishing with figures of 4-108. A masterly 192 from Mohammad Azharrudin ensured there was no let-up in the entertainment, as India established a first-innings lead of 91 and exceeded even the Kiwis' extraordinary run-rate. However, on the fourth day New Zealand's play was attritional as Wright made sure that a series-winning draw could be the only result.

DJ Cameron held no grudge: 'His bat like some biting broadsword, he slayed the Indian bowlers with strokes ranging from brilliant to outrageous.' Smith's 173 remains the world-record score for a number nine in a Test match. However, he lost the record for the fastest 150 to Mahela Jayawardene against a fledgling Bangladesh when he was called in ('retired out') to prevent further torture. Perhaps that record should also still belong to Smith.

VVS Laxman – 281

India v Australia, Kolkata 11-15 March 2001

34

In 2011 India's Test team was crowned as world cricket's leading side for the first time in its history. The foundations for this global domination can be traced to a decade earlier, when a career-defining performance by VVS Laxman helped to turn a whole series on its head as India, in the face of a seemingly unassailable deficit, staged an unbelievable recovery to go on and overpower what many considered to be the finest cricket team ever assembled.

When Australia strode confidently into Mumbai in February 2001, it was on the back of a record 15 consecutive victories, which, after a 10-wicket win to take the first Test, was duly increased to 16, fully five more than even the all-conquering 1980s West Indians had managed. With Adam Gilchrist at his most belligerent, Glenn McGrath having given up a measly 44 runs from 36 overs in the match and Shane Warne described by *Wisden* as 'most guileful', things looked bleak for India.

For the second Test at Kolkata, India, perhaps surprisingly considering the previous failures, made no changes to their batting line-up, though captain Sourav Ganguly had intimated to Laxman that his place might be more secure if he would agree to open – Laxman politely declined. Nevertheless, after giving up a first-innings lead of 274 on a pitch which had been expected to provide a good batting surface, a series-clinching victory seemed within their opponent's grasp. If their first-innings 445 had confirmed the excellence of the pitch, India's first-innings failure confirmed the excellence of Australia's bowlers. Captain Steve Waugh had no hesitation in asking India to bat again, later saying that he had been 'extra keen to keep them pinned down and keep the momentum going'.

When the talismanic Sachin Tendulkar was third out with India still requiring 159 to make Australia bat again, Waugh's decision looked to be unquestionably correct, India appearing at that stage to have virtually no chance of stemming the baggy green tide. However three Indian players had other ideas: Rahul Dravid, Harbhajan Singh and VVS Laxman. Laxman had been the only batsman in the first innings to defy the Australian attack; batting at number six he had scored 59 of a paltry team score of 171, a total which Australia had exceeded with their final two wickets. Waugh, who felt that Laxman was 'playing for his career', also thought that the 'extra time in the middle might have played him into form'. His reward was promotion to number three.

From an absolutely hopeless position, Laxman forged significant partnerships, first with Ganguly and then Dravid, to gradually bring India back from the dead. The best attack in the world of Warne, McGrath, Michael Kasprowicz and Jason Gillespie was taken apart bit by bit and piece by piece with shot after dazzling shot, as Laxman found the boundary no fewer than 44 times with the surgical precision wholly appropriate to this son of two doctors. He regularly came down the track to Warne and looked totally in command against all types of bowling. His fifth-wicket partnership of 376 with Dravid was the highest ever at Eden Gardens and completely turned the game on its head.

The first three days had seen 24 wickets but on the fourth there were none as Laxman batted for ten and a half hours, having been unbeaten at stumps on three consecutive days. At 237 he passed Sunil Gavaskar's Indian record, finally being dismissed from an understandably tired-looking shot to deep gully for a flawless 281. India's highest-ever second-innings total of 657-7 allowed them to declare with a lead of 383. Perhaps most crucial was that Laxman had scored quickly enough to allow his bowlers to press for a win.

Considering that the largest successful run chase in India at that time was 276, the tables had turned to such an extent that Australia, after posting a huge first-innings lead, now needed to bat out the last day to try and force a draw. By the time Harbhajan took his 13th wicket, a haul which included India's first ever Test hat-trick, Australia had been dispatched for 212 and India had, unbelievably, overcome the highest-ever deficit to earn victory after following on. This was only the third occasion that a team had won a Test after the ignominy of two successive innings, and each time Australia had been on the wrong end.

Harbhajan repeated his heroics at Chennai a week later and Laxman, with two more fifties, increased his aggregate to 503 runs at 83.83, the highest ever by an Indian in a three-Test series. This was only Laxman's second century, his first had been a superb 167 in Sydney the previous year representing the third-highest percentage of team runs ever – not too many have opened their account of Test centuries with two such monumental knocks.

The contribution of Rahul Dravid was crucial and has been overshadowed by Laxman's performance – he too was playing for his place. His determination under such pressure was immense – as umpire Peter Willey recalled, "He was dead on his feet." Dravid though was fulsome in his praise of Laxman, acknowledging that watching him was akin to viewing a highlights package and that it was "a defining moment in the history of Indian cricket".

Laxman's own feelings about his innings were as weighty as the performance itself: "This innings is close to my heart because of the precarious position we were in. All the Australians bowled well…they are class bowlers without exception." *Wisden India* felt the same and in 2002 voted this the greatest Indian innings of all time. As Anandam P. Kavoori enthused over Laxman's batting, rich in visual aesthetics as opposed to resolute run-gathering – "He speaks in a dying language."

A decade after the Indians had beaten the world champions as a result of the most unlikely of turnarounds, they stood astride the international cricketing world as number one Test nation and World Cup champions – the confidence gained from this series win had given them the platform to go on and become world-beaters.

Gordon Greenidge – 134

England v West Indies, Manchester 8-13 July 1976

33

Ask any English cricket fan to recall Old Trafford 1976 and it is likely that the first words uttered, doubtless expressed with righteous indignation, will be "Close and Edrich". Sadly the barrage of bouncers sent down by Michael Holding and Wayne Daniel overshadowed a magnificent performance with the bat by Gordon Greenidge, who fashioned two centuries the first of which is rightly lauded as one of the greatest in the history of Test cricket.

The naming of Greenidge in the squad to visit England was a surprise to everyone after a nightmare tour of Australia in the winter of 1974-75, during which Messrs Lillee and Thomson had made life hell for the West Indies' batsmen in general and Greenidge in particular. He bagged a pair in the first Test, was dropped for the next and then managed only 11 runs in the third. Providing counsel to professional cricketers was not the style of skipper Clive Lloyd, who also made dismissive comments about Greenidge in the newspapers leaving his confidence in tatters as he headed home, maroon cap in hand.

Predictably Greenidge was overlooked for the home series against India; however, his familiarity with conditions in England, having moved there from Barbados as a 14-year-old before enjoying a fruitful partnership opening for Hampshire with the great Barry Richards, led to his recall. It was somewhat ironic then that England would enjoy Caribbean-like conditions, as outfields were baked brown by the driest summer for two and a half centuries. Still with much to prove in order to make the team proper, a useful start in the first match saw Greenidge make 84, followed by 82 against the MCC and 115 at Taunton. Lawrence Rowe had opened against India and was his chief rival to share opening duties alongside Roy Fredericks; however, the former missed many of the warm-up games and Greenidge's good form saw him selected to open in the first Test.

He could not build on a good start in either innings at Trent Bridge, a calf strain being partly to blame in the second. Fortunate to be missed early on in the second Test, he would go on to unleash a lone assault on the England attack, being eventually caught in the deep after he had made a fine 84 from a total of only 182. Frustratingly he would make 22 in the second innings and had now made starts in all four innings but had built on only one.

Much of the talk leading up to the third Test concerned the Old Trafford pitch, and after a successful call Lloyd had no hesitation in batting first, believing the surface would not hold up. Scarcely half an hour later four West Indians were back in the pavilion for a scant 26 runs, courtesy of a dream start to Mike Selvey's Test career. Greenidge himself survived two scares; the first an lbw which Selvey thought plumb, but crucially umpire Bill Alley did not, and the second a top-edged hook which Knott should have left for Underwood, with

Greenidge once again in the 20s. That storm weathered, there was to be no stopping him this time. Despite the ball rearing and keeping low in equal measure he alone seemed able to place it where he pleased, as he moved to his fifty from just 78 runs. Debutant Collis King managed to stick around long enough to provide solid support, his 32 from a fifth-wicket partnership of 111 proving vital while at the same time serving to emphasise the dominance of Greenidge's performance.

The century came shortly afterwards from just 146 runs, Greenidge having advanced from 50 in just over an hour, but he was by now rapidly running out of partners. Shortly after tea he finally succumbed to Derek Underwood's quicker ball for 134 with the score at 193-9. During an innings in which only King of the other batsmen had managed more than 10 runs, Greenidge's 134 represented 63.5 per cent of the total, a figure which had only ever been surpassed by Charles Bannerman in the very first Test almost 100 years before.

The brilliance of Greenidge's knock was brought into stark relief by the evils which the West Indies bowlers were able to extract from the pitch – numerous unplayable deliveries found the batsmen wanting and they closed England's innings for a paltry 71, their worst performance in almost 30 years. With Lloyd deciding not to enforce the follow-on and despite numerous rain interruptions, Greenidge built on his earlier exhibition with another stylish display in the West Indies' second innings. The following day he became the first ever to achieve two centuries in a match at Manchester and only the second West Indian to manage the feat anywhere, the other being a certain George Headley.

The West Indies had the luxury of declaring 551 runs to the good, sending England in to survive the remaining 80 minutes of play. 'Survive' is certainly not hyperbole, as Brian Close and John Edrich were subjected to a terrifying assault, leading to widespread condemnation among press and public alike. Michael Holding has since blamed the pitch rather than the bowling; however, his reaction at the time to being warned by umpire Bill Alley suggests otherwise, when the very next ball found Close's ribs. As the next decade or so would confirm, cricket had been changed for good, or rather, forever. Ultimately England were dismissed for just 126, losing by the huge margin of 425 runs.

Another century in the fourth Test gave Greenidge three in succession, his 115 helping the West Indies to seal the rubber. He ended the series with an unbeaten 85, the final Test resulting in another big win for the West Indies, who, after opening with two draws, had now thrashed England 3-0. He finished with 592 runs at 65.77, second only in both measures to Viv Richards. With this performance Greenidge, who considers this innings to be the finest of his career, announced himself as one of the world's greatest opening batsmen – as he recalled in his autobiography: 'After the years of struggle and the mental torment of my failures, the hours after the completion of my second century have to be among the finest of my life.'

Don Bradman – 103*

Australia v England, Melbourne 30 December-3 January 1932-33

32

The groan of the crowd told Australian last man, Bert Ironmonger, that Bill O'Reilly had been dismissed for a duck, which made Australia 186-9, with not-out batsman Don Bradman still there on 98. The *sobriquet* 'Dainty' was typical Aussie humour, with the *avoirdupois* Ironmonger being anything but. Bert was also known as 'the ferret' because he went in after the batting bunnies. So bad was his batting (Test average 2.63), legend has it that on one occasion his wife rang as Ironmonger was heading out to bat. When informed of this she said, "No worries, I'll wait."

Dainty must have been nervous, he was after all the last chance for the Australian people's champion, Don Bradman, to bring up what would be a magnificent century. Under normal circumstances the crowd would have been passionate enough about their team and their Bradman against the traditional enemy, the 'Poms', but this was beyond passion – it was akin to life and death. The reason for this was the visitors' tactics, what the English captain Douglas Jardine christened fast leg-theory but was now, in the second Test, being routinely labelled 'bodyline'. This act of bowling at the body and predominately at the head, was incensing the crowds but, like a car crash, they couldn't look away, with fans flocking to the matches in record numbers. The first Test had almost seen the end of bodyline when Stan McCabe had scored a scintillating 187 not out. It was felt by many that if Bradman could have partnered his fellow New South Welshman, it might have died then and there.

Unfortunately Bradman had been ruled unfit for the first Test and, as bodyline had been conceived with the prime motive of checking his unprecedented dominance, there was some conjecture that Jardine would save it for later. But use it he did and, despite McCabe, it was ultimately successful with England winning by 10 wickets. Still, many believed that, with Bradman back in the team, this evil new method could be exorcised.

The venue for the next Test was the MCG which, at the time, was traditionally the fastest pitch in the country. Perhaps with this in mind, the English captain left out his spinner and brought in a fourth fast bowler, Bill Bowes. Nothing out of the ordinary in 2013 but in 1933 an all-pace attack was unheard of. The pitch however was to favour slow bowlers, with Jardine of the opinion the wicket had been doped to blunt his barrage of fast men.

Bill Woodfull, the Australian captain, had no hesitation batting on the straw-coloured pitch and took Jack Fingleton out with him to the middle. Unfortunately Woodfull was bowled, soon after sustaining a blow to the chest, by the only English bowler who refused to use the bodyline field, the amateur Gubby Allen. Surprisingly, the next man was not Bradman but debutant left hander Leo O'Brien. In the change room, Bradman had been bemused to see O'Brien padding up at the commencement of the innings, saying, "You don't seem to have much confidence in me, Leo" before the newcomer gestured to the batting order pinned on the dressing-room wall.

Bradman entered to one of the biggest cheers ever witnessed on a cricket ground, with Australia 67-2, and then left to one of the most deathly of silences, with Australia 67-3. Bowled first ball by Bowes. Thanks to a brave 83 from a battered and bruised Fingleton, Australia finished with 228. In reply, England collapsed for 169 with Bill 'Tiger' O'Reilly claiming 5-63, on a pitch that was playing slower and lower as the game progressed.

With a first-innings lead of 59 and England without a spinner, Australia just needed a decent second innings to bat England out of the match. 'Just' can be a big word and this England team, even without the use of bodyline tactics, ranks as one of the game's finest and they were to show just why they have earned this praise with a fine bowling performance in the home team's second innings.

Fingleton could not replicate his first-innings heroics, dismissed for one and when O'Brien was out for only 11 Bradman joined his captain with Australia 27-2, his welcome from the crowd just as frenzied as on the previous day. He opened his account with an aggressive pull off Bowes for a boundary and kept backing away to leg when the bowlers pitched short to crash back-foot drives cum cut shots through the mostly vacant off-side field. By the time he had reached 80 and Australia 166-7, Jack Worrall, writing in the *Australasian*, was already enthusing: 'He is now the most scintillating batsman of the world, perhaps the master of all time.' How the rest of the team struggled can be measured by the next best score being just 32.

With three wickets remaining and Bradman needing 20 it looked almost certain 'The Don' would make his century but there he was, on 98, as out shuffled Dainty Ironmonger. As he approached the wicket to take strike he attempted to reassure the young champ with "Don't worry, son, I won't let you down". Bradman may not have been that convinced as both Wally Hammond's two remaining balls just missed the edge of Dainty's bat which was firmly stuck in the block hole. Bradman now faced Bill Voce. The left armer bowled tight and by the time he was at the top of his mark ready to bowl the last ball, the crowd was on edge with Bradman still on 98. The chances of Ironmonger, the worst batsman in the world, lasting another over appeared almost non-existent. Voce bowled the last ball short and Bradman lifted it over the leg-side field to bring up his century amidst wild cheering, especially from the female contingent. Ironmonger was run out in the next over for a predictable duck but, thanks to the efforts of Bradman, England now faced a daunting 251 to win. With conditions in their favour, O'Reilly and Ironmonger tore England to pieces, claiming 5-66 and 4-26 respectively, to level the series. It was to be only a temporary reprieve but a magnificent example of the art of the greatest batsman ever.

Viv Richards – 192*

India v West Indies, Delhi 11-15 December 1974

31

'He shows unmistakeable signs of developing into the first great West Indian batsman from the smaller, less developed islands', was the way Vivian Richards, then 22 and yet to make his Test debut, was described by the official souvenir published by BCCI for the 1974-75 visit to India by the men from the Caribbean.

A century against West Zone in his first innings on the subcontinent ensured that Richards made the side for the first Test, and he spent a grand total of seven minutes at the crease, dismissed in both innings, for four and three, by Bhagwat Chandrasekhar. He did not even have the consolation of being mesmerised by a great bowler at the peak of his powers, Chandra's bowling in the game being, by his own high standards, less than his best.

Despite the lack of any meaningful contribution with the bat by Richards, his side won easily enough, by 267 runs and Richards retained his place for the second Test. In 1979 he wrote, 'I believe that if I had failed again I would have been resigned to an abrupt end to a brief Test career.' It seems highly unlikely that anyone else believed that, or that it was ever on the cards, but the sentiment is interesting simply because it illustrates that even 'the Masterblaster' was not always the epitome of self-confidence that he later seemed.

India were missing both their influential captain, the Nawab of Pataudi Jnr, and their leading batsman, Sunil Gavaskar. Their consolation was the return from injury of Bishan Bedi. With Srinivas Venkataraghavan being stand-in skipper, the selectors had to decide whether to accommodate Bedi by omitting their other top-class off spinner, Erapalli Prasanna, or Chandra. It was the mercurial wrist spinner who missed out, and, considering his problems in the previous Test, Richards' confidence must have grown enormously as news of that change emerged. The measure of his relief can be gauged from his 1991 comment about the first Test: "I seriously doubted if I would ever be good enough to compete with the likes of Chandra. This bowler had terrified me…he could do things with the ball that seemed supernatural."

At Feroz Shah Kotla in Delhi, Venkat won the toss and batted and, after an opening salvo from Farokh Engineer, India proceeded pretty well up until lunch before getting bogged down in the afternoon. The wicket was, at this stage, rather placid although it did have a bit of bounce to keep the quicker men interested. No doubt Chandra's pacy leg breaks and googlies would have been ideally suited to it later in the game.

In the end, the Indians lost their way and paid far too much respect to the West Indian spinners. Admittedly off spinner Lance Gibbs was a great bowler, but surely somebody should have been trying to knock the rather less worldly-wise 21-year-old slow left armer,

Elquemedo Willett, out of the attack, rather than allow him to take a couple of important wickets for just 30 runs in his 13 overs. The early wicket of Greenidge before the close cannot have done much to appease Venkat after his own side were dismissed for just 220.

Next day, the West Indies, in getting to 89-3 by lunch, managed to make batting look as tricky as the home side. It was the fall of nightwatchman Willett at 73 that brought Richards to the crease and it is understandable that he did not look too hard for runs before the interval. What he saw in those few overs was, however, clearly enough to settle him as he and his side added 153 in the two-hour afternoon session, and then another 136 in the 90 minutes between tea and stumps. Richards was unbeaten on 118 at the close having enjoyed significant partnerships for the fifth wicket with his captain, Clive Lloyd, and for the seventh with Bernard Julien. Perhaps Richards' attitude had changed when, almost immediately after lunch, there was a huge appeal against him for a catch at the wicket off Venkat when he was on 12. He has always maintained that he did not hit the ball, and although the Indian fielders were certain that he did, the man who mattered, umpire Gothoskar, agreed with Richards. It was when he was batting with Lloyd that the tempo changed, and although Lloyd's scoring rate was much the quicker it was Richards who was the first to clear the boundary. By the time the innings finished on the third morning he had hit six sixes and 20 fours in an unbeaten 192.

Although Richards batted superbly on the second day it was during the 80 minutes that the West Indies batted on after the rest day that represented the first flowering of the Vivian Richards who was to bestride the art of batsmanship for the next decade or so. He himself added 74 in that short session, causing Indian writer Sunder Rajan to express the view that he 'took one's breath away…he lashed out at almost every ball and hit five sixes in the morning.' So frenetic was the cricket that Gibbs and Andy Roberts were both run out, so depriving Richards of a thoroughly deserved double-century.

By the end of the third day, India, who had begun their second innings with a deficit of 273, had progressed to 239-5. There was overnight rain and the last five wickets produced just 17 runs as West Indies went 2-0 up in the series with an innings victory.

For the third Test, Pataudi and Chandra returned, and India won. They won the fourth as well to square the series before, on winning the toss in the decider, the West Indies piled up 604-6 before declaring. With Gavaskar now back, the home side certainly didn't roll over but they were in an impossible position and the visitors ran out comfortable winners to take the series. For Vivian Richards a memorable career had begun and in many ways his first great innings was the decisive moment of the series. He may have been the fortunate recipient of a blunder by the Indian selectors, but that doesn't alter the fact that he played one very fine knock. Gavaskar had sat out that second Test, but he watched the game and almost 20 years later wrote: 'What a wonderful sight it was to see Viv Richards play.'

Ian Botham – 114

India v England, Mumbai 15-19 February 1980

It was an embattled and chastened England side that arrived in what was still then Bombay for the one-off Golden Jubilee Test with India in February 1980. On the way home from an exhaustingly scheduled experimental split-series tour, England had shared the Australian summer with an ascendant West Indies and ended it very much as the also-ran sideshow to the main event. Their skipper, Mike Brearley, in particular was the butt of such abusive derision from the Australian public as to draw from the host's manager a statement that a section of the crowd had made him ashamed to be an Australian. Losing 3-0 to a home side themselves beaten conclusively by the West Indies, England never threatened to upset the pre-tour odds and only Ian Botham, leading wicket-taker by a distance as well as leading run-maker, had represented the old enemy with any conviction, emerging with reputation undimmed to end the tour with an unbeaten 119 out of 273 at Melbourne.

At just 24 and still in only his third full year as a Test player, Botham landed for the first time in the subcontinent to be welcomed by an Indian public stirred by tales of the man they called Mr Iron Bottom's performances against their side the previous English summer. And, as he would later reveal, with as much Aussie beer crammed into the team's luggage as possible. Daunting evidence, from the perspective of some of the team, of the bumptious boy's determination to banish the 'down under doldrums' off the field as well as on it. And indeed, while reports confirm that a number of his team-mates were left liverish by Botham's relentless pursuit of off-field morale-boosting, out on the Wankhede pitch they would be energised and uplifted witnesses to, statistically at least, perhaps the greatest all-round performance in Test history.

India won the toss and new skipper Gundappa Viswanath elected to bat on a pitch with a good covering of grass left by groundsmen perhaps wary of it turning too quickly and truncating the jubilee celebrations. After a slight delay as large balloons were released to mark the centennial opening and both anthems were sung through twice, the home side, themselves enervated after playing 16 Tests in seven months, started well enough reaching 102-1. But then Botham had an uncharacteristically skittish Gavaskar caught behind by Bob Taylor, the first of his record seven catches in an innings. Supported by the unlucky John Lever, Botham then swung and seamed his way with pace and aggression through the Indian line-up dismissing Kapil Dev, one of his rivals for world's top all-rounder billing, for a duck on his way to a return of 22.5-7-58-6 in an Indian total of 242 all out. "He bowled brilliantly" recalled Dilip Vengsarkar, one of the few Indian batsmen Botham did not dismiss.

The scheduled second day of the match was postponed with the rest day brought forward as India waited for its first total eclipse of the sun since 1898. When England finally took to the field at 3-0, their batting at first continued in the indifferent vein that had characterised the Australian tour. With the ball still moving about and Kapil Dev and Karsan Ghavri using it to skilful effect, the visitors, not helped by some woeful home umpiring which saw off Brearley and Wayne Larkins, slumped to 58-5. When they had reached 85 without further loss, Taylor, then on seven, was given out instantly by umpire Rao in response to Syed Kirmani's lone appeal for a caught behind. Taylor looked flabbergasted before Viswanath, fielding at first slip, and as certain as the batsman that there had been no contact, with a gesture for which the Test will forever be remembered, called him back.

Good deeds seldom get rewarded in the short term and this occasion was no exception as Botham, supported staunchly by the reprieved Taylor, took England to within sight of a first-innings lead. Until he was out, lbw to Ghavri with just 10 minutes of the day left, none of the problems of timing or survival that dogged his team-mates appeared to trouble Botham. He cut the quicker bowlers with ferocity and swept with insouciant arrogance. John Woodcock in his match report for the *Times* said that he 'had never seen anyone sweep much better'. His formidable power enabled him to get away with one or two risky shots but this was an innings built on sound judgement and excellent defence as much as audacious improvisation. As John Emburey said later: "This wasn't one of those innings where he went in and smashed it. He backed his technique...and batted responsibly." In all, he batted for 206 minutes for 114 off 144 balls and hit 17 fours. His stand of 171 with Taylor was England's best ever sixth-wicket partnership against India.

This was Botham firmly on the upward surge towards the summit of his cricketing powers; before the belly and the bombast, before his Headingley deeds in 1981 led him to rely overly on his brute strength and belligerence – a window onto the Test batter he might have become had he not seen himself as perhaps first and foremost a bowler. Sound defence, orthodox technique, fearless confidence and controlled power. The batting quality which would lead Imran Khan, himself one of the four great all-rounders of his or perhaps any other era, to later reflect that "Botham was a better batsmen than all of them".

At the close of the second day, with six wickets and a century to his name, Botham decided to celebrate. Derek Underwood and the *Daily Mirror* correspondent Chris Lander were the principal victims, the latter too ill the following day to make it to the ground and watch an apparently unaffected Mr Iron Constitution take 7-48 and bowl his side to within 100 runs of a duly completed 10-wicket victory. 'It was,' said *Wisden*, 'an extraordinary all-round performance by Botham, whose versatility was in full bloom.' 'Oh what a joy he is,' echoed John Woodcock.

Garry Sobers – 168

Australia v West Indies, Sydney 13-18 January 1961

Max Walker's Cricket Game was a dice entertainment circa 1984, which featured a selection of teams from the ages, with the players ranked in batting and bowling from A to G for batsman and A to D for bowlers. Garry Sobers, because of his longevity, was included in four teams. To my young eyes it was amazing how much the game's greatest ever allrounder's ratings in batting varied.

Team	Batting	Bowling
1955	D	B
1960-61	A	C
1968-69	B	B
1973	E	B

The words these ratings conjure are 'inconsistent' or 'mercurial', depending if you are a glass half-full or -empty type. It's surprising Sobers' batting varies to such a degree while his bowling is rated fairy consistently. After all, his final Test batting average of 57.78 screams more than just simply regular purple patches. His bowling with its three different types and final average of 34.03, would seem more likely to be of a hit-and-miss nature.

As the game's rating suggests, Garry Sobers in the summer of 1960-61 was at his very peak as a batsman, but perhaps they had a point regarding his inconsistency as, apart from his two centuries, he failed to move past 21 in six of his innings in the series. Sobers had followed a great 132 in the first Test, which was also the first tie in Test cricket, with a double failure in the second with scores of nine and nought.

The third Test pitch was expected to favour the spinners, although there was a small green patch at one end. Despite this there was no real surprise when Frank Worrell elected to bat after winning the toss. The easy nature of the surface quickly became apparent with the openers being able to confidently play their strokes off Australia's greatest ever left-arm paceman Alan Davidson, and a wayward and ultimately pathetic figure, Ian Meckiff. Sobers came to the crease with the score at 68-2 but looked anything but confident, seemingly playing more with the edge of the bat than the middle as Meckiff troubled him with his slower ball which Sobers seemed unable to pick. By lunch the West Indies were 93-3. With Sobers out of form and the other not-out batsman, Worrell, suffering from flu, Australia appeared to be just one good session away from inflicting a batting collapse on a flat strip.

After lunch, Sobers slowly started to find his form and brought up his half-century before losing his captain for a stubborn 22 off 81 deliveries, the score an ambivalent 152-4. Without offering any real chances of dismissal, Sobers, who was just existing at the crease, was by tea 80 out of 215-4. Between lunch and tea he had started to master the spin bowlers but the skill of Davidson and that befuddling slower ball of Meckiff would surely account for the left hander shortly, especially as the home team would claim the new ball after the break.

It was said by contemporaries of the great allrounder that he did not appear to sweat, which was frustrating as when he was in form the fielders regularly had to wipe their brow as they chased another ball to the boundary. After tea they sweated bullets as Sobers unleashed all of the shots known to the batsman's art; with a mix of delicate placement and brutal force he scorched 72 runs from 70 balls. If there was one shot that summed up the innings it was a six off Meckiff, whose suspect action would eventually see him labelled a 'chucker' and force him out of Test cricket. Sobers had struggled with the slower delivery all day so when Meckiff released the ball he came forward to play a drive, then, realising he had misjudged the trajectory and speed, amazingly found time to reassess, rock back and launch an almighty swing over mid-wicket that saw the ball scatter spectators in the stands. Later Sobers would say laughingly, "It was him or me." A crestfallen Meckiff retorted, "It was me, who suffered." Showing all the respect for a fellow bowler who has just been hit for six, Davidson quipped to his fast-bowling mate, "You just stuffed up the new ball beautifully, didn't you!"

Sobers' assault had been so faultless it appeared that containment was the only option. But there was no containing him in this mood. Instead, and perhaps fittingly, it was an act of God, (perhaps only God could stop him) in the form of a thunderstorm that brought the day's fun to an end with Sobers 152 not out and the West Indies 303-5.

Next day, Sobers added only 16 to his score before Davidson caught and bowled him, after he mistimed a hook stroke. Sobers said he was in two minds and 'checked' the shot after his captain had told him before he resumed his innings to cut out the hook. The West Indies lost five wickets for just 36 runs, and invited the Australian team back into the match.

The home team were unable to take advantage of their fight back as they crumbled to the spin of Lance Gibbs and the veteran off spinner, one of the 'pals of mine', Alf Valentine for just 202. The only player who seemed able to turn the match around had been the stylist Norm O'Neil who had stroked 71 before Sobers bowled him, after the most versatile bowler in the history of the game was asked to employ his wrist spin by Worrell.

The West Indies, thanks to a fine 82 by the captain, set Australia 463 to win the match which, once more thanks to the bowling of Gibbs and Valentine, proved way too many; they fell 222 runs short. The win had evened the series and given the West Indies the belief that they could eventually triumph. Following perhaps the tensest of all draws in the next match, it all came down to the fifth Test at Melbourne where a world-record Test crowd of 90,000 spectators were treated to more nail-biting action and a home victory by two wickets. The promise of brighter cricket had been fulfilled. Thank you Messrs Benaud, Worrell and Sobers.

Gordon Greenidge – 213

New Zealand v West Indies, Auckland 27 February-3 March 1987

New Zealand went into the second Test, at Eden Park, much boosted after their fightback three days previously in Wellington. They had not lost a home Test in five seasons; the West Indies had not triumphed in a Test in New Zealand since 1968-69, and they had underwhelmed so far on this tour. 'Overall,' wrote Richard Streeton, 'West Indies still give the impression that they find it hard to apply themselves.' This was no less true of Gordon Greenidge than it was of his team-mates, his efforts the previous year in England and Pakistan had been mediocre and, although he'd batted beautifully in the first innings at Wellington, he'd been substantially less comfortable against the turning ball in the second.

Spin was unlikely to feature much at Eden Park, where the wicket was exceedingly green. There had been little rain there of late, but the groundsman was fond of his sprinkler, and the heavy roller brought plenty of moisture to the surface. On a cloudy first morning, Viv Richards won the toss and elected to bat – 'Surprising,' thought *Wisden's* chronicler, 'considering the overcast conditions and the well-grassed pitch.' The ball swung prodigiously and moved a long way off the seam and Richard Hadlee, in particular, provoked considerable bounce, making trouble for both batsmen. He had yet to concede a run when the final ball of his third over reared up at Desmond Haynes. The catch went to third slip and the West Indies were 7-1.

Greenidge survived a confident shout for leg-before, and then found himself beaten, all ends up, by a veritable brute. It struck high up on the bat, but landed safely behind a congested slip cordon. Larry Gomes was out not long after to a nothing shot, bringing Richie Richardson to the crease. The plan was to counterattack, and this he did, driving his first ball down the ground for four. But the momentum was difficult to sustain through three stoppages for rain, which totalled collectively some 50 minutes.

Greenidge had needed all his science and know-how to survive these initial exchanges and interruptions, but as things settled down he began to play with more autonomy, taking two straight boundaries off Hadlee, one aerial and one along the ground. A lofted on drive was succeeded by another straight drive, this time for six, and a mighty sweep for four. Off three deliveries from Stephen Boock he thus hit 14 runs, bringing up his fifty and taking the West Indies into three figures.

A 95-run stand with Richardson was broken when the latter nicked a short ball off Hadlee through to Ian Smith behind the stumps. Richards replaced him and started well, driving Boock coolly for six, then square cutting him for a contemptuous four. He was looking extremely menacing, with the potential to play an innings even greater than the one

Greenidge would record, but in the next over he went only half-forward to Hadlee, and the ball spun back on to his wicket. Undaunted, Greenidge went to his 13th Test century with yet another straight drive off Hadlee. He then survived an awkward spell to reach 112 at the close with his side a respectable 211-4, the opening day's play having lost two hours, the cumulative effect of five disruptions.

His latest partner, Gus Logie, was out early the following morning, caught brilliantly in the gully by Martin Crowe. With proceedings stayed four more times by rain, just 32 runs were added in the 21 overs before lunch, as Hadlee returned with fresh hostility after each intermission. There was still life in the wicket, the ball often keeping low and Ewen Chatfield was proving a handful to all bar Greenidge. But here was the weakness: New Zealand had selected two spinners and the two seamers lacked adequate support. That said, the frequent rain breaks enabled them to operate for considerable spells. The new ball was taken after 88 overs, with the score 258-5.

Not long after lunch, and into his 130s, Greenidge top-edged Jeremy Coney out to deep backward square-leg. It swirled in the firmament before falling through Chatfield's fumbling fingers. As it crossed the boundary, Coney held his head in his hands. Greenidge made things worse, when Chatfield ran in to bowl, by clipping him wristily over mid-wicket for six. Then at 148 he survived another chance, John Wright dropping him at mid-on.

His 150 came up after 395 minutes. He was striking the ball with as much force as ever, and using his feet spryly to put the spinners under strain. Boock, again, was his primary victim. 'There is something of the demolition gang about Greenidge when he is in this form,' wrote Henry Blofeld. 'He comes to meet the ball as if he is angry with it, and the bowler can expect no mercy.' But this innings was no slog; it was the most diligent he had yet played – 'A triumph,' in the words of *Wisden*, 'of technique and temperament.'

Wright let him off again, this time at long-on, when he had 187. (This was no match for fielders – in this innings alone seven chances went begging and the other match centurion, Crowe, benefitted from two dropped catches.) Greenidge made it count, going soon to his third double-century. His partnership with Jeff Dujon, which secured his side's ascendency, was worth 165. He was finally out 20 minutes before the close of play, losing his off stump to Hadlee. At that point in the history of the game, only Wally Hammond had hit more sixes in a Test innings than his seven. But his nine-hour 213 was also a staggering feat of application. Martin Crowe esteemed it one of the three best innings he ever saw.

Richards declared on 418-9, and New Zealand responded with 157 all out. They struggled courageously in their second innings, taking the match into the final hour of the final day (the weather having shortened the match by some 500 minutes), but defeat was rarely, and then only briefly, in any real doubt, Malcolm Marshall and Courtney Walsh sharing 12 wickets. Greenidge was a predictable and worthy man of the match.

Michael Slater – 123

Australia v England, Sydney 2-5 January 1999

27

Sometimes life gives you a second chance, or even two! Not always, but sometimes. It's what you do with those second chances that counts. In the case of Michael Slater, he took his second chances and made as much of them as anyone probably could and, in the process, produced one of the all-time great Test innings.

Lauded as a breath of fresh air, a swashbuckling opener who would rather play the aggressor than the dour run accumulator steadily taking the shine off the cherry so that the middle-order batsmen can make hay, Slater burst onto the international scene with a century at Lord's in only his second Test match. It was as much the nature of his celebration as his batting which raised eyebrows, as few could fail to be moved by the exuberance of his virtual lap of honour on reaching the milestone.

Fast-forward three years and Slater, only three matches removed from a double-century against Sri Lanka, had been dropped for reasons never made clear to him, but which most considered to be the result of his poor shot selection. Indeed, Ricky Ponting had told him over a beer that he would always get out in the nineties because he started slogging whenever he got there, and a quick search shows that 'Punter' had a point – Slater was king of the nervous nineties during the 1990s, sitting atop cricket's nearly-men with no fewer than eight dismissals while in sight of the magical ton, more than any other player in that decade.

Handicapped as he was with *ankylosing spondylitis* and associated arthritis leaving him feeling "like an old man" at times, peppered with a dash of what was later diagnosed as bipolar disorder, Slater nonetheless worked hard to get back into the national side. Selected for the 1997 Ashes tour he unfortunately didn't make the Test team, but by the time of the tour of India he was opening again for his country. However, in four innings he was unable to fashion even 30 runs in total and he found himself once more playing for his place, so it was somewhat ironic that it was a score in the nineties which kept him in the side.

The 1998-99 Ashes found Slater returning to top form and entering the final Test he already had two centuries under his belt, helping Australia to build a 2-1 lead. England were no pushovers however and fine bowling from Darren Gough, who had a hat-trick in the first innings, together with Dean Headley and Peter Such kept things tight. So tight in fact that Australia, who had enjoyed a first innings lead of 102, found things so much of a struggle in the second innings on a turning pitch that nine of their batsmen fell in single figures. The exceptions were Mark Waugh (24) and Michael Slater.

It was while batting with Waugh that Slater received another second chance. Calling for a tight second run when on 33, a fabulous pick-up-and-throw from Dean Headley flattened the stumps from long-on. Virtually everyone in the ground felt that Slater was out, including, it seems, Slater himself as he traipsed off while stripping off his gloves. However, the decision was referred to the only man whose view counted, third umpire Simon Taufel. England officials Graham Gooch and David Lloyd had sent a letter of complaint to the match referee after the Adelaide Test, during which Michael Atherton had been given out after an almost instantaneous review, so it was ironic that the review of Slater's run-out seemed to take forever – careful what you wish for.

Eventually, to the amazement of most of those at the ground and watching on TV, Slater was given not out. Taufel, who was officiating in just his 11th first-class match, had apparently been unsighted on the most telling camera angle by Such and as a result had to give the batsman the benefit of the doubt. Thus reprieved, Slater proceeded to play what Henry Blofeld called "one of the most phenomenal innings in the history of Test cricket", comparing him to the great Denis Compton. While all around him fell like ninepins, Slater carried serenely on, at one point adding 75 in only 91 balls on a pitch which the *Times* described as 'devilishly difficult'. He reached his hundred from a total of just 148, receiving what the commentary team declared was one of the greatest ovations ever heard at the SCG. Eighth out at 180, his final 123 from a team aggregate of 184 represented 66.85 per cent of the total, second only to Charles Bannerman in the very first Test match.

As far as some elements of the British press were concerned, Slater had lived on borrowed time – 'Video Nasty!' screamed the *Daily Mirror* highlighting Taufel's inexperience and the shortcomings of the *ABC* camera positions. The *Birmingham Post* bemoaned 'Slater's Ton of Luck' and pointed out that, having removed his gloves, Slater had indicated his acceptance of the inevitable, though he later claimed that it was because he was sweating. The broadsheets were more gracious in their acknowledgement of Slater's brilliance. Mike Selvey in the *Guardian* thought, 'He might have been batting on a different pitch, against different – and indifferent – bowling rather than on this capricious offering, against bowling that was never less than wholehearted and fielding that bordered on the demonic', while C M-J in the *Daily Telegraph* praised 'an innings replete with brilliant strokes and dazzling footwork'.

That the ACB immediately issued a statement that it was urgently considering the installation of special cameras in line with the crease suggested that it also felt justice had not been served. Sadly the incident tarnished the greatness of Slater's innings at the time, although with hindsight it can take its place among the all-time great Test-match innings, having turned a likely 2-2 series stalemate into a 3-1 victory for Australia.

Ironically, in view of the alleged reasons for his time spent in the international wilderness, Slater commented: "I decided to play my natural game and treat every ball on its merits. There was no point me being there if I wasn't scoring." In so doing, he had shown that, given a second chance, he could make the most of it as few others.

Mark Waugh – 116

South Africa v Australia, Port Elizabeth 14-17 March 1997

Rather watch 20 by Junior Waugh in majestic style
Than 100 by those whom 20-20 orthodoxy defile

Mark Waugh, the most fluent and aesthetically pleasing batsman of his generation but also one of the most frustrating to watch. Often, when he appeared to be a class above the rest and to have the bowling at his mercy, he would play a lazy shot to what appeared, more often than not, an innocuous delivery. And just like that his innings would be over. To make matters worse, he didn't seem to care; he would nonchalantly wander off the field. No shaking of the head or staring back at the pitch to apportion blame. His fans had to learn to accept 30s and 40s instead of centuries and 150s. His concentration, some would say his interest, never seemed to be there in the Test arena. Despite playing some match-winning Test innings, Waugh was never quite able to shake the 'lackadaisical' tag.

But all of these supposed shortcomings were absent when Waugh played what he himself described as 'easily my best innings' during the second Test of a three-match series in South Africa. It was early 1997, a year in which he was destined to average only 31.40 from 15 Tests with just this one century. Mark would draw a stickman on his thigh pad each time he scored a first-class century and this milestone would give him his 61st three-figure score. By this stage his pad was worn so thin he felt every hit 'through to the bone' but it gave him such confidence to see all those stick men that he would not countenance a replacement.

The Australians entered the second Test, in Port Elizabeth, as the number one Test nation. In the first, Australia had cruised to victory by an innings and 196 runs and South Africa seemed destined to yet again fail in their bid to win a first Test series against Australia, and also to lose their first home series, since coming back into the international fold in 1992.

The pitch for the Test was the favourite colour of fast bowlers: green. The opening pair for South Africa were two of their all-time finest in Allan Donald and Shaun Pollock, but they would have to wait for their turn to bowl on this deck as Australian captain Mark Taylor won the toss and, to no-one's surprise, elected to bowl first. Australia also had two quality opening bowlers in Glenn McGrath and Jason Gillespie, who quickly dismissed the Proteas for a barely respectable 209, with Gillespie claiming his first five-wicket haul for Australia. In reply the visitors scored at a snail's pace, taking over 70 overs to score a meagre 108, in the face of Donald who, according to *Wisden*, 'bowled with fearsome hostility and frequently beat the bat'. Although he only claimed one wicket his pressure produced many a false shot at the other end and only 18 runs were scored from his 23 overs.

With a lead of 101, South Africa found themselves back at the wicket on only the second day of the Test. By stumps the Proteas were seemingly well on their way to victory at 83-0 and a lead of 184 with all 10 wickets still in hand. At a team meeting that night Mark Waugh was most vocal, urging his team-mates to attack the bowling, not "to throw in the towel", and making his impressions of the first-innings effort absolutely clear: "Seventy overs for 108 runs is not the way Australians play cricket."

Perhaps inspired by Mark's words, Australia rolled South Africa on the third day for 168, claiming all 10 wickets for just 85 runs in less than two and a half hours. There was more good news for the visitors with Pollock, who had strained his hamstring in the first innings, being unable to bowl. Still, with Donald in superlative form, a lead of 269 runs plus a still uneven and fast pitch, it was short odds on a South African victory.

With plenty of time left on the third day, Mark Waugh went to the crease at 30-2. He found a partner in Matthew Elliott whose driving almost matched the fluidity of his own. The two began to take control, 'Junior' being particularly severe on Paul Adams, whom he described as a "cocky kid", hitting him for a towering six and never letting him settle. Adams stuck to his task and caught and bowled Elliott off a full toss reducing Australia to 113-3. This only seemed to inspire Waugh, as he clipped a boundary off Brian McMillan when he pitched on his legs and, off the next ball, cut him for a succulent four when he dropped one short. Waugh then brought up his fifty with yet another cut stroke, his half-century including eight boundaries and the six off Adams, and at stumps Australia were 145-3 with Waugh unbeaten on 54.

The crowd on day three had been a disappointing 6,517, however with the prospect of a grandstand finish over 10,000 showed up on the fourth, and inevitably, final day. Waugh was in fine touch from the outset, one drive from Donald, whom Mark described as 'superb' in this Test, was nothing more than a block but it flew to the boundary. As he later admitted, when in his 60s he 'feathered' one off Adams, however, as there was almost no appeal, he marched on – it seems Mark Waugh, like most Australians, was not a 'walker'. This 'almost' chance was his only mistake on the way to his century which he duly and appropriately brought up with another well-timed cut, Australia at that stage being 234-5. From the time he brought up his century to his dismissal for 116, off a beautiful inswinger from a baby-faced Jacques Kallis, Waugh looked as if he was playing with the home team's bowlers. As he left the field the Australians needed only 13 runs for a famous victory.

One would imagine Waugh and his team-mates could now enjoy the last rites. However two more wickets saw Australia precariously placed at 265-8 with six still needed and Glenn McGrath, at that stage of his career arguably the worst Test batsman in the world, padded up in the sheds. Cue Ian Healy, the Aussie wicket-keeper, who casually lifted a Cronje inswinger for six and Australia had won a great match and with it the series.

Part Three
Innings 25–1

Pinnacle

Michael Clarke – 151

South Africa v Australia, Cape Town November 9-11 2011

- Keith Stael -

At the beginning of 2011 it became clear that Ricky Ponting's injured finger would not allow him to captain the Australian side in the final Test of that summer's Ashes series in Sydney. Michael Clarke had already been appointed vice-captain in April 2008 following the retirement of Adam Gilchrist and so it seemed the obvious, if not perhaps the unanimous, move to install Clarke as the 43rd Test match captain of Australia. He was duly honoured with the interim appointment but his elevation did nothing to turn the tide as Australia lost that Test to end the series defeated 3-1. Clarke's personal contribution to the cause had been meagre, 193 runs at 21.44. According to the *Sun Herald* it had been 'a summer to forget' and personally 'Michael Clarke had a shocker'. He had been given the top job in Australian cricket, albeit temporarily, but on the down side only a few days later he resigned from his position as T20 captain, a role he had held since 2009. His lack of explosive power as a batsman prevented him achieving the heights necessary in that form of the game. Clarke retained the captaincy of the 50-over team yet even that required the dreaded vote of confidence from national selector Greg Chappell who agreed that he had been out of form all summer but argued that in this format Clarke 'had excelled as captain and will be given every opportunity to lift himself out of his slump.' However, Clarke had problems with the Australian public that went far beyond a mere dip in form.

Three months after that Sydney Test, Ricky Ponting resigned as Australia's Test and one-day captain immediately following their exit from the World Cup at the quarter-final stage. He thought it fit to recommend Michael Clarke as his successor and the appointment duly followed on 30 March. In his press conference accepting the post, Clarke made a revealing remark: "Hopefully I can earn the respect of the doubters who are out there. No doubt it's about how I conduct myself on and off the field." On-field problems might be easy to identify (if not easy to repair), a lack of runs as a batsman perhaps or tactical naivety as a captain, but in referring to awareness about potential problems with his off-field conduct Clarke gave recognition to concerns that had dogged him for a few years, most of his international career in fact. A column that was actually supporting Clarke revealed the extent of his problem. Writing a couple of days after Clarke became captain, Richard Hinds remarked in the *Sydney Morning Herald*: 'I've been trying to hate Michael Clarke, like I'm supposed to.' With friends and supporters like that he clearly had his work cut out. But what exactly was the difficulty Clarke faced?

Put simply and using a ghastly modern version of a word, Clarke's problem was with his 'image', with the general impression he gave to the Australian public. Cricket Australia had taken to the national press in February 2011 to announce that Michael Clarke most definitely did not have an image problem, a claim that could only make matters worse by opening the topic up for further debate. This foray into public relations on behalf of Clarke had been prompted by the embarrassment suffered by Cricket Australia and the player himself as he was jeered by his countrymen on his way to the crease at the 'Gabba two days previously in a one-day international against England. By trying to pretend that those boos emanated only from concerns about Clarke's prolonged lack of runs, Cricket Australia continued a debate that had long festered in Australia about their supposed new Golden Boy since he had made his debut in 2004, a debut that featured a century closely followed by another one on his home bow back in Australia. What then, apart from his current run drought, was wrong with Clarke? What was up with 'Pup's' image?

There is an Australian slang phrase that in its long form accuses those men who dress too ostentatiously as being as 'flash as a rat with a gold tooth.' Used in its shortened version, 'flash', it can also mean that the accused is a bit dodgy in some way, not to be fully trusted. With his abundant tattoos, ever-changing haircut, brand new sports car and model girlfriend, Clarke had presented a lifestyle to the Australian public that allowed them to think of him as flash or, to use another Australian phrase, just not 'fair dinkum'. When the story emerged of his conflicting loyalties (a boozy sing-song with the boys or supper with his girlfriend?) the public took the side of Simon Katich who had forcibly reminded him of what it meant to wear the baggy green. Clarke failed to meet the exacting standards of immediate predecessors such as Mark Taylor, Steve Waugh and even Ponting himself. Those three could be described in many ways but 'flash' would surely never apply. 'Tubs' Taylor was 'a good bloke', Waugh was 'tough' and 'Punter' Ponting was a great player, but flash? Never. Certainly Shane Warne had attracted his fair share of jibes but then he was Warnie, the world's greatest-ever spinner and no amount of flash behaviour could discredit him in the eyes of the Australian cricket-loving public. And he never quite made it to captain – maybe too fancy for the authorities?

When Clarke made his debut as skipper in January 2011, Cricket Australia had already made another venture into the public relations world, taking the opportunity to describe him as Australia's first 'Gen Y Captain'. Whilst taking any member of any group and attributing the stereotype characteristic to them is undoubtedly unfair and usually wrong, nevertheless the public impression of 'Gen Y', indeed its very definition, is of a cohort of narcissists with a strong sense of entitlement and for whom material wealth is very important. Yuppies reborn. With that and their obviously fraudulent claim that Clarke did not have an image problem, here were two very nice pieces of work on behalf of their new captain by his bosses.

And of course we must not forget the problems Clarke had with his Australian team, problems that any captain would have faced. Thrashed by England at home for the first time since 1986-87, Australia were still a team in transition trying to present to the public a hope for a future that might begin to rival the period of dominance they enjoyed from 1995 until 2007, the Ashes of 2005 notwithstanding. With his form in the 'dunny', his bosses unreliable and his team inexperienced and unproven, Clarke had many obstacles to negotiate at the very start of his captaincy career.

Captaincy can do funny and unpredictable things to batsmen who finally get the pinnacle position. Bobby Simpson scored 10 centuries and averaged 54 when bossing the side but scored none and averaged just 33 when taking orders. Mark Taylor, by contrast, averaged almost 50 as a foot soldier but less than 40 after promotion. Don Bradman, as in most things, remains an exception, averaging almost exactly 100 as captain and player. The question for Clarke as he acceded to the job, often referred to in Australia as second only in importance to the prime minister, was whether he would be inspired or intimidated by his new role.

First up for Clarke the captain came a three-match series in Sri Lanka. He headed a squad that featured four uncapped players; Nathan Lyon, Shaun Marsh, Trent Copeland and James Pattinson as well as two players, Usman Khawaja and Michael Beer, who had made their debuts in the Sydney Test defeat against England. Despite this obvious lack of experience Australia won the series 1-0, a significant achievement for a side seeking to establish itself and Clarke made a much improved contribution with the bat, scoring 214 runs at nearly 43 including 112 in the second innings of the third Test. One feature of that innings was that Clarke went to his 100 from only 139 balls, a strike-rate of 72 runs per 100 balls as compared with a career average of 55. The early indications were that the Australian team was responding well to Clarke and he was inspired, or at least not intimidated, as a player. Things were looking up for 'Pup'.

The Sri Lanka series finished on 20 September and Australia's next game was to be the first Test in a two-match series against South Africa starting on 9 November. Anxiety was growing in Australia that a proposed World Championship of Tests featuring the top four ranked sides, earmarked for 2013, might go ahead without Australia as they were far from certain to qualify. Uncertainty about the captain himself still manifested itself in widespread comment. For example, former Test batsman Dean Jones went into print on 8 October arguing that many Australian cricket fans 'still don't rate Michael Clarke, for whatever reason'.

For such an absurdly short series it produced any number of remarkable happenings. In the first game both Australia and South Africa were bowled out in double figures. In the second, Australia turned their fortunes completely around and chased down an improbable target to level the series as debutant Pat Cummins starred with both bat and ball.

That face-saver was still in the future however as Graeme Smith won the toss for South Africa in Cape Town and, rightly anticipating early movement in the air and off the pitch for his formidable seam attack, put Australia in to bat on a damp and overcast morning typical of November. After a delay for rain, Dale Steyn and debutant Vernon Philander, moving the new ball hither and thither, quickly removed Shane Watson and Philip Hughes before the players were sent back into the pavilion with the score at 23-2. Ricky Ponting was next to go, shortly after lunch, and at 40-3, and with no sign of conditions improving, Clarke got off the mark first ball with a nudge into the leg side off a friendly Steyn delivery. That, however, was where the friendliness ended as the finest fast bowler of the 21st century set about 'targeting' Clarke in an unforgettable two-over contest won by the Australian as he straight drove past the bowler off a good length. The quiet start of just three runs from 20 balls was now over and the introduction of a wayward Jacques Kallis for the tiring Steyn brought a new dimension to proceedings.

With the ball still doing plenty, Morne Morkel and Kallis were now treated roughly as Clarke moved from three in 20 balls to 44 from 48 balls. Clearly reasoning that on such a pitch the unplayable ball was inevitable he began unleashing gorgeous shots all round the wicket. His approach was clear – to try and wrest the initiative back from his opposite number who was packing the off-side field. With this in mind, he fetched one ball from Kallis way outside off and pulled it to the mid-wicket boundary as if telling Smith to re-think his field. When the bowlers pitched up too far, straining for the swing that was in the air, he drove through the covers and back past the bowler. Kallis went for 37 in just six overs. Then when the bowlers dropped short, looking for the uneven bounce and sideways movement that had flummoxed the early batsmen, he cut in front of and behind point or even hooked them to the long-leg boundary, a shot the modern-day Michael Clarke usually keeps in his locker. The afternoon session belonged to Clarke – in just under 24 overs he plundered 74 runs off the best fast-bowling attack in the world on a surface they might have designed for their own convenience. At the other end the obdurate Shaun Marsh was out shortly before tea having added 17 in the same time.

The evening session looked to be continuing in a similar vein as far as Clarke was concerned until bad light and then rain caused play to be halted an hour early. In this truncated session 14 overs were bowled and four wickets fell for the addition of 71 runs. That Clarke managed less than half of these was due partly to some quick work by Mitchell Johnson but also to a slightly more restrained approach. But there was nothing restrained about the roar he let out as a glorious drive off Kallis brought up his hundred. Was there maybe a sense of a watershed in the making?

At close of play Australia were 214-8, at first glance not a surprising score against Steyn,

Morkel, Philander and Kallis and on a pitch offering plenty to the bowlers all day. What was remarkable was that Clarke, 107 not out at stumps, had scored exactly half of those runs and had gone to his century from a mere 108 balls. Asked how he rated his century Clarke replied: "I'll let you know in a few days' time." The inference was clear, the innings was meaningless in isolation but as part of a team triumph it may have merit. Nonetheless, Clarke was clearly and rightly proud of his achievement such as it was: "I remember Warnie saying to me years ago that the better the bowling the more positive you have to be," he said. "That was my attitude today. I knew I was facing a pretty good attack in conditions that were going to do a little bit. But I thought I needed to do something to put a little bit of pressure back on them."

Next morning, Clarke's innings should have come to an abrupt halt as he snicked Philander's first delivery to second slip – or rather where second slip should have been if Graeme Smith hadn't miscalculated. This was the reward for his outstanding work the previous day, even Smith was now on the back foot. With Peter Siddle as a resolute partner his innings took on a more circumspect character. The first three overs of the day brought 20 runs but then only 13 came from the next eight as the batsmen decided that survival and slow accumulation was the order of the day. This all changed on Siddle's dismissal and Clarke smashed two more boundaries from Morkel before perishing in an ambitious lunge for a third. He was out for 151, contributing a startling 53 per cent of his team's total of 284. A previously unconvinced Allan Border remarked that Clarke batted as though he were playing on a different pitch to everyone else and the response of the South African players indicated that they, too, thought they had witnessed an extraordinary display of bravery and bravura.

Again, as in Sri Lanka, Clarke had developed his attacking stroke play to a degree that he scored at 86 runs per 100 balls while the other 10 members of the team managed less than 42. But it was the bizarre events that followed which would put his knock in to some context.

The total of 284 then started to look a monumental score as South Africa were dismissed for 96 with Shane Watson taking five very quick wickets; only openers Graeme Smith and Jacques Rudolph reaching double figures. Then, even more remarkably, Australia were themselves dismissed for 47, having been 21-9 and staring down the barrel of Test cricket's lowest-ever score, an ignominy avoided by the combined efforts of Lyon and Siddle. This time Clarke fell to Philander for two. South Africa then resumed something approaching accustomed Test cricket standards of batting as they closed on 81-1 in their second innings. Despite this return to relative normality, no fewer than 23 wickets had fallen on the madcap second day. The general feeling in the bemused press box was that a toxic mix of a difficult wicket, fine bowling and inept batting had led to this almost unprecedented mayhem. This total of wickets in a single day hadn't been exceeded since 1902, just one of many notable 'achievements'. A unique feature was that this was the first time that a batsman from both sides had been dismissed twice in a day – Jacques Rudolph and, of course, Michael Clarke being the record-book entries.

On the following day the South African pair of Smith and Hashim Amla made light of the winning target of 236, both easing to centuries in much improved conditions relegating the events of the previous day to something akin to a delirious dream. One minute, however, brought a surreal air back to Newlands. When South Africa needed 111 runs to win at exactly 11:11 on the 11th day of the 11th month in 2011, the scoreboard read 11:11 11/11/11. Cricket South Africa asked all the fans in the crowd to stand on one leg for the duration of that minute and with the crowd hopping about, umpire Ian Gould got into the spirit too.

The suicide of Peter Roebuck, one of cricket's most eminent writers, rather overshadowed the Test match that week in Cape Town. Roebuck, who threw himself out of a hotel window on Saturday 12 November, the day after the game ended, rated Clarke's innings very highly. Writing in the *Sydney Morning Herald*, Roebuck's take on day one had been that 'Michael Clarke chose a fine time to play the best innings of his career'. He was enthralled by the confrontation between Clarke and Steyn, 'a fit and fierce speedster charging full pelt to the crease and sending down swift swingers and searing bumpers, a combination that troubled every batsmen except one.' But by the time Roebuck wrote what turned out to be the final column of his life, Clarke's first-innings heroics had been drowned in a sea of vitriol directed at a team display that in Roebuck's words was 'shameful and worthy of censure'. Perhaps it is the fate of all great sporting performances to be forgotten somewhat if the team eventually loses. Would we care overly about VVS Laxman's 281 or Ian Botham's 149 without the efforts of Harbhajan Singh and Bob Willis who turned these great feats from potentially heroic failures to match-winning epics? Michael Clarke was not so fortunate; maybe with a Warne or McGrath at his disposal things would have turned out differently but we should remember this innings for its brilliance, technical perfection and outstanding determination against the world's best on a track to suit, even though it turned out to be in a losing cause.

Clarke has a complicated relationship with the Australian cricketing public. Things improved largely because 2012 was an *annus mirabilis* for Clarke the batsman, a year in which he scored 1,595 Test runs at an average of 106.33, passing Ricky Ponting's previous record of calendar-year runs for Australia set in 2005. In January he scored 329 not out against India and also made three other scores of 200 or more. It was hardly surprising when *Wisden* 2013 proclaimed him the world's leading cricketer.

It is not unreasonable to trace the start of Clarke's phenomenal run of scoring to this great knock against South Africa. Certainly it represented ascension to master batsman. Whatever fault Australians could now find with Clarke, lack of runs was not one of them. It's easy to forget though that things had been very different only 12 months earlier at the start of 2011 when Clarke made his debut as captain in that last match of the Ashes series.

Australia

Batter	Dismissal	Runs
SR Watson	c Kallis b Steyn	3
PJ Hughes	c †Boucher b Philander	9
SE Marsh	lbw b Steyn	44
RT Ponting	lbw b Steyn	8
MJ Clarke*	b Morkel	151
MEK Hussey	c †Boucher b Morkel	1
BJ Haddin†	c Prince b Steyn	5
MG Johnson	c Morkel b Philander	20
RJ Harris	c Morkel b Philander	5
PM Siddle	c de Villiers b Morkel	20
NM Lyon	not out	1
Extras (b5, lb7, w1, nb4)		**17**
Total (all out; 75 overs; 349 mins)		**284**

Fall of wickets 1/9 2/13 3/40 4/143 5/158 6/163 7/202 8/214 9/273

Bowling	O	M	R	W
DW Steyn	20	4	55	4
VD Philander	21	3	63	3
M Morkel	18	2	82	3
Imran Tahir	10	1	35	0
JH Kallis	6	0	37	0

Batter	Dismissal	Runs
SR Watson	lbw b Steyn	4
PJ Hughes	c Rudolph b Morkel	9
RT Ponting	lbw b Philander	0
MJ Clarke*	lbw b Philander	2
MEK Hussey	c Prince b Morkel	0
BJ Haddin†	c †Boucher b Philander	0
MG Johnson	c Amla b Philander	3
RJ Harris	c Smith b Morkel	3
PM Siddle	not out	12
SE Marsh	lbw b Philander	0
NM Lyon	c de Villiers b Steyn	14
Extras (0)		**0**
Total (all out; 18 overs; 95 mins)		**47**

Fall of wickets 1/4 2/11 3/13 4/13 5/15 6/18 7/21 8/21 9/21

Bowling	O	M	R	W
DW Steyn	5	1	23	2
VD Philander	7	3	15	5
M Morkel	6	1	9	3

South Africa

Batter	Dismissal	Runs
JA Rudolph	b Harris	**18**
GC Smith*	b Watson	**37**
HM Amla	lbw b Watson	**3**
JH Kallis	c Ponting b Watson	**0**
AB de Villiers	lbw b Harris	**8**
AG Prince	lbw b Watson	**0**
MV Boucher†	lbw b Watson	**4**
VD Philander	c Ponting b Harris	**4**
DW Steyn	not out	**9**
M Morkel	run out (Siddle)	**1**
Imran Tahir	b Harris	**5**
Extras (lb4, w1, nb2)		7
Total (all out; 24.3 overs; 130 mins)		**96**

Fall of wickets 1/24 2/49 3/49 4/73 5/73 6/77 7/77 8/81 9/83

Bowling	O	M	R	W
RJ Harris	10.3	3	33	4
MG Johnson	5	0	26	0
PM Siddle	4	1	16	0
SR Watson	5	2	17	5

Batter	Dismissal	Runs
GC Smith*	not out	101
JA Rudolph	c †Haddin b Siddle	14
HM Amla	c Clarke b Johnson	112
JH Kallis	not out	2

Did not bat
VD Philander, AG Prince, MV Boucher†, Imran Tahir, DW Steyn, M Morkel, AB de Villiers

Extras (lb4, w1, nb2)		7
Total (2 wickets; 50.2 overs; 232 mins)		**236**

Fall of wickets 1/27 2/222

Bowling	O	M	R	W
RJ Harris	14	2	67	0
PM Siddle	12.2	0	49	1
SR Watson	10	0	44	0
MG Johnson	11	1	61	1
NM Lyon	3	1	11	0

Jacques Kallis – 161

South Africa v India, Cape Town 2-6 January 2011

24

-Telford Vice-

Jacques Kallis and most of his accomplishments can be distilled into one short word: cold. It's in the pulseless precision he brings to even his most flamboyant strokes, the world's neither stirred-nor-shaken reaction to him, and the feeling the more mortal among us have when we enter his icy presence.

There is more discernible humanity in Shivnarine Chanderpaul taking a moment to mark his guard with a bail than there is in a day of Kallis at the crease, even though the former is a temporary scratch in the earth and the second is often chiselled into the annals.

Even Kallis' fake hair looks frozen, as unthawable as his perfectly perpendicular bat in the long moment after a lofted drive. He has fashioned one of the great careers with the passion he might have brought to mowing the lawn. This is not to paint Kallis as some bloodless run machine. But it is difficult for those of us who will never finish our lofted drives with perpendicular bats not to think of him as such – as an organism not fully formed unless there are runs to score, creases to occupy, or wickets and catches to take. It's not him. It's us.

Without cricket there would be no Kallis as we know, respect and are befuddled by him. Without Kallis, cricket – in particular South African cricket – would not be half the game it is. These truths and half-truths had been self-evident for so long that there was no questioning them when India arrived in South Africa in the first week of December 2010 to play three Tests.

Even when Kallis walked to the wicket an hour before tea on the second day of the first Test at Centurion, that everything we thought we knew about him was to change was not apparent. How could it be when that change was, in its own context, evolutionary? It took almost six-and-a-half hours to be effected; 389 minutes, in fact, involving 270 deliveries, 15 fours, five sixes, a sacred look at the heavens in dedication to his father and a profane drive off an imaginary golf tee in giddy celebration of the prize of lifetime membership of an exclusive country club that his feat had secured.

It was what Kallis had not achieved in his 50 series, 139 matches and 241 innings that had come and gone before – many lesser players had reached this milestone earlier. It was a Test double-century and it was, as much as any other single event in his life, the making of Jacques Henry Kallis. It was the moment of his global warming, the long and winding instant he became more human than he had ever been, as well as one of three centuries scored by South Africans in reply to India's first innings of 136. They had been roughed up on a pitch designed to accomplish exactly that, and they started their second innings in a hole 484 runs deep. Sachin Tendulkar dug them some way out of it with an unbeaten 111, not just a fine performance but also his 50th Test century. The eruption was heard, felt and seen around the world. How Tendulkar must have envied Kallis: one day, with luck, he will also be allowed to achieve his humanity.

Kallis confirmed his new, merely human, status in his innings of 10 – run out at the non-striker's end after backing up too far – and 17 – dropped on nought but out soon enough fending a brute of a Sreesanth delivery to gully – at Kingsmead, where India, humbled by an innings in the first Test, levelled the series. It was only their second win in 14 Tests in South Africa, and the fact that it was achieved in the wake of a drubbing told the South Africans that they were not dealing with the tabbies the Indians had been on previous tours: this time they were tigers.

And so to Cape Town, where the world's two best teams would try, one more time with feeling, to decide which of them was the best. It is at Newlands that this story begins as well as ends, but the layers of meaning added by the events that preceded it are crucial to its understanding – and to fully appreciating the role that Kallis played in its making.

India had come to South Africa with the No.1 ranking in their hearts and Gary Kirsten in their minds. No-one was surprised when they failed abjectly to come to terms with the conditions at Centurion, and South Africans, who had seen their side go down to Sri Lanka at Kingsmead the season before, knew another defeat in Durban – which seems to have become the last place their national team wants to play – was feasible. But if the Indians had their haughtiness dented by being treated like any other opponents in the first Test, the South Africans seemed offended to have been beaten in the second. Cape Town, then, would offer a cure for both ills. Or would it be for just one, or even none?

MS Dhoni looked up, saw clouds over Newlands, called correctly for only the second time in 15 Tests, and declined to bat. That was India's first mistake, especially as rain and bad light meant just 37 overs were bowled before tea. Their second error was to fail to exploit the limited opportunities they had to apply pressure. But they did manage to remove Graeme Smith before the first rain delay and Alviro Petersen shortly after the resumption.

It was not quite half-past-one on a dreary Sunday afternoon when Kallis walked his imperious walk down the stairs, over the boundary and to the middle. The first delivery he faced, bowled by Ishant Sharma, curled away and was left well alone. Kallis shouldered arms to Sharma's next delivery, an inswinger that found the thigh pad and moved sharply enough to prompt Hashim Amla to make the journey from the other end of the pitch for a chat.

Kallis took nine balls, eight of them Sharma's, to get off the mark, which he did with a nudge to cover-point off Zaheer Khan. Two deliveries later he unleashed a stroke of savage power to put Sreesanth through the covers for his first boundary – back, across, forward, bang. He was 12 when he edged Zaheer onto his back leg and was almost bowled.

Amla, meanwhile, rose above all that to play what for him was an out-of-body innings, a display of flash and dash that looked doomed to be ended sooner than it was – with a miscued pull to a bouncer from Sreesanth. At the other end of the pitch Kallis, who had faced 35 balls for his 17 when Amla got out for 59, showed no flicker of alarm or anything else. Anxious, fidgety AB de Villiers took charge of the next seven deliveries. Kallis kept calm as he did so, then faced four more without scoring or worrying about not scoring. Not so De Villiers, who found a way to drive a swinging ball from Zaheer down the ground for four. Kallis' response was to block three of Sreesanth's efforts and steer the fourth – tossed up invitingly – into the covers for a single.

Tea came with South Africa steady on 125-3. In the moments before play resumed, the Indians buzzed in their huddle and De Villiers was down the pitch, looking to disguise imperfections in the surface. None of that for Kallis, who kept stoic counsel with himself at his end. Not for the first time in his storied career and surely not the last, he was the centre of the game – he waited for it to come to him, not the other way around. This is easily mistaken for arrogance: does Kallis fancy himself bigger than all of cricket? More important than its other protagonists? No. He knows his place, but he also knows that there are few who can share that place with him.

A run accrued to each of Kallis and De Villiers in that first over of the session, which was delivered by Harbhajan Singh. Sharma took charge of the second over and beat Kallis both with outswing and inswing. Then De Villiers took two singles off Harbhajan. Sharma returned, eager to build on his work of an over before. His first ball swung in. Kallis defended. The next delivery splayed full towards the leg side. Kallis dismissed this ordinariness from his presence and to the mid-wicket ropes for four. Whatever pressure Sharma had managed to muster went with it. Kallis also took a single off that over, and three runs off the next – which culminated in De Villiers turning on the style to drive a perfectly pitched, turning delivery from Harbhajan through the covers for four.

Runs did not flow, but they were also not rare. They were coming as and when the batsmen saw fit to take them; a mode of batting that suited the patient, assured Kallis more than it did the urgent nature of De Villiers. Kallis' next boundary was nothing so ostentatious, just a nudge of an angled bat to put Sharma through fine-leg. Three balls later a similarly veering delivery was met with more bat and stabbed between short-leg's planted feet for two. Sharma's next effort was too full, and Kallis squeezed the trigger on a handsome on drive only for Harbhajan to tumble into a fine stop.

This slow but sure rhythm was maintained without significant interruption – save for

De Villiers drilling a wayward offering from Sharma into Cheteshwar Pujara's thankfully protected shin at short-leg – until, in the over after the drinks break, Sreesanth produced a sublime outswinger that took the edge of De Villiers' bat and flew behind to Dhoni.

The partnership was thus ended at 58, South Africa were 164-4, and India thought they saw a chink in the home side's armour. Kallis disabused them of that notion with the next delivery, from Harbhajan, which he leaned into and steered to mid-wicket for the single that took him to 50. The milestone had taken 99 balls to arrive and it was mildly spiced with four boundaries. In other words, exactly to Kallis' and South Africa's tastes.

Criticism of Kallis over the years has tended to label him as selfish; not a team man; more interested in maintaining his average than doing what needs to be done to win or save a match. The truth in this is that Kallis is selfish in the Ayn Rand sense, as in: 'The man who does not value himself cannot value anything or anyone.' And: 'In a free society one does not have to deal with those who are irrational. One is free to avoid them.' Also: 'In order to deal with reality successfully – to pursue and achieve the values which his life requires – man needs self-esteem; he needs to be confident of his efficacy and worth.' Or even: 'Man's basic vice, the source of all his evils, is the act of unfocusing his mind, the suspension of his consciousness, which is not blindness, but the refusal to see, not ignorance, but the refusal to know.'

These are dangerous ideas that go to the extremes of what it means to be human in a world that has to make room for other humans, and are sometimes used as excuses to commit societal brutality by those who refuse to make that room. They are ideas that Kallis – who is entirely likely to wonder 'batsman or bowler?' when asked if he knows who Ayn Rand might be – has probably never entertained.

But he is no less Randian for that. In fact, more so: it is his bedrock nature to be rational and confident of his efficacy and worth, and to focus his mind to the exclusion of any and all else he does not want to think about. He is, in the most worthy way, selfish. He is this way not because he read a couple of fat books called *The Fountainhead* and *Atlas Shrugged*. He is this way because he is this way.

As Kallis stood there, bat raised to accept the gratitude of his home crowd for scoring another sturdy half-century, his selfishness was celebrated as it had been many times before. But proof that Rand didn't have all the answers came with the next ball Kallis faced. It was delivered by Sreesanth, and pitched on a length and leapt up and away. Even Kallis' cold-steel instincts could not prevent him from being drawn towards its line. The edge fell short of the cordon and streaked away for four.

Four balls later Sreesanth was roaring for Kallis to be given out lbw. Simon Taufel shook his head. Hawkeye said Sreesanth had the stronger argument. By then, Kallis had been joined by Ashwell Prince – a left-handed version of himself in terms of grit and powers of same two men, playing on the same ground in 2007, had eroded the visitors' resolve with batting so dour it made manila envelopes look pornographic by comparison. At times in their stands of 77 and 83 off 167 and 229 balls respectively, the earth stopped turning just to see how long they could treat Newlands like their personal Zen garden.

This time, Kallis and Prince kept their opponents and all who watched them more entertained. Their partnership yielded 98 and came off 197 deliveries. Dour it was not. It was a product of intense focus and superb application to the task. An edge by Prince off Zaheer that looped over where a fourth slip would have stood, a direct hit on the non-striker's stumps that found Kallis within his ground, two fours four balls apart – languidly lapped and struck straight – by Prince off Harbhajan, another off the spinner by Kallis, technically driven to fine leg with the help of a radically altered stance, were the most important events of the rest of the first day's play. Kallis was 81 not out at stumps, just 24 of his runs having come in boundaries. And this from a man whose 17 sixes in 2011 was just one fewer than the number hit by De Villiers. But it was that sort of day on that sort of pitch against that sort of opposition.

When South Africa resumed the next day on 232-4, Kallis was in the same sort of mood. Prince rattled the status quo in the morning's third over by driving Harbhajan through the covers for four twice in three balls, first off the front foot then the back. Kallis did unfurl a sumptuous cover drive off Sharma the over after that, but once he reached 90 he faced 15 balls without adding to his score. In that time, he saw Sreesanth use the second new ball to dismiss Prince and Mark Boucher with consecutive deliveries. The previous ball had left Prince. The next one cut a wicked curve through the air and demanded a drive. Prince obliged, and the inswinger bowled him though the gate for 47. Boucher, ham-fisted and flat-footed and in the throes of poor form, could only edge to Dhoni.

South Africa had crashed from 262-4 to 262-6 in an eye blink. Not that Kallis blinked. Instead, he drove Sreesanth through a clumsy Tendulkar at mid-on and smeared him imperiously through mid-wicket for boundaries to move to 99. The look on Kallis' face when he is one run shy of a century is the same as the look on his face when he is 99 runs away. It's the same look as when he is at the top of his run or awaiting a bowler as he stands in the slips. He wore this look when Dale Steyn did the sensible thing and stuck his bat between his throat and a vicious delivery from Zaheer. The catch was taken at gully and South Africa were 272-7. Kallis was still 99 not out.

Despite almost getting himself out twice in the five balls of the over that remained, Morne Morkel survived. Sreesanth began the next over with a full delivery that hooked away from Kallis just as he offered at it: beaten, bowed, but not out. Looking like he was late on his way to commit a crime, Sreesanth came storming in again. His effort strayed too far onto the pads and Kallis waited long enough to dab it demurely past square-leg. Newlands rose to salute the 39th Test century of the finest player of the age, bar bloody none. Off came his helmet. Out came his smile. Up went his arms. Away went any semblance of inhibition.

There is a school of thought that, in his pomp, Kallis was good enough to hit a six whenever he felt like it. He hit none during this innings, but after reaching his century he hit 10 fours – one of them edged – from 82 balls. Thus, of the 61 runs he scored after bringing up three figures, only 21 of them required something so inelegant as running to the other end of the pitch. In doing so Kallis had to put up with a hip strain and with partners, Paul Harris and Lonwabo Tsotsobe, who were entirely likely to do something that deserved a kick up the backside.

They duly did those things but not until Kallis had ensured South Africa squeezed 79 runs, his share being 61, out of their last two wickets before he cut too thinly at Zaheer and was caught behind. As an individual performance it was of the highest quality. As an intervention in a self-destructing innings it was vital. As an example of what Kallis does best it was even better than the undefeated 109 he would score in the second innings to secure the draw.

Ayn Rand would have understood as much about all that as Kallis would of her writing, but she should be proud that her philosophy was padded up and at the crease in Cape Town in January 2011.

South Africa

First innings

Batsman	Dismissal	Runs
AN Petersen	c †Dhoni b Sharma	21
GC Smith*	lbw b Khan	6
HM Amla	c Pujara b Sreesanth	59
JH Kallis	c †Dhoni b Khan	161
AB de Villiers	c †Dhoni b Sreesanth	26
AG Prince	b Sreesanth	47
MV Boucher†	c †Dhoni b Sreesanth	0
DW Steyn	c Pujara b Khan	0
M Morkel	c †Dhoni b Sreesanth	8
PL Harris	c Pujara b Sharma	7
LL Tsotsobe	not out	8
Extras (b1, lb6, w1, nb11)		**19**
Total (all out; 112.5 overs; 522 m)		**362**

Fall of wickets 1/17 2/34 3/106 4/164 5/262 6/262 7/272 8/283 9/310

Bowling	O	M	R	W
Z Khan	29.5	6	89	3
S Sreesanth	29	0	114	5
I Sharma	27	6	77	2
H Singh	27	3	75	0

Second innings

Batsman	Dismissal	Runs
GC Smith*	lbw b H Singh	29
AN Petersen	lbw b H Singh	22
PL Harris	lbw b H Singh	0
HM Amla	b Harbhajan Singh	2
JH Kallis	not out	109
AB de Villiers	b Khan	13
AG Prince	c Sreesanth b Sharma	22
MV Boucher†	lbw b Tendulkar	55
DW Steyn	c sub (Vijay) b H Singh	32
M Morkel	c Sreesanth b H Singh	28
LL Tsotsobe	c Sehwag b H Singh	8
Extras (lb7, w2, nb12)		**21**
Total (all out; 102 overs; 478 mins)		**341**

Fall of wickets 1/50 2/52 3/53 4/64 5/98 6/130 7/233 8/287 9/333

Bowling	O	M	R	W
Z Khan	20	2	64	1
S Sreesanth	24	3	79	0
I Sharma	18	1	62	1
H Singh	38	1	120	7
SR Tendulkar	2	0	9	1

India

First innings

Batsman	Dismissal	Runs
G Gambhir	c †Boucher b Harris	93
V Sehwag	c Smith b Steyn	13
R Dravid	run out (de Villiers)	5
SR Tendulkar	b Morkel	146
VVS Laxman	run out (Harris)	15
CA Pujara	lbw b Steyn	2
MS Dhoni*†	c Prince b Steyn	0
H Singh	c sub (JP Duminy) b Steyn	40
Z Khan	c Prince b Morkel	23
I Sharma	c †Boucher b Steyn	1
S Sreesanth	not out	4
Extras (lb20, w1, nb1)		**22**
Total (all out; 117.1 overs; 536 mins)		**364**

Fall of wickets 1/19 2/28 3/204 4/235 5/237 6/247 7/323 8/341 9/350

Bowling	O	M	R	W
DW Steyn	31	11	75	5
M Morkel	29.1	7	106	2
LL Tsotsobe	26	5	82	0
PL Harris	29	8	72	1
AN Petersen	2	0	9	0

Second innings

Batsman	Dismissal	Runs
G Gambhir	c †Boucher b Steyn	64
V Sehwag	c Smith b Morkel	11
R Dravid	c Prince b Tsotsobe	31
SR Tendulkar	not out	14
VVS Laxman	not out	32

Did not bat MS Dhoni*†, CA Pujara, I Sharma, Z Khan, Harbhajan Singh, S Sreesanth

Extras (b7, w5, nb2)		**14**
Total (3 wickets; 82 overs; 352 mins)		**166**

Fall of wickets 1/27 2/106 3/120

Bowling	O	M	R	W
DW Steyn	18	6	43	1
M Morkel	15	6	26	1
LL Tsotsobe	13	4	29	1
PL Harris	30	19	29	0
GC Smith	4	0	27	0
AN Petersen	2	0	5	0

Virender Sehwag – 201*

Sri Lanka v India, Galle 31 July-3 August 2008

23

-Andy Baynton-Power-

We all know the situation; the brilliant quick bowler with his tail up delivers the ball on a perfect length and line. A hint of swing has it pitching just outside off, before seam movement takes it further away from the right hander who would be well advised, if good enough, to leave well alone. But he only has a fraction of a second to respond and make his decision. Yet somehow this astonishing batsman is neither shouldering arms nor nibbling, he's standing tall and smashing a wicket-taking delivery through the covers, on the up, to the boundary. "Wow," enthuses the commentator, "I'm here to tell you that was some shot." And it was. Next over, same bowler, same ball, same response but instead of that beautiful meaty sound of ball meeting sweet-spot there is a heavy click as a thick edge flies waste high to a grateful third slip. "Gone! And you have to say that was a poor shot – no foot movement."

The gap between brilliant and brainless was some four centimetres. Or was it? Surely the first shot was every bit as reckless and feckless? Our foolhardy batsman got away with his poor shot selection first time but within minutes he went from hero to zero. So who is our thrilling and exasperating protagonist? Take your pick: Victor Trumper, Stan McCabe, Denis Compton, Barry Richards, Gordon Greenidge, Virender Sehwag. This is how they played, the risks they took made them what they were: the most thrilling, watchable and often frustrating batsmen of their respective generations. If you want the highs then you must take the lows, and for each run-a-ball century there will be a horridly inappropriate early-innings catastrophe signalling disappointment for all neutrals.

Virender Sehwag must stand as the prime example of this approach and somehow it has led to an under-appreciation of both his talents and achievements, as if he has somehow not done himself justice and sold himself, and his team, short. Many purists are inclined to scoff when he says, "I don't like to defend and hate to leave deliveries. It's a waste of time", and maybe they have a point. But his approach to batting is built on simplicity and take away the rudimentary approach and you have a confused and confusing mixture of styles. His approach is what it is – there is no plan B against a brilliant bowler on a helpful wicket. On the contrary, all the more reason to chase after him and get him out of the attack before he produces the unplayable ball.

The detractors would stand on safer ground if the statistics spoke in their favour but in the case of Sehwag we can make some interesting comparisons with fellow Indians who represent the antithesis of his method: the restraint and obduracy of Rahul Dravid, the elegance of VVS Laxman and the colossus that is Sachin Tendulkar. In boxing terms these three represent the guile and ringcraft of, say, Marvin Hagler, Thomas Hearns and Sugar Ray Leonard against the head-down pugnacity of Roberto Durán – always coming forward, trading blow for blow and outslugging the opposition. It may not have aesthetic appeal but the figures do stack up. In mid-2013, Laxman's Test record stood at 8,781 runs at 46.0, Dravid had 13,288 at 52.3, Tendulkar 15,837 at 53.9 and Sehwag a paltry 8,586 at 49.3. Round one to Tendulkar with Dravid close behind. But the strike-rates tell another story. Dravid only 42.5, Laxman just short of 50, Tendulkar an estimated 56 (some of his early innings were not measured) and Sehwag at 82.2. Seconds away, round three.

Strike-rate isn't everything but nor is the average and somewhere between the two lies a story. In the general context of Test cricket, which team wouldn't prefer a rapid 49 to a slow 52? In terms of effect on the opposition and likelihood of achieving a positive result, a quickfire 49 would be the weapon of choice. And this from an opener whose bruising methods often leave the opposition reeling on the ropes early in the bout.

So why has Sehwag suffered in comparison with often faint praise? Even during his most prolific periods there was the sense that the real class was in the stellar middle order and that this brazen thrasher was something of a tasty *hor d'ouvres* to sharpen the appetite for the succulent main course. In August 2008 Suresh Menon posed the question: 'Is Sehwag great yet?' He came out undecided, mulling his method, potential and even his Jat working-class background as possible drawbacks. He did strike the nail firmly on the head when he wrote, 'There is an obviousness about Sehwag's batting that upsets people who like complexity and mystery. To be simple is not to be simplistic.' And surely any doubters at this mid-point in his career must have been swayed by what happened in the 12 months from late November 2009. In 23 Test innings he amassed 1,726 runs at an average of 82, although detractors would certainly point to every last run being scored in Asia.

It is surely significant that the question of greatness was being asked at precisely this time. There had already been the memorable triple-centuries against Pakistan and South Africa and wonderful three-figure scores against Australia and the West Indies, but these were the bedrock. There was the feeling that with his undefeated 201 against Sri Lanka at Galle, Sehwag had finally emerged from the shadow of the 'Fab Four' (the 'Prince of Calcutta', Sourav Ganguly, the starry fourth member) and was now the most feared member of India's most illustrious batting line-up, a potential game changer every time he strapped on his pads.

However, flash back to the second half of 2006 and the only thing he appeared to be changing was his legwear as a series of low scores had him seemingly returning to the pavilion with a speed and frequency reminiscent of his boundaries. This drop in form led to a drop from the team and he was to spend a year in the wilderness. A last-minute call for him to join India's tour of Australia in the summer of 2007-08 came as a surprise as his form had not been particularly impressive, and it was probably his success on their previous visit that was on the selectors' minds. Or perhaps it was the buzz from the media: Ian Chappell, for one, suggested that they had 'missed a trick' by not taking a gamble and naming Sehwag in their preliminary squad.

So, at the eleventh hour the selectors took the gamble but they were not prepared to go 'all in' and declined to select Sehwag for the first two Tests both of which India duly lost. However, he returned to the fold to help them win the third and went on to score a match-saving second-innings 151 in the fourth and final Test. He followed this up with his second triple Test century, the fastest-ever, 319 at a strike-rate of 104.93 in a draw with South Africa in Chennai. The Nawab of Najafgarh was back in spades.

In July, India crossed the Gulf of Mannar to take on Sri Lanka for a three-match Test series. They'd drawn 1-1 with South Africa and were looking to go one better before taking on Australia and then England in consecutive home series. It did not start well. In the first Test Sri Lanka won the toss and racked up 600-6 including four individual centuries. They then unleashed their weapon of choice, Muttiah Muralitharan, along with a Test debutant, the 23-year-old Ajantha Mendis, a proper mystery spinner very much in the style of the two Australians, Jack Iverson and John Gleeson, who had bamboozled all and sundry in the early '50s and late '60s respectively. The Indian batting line-up, boasting 106 previous Test hundreds between them, were humiliated, twice, and Sri Lanka won by an innings and 239 runs. Nuwan Kulasekara took the first wicket, that of Sehwag, who had typically biffed five fours off 15 balls before top-edging a hook to square-leg. But then the spinners, master and apprentice, went to work and took the remaining 19 wickets to bowl out India for 223 and 138. Rarely had they succumbed quite so comprehensively to spin.

Five days later, they were in Galle for the second Test. India's captain Anil Kumble said: "There is definitely a lot of experience and resilience in this team. We will fall back on that resilience. We need to win this Test match." Positive words, but the task looked daunting. Sri Lanka had lost just one of their last nine Tests there since July 2000. Muralitharan had taken 91 wickets in 12 Tests there at an average of 16.50 and in four of those matches had taken 10 wickets or more. And in those same 12 matches, master batsman Mahela Jayawardene had scored 1,389 runs at an average of 99.21. Galle was clearly a fortress in more ways than one.

The fort itself stood proudly in the sun but the weather was relatively cool with a strong cross breeze coming in from the sea. It had rained over the previous two days leaving the outfield decidedly soggy. When the covers were taken off they revealed a wicket described by commentator Sriram Veera as 'Janus-faced'. One end was dry with cracks and the other flat and somewhat damp. However, upon winning the toss, Kumble had no hesitation in opting to bat first.

In typical fashion Sehwag got off the mark with a boundary from the second ball he faced. One more ball and then play was held up because the sun was reflecting off cars parked behind the boundary ropes. Perhaps the owners had felt that Sehwag wouldn't last long and their cars were safe. Once the vehicles had been suitably draped play resumed. Kulasekara bowled to the dry cracked end and immediately found plenty of movement, both vertically and horizontally, off the pitch, while the experienced Chaminda Vaas at the other end was using the breeze to make the ball swing. Sehwag and his opening partner Gautam Gambhir, dropped off Kulasekara when 13, played carefully yet forcefully and took the score to 37 after 10 overs, at which point Mendis replaced Vaas. In his second over Sehwag stepped down the wicket and swung him over cow corner to take the first Test six off his bowling. 'Viru' had hit his straps. Kulasekara was taken off after our stocky right-hander hit five fours off his previous three overs, and was replaced by Muralitharan. First ball, Sehwag spanked a doosra to the point boundary to bring up a run-a-ball fifty. The mighty spinners were on but the Indian openers were equal to them – Sehwag was 'picking' the previously mysterious Mendis whose first four overs went for 29 runs – and dominated the morning session. Lunch was taken with the score on a huge 151-0 from just 29 overs. The first breach in the fortress walls had been achieved.

It was the perfect riposte after the hammering in the first Test. Sehwag had hit 91 in 82 balls, and sidekick Gambhir, with a little luck, had reached 50 off 92 balls. They'd seen off the new ball in difficult conditions and used their feet well against the spinners. This was the 22nd time these two had opened together and over the next few years they would forge one of the great opening partnerships in Test cricket, amassing 4,412 runs together at an incredible rate of 4.62 runs per over. And it wasn't all fours and sixes. They ran well and hard together and this, along with their right-hander and left-hander combination, often caused opposition bowlers to lose their rhythm and bowl bad balls which, of course, were never turned down.

During lunch it started raining heavily and play was held up for nearly four hours. On resumption India immediately picked up where they left off. Gambhir took a four and two of the first over and then Sehwag whacked Vaas' second ball almost into the Galle Fort. Three balls later and a blistering on drive brought up his century in 87 balls. Next over Gambhir was deceived by a Mendis two-fingered delivery and trapped in front for 56. The pair had put on 167 in just under 32 overs. A mere three overs later and Dravid, Tendulkar and Ganguly were all back in the pavilion, Mendis and Vaas having scooped out most of the rich filling of the Indian batting order: John, Paul, George and in came Ringo. Laxman settled in, not without some early distress, to give the star turn some rock-solid accompaniment. Only nine more overs were bowled before bad light stopped play for the day, but not before Murali had tried bowling round the wicket to Sehwag who responded by using his feet to smack two glorious cover drives in consecutive balls. The close-of-play score was 214-4 with Sehwag on a chanceless 128 not out. However, Sri Lanka were back in the match.

The next day began under overcast conditions and the fissures at the cracked end had opened up some more. Sri Lanka crowded the leg-side field and bowled to it hoping to force an error from Sehwag, but he adjusted by using his feet and playing inside-out to hit the ball through the vacant areas on the off side. This was typical of our man's career. Plans would be hatched to curb his free scoring: cramp him up with inswingers, bowl short, don't give him room on the off stump, but none worked.

With the score at 251 Sehwag stroked a single to become the 10th Indian batsman to score 5,000 Test runs. The very next ball another single brought him his 150, the 11th time in succession he'd extended his 100 to 150, a Test record. Soon after, he was nearly caught as he top-edged a sweep off Mendis but substitute fielder Chamara Silva couldn't stay inside the boundary rope giving Sehwag his third six. No doubt, if Sri Lanka's lanky opener Michael Vandort had been fielding there, Sehwag would not have attempted the shot!

With the partnership standing at 100, Laxman fell to Mendis for 39. The Sri Lankan spin pair, who had been extracting turn from the slowish pitch and who had, apart from a few early overs from Vaas, been bowling without change, sensed their opportunity. Mendis, bowling to the cracked end, and Muralitharan began to mop up the tail with their carrom balls and doosras respectively. Sehwag's strike-rate slowed as the pressure grew, but he would not be felled. He was on 195 when Zaheer Khan had a wild slog at a doosra to become the ninth wicket down. Sehwag then farmed the bowling to find himself facing Murali on 199. He stroked an easy single off the third ball but refused to take it for fear of exposing last man Ishant Sharma – a rare case of *not* taking one for the team. Two balls later he chose, of all things, a reverse sweep but it went straight to the fielder. Last ball of the over: pressure on, fielders in, Sehwag guided the ball past square-leg to bring up an astonishing 200 – and retain the strike.

Sharma perished soon after to leave Sehwag unbeaten on 201 in a total of 329. He'd faced 231 balls and hit four sixes and 22 fours, the other 10 players had faced 261 balls and managed just 116 runs It was his fifth score in excess of 200 and the first double-century scored by an Indian against Sri Lanka. He became the second Indian batsman to carry his bat (after Sunil Gavaskar). India's score of 329 was the lowest total to include a double-century and it was only the second time a batsman had recorded over 60 per cent of a completed team innings while scoring a double-century, after West Indian Seymour Nurse in 1969.

Mendis finished with 6-117 but had not been able to remove Sehwag. Afterwards the laconic batsman said, "I could pick the ball from Mendis' hand. I attacked him and created a little doubt in his mind. I hit the good balls for fours through cover and point. I was able to read his googly and top-spin." When it came to playing Murali: "I was not able to pick his doosra, so I treated every ball as a doosra and tried to hit it. But I found them to be off spinners. It did not matter much as I was getting boundaries." He added that he felt this was his best innings yet: "My triple centuries in Pakistan and Chennai came on good tracks and I could feel on both occasions that the opposition simply didn't have it in them to get me out, but here wickets were falling regularly at the other end and I batted throughout the innings."

Sri Lanka reached 137-1 in reply before Harbhajan Singh, taking 6 for 102, reduced them to 292 all out, Jayawardene bossing the run-getting with 86. With a lead of 37, Sehwag came out for the second innings and, as one was coming to expect, punched the first ball he faced through mid-wicket for four. He raced to a 49-ball fifty, but then, much to his disappointment, cracked a drive straight down cover's throat. The rest of team fared a little better this time round and knocked up 269 to set Sri Lanka 307 runs to win with still five sessions to come. Mendis had taken four more wickets to record 10 in the match.

An exciting finale seemed to be on the cards, but after 21 balls Sri Lanka were 10-3 with the three half-centurions of their first innings succumbing to the new-ball work of Sharma and Khan. Thereafter, Harbhajan and Kumble span the rest of the team out for just 136. India had won by 170 runs and squared the series. Of course, there was only one contender for man of the match.

In the decider, Sehwag got off the mark with a four in both innings but was out for 21 and 34, undone each time by the debutant quick, Dhammika Prasad. Without enough of his dominating presence, India fell apart once more and lost by eight wickets thanks to a focused 144 from Kumar Sangakkara and 13 more wickets for the spin twins.

Nevertheless, India went on to win their encounters with Australia and England, and Virender Sehwag ended the year being named *Wisden*'s Leading Cricketer in the World for 2008 – a fitting tribute to our man's extraordinary exploits. Surely now the Fab Four had become the Famous Five.

India

G Gambhir	lbw b Mendis	56
V Sehwag	not out	201
R Dravid	c Warnapura b Mendis	2
SR Tendulkar	lbw b Vaas	5
SC Ganguly	c †H Jayawardene b Vaas	0
VVS Laxman	c Samaraweera b Mendis	39
KD Karthik†	lbw b Mendis	7
A Kumble*	st †H J'dene b M'tharan	4
H Singh	b Mendis	1
Z Khan	c †H J'ene b M'tharan	2
I Sharma	lbw b Mendis	0
Extras (b1, lb4, w7)		**12**
Total (all out; 82 overs; 348 mins)		**329**

Fall of wickets 1/167 2/173 3/178 4/178 5/278 6/290 7/317 8/318 9/323

Bowling	**O**	**M**	**R**	**W**
WPUJC Vaas	19	2	74	2
K Kulasekara	8	1	40	0
BAW Mendis	28	1	117	6
M M'tharan	27	1	93	2

G Gambhir	b Mendis	74
V Sehwag	c Dilshan b Vaas	50
R Dravid	lbw b M'tharan	44
SR Tendulkar	c D Jayawardene b Vaas	31
SC Ganguly	st †H Jayawardene b M'tharan	16
VVS Laxman	lbw b Mendis	13
KD Karthik†	c Sangakkara b M'tharan	20
A Kumble*	lbw b Mendis	2
Harbhajan Singh	c & b Mendis	11
I Sharma	run out (Dilshan/†H J'ene)	0
Z Khan	not out	1
Extras (lb7)		**7**
Total (all out; 76.2 overs; 321 mins		**269**

Fall of wickets 1/90 2/144 3/200 4/200 5/221 6/252 7/255 8/257 9/257

Bowling	**O**	**M**	**R**	**W**
WPUJC Vaas	13	4	32	2
K Kulasekara	5	0	31	0
M M'tharan	31	3	107	3
BAW Mendis	27.2	4	92	4

Sri Lanka

MG Vandort	c Dravid b Khan	4
SM Warnapura	c Gambhir b H Singh	66
KC Sangakkara	c & b H Singh	68
D Jayawardene*	c †Karthik b Kumble	86
TT Samaraweera	lbw b H Singh	14
TM Dilshan	c Gambhir b H Singh	0
H Jayawardene†	c Laxman b H Singh	24
WPUJC Vaas	c H Singh b Kumble	1
K Kulasekara	not out	5
BAW Mendis	lbw b Kumble	0
M M'tharan	c Ganguly b H Singh	0
Extras (b10, lb12, nb2)		**24**
Total (all out; 93.3 overs; 388 mins)		**292**

Fall of wickets 1/4 2/137 3/144 4/192 5/192 6/250 7/255 8/291 9/291

Bowling	**O**	**M**	**R**	**W**
Z Khan	9	1	51	1
I Sharma	8	1	36	0
A Kumble	36	7	81	3
H Singh	40.3	8	102	6

MG Vandort	lbw b H Singh	10
SM Warnapura	c Laxman b Sharma	0
KC Sangakkara	c Laxman b Khan	1
D Jayawardene*	c Dravid b Sharma	5
TT Samaraweera	not out	67
TM Dilshan	c †Karthik b Sharma	38
H Jayawardene†	c Ganguly b H Singh	4
WPUJC Vaas	lbw b H Singh	0
K Kulasekara	c Sharma b Kumble	1
BAW Mendis	c Kumble b H Singh	2
M Muralitharan	c & b Kumble	0
Extras (b4, lb2, nb2)		**8**
Total (all out; 47.3 overs; 238 mins)		**136**

Fall of wickets 1/4 2/5 3/10 4/37 5/113 6/130 7/131 8/132 9/135

Bowling	**O**	**M**	**R**	**W**
Z Khan	8	1	18	1
I Sharma	15	8	20	3
A Kumble	10.3	3	41	2
H Singh	14	1	51	4

Colin Cowdrey – 102

Australia v England, Melbourne 31 December-5 January 1954-55

22

-Dave Wilson-

England, holders of the Ashes and having stumbled at the first hurdle in their defence of the title, are set on their way to retaining the cherished urn by an iridescent batting performance, buttressed by a fiery fast bowler in irresistible form demolishing a favoured Australia for 111. "Ah yes, Headingley '81!" I hear you cry. But no – this particular tale of big-bottomed derring-do took place some 26 years before and on the other side of the world.

When I first began following the game in the 1960s, I was initially drawn more to batsmen as it seemed to me that they needed to be perfect – typically they were allowed just one mistake, resulting in their dismissal. Colin Cowdrey was one of the leading batsmen of the time so I was well aware of him, though he was by then well into his thirties, his somewhat corpulent figure usually enhanced even more by being encased in a sweater seemingly two inches thick. So it came as something of a shock to me once I started studying the game's rich history to discover that even as a callow youth Cowdrey had still cut something of a large figure.

Cowdrey's additional pounds became largely irrelevant, however, once he took guard and began to stroke the world's best bowlers to all corners of the ground with as fine a technique as you could wish for, and with little apparent effort. Study any photograph of Cowdrey in action and in every case the follow through will display a classically high left elbow. Such model technique had Cowdrey turning heads at an early age. His dexterity in the slips was also seemingly unimpeded by his bulk. He was awarded his county cap in 1951 aged just 18, the youngest ever for Kent. By 1953 he was turning out for his county's first team though it was while representing the Gentlemen that he scored two good fifties against the touring Australians, a side featuring the great strike bowlers Ray Lindwall and Keith Miller. That performance was to stand him in good stead when the team was selected for the next Ashes contest in Australia.

The following year Cowdrey's numbers dipped somewhat, though this was in part caused by the wettest summer in a long time and this, together with final examinations at Oxford University, tempered any expectations he may have had of making the squad for the upcoming Ashes tour. As it happened, he was playing for Kent against Surrey at Blackheath when the squad was announced and, astonished to hear his name called while Surrey stalwarts Jim Laker and Tony Lock missed out, he hurried away from the ground before he could be accosted by the Surrey players over his inclusion. Cowdrey had not yet scored a Championship hundred, played in a Test or toured overseas, so he was 'blooded' in that summer's final Test against Pakistan, named as twelfth man but only being required to field for 20 nervous minutes.

Skipper Len Hutton, obviously himself surprised by Cowdrey's inclusion and with an eye to Denis Compton's knee trouble, added fellow Yorkshire batsman Vic Wilson as insurance, so that it was an unprecedented 18-strong England squad which gathered at Tilbury ready to board the *Orsava* for what would be a seven-and-a-half-month tour of Australia and New Zealand. Cowdrey, the youngest member of the party by some three years, was impressed by the fact that Hutton made a point of reassuring his father that he would be taken good care of, speaking with Cowdrey senior for a full 20 minutes. Sadly, it would be the last time Cowdrey would see his father alive.

There is a splendid story that, during the long sea voyage, Cowdrey was observed by Frank Tyson being addressed with some passion by a well-dressed man whom Tyson didn't recognize: "When you reach Australia, just remember one thing," exclaimed the older gentleman, "Hate the bastards!" Tyson enquired of scorer and baggage man George Duckworth as to the man's identity: "That," confided the 'bodyline' veteran, "was Douglas Jardine."

On reaching Australia, Cowdrey received a telegram which informed him of the sad news of his father's death. However, after discussions with room-mate Peter May, he decided that nothing was to be gained by returning home. At the welcome dinner later that evening, Hutton did not approach Cowdrey, but afterwards over coffee he put his hand on the young man's shoulder and said "I'm sorry" – that the sentiment was heartfelt was confirmed by the tears in Hutton's eyes. Once the news became public there was a huge outpouring of sentiment towards him with many telegrams reaching his hotel, including one signed by one Robert Menzies, the prime minister of Australia.

Despite this most dreadful start to his time in Australia, Cowdrey played quite well in the warm-up matches. In the sixth game, against a New South Wales side which was at that time the pre-eminent state, Cowdrey finally took his game to a new level with a century in each innings The first at number six after entering with the score at 38-4 and facing Keith Miller, Alan Davidson and Richie Benaud on a lively pitch, the second while opening. In between the two innings, which the *Observer* correspondent Alan Ross described as 'batting of honourable lineage', he received a somewhat cryptic cable: 'See Two Kings Three-Fourteen'. As he later discovered, the cable was a biblical reference which read: 'And the Lord said to Elijah, do it a second time.' "What a lovely message, but I never could reply to the sender", Cowdrey later told *Cricket Today*.

Cowdrey played reasonably well in the first Test at Brisbane, with 40 and 10, but England lost heavily by an innings and 154 runs after Hutton had put Australia in and they had made 601-8 declared. England's much-vaunted attack had been toothless and it was veteran Alec Bedser who paid the price having bowled poorly, although an attack of shingles was a huge mitigating factor. Ironically, conditions at the start of the second Test at Sydney would have ideally suited Bedser, with overcast skies and a green pitch, and England, put in first after the no doubt relieved England captain lost the toss, collapsed to 154 all out. Batting again 74 runs adrift, England were rescued by a scintillating partnership between May (104) and Cowdrey (54), setting up a thrilling climax as Frank Tyson bowled Australia out for 184 to give England an unexpected victory. Despite Australia's collapse, it's not hyperbole to say that had Neil Harvey not run out of partners on 92 his innings would undoubtedly have featured in this volume. Cowdrey had got himself out to a rash shot and sometime later George Duckworth saw him leaving church, commenting: "I should think you had a lot to tell 'im."

Before the third Test, in Melbourne, Hutton asked both Bailey and Bedser to inspect the pitch with him. Whatever he saw, he again decided to leave out Bedser and, as Compton was now fit, Tom Graveney was asked to step aside. However, Compton's rustiness soon saw him dismissed for just four runs, the story of the first morning's play being the bowling of Keith Miller.

Miller's injury status had led many to believe that he would only be called on to bat in Melbourne. However, there is a story that he was persuaded to have a go with the ball by none other than Prime Minister Menzies, perhaps mindful, avid student of the game that he was, of the great performance by the legendary SF Barnes on the same ground some 40 years earlier. It was during the opening session of the 1911-12 Melbourne Test that Barnes had ripped the heart from the Australian batting, posting the startling figures of 9-6-3-4.

A couple of hours later, Miller went in to eat a hearty lunch having produced the remarkably similar figures of 9-8-5-3, including the prized scalps of Edrich, Hutton and Compton. Only two of his 72 balls had been scored off, Miller's dominance over some of England's greatest-ever batsmen being absolute, as he was able to maintain a perfect length on the off stump all morning.

Cowdrey meanwhile had entered at 21-2 – as Alan Ross commented, he was 'yet to come in to bat in a Test match with the drums beating anything but a dirge' – but despite the aggression which was firing his bowling, Miller welcomed him with a hearty "G'day, young Cowdrey". The youthful batsman was fascinated to hear the badinage between the charismatic Miller and the equally-magnetic Compton, who was beaten first ball: "All these years, Denis," said Miller to the man who had once scored 18 centuries in a single summer, "and you don't seem to get any better. You'd think with all this experience I've been reading about you'd at least get a touch." Lindwall meanwhile provided much entertainment to the vast crowd, first with a bouncer which attempted to unbutton Cowdrey's shirt, followed by a yorker right into his toes. Miller then fired a bullet of a ball into Compton's thumb, Harvey taking the catch in the gully; 50 minutes gone and England already four down for 41. Cowdrey was now joined by Trevor 'Barnacle' Bailey or, as the *Melbourne Age* rather less solicitously referred to him, 'Dead Rat'.

Cowdrey soon found his feet, however, turning a well-disguised slower ball from Lindwall to mid-wicket for three with a mischievous grin and, with the crowd now warming to him, England went into lunch at 59-4, remarkably the most runs of any opening session so far. Shortly after the resumption, Cowdrey struck a regal four off Lindwall, then followed up with a luxurious square cut which flew to the pickets. Bailey should, by rights, have been comfortably run out shortly after but Ron Archer missed the stumps. An impudent glance past the slips brought up Cowdrey's fifty, made out of 69 while he was at the crease, and the warmth of the reception was astounding, genuine and heartfelt – the crowd was now most definitely on his side for exhibiting what Denys Rowbotham in the *Guardian* described as 'high seriousness with a schoolboy sense of fun.'

'The Barnacle' now decided to get in on the act, sweeping Benaud for four after which Cowdrey drove another boundary to bring up the hundred. Enough was enough for Australian skipper Ian Johnson, who set about changing the field to stifle Cowdrey's run-making. No doubt mindful of the shot by which he had perished in Sydney, the one for which he had apparently requested God's forgiveness, the Aussie skipper had Bill Johnston bowling to a packed cover field in order to try and entice him to further recklessness. Cowdrey found himself marooned on 56 for fully 40 minutes, causing the crowd to become restless – it wasn't that he wasn't trying shots, rather that the fielders were sticking to their task extremely well, Harvey in particular making several acrobatic dives to prevent additional runs.

Conversely, Bailey had begun to make runs during Cowdrey's hiatus, but was now caught behind for 30, the partnership having realised 74. Finally cracking after 11 straight scoreless overs, Cowdrey came down the pitch and watched heart-in-mouth as a hard-hit shot headed straight for Archer, the same fielder who did for him at Sydney, however the ball just evaded his outstretched fingers and flew to the boundary. At last freed from his shackles, Cowdrey hit Johnson for his ninth and tenth fours and headed in for tea on 68 with England 130-5. He carried on after the break where he had left off, a sublime cover drive eliciting a "Good shot, Col" from Johnston, the young batsman showing his gratitude for this with a sweep to the boundary. A bouncer from Lindwall had Cowdrey rattled somewhat, though he forced a grin and smacked him for four the very next ball.

Godfrey Evans had joined Cowdrey on Bailey's dismissal and, though he initially met with little success, he now provided the crowd with some light relief when Miller returned to the attack. Evans managed to hit a ball that Miller pitched up for four, promptly marching down the pitch triumphantly and ceremoniously shaking hands with the obliging bowler. However, another four convinced Johnson that Miller's injury had now rendered him a spent force and he was promptly taken off. Evans had helped Cowdrey to add 35 in just 40 minutes since tea, but he was now trapped lbw for 20 by Archer, Miller's replacement, with England 169-6 and Cowdrey on 90. Hoping Cowdrey would be nervous in the nineties, Johnson brought himself back on but after seven dot balls the last one went for three. Having retained the strike, he now hit the leaping Archer straight back for his 14th four, taking him to 97.

A brassed-off Archer ensured the next ball was short and Cowdrey forced it to the on side, the crowd's cheers growing in volume with each turn, so that by the time they ran the third, bringing up his hundred, the noise was deafening. Hutton had earlier been absolutely distraught to lose his wicket for 12 and had glumly hidden himself away in the dressing room, but as Cowdrey neared three figures he was persuaded to watch and once the milestone was reached the captain's grin was as wide as anyone's. There was no doubt some sentiment being expressed by the crowd but it was mixed with great admiration for a magnificent, ultimately match-winning performance from a player just turned 22, playing in his third Test with the Ashes up for grabs and in front of 63,000 people. Frank Rostron of the *Daily Express* believed that, 'it was the sort of adulation they reserved for Bradman in his heyday', while Alan Ross noted that, 'the crowd cheered long and movingly', the ovation being apparently comparable only to Bradman's 100th hundred in Sydney. It was a fitting century for an MCG stadium which itself celebrated its centenary that same year.

Nevertheless, there was the small matter of a Test match to be won. However, after adding just two more, Cowdrey was dismissed, though it took a ball out of the blue to dislodge him. Ian Johnson pitched one into the rough patch caused by Bill Johnston's boots and the ball promptly turned approximately two feet, which was about two feet more than any other ball thus far, Cowdrey not even offering a stroke as it cannoned off his pads into the stumps. Disbelievingly he trudged off towards the pavilion as the ovation resumed where it had so recently left off from his century. He had made his 102 out of just 160 and once his guiding hand was lost the remaining four England wickets fell for just 10 runs.

Despite England's low first innings total they were soon right back in the game with Australia at 92-5, although a strong rearguard saw the hosts build a 40-run first-innings lead. England were then buoyed by a fine 91 from Peter May, leaving Australia needing what should have been a reasonable 240 to win. It was not to be. With the pitch by now seriously breaking up, a typhoon called Tyson wrapped up the match, a spell of 6-14 on the final morning sending Australia reeling for just 111, his final figures being 7-27. The mood of the Australians during this collapse can be gauged by this exchange when Keith

Miller came in to bat on the final morning, Tyson having just removed Neil Harvey with only five additional runs added: "Morning Godfrey." "Morning Keith." "I hope that bastard comes off soon!" Miller wasn't the only one to be disenchanted with Tyson's performance; after the match concluded just before lunch, a glum-faced man stormed into the umpire's dressing room, asking: "Who was the chap who gave Bill Johnston out?" "I was," replied Mel McInnes. "Well I'm the caterer and that decision of yours has cost me 10,000 bloody pies!"

To add to his growing collection of telegrams received during this tour, Cowdrey received possibly the most welcome one from MCC president 'Plum' Warner, consisting of just four words: 'Cowdrey. Melbourne. Magnificent. Warner.' England, following the abject humiliation of Brisbane, now found themselves with a 2-1 lead in a series they only needed to draw to retain the Ashes.

Other than the cricket, there had been additional drama earlier in the week as a result of controversy over the pitch used at Melbourne. On the morning of the fourth day, Tuesday, the *Melbourne Age* cricket correspondent Percy Beames, after discussions with some of the Australian players, alleged that the pitch had been watered on Sunday evening; once a match had started, this was against the laws of the game so it represented a serious allegation. The authorities vehemently denied any wrongdoing and, after the Test was over, two civil engineers presented their opinion of what had happened in the form of a long and very detailed letter to the Victorian Cricket Association, claiming that the cause was a combination of very hot temperatures and sweating under the unventilated covers. One critic in a Sydney paper, however, commented, 'Has anyone worked out how the wicket rolled itself out to close up all those cracks?' Whatever the reason, it must be stressed that the whole of Cowdrey's innings had been played before the alleged watering had taken place.

Australia now needed to win both remaining Tests in order to wrest the Ashes from England and, after making several changes they made a promising 323 to start the fourth Test at Adelaide on a perfect wicket. After sharing a 99-run partnership with Hutton, Cowdrey again started to look impatient, so Hutton sent out twelfth man Vic Wilson with some bananas. "What the hell are these for?" asked Cowdrey, who hadn't requested anything. Wilson replied, "Well, the skipper thought you might be hungry. He watched you play a couple of wild shots just now. It rather suggests he is keen for you to stay out here batting a little longer." Suitably chastened, Cowdrey went on to make a fine 79 as England passed Australia's total with 341. When Australia batted again, Cowdrey had his nose broken while fielding and this signalled an Australian collapse. As a result, England required just 96 to retain the Ashes but, at 49-4 an apparently crestfallen and wildly pessimistic Hutton exclaimed: "The buggers have done us!" Compton, standing at his shoulder at the time, had other ideas and safely saw England home.

The fifth Test was all but washed out and England had retained the Ashes with a 3-1 series victory, a result which had been unthinkable after the first Test debacle. Cowdrey's first Ashes tour had been a great one, as he ended up in a low-scoring series with an average of 35.44 (only Graveney, in just three innings, topped 40), and was second only to May in the aggregates with 319. England had, in Cowdrey, May, Tyson and Brian Statham uncovered four young players with huge potential and the series was a triumph of youth over experience.

After such an impressive start to his Test career, there were some who considered that Cowdrey did not live up to that early promise. Brian Johnston wrote, 'I am not the only one to think that, great player as he undoubtedly was, he could perhaps have been the greatest' while Cardus noted, 'His trouble has been a certain introspective modesty; he has never realised quite how great a batsman he is.' A good example of this introspection came during the 1962-63 Ashes series when, having helped win the second Test with innings of 113 and 58 not out, he countered the praise with, "Yes, but now there's the next one to worry about." However, Christopher Martin-Jenkins considered Cowdrey good enough to plump for him in his all-time England XI, and this quote from England spinner Fred Titmus surely confirms his great skill:

> 'Sometimes if a game was drifting to a draw, we'd say "Come on, play us some shots", and John Murray behind the stumps would nominate a particular stroke and he'd play it whatever the delivery. Amazing talent, done without showing off. He was just amusing himself.'

I leave the final words to Cowdrey's good friend John Woodcock, who covered the 1954-55 tour for the *Times*: 'Of all the outstanding Test innings I watched, played by all the best players, I think the one I would most like to live through again is Colin's at Melbourne.'

As the members of the famous Hill at Sydney would have it, "Good on yer, Pearshape."

England

Batsman	Dismissal	Runs
L Hutton*	c Hole b Miller	12
WJ Edrich	c Lindwall b Miller	4
PBH May	c Benaud b Lindwall	0
MC Cowdrey	b Johnson	102
DCS Compton	c Harvey b Miller	4
TE Bailey	c †Maddocks b Johnston	30
TG Evans†	lbw b Archer	20
JH Wardle	b Archer	0
FH Tyson	b Archer	6
JB Statham	b Archer	3
R Appleyard	not out	1
Extras (b9)		**9**
Total (all out; 67.6 overs)		**191**

Fall of wickets 1/14 2/21 3/29 4/41 5/115 6/169 7/181 8/181 9/190

Bowling	O	M	R	W
RR Lindwall	13	0	59	1
KR Miller	11	8	14	3
RG Archer	13.6	4	33	4
R Benaud	7	0	30	0
WA Johnston	12	6	26	1
IWG Johnson	11	3	20	1

Batsman	Dismissal	Runs
L Hutton*	lbw b Archer	42
WJ Edrich	b Johnston	13
PBH May	b Johnston	91
MC Cowdrey	b Benaud	7
DCS Compton	c †Maddocks b Archer	23
TE Bailey	not out	24
TG Evans†	c †Maddocks b Miller	22
JH Wardle	b Johnson	38
FH Tyson	c Harvey b Johnston	6
JB Statham	c Favell b Johnston	0
R Appleyard	b Johnston	6
Extras (b2 , lb4, w1)		**7**
Total (all out; 100.5 overs)		**279**

Fall of wickets 1/40 2/96 3/128 4/173 5/185 6/211 7/257 8/273 9/273

Bowling	O	M	R	W
RR Lindwall	18	3	52	0
KR Miller	18	6	35	1
RG Archer	24	7	50	2
R Benaud	8	2	25	1
WA Johnston	24.5	2	85	5
IWG Johnson	8	2	25	1

Australia

Batsman	Dismissal	Runs
LE Favell	lbw b Statham	25
AR Morris	lbw b Tyson	3
KR Miller	c †Evans b Statham	7
RN Harvey	b Appleyard	31
GB Hole	b Tyson	11
R Benaud	c sub b Appleyard	15
RG Archer	b Wardle	23
LV Maddocks†	c †Evans b Statham	47
RR Lindwall	b Statham	13
IWG Johnson*	not out	33
WA Johnston	b Statham	11
Extras (b7, lb3, nb2)		**12**
Total (all out; 63.3 overs)		**231**

Fall of wickets 1/15 2/38 3/43 4/65 5/92 6/115 7/134 8/151 9/205

Bowling	O	M	R	W
FHTyson	21	2	68	2
JB Statham	16.3	0	60	5
TE Bailey	9	1	33	0
R Appleyard	11	3	38	2
JHWardle	6	0	20	1

Batsman	Dismissal	Runs
LE Favell	b Appleyard	30
AR Morris	c Cowdrey b Tyson	4
R Benaud	b Tyson	22
RN Harvey	c †Evans b Tyson	11
KR Miller	c Edrich b Tyson	6
GB Hole	c †Evans b Statham	5
RG Archer	b Statham	15
LV Maddocks†	b Tyson	0
RR Lindwall	lbw b Tyson	0
IWG Johnson*	not out	4
WA Johnston	c †Evans b Tyson	0
Extras (b1, lb13)		**14**
Total (all out; 31.3 overs)		**111**

Fall of wickets 1/23 2/57 3/77 4/86 5/87 6/97 7/98 8/98 9/110

Bowling	O	M	R	W
FH Tyson	12.3	1	27	7
JB Statham	11	1	38	2
TE Bailey	3	0	14	0
R Appleyard	4	1	17	1
JH Wardle	1	0	1	0

Gary Kirsten – 100*

Pakistan v South Africa, Faisalabad 24-27 October 1997

-Neil Manthorp with Patrick Ferriday-

"It must have been crap to watch."
Gary Kirsten, Faisalabad 24 October 1997

Gary Kirsten was never a great one for self-promotion. Although cricket has always been a sport apparently requiring self-effacement there was an honesty that brooked no argument about Kirsten's words when announcing his retirement: "If anybody had told me in 1994 when I made my debut that I would play 100 Tests for my country I would have asked them what they were smoking." But what he might have lacked in flair was amply counter-balanced by a sound technique, abundant concentration and an ability to recognise weaknesses and address them and in this he was always destined to become a great coach. He became the batting bedrock on which South Africa moved from the often shaky post-isolation side of the early 1990s to the 2004 version that was fast becoming the team-to-beat in world cricket.

When he finally called time on a 10-year Test career, he had amassed 7,289 runs, including 21 centuries, at an average of 45.27. There had been the mammoth and marathon match-saving 275 against England at Durban in 1999, twin hundreds in South Africa's first game at Eden Gardens and centuries against the two bowlers he nominated as the finest he faced, Courtney Walsh and Glenn McGrath. He had been a thorn in the side of opposition attacks all over the world from the seam-friendly surfaces of England and New Zealand to the low-slow turners of the subcontinent. Always a triumph of substance over style, he was a man who designed and built his own igloo-like comfort zone and then bedded down within it, to the exasperation of opposition bowlers the world over. His maxim might have been: 'Find what you're good at and keep doing it', and nowhere was this better displayed than in Pakistan in 1997.

These were delicate times as South Africa rejoined the cricketing world and this trip represented their first visit to Pakistan. The two teams' only previous encounter at Test level had been a one-off game at the Wanderers in 1995, a game which South Africa, and in particular Fanie de Villiers, dominated throughout to win by 324 runs. For South African captain Hansie Cronje, the tour represented the first of two, back-to-back hurdles in establishing his side as world Test champions. The next stop would be Australia. "I do not believe that victory in both Pakistan and Australia is an unrealistic goal. I believe we can do it", he said before departure. In truth, so naive were the South African players in the ways of the subcontinent that victory in Australia seemed more likely. And even that was a forlorn hope.

Pakistan, meanwhile, were celebrating their Golden Jubilee as a nation and a cricketing union, and the Test series against South Africa was the beginning of a mouth-watering schedule for them that included Test series against the West Indies and neighbours India, along with a bumper day-night quadrangular.

Sadly, the first two Tests of the series proved to be something of a damp squib. On day one of the first game in Rawalpindi, the Pakistani top order crumbled to 216-6. But a duo of debutants were to nullify the visitors' early inroads. Opener Ali Naqvi and allrounder Azhar Mahmood racked up remarkable centuries to become the first same-team debutants to score hundreds in the same Test. Their achievement killed the match as a contest however, with a dead pitch offering minimal seam movement and predictable, tennis-ball bounce. The game petered out to a draw with just 26 wickets falling. Kirsten entered the spirit of the thing by top-scoring with 98 in over seven hours of unrelenting concentration as Saqlain Mushtaq and Mushtaq Ahmed sent down 120 overs in the only South African innings.

The second Test, at Sheikhupura, proved to be even less of a spectacle with the monsoon rains permitting just two days of play. The only notable piece of history was a debut for 20-year-old Mark Boucher, who ended Dave Richardson's run of 38 successive Tests for his country since South Africa's readmission in 1992 – the veteran wicket-keeper being withdrawn from the squad due to a groin injury. South Africa were bowled out for 402 in their first innings, and the hosts reached 53-1 in reply before time was called on a forgettable affair. It left the series evenly poised at 0-0 going to Faisalabad.

Pakistan Cricket Board officials, incensed at the lifeless track in Rawalpindi and frustrated in Sheikhupura, demanded something a great deal more lively for the series decider. It was positively emerald green by subcontinent standards. Majid Khan, the PCB chief executive, had instructed the Faisalabad groundsmen to "leave enough grass to encourage results." They did just that, although both sides still elected to retain two spinners, and it laid the platform for a thrilling battle in which Gary Kirsten took centre stage. Hansie Cronje won a toss that he freely admitted he would have preferred to lose. But despite the reunification of the devastating duo of Wasim Akram and Waqar Younis, the South African captain bravely decided that his team would bat first.

Kirsten and Adam Bacher strode to the crease with the unenviable task of seeing off the new ball but the first casualty was Pakistan's Aamer Sohail, picking up a finger injury within minutes. Substitute fielder Mohammad Wasim was quickly in the game, snaffling two difficult chances at second slip to send Bacher and Brian McMillan packing. Now it was the turn of Waqar Younis who quickly trapped Darryl Cullinan and Cronje in front with his signature full-pitched inswingers and suddenly South Africa were 30-4 after only an hour's play. Mushtaq Ahmed then took the ball as the first-change bowler, and three quick wickets from the leg spinner left South Africa on the brink of disaster at 98-7 shortly before lunch. The man who'd stood firm at the other end, watching the procession, was Kirsten. Bristling and bustling with scratchy, scuffling determination, he had taken every opportunity to score and in fact completed his half-century before the team total had reached 100. This was Kirsten at his scrapping best against top-class bowling on a difficult pitch when the series could be decided in the first two sessions of the first day. But he needed help and it arrived in the form of Pat Symcox, who joined him at the crease with his usual swagger and charisma.

'Symmo came to the crease and was as bubbly as ever', Kirsten recalled in his autobiography, *Gazza*.

> 'He wouldn't stop talking and, as usual, he had a theory for everything. I was trying hard to concentrate on the crisis we were in, but Symmo was a welcome and amusing distraction – as much for the bowlers and fielders as me. There is no doubt the distraction helped me rather than hindered me because I was forced to relax rather than tense up, but I'm not sure the Symmo batting method could ever be taught.'

Unorthodox or not, Symcox provided able support to his more established colleague and the pair began to develop a partnership in which the big spinner took the attack to the Pakistani bowlers. Divine intervention even seemed to play a part when Symcox, having made 36 in quick time, was beaten by a Mushtaq googly which slipped under the bat and passed between middle and off stump. Umpire Steve Dunne, in a moment of pure Charlie Chaplin comedy, removed his spectacles and gave them a disbelieving wipe. Having checked to see that the ball hadn't somehow become squashed out of shape, the umpires ascertained that the groundsman had set the stumps slightly too far apart and he was recalled to fix his embarrassing mistake. At least, that was what most observers believed. Actually, it was the umpire's mistake because they are responsible for checking and declaring that conditions are fit for play although they had been confused by a bail being cut too long.

Symcox remained completely unfazed and continued merrily on as captain Saeed Anwar chopped and changed his bowlers to no avail. But this was no wild thrash, as Kirsten fed the strike to his partner and the game began to turn a corner. The decisive stand of 124 finally came to an end as Symcox, who'd contributed 81 from just 94 deliveries, had his stumps knocked over by a slippery Akram inswinger. However, the significance of Symcox's innings was not lost on Kirsten.

> 'Although Symmo scored a Test century against Pakistan a couple of months later at the

Wanderers in similarly dire circumstances, I don't think he would rate this innings much behind the hundred. In both situations the game situation was difficult and tense.'

With just two wickets to fall and the score at 222-8 the early damage had been partially repaired but there was still the tempting prospect of a three-figure score just four boundaries away. New batsman Allan Donald could only survive eight deliveries before falling to the rampant Akram, and it was left to last man Paul Adams to keep his wicket intact as Kirsten tried to reach a century.

'When it was seven or eight wickets down the hundred was completely irrelevant – it wasn't on my mind at all. Well, maybe very occasionally. But when Paul walked to the crease and I was so close then, yes, I was aware of it and quite keen to see if we could get there. Gogga [Adams] did everything he could to stick around and showed what a determined fighter he could be, even at the age of 20. The nervous 90s were even worse than normal because the scoreboard operators weren't the best around and there appeared to be a shortage of certain numbers. It was the original, club-style scoreboard with metal plates and rusty nails. For a while my score just read nine as all the available eights were being used.'

It appeared to be job done some minutes later though, as Kirsten nudged a single off his hip into the leg side that seemingly brought up his hundred. However, after celebrating the feat, his score was promptly adjusted back to 99 at which point Adams was adjudged lbw to Azhar Mahmood with the total on 239 and Kirsten stranded on 99 not out.

'There was some confusion in the crowd when I took the single which prompted the scoreboard operators to change the numbers to 100. The applause started, the guys were cheering on the balcony and the congratulations started. I was aware of the confusion but very happy to take the hundred – I wasn't bothered about any nagging doubts. Still, I waited a few moments to see if anyone was going to spot the mistake, if there had been one, but nobody did. The century was official.'

'The tension and the relief were too much for Paul and he was bowled almost immediately. But my worst doubts came to reality within minutes of getting back into the dressing room where I noticed the television scoreboard had me on 99 not out and I heard there was a discrepancy in the official scorebook. Two of the three scorers had 99 but the senior man had three figures. A few minutes later, it was finally confirmed – 100 not out. South Africa 239. The official scorers were extremely discreet, they never actually confirmed what they had done but, in the spirit of the game, I think they reworked the books. There were rumours that they had been seen rubbing away at the leg byes column and adding a single to my score. Did I care? No!'

A five-hour marathon innings, certainly worth a century, was finally confirmed as such. Nobody ever confirmed the conspiracy theory that his century was manufactured by scorers. The official pencil-pushers were adamant. Perhaps it really was the scoreboard operators. Not for the first time such a controversy was amicably settled and Kirsten became the first South African to carry his bat since Jackie McGlew against New Zealand in 1961, and even more importantly his side was back in the game and the series was still alive. His innings, from 208 balls, included 15 fours.

As I noted at the time, writing the *Wisden* match report, Pakistan's innings followed an eerily similar path to South Africa's, the new ball side-stepping and bouncing eagerly. On the second morning, they were 80-5 before Inzamam-ul-Haq and Moin Khan added 144, making light of the difficulties of their team-mates. At 224-5, just 15 behind, Pakistan were on top. Cronje, sensing tension and maybe fear in his ranks, brought himself on. Desperation or not, within minutes it looked like a stroke of genius. Inzamam, on 96, immediately chased a wide away-swinger to second slip. In Cronje's next over, Moin allowed another wobbler to sneak on to off stump. But Aamer Sohail, batting at eight with a damaged finger, and Waqar pushed on to a lead of 69. With an hour still to play on the second day, Pakistan took the opportunity to add to their advantage by dismissing both openers leaving South Africa on 21-2, the first-innings centurion falling to Wasim Akram for just four.

The following day Symcox, the nightwatchman in South Africa's second innings, reprised his first-innings performance, standing very still and hitting hard anything pitched up to him. This simple form of batting earned him another fifty, including one of his customary sixes over long-on. 'Neither side batted well for the entire match although it was a personal triumph for Symmo, who added 55 as nightwatchman in the second innings to, once again, keep us alive', said Kirsten.

Mushtaq and Saqlain took seven wickets between them, though, and the confident Pakistanis bedded down on the third evening at four without loss, needing 142 to win – in two days. On the bus back to the hotel, Symcox delivered an impassioned speech to his downcast team-mates about seizing the moment: "This game can be won", he yelled. Most were, initially, unmoved. 'But we were all listening by the end', said Kirsten. 'Despite Symmo's efforts, nobody gave us a real chance of defending 145 in the fourth innings.' Certainly the local authorities didn't, as they declared the following day a holiday in anticipation of a famous victory.

In the morning, Sohail carved Donald for two fours – but his third slash went to point. Then Shaun Pollock, bowling with impeccable discipline to a specific plan for each batsman, took four in seven balls, all top-order and high-class players. The batsmen played like rabbits in headlights but it was Pollock's headlights which paralysed them. Lunch was taken at 79-6 – "I don't know how they felt," said Pollock, "but we couldn't eat a thing. We all just sat, staring at the clock, willing the minutes to go by."

Cronje brought Symcox on straight afterwards and the grizzled bear turned cunning fox tossed the ball up so sweetly it was impossible for the terrified batsmen to resist. He removed Wasim, swatting across the line in panic, and Saqlain, deflecting the ball to short-leg. Finally, Moin, after a gutsy 32, pulled him to deep mid-wicket, where Donald took a throat-high catch and sprinted 60 meters to join a celebrating crush of bodies.

'The greatest challenge that evening was how to celebrate appropriately. Even in the most excited moments we were always aware of the conflict of interests between Muslim culture and our preferred method of toasting a victory, and we were careful not to offend', Kirsten recalled.

> 'SA Breweries had once again worked a piece of diplomatic magic through the SA Embassy in Karachi and several (quite a few, to be honest) cases of Castle lager had been subtly delivered to the hotel. We shut off the team room, made it as noise-proof as possible and – let rip. It was a fantastic celebration and release of tension. We were as strong a unit that night as I ever saw. It wasn't like being at home, or in England, Australia, or anywhere else. In those places people have preferred destinations and the team fragments. That night we felt like 14 brothers.'

The 37-year-old Symcox, who'd played the role of batsman, bowler, and team motivator – and been able to get under the skin of the Pakistanis – was duly named man of the match, while Pollock's four wickets in seven balls in the fourth innings had proved pivotal. But it was Kirsten's odds-defying innings amidst the carnage around him that had carved out any possibility of his team winning the match and the series and he was rightly named man of the series.

Many say that a Test match can't be won on the first day but that it most certainly can be lost. Had 98-7 at lunch been 98-8 – including the wicket of Kirsten – South Africa's fate may well have been sealed and Saeed Anwar's men would, in all likelihood, have been the ones celebrating a series win. Instead Kirsten's defiance and tenacity kept one of the world's greatest bowling attacks at bay in extraordinarily difficult conditions, and enabled his team to go on and make history.

> 'After my first year of Test cricket, I couldn't help setting goals for myself – or at least dreaming of the achievements I felt would be most special – the most I could hope for in what I hoped would be a career of five or six years. I rarely made these targets, or dreams, public, but it was important to push myself. The top three, in no particular order, were to score two centuries in

> a Test, make 10 Test centuries and carry my bat through an innings. In Faisalabad, I achieved the last one.'

A thing of beauty it may not have been but if great batting is measured by context and consequence then this innings was right up there with the very best of them, aided and abetted by a ball passing through the stumps and some helpful pencil work. A funny old game indeed but a suitable reward for a hugely competitive and determined batsman blessed with more skill than he is usually given credit for.

South Africa

Batsman	Dismissal	Runs
G Kirsten	not out	100
AM Bacher	c sub (M Wasim) b W Akram	1
BM McMillan	c sub (M Wasim) b W Akram	2
DJ Cullinan	lbw b Waqar Younis	0
WJ Cronje*	lbw b Waqar Younis	9
SM Pollock	c Aamer Sohail b M Ahmed	5
DJ Richardson†	c S Mushtaq b M Ahmed	8
L Klusener	c Ijaz Ahmed b MAhmed	18
PL Symcox	b Wasim Akram	81
AA Donald	c M Ahmed b W Akram	2
PR Adams	lbw b Azhar Mahmood	1
Extras (b4, lb3, nb5)		**12**
Total (all out; 68.4 overs)		**239**

Fall of wickets 1/2 2/11 3/12 4/30 5/40 6/64 7/98 8/222 9/230

Bowling	O	M	R	W
W Akram	16	6	42	4
W Younis	10	1	36	2
M Ahmed	22	3	81	3
A Mahmood	10.4	2	36	1
S Mushtaq	10	2	37	0

Batsman	Dismissal	Runs
AM Bacher	lbw b M Ahmed	14
G Kirsten	c M Ahmed b W Akram	4
BM McMillan	c †Moin Khan b M Ahmed	21
PL Symcox	lbw b S Mushtaq	55
DJ Cullinan	lbw b M Ahmed	15
WJ Cronje*	c A Mahmood b W Younis	21
SM Pollock	not out	21
DJ Richardson†	lbw b WYounis	0
L Klusener	lbw b S Mushtaq	38
AA Donald	b S Mushtaq	8
PR Adams	c & b M Ahmed	0
Extras (b3, lb13, nb1)		**17**
Total (all out; 69 overs)		**214**

Fall of wickets 1/16 2/21 3/63 4/97 5/140 6/140 7/140 8/187 9/201

Bowling	O	M	R	W
W Akram	11	0	46	1
WYounis	14	2	43	2
M Ahmed	22	6	57	4
S Mushtaq	15	6	36	3
A Mahmood	7	2	16	0

Pakistan

Batsman	Dismissal	Runs
Ali Naqvi	b Donald	11
Saeed Anwar*	lbw b Pollock	3
Ijaz Ahmed	lbw b Adams	16
I-ul-Haq	c McMillan b Cronje	96
A Mahmood	b Klusener	19
W Akram	c †Richardson b Klusener	2
M Khan†	b Cronje	80
A Sohail	c Donald b Pollock	38
S Mushtaq	c Bacher b Adams	6
W Younis	c Cronje b Donald	34
M Ahmed	not out	0
Extras (lb1, w1, nb1)		**3**
Total (all out; 89.4 overs)		**308**

Fall of wickets 1/10 2/18 3/42 4/74 5/80 6/224 7/229 8/246 9/304

Bowling	O	M	R	W
AA Donald	17.4	1	79	2
SM Pollock	20	5	64	2
PR Adams	23	5	69	2
PL Symcox	9	2	39	0
L Klusener	8	1	30	2
BM McMillan	7	1	20	0
WJ Cronje	5	3	6	2

Batsman	Dismissal	Runs
Ali Naqvi	c Cullinan b Pollock	6
A Sohail	c Bacher b Donald	14
Saeed Anwar*	c †Richardson b Pollock	0
Ijaz Ahmed	lbw b Pollock	0
I-ul-Haq	c McMillan b Pollock	5
A Mahmood	c †Richardson b Klusener	6
M Khan†	c Donald b Symcox	32
W Akram	c Kirsten b Symcox	9
S Mushtaq	c Bacher b Symcox	0
WYounis	b Pollock	0
M Ahmed	not out	4
Extras (b4, lb6, w1, nb5)		**16**
Total (all out; 37.3 overs)		**92**

Fall of wickets 1/23 2/24 3/24 4/29 5/31 6/68 7/85 8/87 9/88

Bowling	O	M	R	W
PR Adams	5	2	10	0
PL Symcox	9.3	5	8	3
SM Pollock	11	1	37	5
AA Donald	6	1	14	1
L Klusener	6	1	13	1

Neil Harvey – 167

Australia v England, Melbourne 31 December-5 January 1958-59

20

-Martin Chandler-

Cricket lovers are an optimistic breed. Every so often the game throws up a genius and, just once, a batsman who transcended even that exalted status. Sir Donald Bradman's records have never been approached, yet more than a few young Australian batsmen have been dubbed the 'New Bradman' by their hopeful followers. Neil Harvey was one of the first to wear that particular millstone around his neck. Statistically he fell further short of the great man than most who have suffered the comparison but Harvey, who as a 21-year-old averaged 106.55 at the end of his ninth Test, was one of the very best.

In fact there are sound reasons, which do not detract in any way from his ability, as to why Harvey's career average is no higher than 48.41. The opposition he faced was particularly strong, the seasons when he was in his prime coinciding with what surely remains as good an England side as there has ever been. There must also be factored in the wickets that Harvey encountered, Australian writer Ray Robinson, previewing the 1958-59 Ashes series for the *Cricketer*, making the point that 'Neil Harvey has never known a season of good Test wickets against English bowling in Australia.' And apart from his first tour, back in 1948 with Bradman's 'Invincibles', the position was much the same in England. In 1953, by his own standards, Harvey had a lean series, and in 1956 he did so by anyone's standards. In the first of those seasons he had to put up with conditions that suited the seam bowlers, and Alec Bedser in particular. In the latter he was dismissed six times by Tony Lock, and twice without scoring at Old Trafford by Jim Laker as the England off-spinner joined the game's immortals. Harvey was generally a superb player of spin bowling, his travails that summer being amongst the most obvious indicators that the Test pitches were prepared to suit the Surrey spin twins rather than either side's batsmen.

In addition, South Africa and West Indies lost little in comparison with the teams led by Peter May and Len Hutton. India, Pakistan and New Zealand, the only other Test-playing nations in Harvey's time, were nothing like as strong, but he never played against New Zealand, and just twice in Australia against India, his first two Tests when he was still a teenager. His other 12 Tests against India and Pakistan took place on the sub-continent, and they were never minnows there.

Despite the overwhelming defeats that England suffered in the first three post-war Ashes series, Harvey was as popular a man in England as any Australian cricketer has ever been. In 1953, his relative lack of success in the Tests notwithstanding, he scored over 2,000 runs at an average of more than 65 on the tour as a whole and was selected as one of *Wisden's* Five Cricketers of the Year. Amongst his 10 centuries that summer were two at Old Trafford, one against England and one against the county of the Red Rose. Perhaps that is when one Lancashire lass fell under his spell to such an extent that 10 years later she named her son after him. It was a prescient move, as Neil Harvey Fairbrother grew up to be another diminutive and stylish left-handed batsman. His record shows that he wasn't quite up to the standards of the 'Fitzroy Urchin', but his reputation does provide food for thought – just how good might the original Neil Harvey have been in the limited-overs game?

It was the twinkling footwork and the perfect balance at the crease that so enraptured the neutral. 'The ball can't turn if it doesn't bounce' was Harvey's rationale for leaving the crease so often in his pursuit of runs from slow bowlers. He had a reputation for not being able to pick a googly, but with this philosophy it hardly mattered. If he was strong on the drive he was just as effective square of the wicket having, like many short men, a powerful hook that he was always ready to deploy. He was equally forceful when square cutting, although some critics complained about the way he fell away from the shot when playing it. That was part of a general impression that he was vulnerable outside off stump, although in truth the weakness was nothing technical. Harvey in a scrap could defend his wicket as well as anyone, but he only batted defensively in a crisis, and even then was constantly on the look-out for scoring opportunities, and that desire to keep the scoreboard moving, rather than any deficiency of technique, could on occasions be his downfall. His captain in 1958-59, Richie Benaud, described him as 'one of the greatest crowd-pleasers the cricket world has known'.

As one of the 'Invincibles', Harvey had found out what it was like to be an Ashes winner before he turned 20. Two years later he had helped Lindsay Hassett retain the urn but thereafter had lost to the old enemy three times. In 1957-58 he was part of the side that convincingly defeated South Africa and at last created real expectation that the Ashes tide might be turning again. On a personal level Harvey had scored plenty of runs outside the Tests but, after a broken finger caused him to miss the first match of the series, he endured a lean time in the big matches. He also gave some serious thought to settling in South Africa, particularly as it was his wife's homeland. Quite naturally he was concerned about his family's future – he had two young children and was, as were all Australians, technically an amateur. In the end he decided against South Africa but appeared on television on his return and, in passing, talked about his desire to obtain better employment. Initially the programme was screened only in his native Melbourne, but was then aired again in Sydney a week later – an offer of a business opportunity was forthcoming and Harvey moved from Victoria to New South Wales.

Harvey had, as many players do, ambitions to captain his country. He had been disappointed on the South African trip when Ian Craig was given the job, but at least he had been made vice-captain. When Craig decided he had to take a break from cricket in '58-59 Harvey could have expected to get the job, particularly when he was drafted in as a late replacement for Craig to captain an Australian XI at the Sydney Cricket Ground a couple of weeks before the first Test. For once May's men won convincingly, by 345 runs, but it was not Harvey's fault. He had only been given four bowlers, two of them left-arm wrist spinners, and the writing was on the wall as soon as he lost the toss. In the fourth innings Laker and Lock ran riot with a pitch badly damaged by the quicker bowler's run-ups. The scratch side were all out for 103. Harvey top scored with 38, an innings that team-mate Norman O'Neill considered to be one of the best he had ever seen. But the big defeat must have counted for something as, when the decision came, the selectors plumped for Richie Benaud.

In his series preview, Ray Robinson wrote: 'The Australians have built up team spirit and gained confidence from outplaying a team [South Africa] that had held its own against England.' Despite that, fellow Aussie scribe and former Test opener Jack Fingleton still spoke for the vast majority when he described Peter May's team as: 'On paper at least, one of the strongest teams ever to represent England abroad.'

The English fast bowling was headed by the heroes of 1954-55, Frank 'Typhoon' Tyson and Brian Statham. Tyson's career had, if anything, gone backwards since his glory days four years previously, but he was still only 28 and returning to the scene of his greatest triumphs. Statham was the same age, and he was at the peak of his powers. Also selected were Fred Trueman, then aged 27 and unarguably one of England's finest ever quick men, and Peter Loader, who lost little in comparison with the competition. At 29 Loader was a year older than Tyson and Statham, and he only ever played 13 Tests but would certainly have managed many more in any other era. As it was, his 39 Test wickets cost him just 22 runs each. The two spinners who made the party were Laker and Lock, to whom the Australians needed no introduction.

The visitors' batting, on the other hand, did not look quite as strong as it had earlier in the decade. Hutton, Denis Compton and Bill Edrich had all retired, but May and Colin Cowdrey were of the highest class. Tom Graveney's best years still lay ahead of him but he, Peter Richardson, Raman Subba Row and Willie Watson were a talented bunch, and there was always Trevor Bailey, approaching the end of a fine international career, but still the best allrounder in England.

As for Australia, Harvey was bitterly disappointed not to get the captaincy, but there was never any question that his great friend Benaud would get his full support. England did not start the tour well but the huge win against the Australian XI Harvey had skippered raised expectations for their chances in the first Test at the 'Gabba. Those hopes were to prove ill-founded as Australia won the match by eight wickets. It was the dreariest of matches exemplified by Trevor Bailey's 450-minute 68 in England's second innings. The trenchant English journalist EM 'Lyn' Wellings, who did as much as anyone to fan the flames of the throwing controversy that the series is best remembered for, wrote: 'England lost the match. They richly deserved to lose it.' And while Benaud celebrated the victory, he acknowledged that the match "produced some of the slowest and worst cricket imaginable". With 14 and 23 Harvey got a start in both innings but even he couldn't raise the tempo.

The second Test was to be played at the Melbourne Cricket Ground, something of an unknown quantity as the wicket had been relaid. In between the Tests England had drawn a couple of games in Tasmania and then moved on to Adelaide where South Australia's last wicket pair had prevented May's men going in to the Test on the back of a victory. The England captain drew first blood by winning the toss, but then disaster struck as Alan Davidson removed Richardson, Watson and Graveney in his second over to reduce the tourists to 7-3. After a start like that it was to their credit that between them May himself, with a superb century, Bailey and Cowdrey got England to 259 before Statham quickly removed Jim Burke to bring Harvey to the crease just before tea on day two. By the close Harvey and Colin McDonald had taken Australia to 96 without further loss. Of those Harvey had scored 60, including 10 fours. With a playing area of not far short of 200 yards across, the quality of Harvey's timing was well illustrated. Fingleton described his batting in that session as 'a delight to watch...he didn't make a false move or an error of judgment.'

May might have missed a trick by not giving Lock the opportunity to bowl at the man he had dismissed six times in the 1956 series and once again at Brisbane, particularly after the way he had bowled in the Australian XI game, but Lock seldom bowled well in this series. It was mainly Bailey and Laker who were pitted against Harvey at the MCG, but he was untroubled by either, helping himself to four boundaries from each on a true wicket that had some pace in it.

Resuming on the third morning, the nature of the game changed. May went straight on to the defensive, Bailey bowling as wide on the leg side as he dared with five on-side fielders. It was frustrating for the batsmen who were able to add only 39 in the 90-minute session to lunch, but for once Harvey was patience itself, taking singles where he could and biding his time.

McDonald did not survive too long after lunch as he was dismissed for 47 with the total on 137. His innings did not contain a single boundary, which puts Harvey's batting the previous evening in context. This dismissal brought O'Neill to the crease, in the eyes of most Harvey's heir apparent as Australia's favourite stroke-maker, but this day the older man was still centre-stage. All the England bowlers pinned O'Neill back on his leg stump and he had to rely largely on nudges, deflections and his senior partner's peerless running between the wickets in order to make any headway. For Harvey, with his additional experience, the runs came more easily and while he was not able to recapture the freedom of the previous evening he gradually accelerated. He briefly dallied in the 90s, but once he brought up his century he pulled smoothly away. By tea Australia had reached 216, with Harvey on 140 and O'Neill 25. The partnership was worth 79. The big test would come after tea, May having held back on taking the new ball that was by then available.

For a while after the break it looked a different game, the persistent Statham actually managing to get a couple of deliveries past the edge of Harvey's bat, but eventually a straight drive went back past the Lancastrian to the boundary, the score went to 226, and the runs too flowed again as England's total began to look inadequate. After 118 had been added, and the deficit was just four, Statham managed to catch the edge of O'Neill's bat to give 'keeper Godfrey Evans a straightforward chance that, at the second attempt, he held on to. As so often happens with long partnerships it was, two runs later, to be two new men at the crease as Harvey, by now on 167 out of 257, went on to his front foot to drive Loader. He turned the delivery into a yorker and, despite the ball not seeming to deviate, missed it and was clean bowled. He had added six more boundaries to the 10 of the previous evening, had batted for six hours altogether and at the point that he was dismissed had scored almost 65 per cent of the Australian total. *Wisden* made the comment that 'Harvey demoralised England in a brilliant innings'. Never a truer word. Neil Harvey had presided sublimely over a passage of play that firmly reinforced the hard-won ascendancy of the Australian victory in the first Test. On a pitch and ground and against an attack that had rendered boundaries an almost obsolete currency he managed no fewer than 16, keeping the scoring rate respectable and steering his side from a position of peril to one of strength – a position they were not to surrender for the rest of the series. If May's first-day century had been a fine piece of art then this was truly a masterpiece.

After Harvey's departure, the English lion finally roared and Statham and Loader restricted the Australians to a total of 308, a mere 49 in front. They may well have been fortunate to have had as many runs in hand as that, Keith Miller, for one, being convinced that Davidson was plumb lbw to Statham from the very first delivery that he faced. Davidson went on to score 24 valuable runs. Statham bowled superbly, his 7-57 being comfortably the best figures he achieved against Australia in his distinguished career and that on a wicket that gave him no discernible assistance.

Sadly for any neutrals the match was over as a contest as soon as England lost five wickets before they even regained the lead. Australia's victory target was, after England subsided to 87 all out, just 39. They lost a couple of wickets in getting there, and that meant that, fittingly, Harvey was there at the end, but the catalyst for England's second innings nightmare was the 'bowling' of Ian Meckiff. For five years a 'chucking' controversy rocked the cricket world, implicating Lock in England, Geoff Griffin in South Africa and Charlie Griffith in the West Indies as well as Meckiff although it wasn't until 1963 that he was finally no balled. Unfortunately for Harvey, as well as the wider interests of the game, it was this controversy for which the second Test and the series tends to be remembered, rather than the innings of which Fingleton wrote: 'Harvey will not forget the reception he got as he walked off. This was his 17th century in 54 Tests. I doubt whether he has played a better one.'

As for the England players they recognised the significance of Harvey's innings in finally throwing off the shackles of 1956. May later wrote: 'Neil Harvey played an innings of great quality, repaying Jim Laker for a few of the indignities suffered in 1956', and Graveney underlined the fact that it was Harvey, rather than the Australians generally, who mastered the game's finest off spinner with the comment:

> 'Neil Harvey was the only man to sort out Jim, despite the fact that all the others would have given him a terrific hiding had they found half the chance. Laker's wicket-taking exploits of the 1956 series hadn't exactly endeared him to Australian batsmen.'

But it wasn't just Laker who Harvey mastered, and confirmation of that came from Laker himself who, whilst acknowledging that Harvey's knock was 'one of those innings I shall remember to my detriment' also added that 'the Australian first innings boiled down to a stirring battle between Neil Harvey and Brian Statham' and he noted that 'even Trevor Bailey couldn't bowl defensively at him.'

In the next Test, at the Sydney Cricket Ground, Laker showed that he wasn't quite finished and, in England's best performance of the series, he took seven of the 12 Australian wickets to fall. He extracted a measure of revenge for the liberties Harvey had taken at the MCG by bowling him for seven in the first innings, although had there been another couple of hours in the game Harvey might well have taken Australia to victory. That draw was the only occasion England avoided defeat in a series that most of their supporters remember, if they recall it all, for reasons that are not strictly cricketing ones.

England

PE Richardson	c †Grout b Davidson	3
TE Bailey	c Benaud b Meckiff	48
W Watson	b Davidson	0
TW Graveney	lbw b Davidson	0
PBH May*	b Meckiff	113
MC Cowdrey	c †Grout b Davidson	44
TG Evans†	c Davidson b Meckiff	4
GAR Lock	st †Grout b Benaud	5
JC Laker	not out	22
JB Statham	b Davidson	13
PJ Loader	b Davidson	1
Extras (b1, lb2, w3)		**6**
Total (all out; 98.5 overs)		**259**

Fall of wickets 1/7 2/7 3/7 4/92 5/210 6/218 7/218 8/233 9/253

Bowling	**O**	**M**	**R**	**W**
AK Davidson	25.5	7	64	6
I Meckiff	24	4	69	3
KD Mackay	9	2	16	0
R Benaud	29	7	61	1
LF Kline	11	2	43	0

PE Richardson	c Harvey b Meckiff	2
TE Bailey	c Burke b Meckiff	14
W Watson	b Davidson	7
TW Graveney	c Davidson b Meckiff	3
PBH May*	c Davidson b Meckiff	17
MC Cowdrey	c †Grout b Meckiff	12
TG Evans†	run out	11
GAR Lock	c & b Davidson	6
JC Laker	c Harvey b Davidson	3
JB Statham	not out	8
PJ Loader	b Meckiff	0
Extras (b1, lb1, nb2)		**4**
Total (all out; 31.2 overs)		**87**

Fall of wickets 1/3 2/14 3/21 4/27 5/44 6/57 7/71 8/75 9/80

Bowling	**O**	**M**	**R**	**W**
AK Davidson	15	2	41	3
I Meckiff	15.2	3	38	6
R Benaud	1	0	4	0

Australia

CC McDonald	c Graveney b Statham	47
JW Burke	b Statham	3
RN Harvey	b Loader	167
NC O'Neill	c †Evans b Statham	37
KD Mackay	c †Evans b Statham	18
RB Simpson	lbw b Loader	0
R Benaud*	lbw b Statham	0
AK Davidson	b Statham	24
ATW Grout†	c May b Loader	8
I Meckiff	b Statham	0
LF Kline	not out	1
Extras (b3)		**3**
Total (all out; 100.2 overs)		**308**

Fall of wickets 1/11 2/137 3/255 4/257 5/261 6/262 7/295 8/300 9/300

Bowling	**O**	**M**	**R**	**W**
JB Statham	28	6	57	7
PJ Loader	27.2	4	97	3
TE Bailey	16	0	50	0
JC Laker	12	1	47	0
GAR Lock	17	2	54	0

CC McDonald	lbw b Statham	5
JW Burke	not out	18
ATW Grout†	st †Evans b Laker	12
RN Harvey	not out	7

Did not bat NC O'Neill, KD Mackay, RB Simpson, R Benaud*, AK Davidson, I Meckiff, LF Kline

Extras		**0**
Total (2 wickets; 17.1 overs)		**42**

Fall of wickets 1/6 2/26

Bowling	**O**	**M**	**R**	**W**
JB Statham	5	1	11	1
PJ Loader	5	1	13	0
JC Laker	4	1	7	1
GAR Lock	3.1	1	11	0

Dennis Amiss – 262*

West Indies v England, Kingston 16-21 February 1974

19

-Martin Chandler with Dennis Amiss -

False dawns are not unusual in sport, and English cricket has had its fair share, but the achievement of Ray Illingworth's side in 1970-71 in reclaiming the Ashes on Australian soil for the first time since Douglas Jardine's men in 1932-33, and doing so with a degree of comfort, is as good an example as any. After that famous victory little went right for England. In 1971 Pakistan were beaten, albeit unconvincingly, and then a home Test series was lost to India for the first time. The following summer the hold on the Ashes was maintained with a 2-2 draw but the following winter England, under Tony Lewis while Illingworth gave the tour a miss, lost to India again before drawing all three Tests with Pakistan. New Zealand were beaten in the first half of the 1973 summer, but the visitors were much more competitive than had been expected, and with a little more luck might have squared the series. And then it was Rohan Kanhai's West Indies. There was a heavy defeat at The Oval, and an even more substantial one at Lord's, and suddenly the Illingworth era was over.

Dennis Leslie Amiss, born on 7 April 1943, struggled to come to terms with the demands of Test cricket in his early career and thereafter was, in many ways, symptomatic of the period with innings of great promise being followed by failure. His rise to the pinnacle of the English game was anything but meteoric, and is a testament to his determination to succeed. He joined the county of his birth, Warwickshire, as soon as he left school in 1958, but it was 1960 before he made his first-class debut, and 1965 before he was able to command a regular place. That first full season was one of consolidation, Amiss' record steady rather than spectacular. He improved markedly the following year, but it was still a bolt from the blue when he learnt from a local journalist that he had been selected for the final Test against Garry Sobers' West Indians. The visitors were 3-0 up and the selectors under the cosh as a result, so perhaps he shouldn't have been so surprised. The match itself was one of the more remarkable in the history of the game. England found themselves 166-7, still 102 short of the West Indies first-innings total, at which point there was a total reversal of momentum as the last three wickets added 361, and an innings victory followed. Amiss did score more runs than Geoff Boycott, Basil D'Oliveira, Brian Close and Ray Illingworth put together, but it was only 17, before Wes Hall trapped him lbw.

With no full England tour scheduled for 1966-67, Amiss had to content himself with a trip to Pakistan with an MCC under-25 party where he averaged over 90 in the representative matches. There followed a none-too-testing summer for England against

India and Pakistan. Amiss was involved throughout, but only made the starting XI three times, and he failed to take advantage. Outside the Test arena however he was in fine form, so it was a blow when he was not in the party that toured the Caribbean in 1967-68. He had been assured by then-skipper Close that he would be involved, but then the Yorkshireman lost the captaincy courtesy of a bit of gamesmanship of which WG Grace would have been proud, ironically enough at Edgbaston. Another chance against the 1968 Australians followed, and a pair, after which Amiss dropped off the selectors' radar. It seemed that might be the sum total of his Test career. The root cause of his disappointing start was a combination of jangling nerves and bad luck. Why the nerves? Looking back over 40 years Amiss has no difficulty now in articulating the reason as:

> "Wondering how you could be good enough to be in the same team as some of your heroes. I played a Test or two with each of Kenny Barrington, Tom Graveney and Colin Cowdrey. I struggled to come to terms with the fact that I could play well enough to even begin to emulate their achievements."

For the next three summers Amiss did enough to cement his place in the Warwickshire side and, in 1971, persuaded the selectors to take another look and got four more outings against Pakistan and India. In an era when selectors were rather less forgiving than they are now, that constituted a fair run. In the first Test against Pakistan he scored four and 22 followed by an unbeaten 19 in the second. Scores of 23 and 56 in the third match represented a very real contribution to England's narrow series-clinching victory and he glimpsed the light at the end of the tunnel. Sadly for him however in the first Test against India he got nine and a duck and was discarded again. In the first innings he clipped his foot with the bat and answered the earnest Indian appeal by walking. Amiss was always a 'walker', but on this occasion wrongly. Non-striker Alan Knott told him in no uncertain terms at the next interval that his bat had got nowhere near the ball. In the second innings he was run out, going for a single that wasn't there. Nerves and ill-luck had cost him again and that could so easily have been that with just 258 runs from nine matches.

It was no surprise to Amiss that he did not figure in the selectors' plans for the 1972 Ashes, but that season even his county game faltered, and he was dropped by Warwickshire. At 29, and with a young family, Amiss had to rethink his future. Another county or leaving the game altogether were options, but in the end, looking at Warwickshire's crowded middle order of Rohan Kanhai, MJK Smith and Alvin Kallicharran, he chose to reinvent himself as an opener. He needed a bit of luck in his first innings at the top of the order, but a flawed unbeaten 151 secured a 10-wicket victory. Four more centuries followed before the end of the season, and with two of England's best openers, Boycott and John Edrich, declining to tour India and Pakistan that winter a berth opened up for him. He failed again in India, scoring just 90 runs in six innings before being dropped, but he was back against Pakistan and finally got a century in the first Test, and then another in the second, before failing to make it a clean sweep in the third by just a single. Amiss built on that success in the summer series against New Zealand (won 2-0) and the West Indies (lost 2-0) in 1973, and was now a certain starter for the 1973-74 trip to the Caribbean.

The home defeat by the West Indies was a heavy one so the interest in England surrounded the selection of Illingworth's successor for the poisoned chalice of captaincy – with no outstanding candidate, the job went to Mike Denness. There was little controversy over the selection of the team itself, although 40 years on the choice of Mike Hendrick over John Snow, and Frank Hayes and John Jameson rather than two of Colin Cowdrey, Brian Luckhurst or John Edrich looks odd. After the recent reverse, there was not a great deal of optimism in England and the West Indies were on the rise again after a disappointing few years. Former England allrounder Trevor Bailey believed their batting to be stronger even than the sides he had faced, which had been able to field the three Ws.

After the first Test it seemed as if the series was to be a continuation of the previous one as the visitors collapsed to 131 all out after Kanhai invited them to bat. Only after a deficit on first innings of 261 was conceded did England begin to fight, Boycott and Amiss putting on 209 for the first wicket. Shortly after lunch on the fourth day, at 328-1, a remarkable comeback beckoned. In the event the sub-editors had to save their ideas for the next Test as, despite Amiss' 174, there was a mighty collapse at the hands of Sobers and Lance Gibbs. England were all out for 392 and the West Indies won comfortably enough by seven wickets.

Moving to Sabina Park for the second Test, Denness won the toss, and had no hesitation in choosing to bat. The Jamaican sun was shining brightly and he was greeted by a grassless pitch, the soil dark brown in colour. The groundstaff had been shining the wicket for a couple of days, a tactic dating back to the days of Hall and Charlie Griffith. It was done by spinning the roller, the intended effect being to make the ball bounce more and fly faster off the pitch. For the first hour it worked, but as the quicker bowlers tired the wicket became a very good one.

Considering the conditions, England's first innings 353 was rather disappointing. Amiss weathered the early storm from Keith Boyce and Bernard Julien but then, on 27, he lost his wicket to the leg spin of Arthur Barrett. In his account of the tour, Christopher Martin-Jenkins reported that Amiss 'essayed a savage square cut to a short leg-break and Kanhai, fielding at extra-cover, dived forward to hold a brilliant catch.' The man himself is rather more blunt: "I committed suicide on that wicket. It hurt like hell and I was determined not to let it happen again in the second innings."

When the West Indies replied, they took full advantage of the easy wicket. There was little in the pitch for pacemen Chris Old and Bob Willis, and both bowled too many short-pitched deliveries. Most of the bowling fell to the spinners, Derek Underwood, Pat Pocock and, giving his new style of slow-medium off-breaks its first public outing, Tony Greig. None of them got much turn or bounce, but they were all accurate, and keen fielding prevented the home side scoring as quickly as they would have liked. In the end it took them until lunch on the fourth day before, after 196 overs, Kanhai declared at 583-9, a lead of 230.

With five sessions left in the match a sound start by Amiss and Boycott was important. The latter was not always the easiest man to bat with, and he had been considerably less than happy with Amiss after a run-out at Trent Bridge in 1973 but by Sabina Park '74 the relationship had got over that and was working well, and Amiss enjoyed batting with Boycott. They quickly hit upon a tactic to inconvenience the West Indies spearhead, Keith Boyce. Nowadays, Boyce's name is largely hidden in the shadows of his illustrious successors, but he was a fine bowler and on his day sufficiently fast that he would not have been out of place in any of the fearsome pace quartets that the Caribbean islands were to produce over the next 20 years. One fault Boyce did have was a tendency to over-step and the vigilant Amiss and Boycott would pointedly, for the umpire's benefit, draw a line across the crease to demonstrate what had been missed. With the umpires duly alerted, the extra deliveries tired Boyce more quickly, and reduced the length of his spells. This was important in that second innings because Boyce, in Martin-Jenkins' words, 'brought this apparently somnolent pitch to life'. Clearly looking for the mistimed hook, a trap Boycott was known to fall into, Boyce went round the wicket with as many as three fielders on the leg side waiting for the mishit. A short one did indeed account for Boycott, for just five, but not from a hook, a straight one tucking him up and causing him to fend the ball away to 'keeper Deryck Murray. It was Amiss who had to deal with most of the short leg-side stuff, hooking it with some success and, more importantly, without looking vulnerable. When his turn came to get the sort of snorting delivery that had accounted for Boycott he raised his arms out of the way. The fielders behind him clearly thought there had been contact with his glove, as there was a big appeal, but both Amiss and the umpire were unmoved.

He then added 70 with his Warwickshire colleague Jameson before, as was always likely, the spin of Barrett accounted for a man who was much more at home against the quick bowlers. By now Amiss, to use Martin-Jenkins' words:

> 'Began to flow with cover drives, square cuts, and those magnificent flicks off his toes to mid-wicket or square-leg. Occasionally he also drove straight, not with a full flourish, but with superb timing, the power coming from the impetus of his high backlift.'

The last thing England needed, in this sort of situation, was a run-out, but in the event there were two. The first was Hayes for a duck, just five runs after Jameson left. Amiss stroked the ball into the covers, where the predatory Clive Lloyd prowled. It was Amiss' call, but there was a momentary hesitation from Hayes (could it be those years of playing with Lloyd at Lancashire?), a man noted for his speed between the wickets, and he just failed to beat the throw. Today Amiss takes the blame, as indeed he did at the time, but all contemporary reports suggest the call was not so much a bad one as unnecessarily optimistic given the match situation.

If Amiss was unsettled by the run-out he certainly didn't show it and, with his captain batting well, for a time after tea all went well. Denness then fell to a bat-pad catch at short-leg and when Tony Greig was also dismissed before the close, the game looked to be up. England ended the day still 12 short of making the West Indies bat again, with just Alan Knott and the bowlers to come. Amiss, as steady and reassuring as in his second innings of the first Test, was on 123. Underwood had come in as nightwatchman to protect Knott.

The fifth and final day was to cement Dennis Amiss' place in the affections of the English cricket-loving public, but it almost didn't happen. His great innings' only blemish came from the third ball of the day when he turned Lance Gibbs round the corner to where Sobers stood. Gibbs found a little extra bounce, and pitched the ball fractionally short. The 'Lion of Cricket' had anticipated the shot and dived forward. The ball was in his hand but he just failed to cling on. Amiss says:

> "He gave a cry of anguish because he knew he nearly had me. I replied to the effect that I hadn't expected anyone to get near it, but I should have known he was there, and played the ball differently."

As to what then transpired, Martin-Jenkins' words speak volumes:

> 'Amiss never gave another chance. The ball hardly passed his bat in the next five and a half hours. He stood four square like a yeoman soldier and, try as they might, the enemy could not get through.'

Inevitably credit must go to the men at the other end too, and while their contributions, in terms of runs scored were slight, their roles were vital. Amiss says:

> "Batting with the tailenders was magnificent. They all batted brilliantly, and I couldn't have done it without them. There was Chris Old, Pat Pocock and 'Deadly' Derek Underwood, who took the force of Keith Boyce on the fifth morning with the new ball."

151/Masterly Batting

Underwood resisted for over an hour on the fifth morning but anyone told at the start of the day that England would save the game would have expected a major contribution to come from Knott. As it was he was at the crease for just 13 minutes before being run out in what was virtually a carbon copy of the Hayes dismissal. Again it was a close call, and Amiss concedes that he had forgotten that it always took Knott a while to get the stiffness out of his legs at the start of an innings. It seems he was probably more culpable with Knott's dismissal than Hayes', but Amiss did pay a price, Knott's pained "Oh no, Den" still haunting him almost 40 years on.

Then it was the turn of Chris Old and he wasn't found wanting – 101 minutes for his 19 runs. England were now leading by 113 midway through the penultimate session and just an hour from safety. One last thrust from the home attack couldn't shift Amiss or his new partner Pat Pocock and by the time the Surrey spinner was finally dismissed, after 83 minutes and four runs of resistance, England had saved the game and Kanhai threw in the towel by giving all his batsmen the chance to turn their arms over.

After batting for so long, Amiss was too tired to go for a triple-century. He did mention to last man Willis he would 'carry his bat' if the big fast bowler were to be dismissed. "I'm not getting out. If I do I'll have to bowl again, and I don't want another thrashing", was Willis' reaction, so they gently played out time, Amiss remaining unbeaten at the end on 262. No-one else contributed more than Jameson's 38. Back home the *Daily Mail* captured the mood with a headline proclaiming 'Amiss Rescues the Lost Test'. The report went on:

> 'Dennis Amiss yesterday completed one of the epic innings of cricket to deny West Indies victory…he led England's great escape with a masterly display of unbelievable concentration.'

The third Test saw yet another English rearguard action. As in the first Test they found themselves put in by Kanhai, and again were a long way behind on first innings, this time 201. At 106-5 in the second innings they were in real danger of defeat but this time it was Keith Fletcher and Knott who rescued them. The fourth Test, due to the weather, never really got going, but there was another century for Amiss in England's 448. So the West Indies needed just a draw in the final Test to win the series. They nearly won the game but, courtesy of some remarkable bowling by Greig and batting by Boycott, eventually lost by 26 runs. England had squared the series. It was to be nearly 16 years before they beat the West Indies again.

England

G Boycott	c Kanhai b Sobers	68
DL Amiss	c Kanhai b Barrett	27
JA Jameson	st †Murray b Gibbs	23
FC Hayes	c Boyce b Sobers	10
MH Denness*	c Fredericks b Boyce	67
AW Greig	c Fredericks b Barrett	45
APE Knott†	c †Murray b Barrett	39
CM Old	c †Murray b Julien	2
DL Underwood	c Fredericks b Sobers	24
PI Pocock	c Gibbs b Julien	23
RGD Willis	not out	6
Extras (lb7, nb12)		**19**
Total (all out; 157 overs)		**353**

Fall of wickets 1/68 2/104 3/133 4/134 5/224 6/278 7/286 8/3222 9/333

Bowling	**O**	**M**	**R**	**W**
KD Boyce	19	2	52	1
BD Julien	18	3	40	2
GS Sobers	33	11	65	3
AG Barrett	39	16	86	3
LR Gibbs	40	16	78	1
RC Fredericks	4	0	11	0
CH Lloyd	4	2	2	0

G Boycott	c †Murray b Boyce	5
DL Amiss	not out	262
JA Jameson	c Rowe b Barrett	38
FC Hayes	run out	0
MH Denness*	c Rowe b Barrett	28
AW Greig	b Gibbs	14
DL Underwood	c †Murray b Sobers	12
APE Knott†	run out	6
CM Old	b Barrett	19
PI Pocock	c sub b Boyce	4
RGD Willis	not out	3
Extras (b10, lb11, w1, nb19)		**41**
Total (9 wickets; 183 overs)		**432**

Fall of wickets 1/32 2/102 3/107 4/176 5/217 6/258 7/271 8/343 9/392

Bowling	**O**	**M**	**R**	**W**
KD Boyce	21	4	70	2
BD Julien	13	3	36	0
GS Sobers	34	13	73	1
AG Barrett	54	24	87	3
LR Gibbs	44	15	82	1
RC Fredericks	6	1	17	0
CH Lloyd	3	1	5	0
RB Kanhai	3	1	8	0
LG Rowe	2	1	1	0
AI Kallicharran	3	0	12	0

West Indies

RC Fredericks	b Old	94
LG Rowe	lbw b Willis	120
AI Kallicharran	c Denness b Old	93
CH Lloyd	b Jameson	49
RB Kanhai*	c Willis b Greig	39
GS Sobers	c Willis b Greig	57
BD Julien	c Denness b Greig	66
KD Boyce	c Greig b Willis	8
DL Murray†	not out	6
AG Barrett	lbw b Willis	0
LR Gibbs	not out	6
Extras (b16, lb18, nb11)		**45**
Total (9 wickets dec; 196 overs)		**583**

Fall of wickets 1/206 2/226 3/338 4/401 5/439 6/551 7/563 8/567 9/574

Bowling	**O**	**M**	**R**	**W**
RGD Willis	24	5	97	3
CM Old	23	6	72	2
PI Pocock	57	14	152	0
DL Underwood	36	12	98	0
AW Greig	49	14	102	3
JA Jameson	7	2	17	1

Doug Walters – 104*

New Zealand v Australia, Auckland 22-24 March 1974

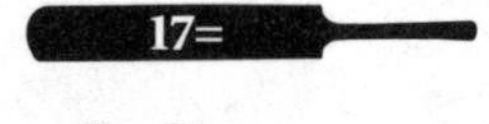

-Ken Piesse-

Every cricketer, no matter how gifted, has his Waterloo. From Don Bradman's famous last match duck in 1948 to Shane Warne's ugly, discrediting one-on-one with Marlon Samuels in his own home town in 2013, the game has a habit of catching even the most inspired. Green wickets were Doug Walters' undoing. Billed as 'another Bradman' alongside Ian Craig and Norman O'Neill on his stunning entry into Ashes cricket, Walters' habit of decimating attacks from Brisbane to Perth and on to the Caribbean made him a star attraction of Australia's middle-order from the mid-1960s.

Yet in England, where the pitches were more sporting and offered seam and swing opportunities for even the most innocuous trundlers, Walters seemed nonplussed and out of his comfort zone, especially in the games that mattered. Captains soon learnt to employ two gullies just for Doug and he'd invariably oblige with nicks behind. On his first trip to England in 1968, having only just returned to cricket after National Service, he averaged 38. Four years later it was seven. He may have had the eye of an eagle, but on challenging wickets which offered disconcerting sideways movement, he displayed a vulnerability which stopped him from joining the pantheon of Australia's true batting greats. On song, however, and with a little good fortune early, he was Stan McCabe reincarnated.

Barry Richards once told me that if he knew Mark Waugh was going to make a century, he'd cancel golf and not miss a ball. If Steve Waugh was to make a ton, however, he wouldn't bother crossing the road. Kevin Douglas Walters had all of Mark Waugh's majesty, the pull shot, the sparkling feet and the will to dominate the spinners like few of his or any era. He was a match winner and a hero of the nation.

His misfortunes in England had puzzled us all. He might not have had the classic perpendicular bat swing of Greg Chappell or the bulldog determination of Ian Redpath, but previously he'd always been able to find a way with his flair and attitude. So good was his eye that team-mates felt he'd follow seaming balls which others would simply miss. Un-Walters-like scores of 17, 20, 1, 2, 7, 4 and 3 saw him lose his place for the deciding Test in England in '72, the game in which Ian Chappell's young Australians were to square the series with a famous victory at The Oval. In the county games against lesser attacks that summer it had been the same old thrill-a-minute Doug. He peeled off three centuries and averaged 50-plus. Come the Tests he was hesitant and so unconvincing that even his mate, Chappelli, temporarily lost faith.

Chappell's vision was always to dominate the cricket world – his way. Doug Walters was one of his first players chosen, not only for his on-field flair but for his fun-loving, knockabout ways. Ever since he was 21 and old enough, finally, to attend the licensed clubs, he liked to have a drink and a smoke and was hugely popular amongst his team-mates, from the Chappells down.

Coming off a thrashing in South Africa in 1970 and an Ashes-losing summer against England in 1970-71, Chappell was building the nucleus of one of Australia's most formidable combines. Newcomers to Australia's elite XI included expressman Jeff Thomson who sauntered in from 10 or so yards and just went 'wang' – propelling the ball close to and above 160kph. The Chappell brothers, Keith Stackpole and Walters remained cornerstones of the batting. So outstanding was Greg Chappell that many began to rate him as Australia's finest since The Don. Brother Ian batted with new consistency and his captaincy was proactive and often inspired. He had this happy knack of backing his hunches and forever staying ahead of the game. Conservative he wasn't but successful he was.

Walters had regained his favourite-son status after a mixed campaign in South Africa where he'd made three half centuries only to scrape together less than 50 runs in five other innings. A photograph of his ungainly attempt to avoid a short ball from Mike Procter with his bat high in the hair, like a periscope, prompted suggestions that the golden child may be losing some of his lustre. His technique was tested like never before. But his unbeaten 70 in the opening Rest of the World international in Brisbane was followed by centuries in Perth and Melbourne. Inexplicably, after a double-failure in home-town Sydney, Walters was relegated to twelfth-man duties for the deciding game in Adelaide. Had it been an Ashes Test there would have been a hue-and-cry.

On becoming Australia's new captain, Chappell had asked Walters to play his natural attacking game, no matter what. Few could change a game in a session like the laconic country boy from the Hunter Valley. England, 1972, may have been Walters' low point but all was forgiven come the West Indies in 1973 where he played with all his old dash and adventure on wickets which were fast, true and on occasions, spun almost square. Against all odds, Australia won the series despite injuries and form issues with their frontline pacemen Dennis Lillee and Bob Massie. Walters' roomie was Terry Jenner, a knockabout leg-spinner jettisoned into the squad at the eleventh hour when Ashley Mallett decided there was better money in journalism than cricket. Jenner and Walters shared a love of cold beer and cigarettes and set up a party room, bolstered by two kegs delivered by tour sponsors Red Stripe. "If there was meant to be a limit on fun," said Jenner, "someone forgot to tell us during that tour." On a raging turner at Port of Spain, Australia won a match it had no right to thanks to a breathtaking century in a session from Walters against a three-pronged spin attack of Lance Gibbs, Elquemedo Willett and Inshan Ali. Chappell was at his most inspirational, refusing-to-be-beaten best in this game, his colourful address to the team at the luncheon interval on the final day prompting a remarkable comeback when the Windies seemed to be cruising towards a series-squaring win. Few could swear like 'Chappelli' and the air was blue as he told his team that no matter what, they weren't going to be beaten. "All we need is another #$%@ing wicket," he said. "We're not #$%@ing giving this up. No #$%@ing way."

With almost 500 runs in the Tests, Walters had again confirmed his ranking among the world's top 10 batsmen. And there was more to come, including another exhilarating, match-winning century at Auckland's Eden Park, pivotal in the squaring of the series with a newly-competitive New Zealand, intent on finally winning some respect from a cocky neighbour who didn't think they could play. Given Walters' woes on green wickets, this was to be one of the most satisfying innings of his headlining career, right up there with his brilliant Sydney double of 1968-69, his starting 155 at the 'Gabba in 1965-66 and the highest score of his Test career, 250 at Christchurch's Lancaster Park in 1976-77.

Having defeated the Kiwis 2-0 in the first-ever Trans-Tasman Test series in Australia in 1973-74, the Australians reciprocated with a three-Test tour, drawing at Wellington and, to the jubilation of success-starved locals, losing at Christchurch after back-to-back centuries from the Kiwi's master opener Glenn Turner. New Zealand had never before defeated an Australian team in a Test. There was much angst against Chappell's hardline behaviour, Turner accusing the Australians of sledging which went way beyond the lines of decency. When he complained, he received a torrent of abuse – but no apology. Others in the home team like Ken Wadsworth and Brian Hastings had learnt not to speak or reply to the Australians. After the first Test in Wellington, not one word was spoken to either of them.

The decider was at Auckland where the weather had been poor and the centre wicket table soft and tacky even 24 hours before the scheduled Friday match start. Walters recalls:

> "One half of the wicket was wet and the other quite normal. You don't get those sorts of wickets anymore. It took me back to my childhood days. You'd do anything and play on anything if it meant getting a game."

One of New Zealand's frontliners, Mark Burgess, was an Auckland local. Never before had he seen an Eden Park wicket so soft, nor as confronting. Team-mate Turner agreed:

> "Either they had too much rain in Auckland or the curator [Bob Beveridge] had made a miscalculation, for the wicket was far too wet for the start of a game...you didn't need to be very clever to know that the ball was going to do some funny things."

Ian Chappell was to later call the pitch "bloody awful" and compare it with an under-prepared Adelaide club wicket in October. Eye witness Richie Benaud, writing in *Australian Cricket* magazine, said:

> 'Everyone expects a little moisture in the pitch at the start of the game. Indeed fast bowlers are entitled to some joy from life, but I have no doubt that this pitch was excessively watered in error on the part of the groundsman.'

Home captain Bevan Congdon had a history of losing tosses but having won one at Christchurch he now made it two in a row, Ian Chappell again calling incorrectly, and having consulted both Burgess and his other 'senior pro', Glenn Turner, Congdon told Chappell he could bat. Sending in the opposition was considered to be the greatest of gambles but on a pitch such as this there were no certainties.

With the Hadlee brothers and the ever-so-tall left armer Richard Collinge, the Kiwis had the pace arsenal to embarrass even the most star-studded batting line-up. On a made-to-measure wicket, complete with the large wet patch at the bottom end, the Australians knew a score of even 200 would be competitive, especially after losing vice-captain Stackpole to the first ball of the match – a Richard Hadlee head-high full toss which he fended in self-preservation to slip.

Within an hour, it was 4-37, Redpath, Greg Chappell and Ian Davis all out to Collinge. "The ball was going through the top and Collinge regularly landed it just short of a good length and made it rear past your ear," said Davis, who, like Stackpole and Greg Chappell, was out without scoring.

> "It was tough out there, yet Dougie was playing his cuts and pulls like he was in a completely different match to the rest of us. It probably has to be his best innings, especially on a wicket like that. He was simply awesome."

Other than a blazing century in a session against Northern Districts in the first fortnight of the tour, Walters, in at number six, had been consistent without hitting the headlines. When Ian Chappell attempted a bold lift over mid-off and holed out, again to Collinge, Australia were 5-64 and on the precipice. So discomforting was the bounce at the bottom end that New Zealand's wicket-keeper Ken Wadsworth was forced to retreat from the stumps even for Congdon's normally gentle slow mediums. Even 125 looked a target too far away. Most thought Australia would be fortunate to survive even to lunch. Walters relishes the memory:

> "The wet patch was a little short of a length and while the ball did rear, it gave you an opportunity to get onto the back foot and play your hooks and cuts. It was like being a kid again playing on the wickets back home. We knew whatever score we could get, New Zealand would have to get them and it wasn't going to be easy."

Both Walters and Rod Marsh, in at seven, played aggressively, lifting the scoring rate above five an over. The lunchtime score of 5-93 soon became 5-150 before Marsh, who made 45, holed out, giving Collinge five of the first six wickets to fall. The pair dieted on many short-pitched deliveries from the Hadlee brothers and hit a swag of boundaries to point and square-leg. "I bowled utter rubbish," lamented Richard Hadlee. "I was severely handicapped [by general soreness] and could not put the ball where I wanted." His nine overs went for 45. His brother Dayle was almost as expensive, conceding 41, also from nine. "We ought to have been able to have bowled them out for not much more than 100," said Turner. "On such a sticky wicket, Walters played tremendously well, even though our bowlers dished up more loose deliveries than you would have expected them to."

Walters' team-mates shook their heads in wonder at his pyrotechnic show. He deliberately lifted his square cuts up and over the ring and pulled forward of square with savage intent. On the occasions when the New Zealand mediums did pitch up, he drove them through the covers. It was a dazzling display. "The game was won and lost in those 75 minutes of batting mayhem from Walters and Marsh," said eyewitness Don Neely, later a New Zealand Test selector. "The runs came at a giddy rate. If courage is defined as the ability to press on regardless of doubt and fear then Walters and Marsh displayed it for all to see and admire." Walters took 99 minutes for his first 50 and less than an hour for his second. "It was all dash and dazzle," said Neely, "as he alone scored what Australia as a team should have been dismissed for."

Walters was 82, and Australia 9-191, when he was joined by last man Ashley Mallett whose ability to stick was underrated. His only thought was to somehow help his mate to a century-to-remember – and avoid being decapitated in the process. Richard Hadlee's only wicket had come from the first ball of the game, one which didn't even land. He was desperate to make an impression and just as he tore in ready to bowl, Mallett pulled away and asked for the sightscreen to be adjusted. "But it can't be," said the umpire. "It's stationary!"

Hadlee glared at Mallett and forgot about hitting the top of his off-stump and proceeded to bowl short, Mallett ducking and weaving like a boxer in retreat. "I was able to survive long enough for 'Freddie' to get his 100. We must have added 30 or so, of which I am still very proud of my seven. Only Dougie could have played that well on such a [seaming] wicket."

Walters' undefeated 104 had included 15 fours and come in just 167 minutes of superlative batsmanship. The roars of approval from the rooms and the backslaps for a favourite son were prolonged. The Australians may have been bowled out in two sessions, but they were back in the game – and the series. "It was an incredible piece of batting," said Chappell, "especially on a wicket which bounced and popped so much."

The degree of difficulty for the batsmen was highlighted in the final session when New Zealand slumped to 8-85, in reply to Australia's 221 and a near-record 18 wickets had fallen in the day. In the circumstances, opener Turner's 34 not out was remarkable. In the overcast conditions he'd played and missed only twice. Like Walters a few hours earlier, it was if he was on a different pitch to all of his team-mates. At the wetter end he stood up more in his stance and tried to play more on top of the bounce. At the other drier end, he allowed the ball to come to him before committing to a stroke. While he was to make only 41 it was a masterly cameo and with 72 in the second in a game the Australians won in just two and a half days, he laid claim to be the outstanding batsman in the world.

Many felt the match should have started a day later on a far-drier wicket, but then again we may not have witnessed Walters' brilliant 104 not out. Like his masterly century in Port of Spain exactly 12 months earlier, it was unfortunately not televised back in Australia – otherwise both innings would still be talked about as being among the best ever.

Australia

KR Stackpole	c Parker b RJ Hadlee	0
IR Redpath	c †Wadsworth b Collinge	13
IM Chappell*	c Turner b Collinge	37
GS Chappell	c Howarth b Collinge	0
IC Davis	c Hastings b Collinge	0
KD Walters	not out	104
RW Marsh†	c Hastings b Collinge	45
KJ O'Keeffe	c Morrison b Congdon	0
GJ Gilmour	c Morrison b Congdon	1
MHN Walker	c Burgess b Congdon	7
AA Mallett	c Turner b Congdon	7
Extras (b4, lb1, nb2)		**7**
Total (all out; 46.2 overs)		**221**

Fall of wickets 1/0 2/32 3/37 4/37 5/64 6/150 7/154 8/162 9/191

Bowling	**O**	**M**	**R**	**W**
RJ Hadlee	9	1	45	1
RO Collinge	18	4	82	5
DR Hadlee	9	0	41	0
BE Congdon	10.2	0	46	4

KR Stackpole	c Congdon b Collinge	0
IR Redpath	not out	159
IM Chappell*	lbw b Collinge	35
GS Chappell	c †Wadsworth b Howarth	38
IC Davis	c Parker b Howarth	5
KD Walters	c Parker b Congdon	5
RW Marsh†	c RJ Hadlee b Howarth	47
KJ O'Keeffe	c Burgess b Collinge	32
GJ Gilmour	b RJ Hadlee	4
MHN Walker	b RJ Hadlee	0
AA Mallett	c Parker b Collinge	6
Extras (b4, lb4, w1, nb6)		**15**
Total (all out; 79.4 overs)		**346**

Fall of wickets 1/2 2/69 3/118 4/132 5/143 6/230 7/315 8/330 9/330

Bowling	**O**	**M**	**R**	**W**
RJ Hadlee	9	1	50	2
RO Collinge	16.4	0	84	4
DR Hadlee	7	0	48	0
BE Congdon	19	1	66	1
HJ Howarth	28	5	83	3

New Zealand

GM Turner	c GS Chappell b Mallett	41
JM Parker	lbw b Gilmour	11
JFM Morrison	c †Marsh b Walker	9
BE Congdon*	lbw b Gilmour	4
BF Hastings	b Gilmour	0
MG Burgess	c †Marsh b Gilmour	7
KJ Wadsworth†	c †Marsh b Gilmour	0
HJ Howarth	c Gilmour b Mallett	0
DR Hadlee	b Mallett	4
RJ Hadlee	c IM Chappell b Mallett	13
RO Collinge	not out	8
Extras (b4, lb1, nb10)		**15**
Total (all out; 30.2 overs)		**112**

Fall of wickets 1/16 2/28 3/34 4/40 5/62 6/62 7/63 8/72 9/102

Bowling	**O**	**M**	**R**	**W**
MHN Walker	10	4	11	1
GJ Gilmour	15	3	64	5
AA Mallett	5.2	0	22	4

GM Turner	c IM Chappell b Walker	72
JM Parker	c †Marsh b Gilmour	34
JFM Morrison	c †Marsh b Gilmour	0
BE Congdon*	c †Marsh b Walker	4
BF Hastings	lbw b Walker	1
MG Burgess	c Stackpole b Walker	6
KJ Wadsworth†	c GS Chappell b Mallett	21
DR Hadlee	c Walters b Mallett	4
RJ Hadlee	b O'Keeffe	1
HJ Howarth	not out	3
RO Collinge	c IM Chappell b O'Keeffe	4
Extras (b3, lb2, nb3)		**8**
Total (all out; 53 overs)		**158**

Fall of wickets 1/107 2/107 3/112 4/115 5/116 6/127 7/145 8/147 9/147

Bowling	**O**	**M**	**R**	**W**
MHN Walker	19	8	39	4
GJ Gilmour	16	0	52	2
AA Mallett	13	6	51	2
KJ O'Keeffe	5	1	8	2

Brian Lara – 213

West Indies v Australia, Kingston 13-16 March 1999

-Patrick Ferriday-

Has a captain ever gone into a Test match under greater pressure than that faced by Brian Lara at Sabina Park in March 1999? When, on losing what looked to be a crucial toss, he said to his opposite number Steve Waugh, "Thank goodness I'll not have to go through this again", who could have blamed him? Given his own form, the parlous state of his team, the utterances of the West Indian Board, the identity of his predecessor and the eyes of the cricketing world it seemed that the assembled gallery had come to bury Lara, not to praise him. *Et tu* Courtney Walsh. *Et tu*?

The mid-1990s saw a calamitous collapse in West Indian cricket, the imperious dominance of the previous decade had unravelled as age picked off the great names one by one. The Frank Worrell Trophy, held by the West Indies since 1978, had changed hands in 1995 and then been retained two years later. By then it was clear that it wasn't only the Australians that had the beating of the once-mighty West Indies. They had been routed by an exceptionally talented Pakistan side in a three-match series and the inevitable ascendancy of Brian Lara to the captaincy, in place of Courtney Walsh, was the first consequence. It was his good fortune that his first opponents, England, were a relatively soft introduction to the rigours of life at the top.

Although the series started farcically, as the Kingston Test was abandoned after 10 overs with English batsmen protecting life and limb on a sandpit full of springs, it finished triumphantly for the home side and their new leader with a 3-1 win. On the surface a very satisfactory outcome, but in reality more indicative of the penetration of Curtly Ambrose (30 wickets at 14 each) than a national cricketing regeneration. An ICC world rating of fourth was just about right and the next series would be a very different kettle of fish – five matches in South Africa beginning in November 1998.

As if the prospect of facing Allan Donald, Shaun Pollock *et al* was not intimidating enough, the West Indies squad first became involved in a protracted stand-off with their Board – at The Excelsior hotel, hard by London's Heathrow Airport. Team manager Clive Lloyd, WICB president Pat Rousseau, captain-cruising-for-a-sacking Brian Lara, his unwilling purported replacement Courtney Walsh and Ali Bacher, armed with a personal plea from Nelson Mandela, were the main players in a four-day drama monitored closely by a greedy press corps. Eventually a compromise was hacked out that would enable the tour to go ahead but there were few smiles – the players had stuck grimly together and demanded the leadership of Lara, and financial expediency had forced all interested parties to accede to their demands. The tour could proceed but a residual air of distrust remained; was it just coincidence that such an impasse had occurred within a year of Lara taking charge? At any event there seemed little doubt that he had the support of his team as he endeavoured to seek improvements in pay and conditions even if many outsiders saw arrogance bordering on insurrection.

For the first three days of the series the West Indies side held its own, thereafter they were simply blown away by the pace trio of Donald, Pollock and Jacques Kallis (69 wickets between them at 17). Lara's admission that "we are not together as a team" was hardly a surprise and the Board's tour report spoke darkly of 'weakness in leadership' and required a 'significant improvement in his leadership skills'. The knives were out and with the Australians due to arrive in the Caribbean a month later, Lara was given a two-match probationary period to put his house, and that of his team, in order.

The pressure, of a different kind, was also on Steve Waugh, having taken over from Mark Taylor following a fifth successive Ashes success. Of course he was inheriting a magnificent and successful team – but the only way was down, hardly a direction that would appeal to the master of mental disintegration.

The first of the four Tests took place at Port of Spain and merely continued the calamitous route that had been established in South Africa, a triumphant homecoming for the captain it was not. Set an improbable 364 to win, the West Indies subsided to an ignominious 51 all out in 19.1 overs, their lowest-ever international score. Despite a fine 62 in the first innings, Brian Lara's stock had hardly risen and his probationary period was due to come to an end one week later, after the second Test in Jamaica.

Still lacking Shiv Chanderpaul and Carl Hooper, Lara was about to lead the most inexperienced West Indian side for 20 years and on top of that the mood throughout the Caribbean was now downright hostile. Michael Holding and Colin Croft, amongst others, made no secret of their opposition to the retention of the captain after the whitewash in South Africa and the *Weekend Independent* in Lara's own island of Trinidad reported reliable information that Chanderpaul would be taking charge for the third Test. The *Express* blazoned the insult: 'From 501 to 51. What A Difference A Zero Makes' and, while director of coaching Reg Scarlett made optimistic noises about the long-term health of the game, the short-term looked riddled with disease and primed for a mercy killing.

Inside Sabina Park itself, the atmosphere was mixed. While many bemoaned the state of West Indian cricket and the demotion of local hero Walsh, there were also scores of supporters that felt it was their duty to rally round their team although the fact that the ground was only half full was an indication that hopes were far from high. Lara tried to distance himself from all the pre-match speculation:

> "I'm going out there to play to the best of my ability and try to level the series. Whatever the Board decides after that, it's still my priority to play West Indies cricket in whatever capacity they see fit."

On a pitch re-laid after the farce of the abandoned Test the previous year, Steve Waugh was delighted to win the toss and bat on a surface he believed "is going to turn square" – with Shane Warne and Stuart MacGill in his side he had reason to allow himself the luxury of a rare grin.

Within 80 minutes, however, the grin had become a grimace as he joined his brother at the crease with Australia wobbling on 46-3, all the wickets going to an inspired hometown hero, Courtney Walsh, who could hardly have found a better way to express his loyalty to his captain – no Brutus he. There wasn't much in the pitch but Walsh, in the words of Peter Willey, "would get wickets on one leg". Four years earlier, on the same ground, the same pair of twins had driven the West Indies to distraction and secured a series victory and they now set about repeating the dose. The score rose ominously during the afternoon and the 100 partnership was recorded before Mark Waugh received a brute of a shooter from debutant off-spinner Nehemiah Perry. The spell was broken and the remaining batsmen were hustled out by the impressive Pedro Collins, surviving just long enough to allow their captain to complete his century. The final total of 256 was at least 100 shy of what had been envisaged but the upside was that Glenn McGrath and Jason Gillespie would have an hour to attack the fragile top order.

And attack it they did – taking a wrecking ball to the crumbling edifice. Within 45 minutes, four wickets were down and Brian Lara and nightwatchman Collins were looking desperately at the umpires as the light faded. They survived but, with the score at 37-4, only Jimmy Adams of the recognised batsmen still to come and on a pitch destined to turn significantly sooner rather than later, it seemed that defeat was imminent.

The second day dawned bright and sunny and Brian Lara was, as usual, late for the team bus to the ground. As he hurtled out of the hotel and past umpire Peter Willey he called out laughingly, "I'm gonna bat all day". Was this misplaced arrogance or endearing confidence from a man who hadn't scored a Test century in two years and was now facing the cricketing equivalent of walking the plank? The next eight hours would tell.

Lara's entrance the previous evening had been greeted with a mixed reception but now the crowd was much more supportive. They knew instinctively that a minimum of two sessions from their champion would be required to keep the game alive. After playing and missing the first ball, in typical fashion he set about his work; careful construction, bit by bit gaining the pace of the pitch and the angles of attack, searching out the dangers and gently probing for weaknesses. Allowing the bowlers 'their hour' had always been at the heart of his method before deciding that the time was ripe for payback. The morning session was one of careful accumulation as first the two quicks and then the leg spinners pushed for the ball that would change the match. The Australian conviction that Lara's weakness, particularly early on, was accurate bowling at the head was given an airing and McGrath had the temporary satisfaction of putting him on his back, but the only victim of these two hours was Collins, forced to retire hurt after receiving a blow to the box from Jason Gillespie. Jimmy Adams replaced the injured party and dropped anchor to secure the listing ship.

Shortly after lunch came the slice of luck that so often defines sporting history as Mark Waugh threw himself to his left but failed to cling on to a chance that most other fielders would barely have seen as it flew past. Soon afterwards the half-century, accurately described as 'solid rather than scintillating' was completed and within minutes a sea change was signalled as, for the first time, Lara skipped down the wicket and deposited Warne into the stands behind long-on.

As the afternoon wore on so the tempo quickened and as the tempo quickened so the mood inside Sabina Park changed. From a morning of tension, the aching muscles were allowed a degree of relaxation; clenched teeth were parted to partake of restorative refreshment and boundaries were celebrated – an expectation of great things hung in the air. Driving, pulling and dashing twos, the total crept up; at 164-4 Lara passed the 5.000 Test-run mark – into the 80s and now in full flow he took three successive boundaries off MacGill as the century loomed temptingly into view. And it was this wicked sorceress that almost undid the best-laid plans. At 99 and dashing for a single, Justin Langer threw down the wicket and as the hordes invaded the playing area Steve Bucknor called for the third umpire. Those on the pitch were either unaware or unconcerned that they might be dancing in the dark – Lara retired to the boundary as the evidence of one camera was analysed by third official Wilson. Eventually he came to the only possible conclusion – not proven and not out.

The first fifty had taken 140 balls to accumulate, the second just 55. All the time at the other end was straight man Jimmy Adams, cajoling, cautioning and encouraging in turns while flying for any quick runs on offer and carefully adding to his own, almost secret, stash. The perfect foil.

Tea arrived with the score at 227-4, just 29 behind now and with a final session that could make or break but with both batsmen brimming with measured confidence even the mighty Australians began to wilt. Two successive sixes off MacGill took Lara towards 150, Adams passed his fifty and the partnership was worth 200. As the shadows lengthened and the crowd revelled in the beauty and power of it all, Lara kicked on again taking four boundaries off consecutive Greg Blewett deliveries to sit on 199. The second new ball had done nothing to slow the run-rate and the fourth fifty arrived in 60 balls followed by the inevitable invasion, more words from Adams and, shortly afterwards, stumps. No less than 340 runs in a day and not one wicket lost, Lara's share being 205. The previous record fifth-wicket partnership, held by Garry Sobers and Seymour Nurse, had long since been shifted from the history books to the memory banks.

Peter Willey stood the full six hours and was quite sure he'd seen an exceptional innings:

> "After McGrath worked him over in the Test match before, I think they were hoping McGrath and Gillespie could sort him out with a few short balls…he wasn't the Brian Lara who'd smack any quick bowler about, he'd lost a little bit. But even Warnie didn't trouble him, none of them did, then, bloody hell, he's got 200."

If day three was to be an exercise in rubbing salt into Australian wounds, it certainly didn't start in the fashion expected. Within minutes the star of the previous day was gone, caught behind off McGrath, after adding just one to his overnight total. Twenty runs later his staunch ally followed, just six short of what would have been his first century against Australia in 22 attempts. Some minor hitting from the tail saw the innings close just after lunch on 431, a lead of 175. With masses of time remaining and on a pitch still playing pretty well but likely to get worse, the West Indies had failed to close out the match and now needed their big guns to fire once more. Courtney Walsh immediately had Michael Slater dragging an attempted cut onto his stumps and from there on the unsinkable ship lurched as if breached below the waterline by the batting of the previous day. None of the vaunted batsmen managed to pass 30 as Nehemiah Perry picked through the wreckage – by the close the deed was as good as done with the score 157-8.

A mere 30 minutes was required next day to complete the formalities as Perry claimed a fifth wicket and then the West Indian openers needed just three balls to secure a famous victory. A little later, a relaxed and smiling Brian Lara could afford to be both generous and compliant in the press conference:

> "For the future Test matches, I would love to continue on this sort of high and see how best we can win back the Sir Frank Worrell Trophy. If the Board doesn't see it that way, I've always said that my love for West Indies' cricket and my commitment to it is unconditional. I'm just happy to be back among the runs, happy to be in a winning team and happy to play that sort of role…I would not pinpoint any one thing that has changed because I think this has been an all-round effort. You have got to realise that no one individual could be responsible for something as disastrous as South Africa. I played a part and I must take some responsibility. Everybody has their weaknesses but the main thing is that whatever happens to me I learn from it."

In assessing his innings he stated what was now the bleeding obvious when he said: "Leading from the front brings out the best in me" and he judged it to be his "most important" but was quick to warn that the job was not yet done:

> "I would love it to be the turning point. But I think we've got to be very cautious when we're talking about the Australians. They are the best Test-playing team in the world, they are accustomed to winning and I think they are going to come back at us hard in the next Test. They are not going to mess up easily."

The Caribbean press was less circumspect – 'King Lara Discovers Royal Form' bellowed the *Barbados Nation*. Guyana's *Stabroek News* thought 'he batted with the deep concentration of George Headley and the breathtaking flair of Rohan Kanhai' while Tony Cozier called Lara's innings quite simply 'the most significant ever by a West Indian.' His opposite number was generous and analytical – 'A brilliant innings highlighted by his extraordinary precision.'

The re-appointment to the captaincy was inevitable – Brian Lara and his team-mates now had 10 days to prepare themselves for the crucial third Test.

Australia

MJ Slater	c †Jacobs b Walsh	22
MTG Elliott	c Lara b Walsh	0
JL Langer	c †Jacobs b Walsh	8
ME Waugh	b Perry	67
SR Waugh*	c Joseph b Collins	100
GS Blewett	lbw b Walsh	5
IA Healy†	run out (Joseph/Perry)	6
SK Warne	c Joseph b Collins	24
JN Gillespie	b Ambrose	1
SCG MacGill	c Joseph b Collins	0
GD McGrath	not out	2
Extras (b1, lb3, nb17)		**21**
Total (all out; 71.3 overs; 332 mins)		**256**

Fall of wickets 1/8 2/28 3/46 4/158 5/171 6/179 7/227 8/242 9/248

Bowling	O	M	R	W
CEL Ambrose	17	9	33	1
CA Walsh	20	6	55	4
PT Collins	16.3	2	79	3
NO Perry	17	1	79	1
JC Adams	1	0	6	0

MTG Elliott	lbw b Perry	16
MJ Slater	b Walsh	0
JL Langer	c †Jacobs b Perry	24
ME Waugh	c Walsh b Ambrose	21
SR Waugh*	c †Jacobs b Perry	9
GS Blewett	c Lara b Perry	30
IA Healy†	run out (Collins/†Jacobs)	10
SK Warne	c Joseph b Walsh	23
JN Gillespie	c †Jacobs b Walsh	7
SCG MacGill	c Joseph b Perry	7
GD McGrath	not out	11
Extras (lb3, nb16)		**19**
Total (all out; 66 overs; 288 mins)		**177**

Fall of wickets 1/4 2/36 3/51 4/63 5/86 6/107 7/137 8/157 9/159

Bowling	O	M	R	W
CEL Ambrose	14	4	28	1
CA Walsh	18	3	52	3
NO Perry	26	8	70	5
PT Collins	8	0	24	0

West Indies

SL Campbell	b McGrath	12
S Ragoonath	lbw b Gillespie	0
LA Roberts	c Warne b McGrath	0
BC Lara*	c †Healy b McGrath	213
DRE Joseph	c Blewett b McGrath	14
PT Collins	c ME Waugh b MacGill	13
JC Adams	c Elliott b McGrath	94
RD Jacobs†	c Gillespie b Warne	25
NO Perry	not out	15
CEL Ambrose	b MacGill	3
CA Walsh	lbw b MacGill	0
Extras (b12, lb8, nb22)		**42**
Total (all out; 132.3 overs; 604 mins)		**431**

Fall of wickets 1/4 2/5 3/17 4/34 5/378 6/398 7/420 8/427 9/431

Bowling	O	M	R	W
GD McGrath	35	11	93	5
JN Gillespie	33	7	79	1
SK Warne	30	8	94	1
SCG MacGill	22.3	3	84	3
GS Blewett	10	1	48	0
ME Waugh	2	0	13	0

SL Campbell	not out	1
S Ragoonath	not out	2

Did not bat DRE Joseph, BC Lara*, JC Adams, LA Roberts, RD Jacobs†, NO Perry, PT Collins, CEL Ambrose, CA Walsh

Total (0 wickets; 0.3 overs; 2 mins) **3**

Fall of wickets N/A

Bowling	O	M	R	W
GD McGrath	0.3	0	3	0

Doug Walters – 242

Australia v West Indies, Sydney 14-20 February 1969

-Ken Piesse-

Few possessed the dancing feet and dare-devilry of Doug Walters, hero for almost every cricket-obsessed Australian boy growing up in the '60s and '70s. As a lad of 10, allowed home early from school because of the December heat, I watched the final session from the 'Gabba on *ABC* TV transfixed as Walters motored to a sublime century. Few debutants had announced themselves at Ashes level with such balance, brilliance and relaxed aplomb. The 19-year-old *wunderkind* pulled the pacemen and advanced at the spinners, hitting them wide of mid-on with the power of Norman O'Neill and the timing and sublime placement of Neil Harvey. He was a natural, born and bred in the New South Wales bush, a graduate of a red ant-bed wicket which he and his brother had sculpted at the family farm at Dungog. One very hot Christmas a giant crack developed on a good length, forcing Walters to use his feet like never before. He learnt to skip at his brother's bowling, clicking his heels together to add to his momentum before driving him straight or to mid-on. If it was shorter, he'd pull the ball with gusto, his bat finishing high over his head like he'd unleashed a No.1 wood. His technique wasn't classical, but he had an eagle eye and the flair and sense of adventure to play his shots. He was to become a talisman in a brilliant new entertaining era for Australian cricket.

Not even the Chappell brothers were to make as many centuries in a session as Walters. One, at Port of Spain in 1973, was rated by his captain Ian Chappell as the finest he'd ever seen on a turning wicket. That was the tour party-animal Doug famously slept in one morning in Jamaica and arrived at Sabina Park 10 minutes after play had resumed. An unimpressed Chappell had him running from fine-leg to third-man. Sighting a pushbike leaning up against the third-man fence, Walters momentarily considered borrowing it to help ferry him to the opposite end of the ground but thought he may be pushing his luck. During a drinks' break, Chappell looked him in the eye and said: "It won't happen again Freddie, will it?" "Chappelli," said Walters "I hope it doesn't, but I can't guarantee that!"

Chappell loved Walters like another brother, despite Doug's disdain of time and many of the normal protocols, like practice. During the 1972 tour to England, Chappell's first in charge, he told his team his door was open any time day or night – "as long as it is before three o'clock in the morning". One very thirsty night Walters got into a two-man school with Rodney Marsh and the pair knocked on the captain's door at 2.59 am!

Always a free spirit – he famously once consumed 42 cans on the flight from Sydney to London and on another boozy night in Perth shared a record 26 long necks with fellow 1972 Ashes tourist Graeme Watson – Walters drank and smoked like there was no tomorrow. He also loved a punt and remained totally unaffected by his fame. He'd been drafted into the Army with open arms, despite telling the medicos how he'd had hepatitis as a 16-year-old and had very, very flat feet. The elderly doctor looked him in the eye and said: "I've seen every [Sheffield] Shield game at the Sydney Cricket Ground since 1901 and you look fit enough for me!"

His Army mates called him 'Hanoi' – they reckoned he was bombed every night! He could hardly fire a rifle and was better at missile throwing. When his superiors reckoned he'd be an asset in Vietnam and invited him to sign up with his platoon, Walters asked: "Sir, can you guarantee me a return ticket?" And that was that. Six weeks later, his enforced two years of National Service was up. He was a cricketer again.

The season of his life came in 1968-69 against the touring West Indians when he averaged 100-plus having been ruled out of the first Test match in Brisbane when in a moment of jest he informed the team doctor that he was fine (after a minor hamstring strain) "but probably couldn't open the bowling". His innocent throwaway line cost him his place.

On his return, in a summer of mega-scores, Walters amassed 76, 118, 110 and 50 before a magical double of 242 and 103 in the final Test of the season in hometown Sydney It was the first time any batsman had made a double-century and a century in the same Test and it came against the still-menacing pace pair Wes Hall and Charlie Griffith, together for the first time all series, alongside swing specialist, West Indian captain Garry Sobers.

Entering the stellar match of his life, Walters had badly bruised his back after slipping on a concrete staircase taking out some rubbish at the back of his Parramatta unit. Wearing thongs, he tripped and bounced down the whole 20 steps. Badly shaken and bruised, but cleared of bone damage, it took twice daily physiotherapy treatment before he was named in the XI for what was the decisive match of the series.

Sydney and its environs had been awash for most of February, with seven inches of rain in four days promoting a wave of toadstools in the outfield. Long-time curator Athol Watkins had been unable to use a mower or even the lightest roller on the wicket since the rains had begun. Eyeing the saturated square, he termed it the most worrying lead-up to a Test he'd faced in a decade. The Australians were leading 2-1 in the race for the Frank Worrell Trophy and they needed to win or draw the decider. Test-great Bill O'Reilly was salivating at the prospect of an old-time greentop, a soft, sticky, under-prepared 22 yards likely to offer bowlers a rare respite from a summer of tall scores. 'My mouth actually waters as I think about it,' he wrote in the *Sydney Morning Herald*. 'Get there early. Take your pick and don't miss the fun. I will be pleasantly surprised if this game goes the full distance.' A sixth day had been scheduled and there was talk that, if a start was impossible on the Friday, the

Monday rest day be used so all six days could be utilised.

The Windies, many of whom were touring Australia for the first time, had been hero-worshipped everywhere they went from the mainland cities to the country strongholds of Kalgoorlie, Gunnedah and Mildura. Roy Fredericks commented how friendly the Australians were. "Everywhere I go they keep waving to me", he said before being told that the flies were particularly bad this summer. Flying over country New South Wales one day, soon after the breathalysers had been brought in, the team plane was thrown around in a squall and Joey Carew commented: "I think they'd better put the breathalyser on this pilot."

The team's determination to retain the Frank Worrell Trophy was paramount and Griffith's rapid recovery after being injured against the Victorians had re-energised the whole group. Sure Hall and Griffith may have been 31 and 30 and in their twilight but the likelihood of a responsive wicket encouraged an old-time salvo and so it proved with Sobers sending the Australians in to bat after an abnormal delay in which he initially reserved his decision having won the toss. Opposing captain Bill Lawry came off the ground not knowing who would bat. After a further mid-pitch conference with the West Indian hierarchy, including manager Berkeley Gaskin, Sobers walked across the SCG members' bar from the visitors to the home rooms and informed Lawry that the Windies would be bowling first. No West Indian captain had ever before sent Australia in. Less than 12 months earlier, at Port of Spain, Sobers had lost a Test after a final-day declaration which saw England score 3-215 in 162 minutes, winning with three minutes to spare.

As promised, Hall and Griffith were short and feisty, peppering both Lawry and his opening partner Keith Stackpole with bouncers. Just nine eight-ball overs were bowled in the first hour as Sobers fussed over the field and consulted regularly with his bowlers. Soon after, Stackpole succumbed to a fuller one for 20. Bowling at first change, Sobers soon dismissed in-form Ian Chappell for one and Ian Redpath without scoring. His each-way late swing was reminiscent of the great Alan Davidson in his pomp. At 3-51, the West Indies' gamble had reaped a handsome early dividend. Game on.

Twenty-three-year-old Walters emerged from the pavilion half an hour before lunch to a welcome reserved only for favourite sons. Just over 10,000 were in but it seemed all were standing for the popular, unaffected country kid whose Test career had been temporarily on hold while he'd completed National Service and had all but been sent to fight overseas.

As always, Walters seemed nerveless, as if he was batting in a Parents v Kids Sunday school social. Lawry had marvelled at the boy wonder's ice-cool composure on his debut in Brisbane three years earlier. He regarded him as an exciting new successor to his own boyhood hero Neil Harvey. It had been a career highlight for Lawry to bat with the 19-year-old during his wondrous debut Test. Now another stirring rescue mission was needed –

and at the most pivotal time in the series.

Playing his natural, instinctive game, despite giving a half-chance to slipsman Seymour Nurse at three, Walters drove a full-length Sobers inswinger to within feet of the long-off fence before imperiously crashing Griffith to the point boundary.

With Sobers taking two for none in six balls, the scoring rate had slowed before Walters' entry. Lawry had defended the straight ones and studiously ignored anything wider. He wanted to see off the pacemen and several times took short ones on his body rather than risk a defensive shot being taken by one of the flotilla of close-in catchers who all seemed just a step or two away, within hugging distance. By the end of play he was black and blue – and unconquered.

Despite the limited preparation, the wicket played truly, slow, without too many height variations. With his considerable swing, Sobers proved to be a bigger danger than either of his two much-vaunted speedsters although Hall was unfortunate to have Chappell dropped twice in the slips before he'd scored, once by Sobers who shook his hand in pain after the ball struck him just below the thumb. So bruised and swollen did his hand become that he was unable to bowl from mid-afternoon, reducing the West Indian attack to three specialists, Hall, Griffith and the off spinner Lance Gibbs.

As the pitch hardened and Hall pitched fuller, both Walters and Lawry played some excellent drives, Lawry through his favourite extra-cover area and Walters straight and through mid-off. Sensing that both players were now set, the crowd of 13,000 relaxed and enjoyed the comeback. At 44 Lawry misjudged a Sobers out-swinger which he edged at comfortable height towards Nurse, only for Fredericks, diving across him, to drop what was a regulation chance. Lawry re-marked his guard and doubled his resolve. No-one else in world cricket, not even the self-interested Yorkshireman Geoff Boycott, was more adept at batting time. He'd make them pay.

The lunch-to-tea session had been intensely fought, Gibbs bowling good lines and being backed by athletic fielding. Griffith was a disappointment, conceding almost five an over and seeming past the cut and thrust of Test cricket. He'd been replaced after just four relatively innocuous opening overs. His second spell was more spirited, however, one vicious short one to Walters grazing his forehead as he tried to duck out of the way. Later he conceded it had been the most lethal single delivery he'd ever faced.

Walters had threatened to produce his full arsenal of shots in the final overs before tea. Immediately afterwards he went on the full attack, scoring 46 runs in an exhilarating first hour. At 75 he was fortunate to survive a muffed chance to slipsman Rohan Kanhai but carried on, driving the spinners with exhilarating freedom. The crowd hushed as he reached his 90s only to explode into delighted chatter and cheering as he struck two fours in a row from the change bowler Carew to reach three figures in three hours and 22 minutes. It was his fifth hundred in 16 Tests.

Eyewitness Bob Gray, long-time cricket writer for the *Australian*, said Walters played with the same reassuring freedom as he had displayed in Brisbane in 1965. 'Some of his strokeplay yesterday touched the height of greatness,' he said, 'and the two ferocious pull shots he produced off successive balls from Carew to reach his century will never be forgotten…there is no doubt that Walters has at last recovered the magic of his initial days on the Test scene and he must rank – both in temperament and ability – as one of Australia's greatest post-war batsmen.'

From the hunted to the hunters, Australia had established a commanding position at 3-268 at the close with Lawry 117 and Walters 122, their stand a massive 217 in 270 minutes. Between them they scored 26 boundaries, Walters leading 16 to 10. He had given Lawry an hour-and-a-half and 27-runs start and beaten him by two to his century, his third of the summer. Lawry's first fifty had taken three hours, his second two. He was struck twice around the shoulder blades and four times around the thigh and upper arms by both Hall and Griffith, but revelled in the challenge and was elated when he also reached his third century of the summer.

"We wasted it," Sobers told Phil 'Redcap' Wilkins, cricket writer for the *Sydney Morning Herald* in the rooms after play. "You can't win matches if the catches aren't held." Sobers' gamble was clearly misfiring. His bowling back-ups had struggled in the frontline. 'What were Joey Carew and Clive Lloyd doing bowling in a Test match on the first day with Australia's score still under 200?' asked colourful Test legend Keith Miller. 'Neither would get a bowl in a second grade Saturday afternoon match.'

Miller applauded Lawry for producing an important century when it counted – 'there's not a better fighter in the game' – but said his ton had come 'at the sake of driving everyone from the ground.' Just over 13,000 had attended the opening day. 'Tiger' O'Reilly was more generous saying he'd rarely seen Lawry play a more important innings at such a crucial time.

The West Indies had been outfielded all summer and the dropped catches were to cost them any chance of staying in the game. Griffith later conceded that he and Hall 'may have lost some of our fire…but the Australian bowling was not superior to ours or more venomous, [and] our batsmen were the equal of theirs.'

With the second new ball just five overs old and with an extra day scheduled should it be needed to allow a result, the West Indies felt early wickets on the Saturday might retrieve their position. Fit again to bowl, Sobers opened with Hall but in sunnier, less humid conditions was unable to command the same potent swing as on the opening morning. Cornering the strike, Walters went for his shots again to the delight of a crowd which was to peak at 25,500 by early afternoon.

Runs flowed at almost a run a minute from the start, Lawry and pacemaker Walters establishing a new record stand against the West Indies and the latter crafting the highest score in the history of Australia-West Indies Test cricket – ahead of Don Bradman's 223 against Jack Grant's first-time Caribbean tourists in Brisbane almost 40 years earlier. Next man in, Paul Sheahan, had had the pads on for almost a day – "But there was no chance of a rest or taking them off briefly as the captain was out in the middle", he said.

News that Hall and Griffith had been omitted from the Windies' touring squad to England had been conveyed to them late on the first morning of the match. While Hall gave yeoman service on a pitch more suited to seam than speed, Griffith rarely worried the Australians, except during his second spell to Walters which was sharp and suspect. The timing of the team's announcement was surely inappropriate.

Walters played some audacious shots including a lofted drive over cover against Sobers, his uninhibited strokeplay regularly prompting standing applause. On 182, to screams of dismay, he lifted a drive from Hall into the covers but Griffith could take the ball only on the half volley. In the same over as Lawry reached 150, Walters scored his 200th run, courtesy of two leg glides and a back cut from Griffith. Hundreds of children raced onto the ground to congratulate him, ground invasions being all the rage in the late '60s. His second century had taken 193 minutes. He'd made 73 between the resumption of play and lunch.

Having extended their stand to 336, Lawry finally succumbed. He'd batted 500 minutes for 151. But Walters wasn't finished yet. He added another 48 with Paul Sheahan, who fell to Griffith, before tiredness finally took its toll. Trying to cut Gibbs off his stumps, Walters missed and was bowled, his majestic 242 having taken eight hours. The reviving and record-breaking stand had ensured the Frank Worrell Trophy. All 25,500 fans, and many in the press box, stood and clapped him from the ground. Old timers said it was the most stirring ovation accorded a batsman since the days of Don Bradman.

The Australians were to bat into a third day, amassing 619. It was the fourth Test in a row they'd scored 500-plus. After Alan Connolly had torn through the West Indies top order and they had been dismissed for 279 and even with a first innings lead of 340, Lawry refused to enforce the follow-on, saying he wanted the West Indies to bat on the final days when the wicket was at its dustiest.

Walters was a beneficiary, helping himself to a second century in the match – reaching three figures from the third last ball of the fourth day's play – before Lawry belatedly declared, setting the West Indies 735 to win. Centuries by Sobers and Nurse couldn't lift the Windies to even half the target and the Australians duly triumphed by 382 runs.

No other Test player, not even the Don, had made a double-century and a century in the same match, the nearest being the South African Alan Melville who scored 189 not out and 104 against England at Trent Bridge in 1947. "I'm rather glad Bill made the decision [not to enforce the follow-on]," said Walters. "Not a bad match that one for me!"

Walters' unprecedented double prompted hearty congratulations from fans Australia-wide, including this letter from No.2 Holden St., Kensington Park, South Australia:

> Dear Doug
>
> My heartiest congratulations on your record-breaking achievements in the fifth Test. My own performances v West Indies were due to be beaten and I am glad you did it.
>
> More important still is the pleasing manner in which you have been getting your runs this season.
>
> It is essential in the interests of cricket that batsmen are alive to the necessity to play shots and be aggressive. This does not imply any lack of soundness but in the end, with discretion, the strokemaker will get more runs. You have had a wonderful season and more than fully recaptured your early form and I hope and expect to see many more fine performances from you to delight everyone. Keep it up.
>
> With best wishes
>
> Yours truly
>
> **Don Bradman**

Walters aggregated 699 runs at an average of 116.50 for the series with one double-century and three centuries. His 242 was to be his highest score in a Test on Australian soil, surpassed only by his 250 against New Zealand in Christchurch in 1976-77. So much for the talk of him having lost a little of his powers during his time in the Army.

Australia

WM Lawry*	b Griffith	151
KR Stackpole	b Hall	20
IM Chappell	lbw b Sobers	1
IR Redpath	c Nurse b Sobers	0
KD Walters	b Gibbs	242
AP Sheahan	c Fredericks b Griffith	27
EW Freeman	c †Hendriks b Griffith	56
GD McKenzie	b Gibbs	19
HB Taber†	lbw b Hall	48
JW Gleeson	c †Hendriks b Hall	45
AN Connolly	not out	1
Extras (lb2, w1, nb6)		**9**
Total (all out; 152.7 overs)		**619**

Fall of wickets 1/43 2/51 3/51 4/387 5/435 6/453 7/483 8/543 9/614

Bowling	**O**	**M**	**R**	**W**
WW Hall	35.7	3	157	3
CC Griffith	37	1	175	3
GS Sobers	28	4	94	2
LR Gibbs	40	8	133	2
MC Carew	10	2	44	0
CH Lloyd	2	1	7	0

WM Lawry*	c Fredericks b Griffith	17
KR Stackpole	c Carew b Hall	6
IM Chappell	c †Hendriks b Hall	10
IR Redpath	c Sobers b Gibbs	132
KD Walters	c Fredericks b Gibbs	103
AP Sheahan	c †Hendriks b Sobers	34
EW Freeman	c Carew b Sobers	15
GD McKenzie	c Carew b Sobers	40
HB Taber†	not out	15
JW Gleeson	not out	5
AN Connolly	did not bat	
Extras (b4, lb6, w1, nb6)		**17**
Total (8 wickets dec; 92 overs)		**394**

Fall of wickets 1/21 2/36 3/40 4/250 5/301 6/329 7/329 8/388

Bowling	**O**	**M**	**R**	**W**
WW Hall	12	0	47	2
CC Griffith	14	0	41	1
GS Sobers	26	3	117	3
LR Gibbs	33	2	133	2
MC Carew	5	0	26	0
CH Lloyd	2	0	13	0

West Indies

RC Fredericks	c †Taber b Connolly	39
MC Carew	c †Taber b Freeman	64
RB Kanhai	c †Taber b Connolly	44
GS Sobers*	c †Taber b Connolly	13
BF Butcher	c Sheahan b McKenzie	10
CH Lloyd	b McKenzie	53
SM Nurse	c Stackpole b Connolly	9
JL Hendriks†	c †Taber b McKenzie	1
CC Griffith	c Freeman b Gleeson	27
WW Hall	b Gleeson	1
LR Gibbs	not out	4
Extras (b2, lb4, nb8)		**14**
Total (all out; 76.6 overs)		**279**

Fall of wickets 1/100 2/154 3/159 4/179 5/179 6/190 7/193 8/257 9/259

	O	**M**	**R**	**W**
GD McKenzie	22.6	2	90	3
AN Connolly	17	2	61	4
EW Freeman	12	2	48	1
JW Gleeson	19	8	53	2
IM Chappell	6	1	13	0

RC Fredericks	c †Taber b McKenzie	0
MC Carew	b Connolly	3
RB Kanhai	c Connolly b McKenzie	18
BF Butcher	c Gleeson b Stackpole	31
GS Sobers*	c Redpath b Gleeson	113
CH Lloyd	c Freeman b Stackpole	11
SM Nurse	b Gleeson	137
JL Hendriks†	c Stackpole b McKenzie	16
CC Griffith	b Gleeson	15
WW Hall	c Sheahan b Chappell	0
LR Gibbs	not out	0
Extras (b1, lb5, nb2)		**8**
Total (all out; 64.2 overs)		**352**

Fall of wickets 1/0 2/10 3/30 4/76 5/102 6/220 7/284 8/351 9/352

Bowling	**O**	**M**	**R**	**W**
GD McKenzie	16	1	93	3
AN Connolly	18	4	72	1
EW Freeman	2	0	16	0
JW Gleeson	15.2	1	84	3
IM Chappell	6	0	22	1
KR Stackpole	7	0	57	2

Virender Sehwag – 293

India v Sri Lanka, Mumbai Brabourne 2-6 December 2009

15

-David Mutton & Dave Wilson-

"Find out where the ball is. Go there. Hit it"
"If there is a ball there to be hit, just hit it"

Two remarkably simple and similar philosophies, reflecting an uncomplicated attitude to batting. It will probably come as no surprise that one of these quotes is attributable to the quintessential Crown Prince of Simplicity, Virender Sehwag. What is more surprising is that the other quote belongs to the actual prince of the batting art, KS Ranjitsinhji; very few traditionalists would mention Ranji and Sehwag in the same breath, yet their approach was, in this essential philosophy, the same.

The second quote is taken from an interview with Sehwag following his 293 against Sri Lanka in Mumbai, the subject of this essay, and accurately summarises the simple but not simplistic attitude of a player who in the first decade of this century turned Test match cricket on its head, spearheading a reshaping of the game and taking it into the new millennium, the era of T20 cricket. He played the long game as if he was playing the short game, looking to entertain the crowd and paying absolutely no heed to the calibre of the attack, the state of the pitch or even the situation of the match.

Crowned the *Wisden* Leading Cricketer in the World for 2008, Ravi Shastri noted that Sehwag had scored at a faster rate than any other opening batsman has ever done on a regular basis in Test cricket, 85 runs per 100 balls. The following year, in retaining the crown, both for his Test and one-day work, he jettisoned the qualifier 'opening batsman'. During this period a run a ball was the norm and no batsman in any position in Test cricket, not Viv Richards, not Adam Gilchrist, had ever approached this level of consistency.

Even after two years as *Wisden*'s champion, he didn't let up one iota going into the following year. It's illuminating to compare his performance in the year from November 2009 to November 2010 with that of his illustrious compatriot, Sachin Tendulkar who also enjoyed a remarkable run. They both batted 19 times, with similar aggregates, 1,502 for Sehwag to 1,415 for Tendulkar, and averages, 79.05 and 83.22 respectively. However the manner in which the runs were made can be gleaned from these numbers: strike-rate – Sehwag 96.90, Tendulkar 56.06; fours – Sehwag 221, Tendulkar 153. And this is no cherry picking, as their career figures show – Sehwag's strike-rate being 82 against Tendulkar's 56 and his percentage of runs in boundaries being 64 compared to the 54 per cent of his more illustrious countryman. That Tendulkar is a batting genius is accepted universally; that Sehwag was a genius of a completely different kind, there can now be no question.

And it is the manner in which Sehwag scored his runs which so revolutionised the game; first, his hunger for boundaries ensured endless entertainment for the cheering thousands watching open-mouthed at his apparent audaciousness; second, he scored at such a rate that the state of the match could be turned on its head at a stroke – likely the kind of stroke no other batsman would or could play. Nowhere was this more apparent than his 83 off 68 balls against England at Chennai in 2008, inspiring his colleagues to the highest successful run chase ever seen in Asia.

Suffering the ignominy of demotion to number seven and then being dropped in 2007, Sehwag returned from an enforced period of introspection to face the Australians on their own patch. His first four innings following his return progressed thus: 29 at a strike-rate of 49, 43 at 70, 63 at 70 and 151 at 64. Yet after just two matches he'd had enough of such circumspection; back in the welcoming bosom of his homeland, he threw off the shackles. His 319 against South Africa at Chennai, the quickest triple-century ever, was followed a few months later by a phenomenal unbeaten 201 against Sri Lanka at Galle. After that he again fell on hard times, as his next 20 Test match innings leading up to the three-Test home series against Sri Lanka in late 2009 did not produce a century.

The first match against Sri Lanka did not start well for Sehwag, a quick-fire 16 contributing to India's first innings collapse to 32-4, though in the second innings he managed 51 in 67 balls trying to inject some pizazz into a match that *Wisden* described as a 'snooze-fest'. Dileep Premachandran warned on *Cricinfo* that 'dead pitches [are] killing Test cricket in India' – but not if Sehwag had anything to do with it. In the second Test, at Kanpur, he forged a blistering 131 in just 122 balls, having made a prudent four from the first 20, inspiring his team-mates to a monster total of 417-2 on the first day. It was described as 'a vintage Sehwag innings', as 233 were plundered in a spell of 41 overs while Sehwag was at the crease – a relatively lean spell of 18 months seemed to be closing for 'Viru'. Sri Lanka were ultimately vanquished by an innings, meaning nothing short of victory for the visitors in the third and final Test would suffice.

This decider was to be played at the Brabourne Stadium in Mumbai, which had not hosted a Test match since 1973. Only the Wankhede Stadium's renovations in readiness for the 2011 World Cup allowed it to bask in attention once more, its faded grandeur a reminder of the country's early days in international cricket and a time before the riches of T20 cricket. The Sri Lankans had more prosaic concerns – they had never won a Test in India, were one-nil down in the series, their two main fast bowlers were injured, and Muttiah Muralitharan was finally beginning to show his age.

Captain Kumar Sangakkara must have been relieved, therefore, to win the toss – the wicket looked like a paradise for batsmen and Sri Lanka's best hope for levelling the series was establishing a commanding first-innings total. Yet by the end of the first day the visitors had reached 366-8, and they were all out less than six overs into the following morning. They had scored quickly but with a profligacy that they would later regret with only a Tillakaratne Dilshan century and Angelo Mathews, unfortunately run out for 99, offering any substance.

In reply Virender Sehwag and Murali Vijay opened for India, the latter a replacement for Gautam Gambhir, who had opted out of the game in favour of his sister's wedding. Sehwag started slowly, reaching 20 from 35 balls, part of a new strategy to contain his natural aggression at the beginning of an innings. In the eighth over he smashed a boundary through the covers and in the ninth really signaled his intent when he danced down the wicket to Rangana Herath and slapped him straight back over his head for six runs. The next over Sehwag launched into the innocuous Chanaka Welegedara, first with a dismissive cut off a long hop followed up with a sumptuous on drive. His second six of the innings from Herath, a flat-batted but effective swipe, brought him to 6,000 Test match runs. By the time Sehwag reached his fifty the Sri Lankans had already ominously regressed into defence, with a solitary slip the only fielder close to the bat. He lunched on 53 and the prospect of plunder, and straight after the interval unleashed a delicate late cut and then his first reverse sweep off Murali, treating the veteran spinner with disdain.

Fully set, Sehwag now began to dispatch balls, both good and bad, to all parts of the ground, unfurling nearly every stroke in the textbook and plenty that were of his own invention. His technique was far from standard, little elegance and very far from beautiful but extraordinary hand-eye coordination mitigated the need for footwork and allowed him to reduce the game to its simplest form: '*If there is a ball there to be hit, just hit it*.' It was this basic premise that facilitated a mixture of brute aggression with surprising deftness. It also made setting fields almost impossible. When the Sri Lankans tried to dry up runs by bowling to an off-side field, Sehwag shuffled his stocky body across the stumps and flicked a ball pitched outside off through the empty leg side. Little wonder that the bowler, Welegedara, was reduced to screaming in frustration.

Sehwag reached his 17th Test match century with a fine sweep off Murali. The following over he slogged the persevering but unthreatening Herath away for another maximum into the vacant leg side. By this stage his mastery over the bowling attack was absolute. He played Murali and Herath, who would scalp Test match batsmen 1,000 times between them, with total control, and scored 141 runs from their bowling. The seam bowlers, Welegedara and Nuwan Kulasekara, were treated like cannon fodder, and at times appeared eager to wave the white flag of surrender.

As India passed the 200 mark without losing a wicket, Sehwag was scoring at a run a ball.

He struck another six, the biggest yet, past the long-on fielder and into the crowd. While Sehwag was destroying the Sri Lankan attack his batting partner, Vijay, in only his second Test match, calmly constructed his own innings until he missed a sweep off Herath and was plumb lbw for 87. This could not have lifted the Sri Lankans too much as it brought Rahul Dravid to the wicket with the score on 221, with Sachin Tendulkar, VVS Laxman, and MS Dhoni still to come.

Dravid proved the perfect foil for Sehwag, encouraging his partner to continue the assault while not deviating from his own glorious orthodoxy. The only problem for Sehwag came not from the Sri Lankans but his back, which caused him enough pain just before tea that there were fears that he would retire hurt. Thankfully he returned after the interval and, with renewed brio, hit the first ball for four and in the second over after the break cut a typically loose ball from Welegedara for another boundary before rattling a dismissive six over extra-cover.

Four more boundaries followed off Kulasekara in the 57th over, and the double-century arrived from the final ball of the over. It was the sixth time that he had reached the landmark, and it came from only 168 balls. That this was the second fastest double in Test cricket was perhaps less remarkable than the fact that Sehwag had scored five of the 10 fastest, including three of the quickest four.

The innings contained Sehwag's trademark adventurous derring-do. He took only a further 39 balls to move to 250, in which he highlighted his unique brand of controlled arrogance, exquisite placement and muscular brutality. There was a checked drive to a ball pitched a foot outside leg stump which split the off-side boundary riders, a six off Murali as he danced down the pitch and struck the ball into the second tier of the stand beyond long-on, two glides down to vacant third-man, a heave for four through mid-wicket, and a thumping cover drive. His 250 then came up with the finest of reverse sweeps from the bowling of Murali, almost letting the ball hit the wicket before caressing it just wide of the wicket-keeper.

Sehwag offered his first real chance towards the end of the day. On 273 he attempted a late cut off Dilshan but succeeded only in sending the ball to Mahela Jayawardene at slip, who dropped a sharp but eminently catchable opportunity. Earlier in the innings there had been a couple of optimistic shouts for leg before wicket, and a lazy drive off Kulasekara on 142 which just looped over mid-on but beyond this Sehwag had offered as much encouragement as a mule in a strop.

At the close of play on that second day Sehwag had reached 284 and India were already in the lead. Only Don Bradman and Walter Hammond had scored more in a single day, and there was eager speculation that evening of Sehwag soaring past Brian Lara's Test match record.

The ground was full the following morning, with Mumbai out in force anticipating more dramatics from Sehwag; alas it was not to be – in the fourth over of the day he chipped a dipping Murali delivery straight back to the bowler. He juggled the catch before gratefully holding it at the second attempt, and then wheeled away more in relief than joy. The twinkle had left the great spinner's eyes just as the mystery had been exorcised from his bowling, and he would go on to play just one more Test match before retiring from the international game.

The dismissal proved to be a false dawn for the Sri Lankans, if such a thing was possible with a scoreboard reading 458-2. Dravid, Tendulkar and Laxman all contributed half-centuries before Dhoni hit a measured hundred as India ploughed on to 726, the highest score in their history. The impact of Sehwag's innings was more than merely his runs; his sheer speed had opened a two-day window to bowl at the Sri Lankans with a lead of 333 runs. Unsurprisingly they wilted after this two-day bruising and folded to defeat by an innings and 22 runs early on the final day.

Interviewed after the match, Sehwag was realistic regarding falling just short of an unprecedented third triple-century:

> "I am very glad I got at least 293 – I am proud of what I achieved. Not many people have got two triples and followed that with 293 – so there is nothing to be disappointed about.
>
> [On his dismissal] "I tried to take my time, but maybe the ball was not there to be hit. I misjudged the length and the ball went straight to Murali's hands. I always tell myself to bat the full day, and *if there is a ball there to be hit, just hit it*."

The records which fell as Sehwag plundered the Sri Lankan attack were impressive and bounteous. He reached 250 off 207 balls, the quickest ever and, had he reached 300 that would undoubtedly have been the fastest too, as he still had 23 balls to score just seven more runs needed to beat his own record. In any case, he joined Don Bradman as the only other player to have three scores over 290. His 200 in 168 balls was the second-quickest ever after Nathan Astle's on a flawless drop-in pitch, and the second hundred took just 67 balls.

In March 2008 India had played South Africa in Chennai where, for the first time ever in the history of Test cricket, both the first and second wickets enjoyed partnerships in excess of 200 runs. Incredibly, less than two years later the feat was repeated in this match – all four partnerships had featured the incomparable Sehwag. Even his dismissal resulted in a record, Murali equalling Anil Kumble's record with his 35th caught-and-bowled.

What would we be saying about Sehwag now had he scored seven more runs? A third triple would have seen him leave behind even Bradman and Lara – would he then have taken his place in the great pantheon of the very best ever? Absolutely not – he is not even considered to be the best batsman produced by his own country, in fact he may struggle to make the top five. A recent ranking has him listed at number 43 all-time – incredible.

Though he is decried as lucky, it's just possible that he realised that he could not only get away with playing the way he did, but could prosper by it. It may just be that all of those shots which just evaded a fielder's outstretched hands were intentional and that he didn't move his feet much because he didn't need to. It's just possible that nobody else played this way because they couldn't. If he was just lucky and had poor technique, wouldn't the world's greatest bowlers have figured him? Instead, he got better and better and faster and faster; his first four Test hundreds were made at a strike-rate of 62 and averaged 122, the four ending with this 293 were made at a crazy strike-rate of 104 and at an average of 315!

Although he scored a few more hundreds, the 293 at the Brabourne was his last truly epic innings. Ian Chappell described it as 'the feat of the year', calling Sehwag 'the greatest destroyer since the U-boat.' Ravi Shastri called him 'a marvel of modern times, a genius who has confounded conventional wisdom, whose daring is now part of cricket's folklore.'

Sehwag spearheaded India's gradual rise to the pinnacle of Test cricket every bit as much as Tendulkar, Dhoni or Harbhajan Singh, this innings and this victory bringing the series win that confirmed the Indians at the top of the Test match rankings for the first time. The Brabourne Stadium had been there almost since the start, and had seen many of the batsmen that helped define Indian cricket: the epic batting of the Vijays, Hazare and Merchant, Vinoo Mankad's double-century to defeat the New Zealanders and another from Dilip Sardesai to rescue them after following on against the same opponents, plus an array of inspiring rearguard fights from Mansoor Ali Khan. It had witnessed India's rise to maturity as a nation and a cricketing power – now it had hosted their ascension to the top with the best innings played on its soil.

Sri Lanka

Batsman	Dismissal	Runs
NT Paranavitana	c Dravid b H Singh	53
TM Dilshan	c Vijay b H Singh	109
KC Sangakkara*	c †Dhoni b Ojha	18
D Jayawardene	c Sehwag b Sreesanth	29
TT Samaraweera	c Vijay b H Singh	1
AD Mathews	run out (T'kar/†Dhoni)	99
H Jayawardene†	c H Singh b Ojha	43
KKulasekara	c †Dhoni b Khan	12
H Herath	c Dravid b H Singh	1
M M'tharan	not out	4
U Welegedara	lbw b Ojha	8
Extras (b4, lb6, w2, nb4)		**16**
Total (all out; 94.4 overs; 415 mins)		**393**

Fall of wickets 1/93 2/128 3/187 4/188 5/262 6/329 7/359 8/362 9/379

Bowling	O	M	R	W
Z Khan	19	2	70	1
S Sreesanth	16	1	82	1
H Singh	32	3	112	4
PP Ojha	23.4	1	101	3
Yuvraj Singh	4	0	18	0

Batsman	Dismissal	Runs
NT Paranavitana	lbw b Sreesanth	54
TM Dilshan	lbw b H Singh	16
KC Sangakkara*	c †Dhoni b Khan	137
D Jayawardene	c †Dhoni b Khan	12
TT Samaraweera	c Laxman b Khan	0
AD Mathews	c †Dhoni b Ojha	5
H Jayawardene†	lbw b Ojha	32
K Kulasekara	c Laxman b Khan	19
H Herath	c Ojha b Khan	3
M M'tharan	c †Dhoni b H Singh	14
U Welegedara	not out	0
Extras (b12, lb1, w1, nb3)		**17**
Total (all out; 100.4 overs; 418 mins)		**309**

Fall of wickets 1/29 2/119 3/135 4/137 5/144 6/208 7/278 8/282 9/307

Bowling	O	M	R	W
H Singh	34.4	5	80	2
PP Ojha	23	4	84	2
Z Khan	21	5	72	5
S Sreesanth	13	4	36	1
V Sehwag	9	2	24	0

India

Batsman	Dismissal	Runs
M Vijay	lbw b Herath	87
V Sehwag	c & b M'tharan	293
R Dravid	c † J'dene b Welegedara	74
SR Tendulkar	b Kulasekara	53
VVS Laxman	c Kulasekara b M'tharan	62
Yuvraj Singh	c Mathews b Herath	23
MS Dhoni*†	not out	100
H Singh	b M'tharan	1
Z Khan	c Kulasekara b M'tharan	7
S Sreesanth	lbw b Herath	8
PP Ojha	not out	5
Extras (lb3, nb10)		**13**
Total (9 wickets dec; 163.3 overs; 705 m)		**726**

Fall of wickets 1/221 2/458 3/487 4/558 5/591 6/610 7/615 8/647 9/670

Bowling	O	M	R	W
U Welegedara	30	3	131	1
K Kulasekara	20	1	105	1
H Herath	53.3	2	240	3
M M'tharan	51	4	195	4
AD Mathews	6	0	36	0
TM Dilshan	3	0	16	0

Bruce Mitchell – 164*

England v South Africa, Lord's 29 June-2 July 1935

-Richard Parry-

Bruce Mitchell would have been surprised and not a little embarrassed by his inclusion in this book. As a player, he never really enjoyed the acclaim for his achievements, blushing and acknowledging significant milestones with a shy wave of the bat. But his apparent diffidence, even in a diffident era, hid a steely determination to succeed, an ability to build and implement a technique to meet the challenges he faced and the flexibility and selflessness to sublimate his natural, free stroke play in the service of a team often under pressure. There have been, as John Arlott put it, 'few less obvious, or more interesting, men in cricket today'.

These qualities do not suggest that any of his innings would naturally find a home in this list. Derek Lodge's statistical analysis of the greatest innings in *Figures on the Green* dismissed Mitchell's efforts on the basis that they were too slow and too well supported but 'Emma' Mitchell's unbeaten 164 at Lord's in 1935 was a perfect example of an innings which was singular in both character and impact, and deserves inclusion in this august company.

This innings made history for his team. It was an isolated golden moment in 50 years of pain. Before Mitchell's inspiration, South Africa had played 16 Tests in England, without a single win. His innings proved the decisive factor in breaking this sequence, and ultimately South Africa were able to cling on their slender 1-0 advantage to take the series. It took a further 28 Tests for the Springboks to record their next victory, in 1951 against Freddie Brown's England.

A South African win away from home therefore required the conjunction of the exceptional – in effect a perfect storm. Lord's, of course, seldom fails to inspire overseas players who may get to experience it once or twice in a lifetime. But in this case, conditions were unprecedented, favoured the visitors, and enabled an exceptional performance by Mitchell beyond anything this highly-talented and massively-organised achiever had managed to produce elsewhere.

He did not, however, win the Test on his own. It required others to perform at the top of their potential, and for the team as a unit moulded by skilful captaincy to achieve much more than the sum of its parts.

It does not detract from Bruce Mitchell's achievement to suggest that he alone was not responsible for the victory. Cricket is a team game where individuals inspire each other to achieve performances which surpass what might otherwise be beyond them. At Lord's in 1935, apart from Mitchell's performance, Xenophon Balaskas and Jock Cameron had their finest Tests with ball and bat respectively, and Chud Langton produced his best all-round effort. These contributions could have been match winners on their own in any other game, and Eric Dalton too chipped in with a match-changing contribution with the ball. Crucially, for the perfect-storm scenario, Herby Wade contributed a captaincy master class, combining planning, judgement and exceptional motivational ability with a healthy element of luck, including winning the toss. Mitchell, a man inspired, played in an inspired team.

The Lord's Test was the 20th game in a 40-match tour (12 of which had been won and seven drawn). The close knit community of 15 players were two months into the tour – and fully acclimatised without yet being exhausted – having been moulded by an astute and highly respected skipper into a unit that transcended the capabilities of the individuals.

The South Africans were coming into this second Test of a five-match series undefeated mainly because the MCC had decided, rather patronisingly, that the series was to be made up of three-day Test matches. This allowed South Africa to escape in Nottingham teetering on 17-1, 147 runs from an innings defeat after rain washed out the final day. And their performance in the week prior to Lord's had provided essential momentum. South Africa had thrashed Yorkshire in Sheffield, during which Jock Cameron, South Africa's stylish and aggressive wicket-keeper, hit Hedley Verity for 30 in an over – 4,4,4,6,6,6 – prompting the famous comment from Yorkshire wicket-keeper, Arthur Wood: "Never mind Hedley, tha has him in two minds, he doesn't know whether to hit thee for four or six." Meanwhile the exotically named leggie and googly bowler, Xenophon 'Bally' Balaskas, took 12 wickets. Both had come into form with a bang. But could lightning strike twice?

This momentum was given further steel by a dose of adversity with two key batsmen in the wars. Mitchell had been struck over the eye a couple of days before the Test and carried stitches in his eyebrow and Eric Rowan was deaf from drugs taken to combat an ear infection.

For the only time in the series, Wade was able to call upon a full-strength attack of Sandy Bell, Bob Crisp, Balaskas (in only his fifth game of the tour) and Langton. England replaced Walter Robins with the Derbyshire spinner, Tommy Mitchell, and brought in another left armer to partner Verity; James Langridge.

But captain Herby Wade's biggest slice of luck came when he saw the pitch and then won the toss and elected to bat. The surface had been attacked by leatherjackets – the larvae of crane flies – which had destroyed the grass at the roots and produced a dusty, bouncy pitch which encouraged sharp turn at bewildering angles and paces. It was clear to both sides what the pitch would do, but which team would exploit it better?

Bruce Mitchell, after passing a fitness test and sporting a large sticking plaster across his eyebrow, and Jack Siedle strode out to bat on a sunny Saturday in front of 35.000 spectators. Verity and the other Mitchell got the first chance to lay down a marker, knowing that England would be batting last. Tommy Mitchell's googly defeated Siedle early on, but Bruce Mitchell batted patiently for an hour and a half before being adjudged lbw to a Stan Nichols inswinger, for 30, with the score on 59-2. His innings was competent and while unspectacular it provided a crucial platform for the other batsmen and a confidence booster for himself in the second innings. His was the first dismissal under a new experimental lbw law (allowing for a ball pitching outside off but hitting in line) but over the course of the match the rule worked more in favour of the South Africans than England. Dudley Nourse followed quickly, playing back to Verity, and it was 98-4 and early afternoon when Cameron replaced Rowan, with the balance beginning to slip towards England.

Despite, or perhaps because of, being interrupted by a presentation to King George V, Cameron carried on where he had left off against Verity and Yorkshire the previous week. He launched a ruthless and sometimes frenzied attack punctuated by occasional moments of sound defence, defying the spin-friendly conditions and wresting the game out of England's grip. At one stage he hit 58 out of 60 scored in half an hour. When Nichols finally bowled him with another inswinger for 90, he walked back to an unforgettable ovation, having hit three sixes and six fours, out of 126 scored while he was at the wicket. South Africa succumbed soon after for 228, by no means a match-winning total despite the leatherjackets.

As the first hero in a game of South African heroes, Cameron had played the innings of his tragically short life. Within a few months he was dead of enteric fever, contracted on the trip home, at the age of 30. This tragedy hung a long shadow over South African cricket, which was understandably very slow to recover from the loss of such a charismatic and talented performer with both bat and gloves, not to mention his bravery and spirit of adventure.

By close of play, England were 75-2, Balaskas having bowled Maurice Leyland with a straight long hop, much to Leyland's annoyance, after cleaning him up the previous week in Yorkshire colours with a huge leg-break. When play resumed on the Monday, Balaskas bowled unchanged for two and a quarter hours, with barely a bad ball, and earned the best figures of his Test career – 32-8-49-5.

'Bally' was known for bowling six different balls an over, often sacrificing control for variety. But his control on the Monday, with his change of pace, huge turn from the dusty and grassless wicket and uneven bounce, gave South Africa a highly significant 30-run lead. He was bowling to three slips and two silly-covers for much of the time.

In the field, Wade pulled rabbits out of hats with almost every decision. His fielders were magnificent, and Eric Dalton, very much a part-time spinner at best, was given his first bowl for almost a month and bowled Wally Hammond before having England's captain, Bob Wyatt, well set on 53, caught superbly by Nourse at square-leg.

South Africa's openers came through the Long Room and down the Lord's steps with a suitably Wagnerian thunderstorm brewing, clearly inspired by their performance in the field. The normally sedate and unemotional 'Emma' Mitchell drove Nichols' first delivery of the innings for four through the vacant mid-off region, picked up a two and a single off the next two balls and Siedle drove the last ball wide of cover for another boundary. The batsmen, as well as possibly betraying a trace of nerves, showed the team's intent to start positively and maintain the psychological advantage.

But within a few overs Tommy Mitchell was also bowling leg breaks to three slips getting sharp turn and irregular bounce. Siedle was quickly caught behind off one that turned square while Verity's control forced Mitchell into playing four consecutive maidens. This was the South African in his element. He was a professional in the modern sense of the term, a cricketer before his time, bringing thorough preparation, discipline and concentration to the task in hand, but with the ability to cut loose when it was time to do so.

His value to the team was not just a matter of statistics yet the numbers are mighty impressive. In 42 Tests, in a consistently losing team, he averaged 48.88 with eight hundreds (seven of which were against England). His tension was apparent as he plucked at the shirt on his right shoulder, shrugged his shoulders or fidgeted with his cap, and went through his routine of standing in the blockhole, raising his bat vertically and looking down the wicket after every ball. But his game rested on a solid and uncomplicated technique, as well as huge powers of concentration, and a lion-hearted determination. He had been spotted early, playing among the mine dumps of the Witwatersrand by 'Barberton' Halliwell, legendary South African wicket-keeper in the 1890s. Halliwell coached him and predicted when he was still a small boy that he would play for South Africa as a teenager. He was only a year out.

Mitchell's cricketing education was continued by Herby Taylor, South Africa's first batting master who passed on his sideways stance and mastery of back-foot play, vital in combating the turn and bounce on matting pitches, which Lord's, thanks to the leatherjackets, so closely resembled. Mitchell's characteristic pendulum style was grooved to deal with the ball spitting off the stretched mat. In defence, he used a short backlift, a half stride to the ball, and no follow through as the ball hit the bat under his nose. But when the mood hit him there was no better driver in the game through the covers and straight, with superb timing and power of stroke. He had been asked to put his normal attacking game on ice and take on opening in 1929 and batted for seven hours for 88 in the Edgbaston Test of 1929, facing Larwood, Geary, Tate and Freeman. Just occasionally, when the time was right, he was able to defrost his normal game and play with a freedom that defied the circumstances.

Verity's four consecutive maidens were ended by a sumptuous Mitchell straight drive for four which wounded England, not least by forcing the chasing Herbert Sutcliffe off the field with a strained thigh muscle. Eric Rowan entered after the fall of Siedle and found Mitchell in the middle of a master class, all ease and grace off front and back foot. He brought up his half-century after 95 minutes, before almost being bowled by a Verity delivery that shot along the ground, but he had few other alarms on a pitch that wasn't far from unplayable. He and Rowan, however, hammered home the advantage.

Shortly after tea, the partnership of 104 was ended, with Rowan's contribution an invaluable 44. Nourse quickly followed, bowled by a Verity scuttler for two, Cameron was caught at deep mid-on for three, and Wade and Dalton both went to Verity without troubling the scorers. South Africa were on 177-6, 207 ahead, and Mitchell had reached an imperious hundred. Nonetheless, much work still remained to be done, and the collapse meant South Africa were on the verge of losing the advantage that Mitchell and Rowan had fought so hard for. But Langton, the fourth Transvaal batsman in the line-up, stayed with Mitchell until stumps with South Africa on 208-6 and Mitchell on 129. This 30-minute period before stumps was of critical importance, another wicket and England may well have been batting and chasing a target of around 220 on the last day.

Next day, the third and final, the weather greatly favoured the overnight batting side. A downpour before start of play softened the uncovered pitch making it easier to bat for the morning session, but it was bound to get more difficult as it dried. Mitchell moved serenely on and maintained his absolute mastery of the bowling, confidently driving through the covers, cutting square and pulling loose balls to the square-leg fence. Wally Hammond commented caustically to his skipper that they were lucky that Mitchell didn't have two eyes.

Wade's challenge was when to close the innings and unleash Balaskas. After Langton's excellent and critical innings finally came to an end, caught and bowled by Hammond for a pugnacious 44, Wade declared giving England 45 minutes batting before lunch. England faced a target of 309 in 285 minutes.

Mitchell had made 164 not out from 278-7. He had demonstrated a mastery of conditions and an ability to dictate the game which none of his team-mates or the opposition were able to approach. Sutcliffe, himself a proven master on spinner's wickets, edged into the Springbok dressing room as Mitchell was peeling off his pads, shook his hand, and told him that he had "just played the finest innings on a wearing wicket I have ever seen".

The total looked beyond the England batsmen, given the state of the wicket, but could the South African bowlers, with the weight of history on their shoulders, close out their advantage? Sutcliffe and Wyatt survived until a very tense lunch, and the match was in the balance when Balaskas came on from the Nursery End, immediately inducing Wyatt to play on. Crisp brought one back through Leyland's defences and England were 45-2. But Sutcliffe and Hammond, England's best batsmen, were more than capable of thwarting South Africa. Hammond was playing fluently against Crisp's pace, but Wade, Balaskas and the rest fielded as if their lives depended on it which, given the significance of the occasion, they almost did.

Sutcliffe was surprisingly allowed to use the twelfth man as a runner, following his earlier muscle strain, but was not prevented from playing the shot of the game against Mitchell's high-flighted spin. He waited for the ball and drove it backwards past the startled 'keeper to the fence, a shot worthy of the Indian Premier League. But the breakthrough was not long in coming, and it was Chud Langton who for the second time in a day made the decisive impact. Hammond inside edged a Langton inswinger to Cameron and a run later he trapped Sutcliffe leg before. He then yorked Holmes for eight, and finally trapped Ames in front for the same score. Langton had taken four quick wickets in the post-lunch session, destroying English resistance, with some help from the new lbw law. No miracles were forthcoming for England and Balaskas joined the exultant Langton in wiping out the tail. The last eight wickets had fallen for 62 runs.

South Africa had played the perfect game. Herby Wade thanked the crowd for their fairness, and the following morning's headlines referred to Mitchell's match, to Cameron's innings, to Balaskas' spin which 'foozled' them, and to the triumph of teamwork. All were true.

But in a stupendous game of Test cricket at its best, in which South Africa outplayed their opponents in all areas, it was Mitchell's innings which provided the foundation on which the victory was built. It was the highest score made by a South African in England in a game when the next highest score was Wyatt's 53. It was an innings of patience and determination, the ultimate acceptance of responsibility by a man who was able to lift his performance and to seize the moment. Not only that, his innings was filled with classic batting from a talented natural stroke player who had built his international career restraining his attacking instincts in the service of a weak team. Douglas Jardine described his 164 as 'five hours of mastery' and C.B. Fry thought he had batted 'as the school-master of all the bowlers ever born.'

All of South Africa's four key batsmen in this Test were from the Transvaal, where they had grown up on bouncing and turning matting wickets, laid on clay. The highest individual score from a non-Transvaal South African was Wade's 23. If the Lord's groundstaff wanted to produce a surface most likely to benefit the visitors and disadvantage their own side, this is the wicket they would have prepared. But it was the leatherjackets which wore green and gold. It would take many years before the perfect storm would happen again for South Africa.

The performance was deliriously celebrated back in Johannesburg and Durban, a rare shaft of sunlight in the depression of the '30s, and Bruce Mitchell's status as an authentic South African hero was confirmed. But South Africa had deeper problems than the depression and the storm clouds of war in Europe. The last building block in the system of racial segregation, which in the post-war period would become known as apartheid, was put in place when the property-based franchise in the Cape Province, and any possible formal political involvement by black South Africans, was ended. White South Africa, with approximately 13 per cent of the population, had created a racially exclusive political system, as well as prohibited access by non-whites to land, property, jobs and freedom of movement.

In cricket, black players had been prohibited from playing for South Africa since the start – thanks to the intervention of Cecil Rhodes which ended the aspirations of the exceptional black player, Krom Hendricks, in the 1890s. This policy had been unsuccessfully challenged by Barberton Halliwell, Mitchell's boyhood mentor, who as wicket-keeper wanted to see the best South African bowlers selected.

Meanwhile, Bruce Mitchell had a shadow. Frank Roro, a black Transvaal batsman working on the mines, accumulated over 100 centuries in racially segregated domestic cricket between the 1920s and early 1950s. His career ran parallel to Mitchell's in the same city at the same time, but sadly never on the same pitch. How different South Africa's cricketing achievements, and indeed the future of the country itself, might have been if racism had not denied Frank Roro the opportunity of batting with Bruce Mitchell in the Lord's sunshine.

South Africa

B Mitchell	lbw b Nichols	30
IJ Siedle	b Mitchell	6
EAB Rowan	c †Farrimond b Verity	40
AD Nourse	b Verity	3
HF Wade*	c Hammond b Langridge	23
HB Cameron†	b Nichols	90
EL Dalton	c & b Langridge	19
XC Balaskas	b Verity	4
ACB Langton	c Holmes b Hammond	4
RJ Crisp	not out	4
AJ Bell	b Hammond	0
Extra (b1, lb1, w1, nb2)		**5**
Total (all out; 91.3 overs)		**228**

Fall of wickets 1/27 2/59 3/62 4/98 5/158 6/187 7/196 8/224 9/228

Bowling	**O**	**M**	**R**	**W**
MS Nichols	21	5	47	2
RES Wyatt	4	2	9	0
WR Wammond	5.3	3	8	2
TB Mitchell	20	3	71	1
H Verity	28	10	61	3
James Langridge	13	3	27	2

B Mitchell	not out	164
IJ Siedle	c †Farrimond b Mitchell	13
EAB Rowan	lbw b Nichols	44
AD Nourse	b Verity	2
HB Cameron†	c Ames b Mitchell	3
EL Dalton	c Wyatt b Verity	0
HF Wade*	b Verity	0
ACB Langton	c & b Hammond	44

Did not bat XC Balaskas, RJ Crisp, AJ Bell

Extras (b3, lb5)	**8**
Total (7 wickets dec; 121.4 overs)	**278**

Fall of wickets 1/32 2/136 3/158 4/169 5/169 6/177 7/278

Bowling	**O**	**M**	**R**	**W**
MS Nichols	18	4	64	1
RES Wyatt	4	2	2	0
WR Wammond	14.4	4	26	1
TB Mitchell	33	5	93	2
H Verity	38	16	56	3
James Langridge	10	4	19	0
ERT Holmes	4	2	10	0

England

RES Wyatt*	c Nourse b Dalton	53
H Sutcliffe	lbw b Bell	3
M Leyland	b Balaskas	18
WR Hammond	b Dalton	27
LEG Ames	b Balaskas	5
ERT Holmes	c Bell b Balaskas	10
James Langridge	c Mitchell b Balaskas	27
W Farrimond†	b Balaskas	13
MS Nichols	c †Cameron b Langton	10
H Verity	lbw b Langton	17
TB Mitchell	not out	5
Extras (b4, lb5, w1)		**10**
Total (all out; 80.3 overs)		**198**

Fall of wickets 1/5 2/46 3/100 4/109 5/116 6/121 7/158 8/161 9/177

Bowling	**O**	**M**	**R**	**W**
RJ Crisp	8	1	32	0
AJ Bell	6	0	16	1
ACB Langton	21.3	3	58	2
XC Balaskas	32	8	49	5
EL Dalton	13	1	33	2

RES Wyatt*	b Balaskas	16
H Sutcliffe	lbw b Langton	38
M Leyland	b Crisp	4
WR Hammond	c †Cameron b Langton	27
LEG Ames	lbw b Langton	8
ERT Holmes	b Langton	8
James Langridge	lbw b Balaskas	17
W Farrimond†	b Crisp	13
MS Nichols	not out	7
H Verity	c Langton b Balaskas	8
TB Mitchell	st †Cameron b Balaskas	1
Extras (lb4)		**4**
Total (all out; 67 overs)		**151**

Fall of wickets 1/24 2/45 3/89 4/90 5/102 6/111 7/129 8/141 9/149

Bowling	**O**	**M**	**R**	**W**
RJ Crisp	15	4	30	2
AJ Bell	12	3	21	0
ACB Langton	11	3	31	4
XC Balaskas	27	8	54	4
B Mitchell	2	0	11	0

Brian Lara – 226

Australia v West Indies, Adelaide 25-29 November 2005

13

-Patrick Ferriday-

"What a moment for Lara, and cricket as well." That slight pause, the trademark of Richie Benaud, implanted the event simultaneously with joy and gravitas. The shot he had just described was a curiously unorthodox paddle down to fine-leg that had left two stumps exposed and surely infuriated bowler Glenn McGrath. The resultant single took Brian Lara to 214 for the innings and 11,175 for his Test career and with it he had overtaken Allan Border.

Of course it was a great moment for Lara, but why 'cricket as well'? This was the same Richie Benaud who had been thrilled by the approach of Frank Worrell and Garry Sobers, the same Benaud who plotted and delivered 'brighter cricket' when the game was being strangled by method in the late '50s. Perhaps the greatest ever Test series, 1960-61 against the West Indies, was his greatest testament. Here was a modern-day representative of that same approach – how could he not have a soft spot for this supremely talented left hander any more than he could avoid a small twinkle every time Shane Warne googled a Pom.

Lara's achievement was hardly a surprise. From the moment he exploded across the international cricket horizon with a flawless 277 at the SCG in 1993 and then took Sobers' record 15 months later, it was clear that here was a batsman equipped to collect virtually every record in the books given mental and physical fitness over the following 15 years. But no great player (with the possible exception of Sachin Tendulkar) can have a seamless rise to, and stay at, the top and Lara was to endure his share of vilification over the years. Accusations of selfishness, mental instability, greediness and poor judgement both on and off the field dogged his career. Usually these broadsides reached a crescendo when either Lara wasn't scoring bucket-loads of runs or the West Indies were taking a beating – the two frequently coinciding.

Yet it was the regular ability to come out fighting in the face of adversity that punctuated his career and provided the great peaks, what the romantic poet Coleridge termed 'obstinate in resurrection'. Three centuries in successive Tests in England in 1995, a wonderful 132 at Perth in 1997, the career-defining pair of centuries at home to Australia in 1999 and the 196 against South Africa after an eight-month absence in 2005. There were also the softer options, notably the 375 followed by 400 against England.

It was at Adelaide in November 2005 that Lara was facing another such hiatus and it was here that he produced one of his greatest ripostes. This time the criticisms were darker than ever – at 36 years old it was about waning and, in particular, a nervous inability to deal with fast short-pitched bowling. This weakness could prove, in cricketing terms, terminal and Australia had Brett Lee, the most consistently fast bowler in the world. On the positive side, Allan Border's record was within touching distance at the start of the Australian summer which would feature one Test between the ICC World XI and Australia followed by a three-match series between the hosts and the West Indies. Lara had four matches to score 356 runs but would the Australian crowds be treated to a final burst of glory to crown a glorious career or was the more likely scenario the exhausted athlete dragging himself across the line before being ushered into respectable retirement lest the lustre fade and pity flourish?

There had been little wrong with Lara's form prior to the Australian trip (four centuries in five home games against South Africa and Pakistan) but there was plenty wrong with his team; one victory and three defeats had given more than an inkling of the enormous challenge that lay ahead against the mighty Australians, although an Ashes defeat during that English summer had at least suggested a sense of fallibility. But they were still unbeaten in 13 years in a home series and after an easy win against the World XI (Lara chipped 41 from his Border-target) Australia were overwhelming favourites to gobble up callow visitors boasting only three top-class batsmen and a mediocre bowling attack.

The first Test, at Brisbane, went as expected: the West Indies thumped by 379 runs (Lara 44 runs and one terrible umpiring decision). The second, at Hobart, followed much the same course – defeat by nine wickets, Lara 58 runs and again victim of an umpiring howler. Going into the final match the series was already lost and Brian Lara was still 213 adrift of the record figure. An opportunity to quietly slink off into the sunset, rest and wait for the easier prospect of New Zealand in early 2006 or front up and dismantle the best bowling attack in the world? Lara, as was his wont, chose the latter course.

On a bright and sunny November morning, Shiv Chanderpaul called correctly and, without any great confidence in a positive outcome, chose to bat. Within half an hour the familiar proceedings had started, Brett Lee having both openers caught by Matthew Hayden in his third over. As Lara walked out to a thunderous ovation, high up below the roof of the stand Tony Greig's endearing enthusiasm was informing viewers that "Brett Lee's on fire" – not 'literally' at least. This pair had history too – two years earlier, Lee had subjected Lara to a frightening fusillade in Trinidad that he had weathered despite taking a number of blows to the body. Lee was barely slower now but Lara was older and he could have little illusion about what awaited at the hands of Lee and his half-decent supporting cast of McGrath, Warne, Stuart MacGill and new boy Andrew Symonds.

Brett Lee was no tearaway firebrand though and knew that a succession of bouncers would be a waste – his first ball was a beauty, fast, on a good length, and on the off stump. The batsman found himself squared up and looked perhaps fortunate to survive after thick-edging down to the third-man boundary. In fact it wasn't fortune, it was skill. Lara hadn't pushed with a nervous iron grip as shaky starters are prone to do, hence the ball angled safely and low but there was still plenty in that moment to encourage the bowlers.

Nerves remained evident for the period up to lunch; with two early wickets gone and then Ramnaresh Sarwan becoming Lee's third victim at 53 it was clear that the match could be virtually decided by tea and indeed Australia believed they had got their man when Lara unwisely padded-up in Symond's first over. On such brittle foundations can great things be built – Aleem Dar called it right, the ball had pitched just, and only just, outside leg. Maybe this was the point where Lara began to believe that this would be his day after the misfortunes of the previous weeks. He later summed up his early approach by saying: "You give the bowlers their hour and after that you've got to know the pace and bounce of the pitch, what the bowlers have to offer, and don't be intimidated." It had been a hairy session but the lunch interval was reached with no further loss, 71-3.

The break seemed to have refreshed at least one of the batsmen and ominous signs for the Australians were now appearing. The wicket was relatively flat and some of the more extravagant shots were about to make their entrance – Lara himself said that "at some moment you've got to pick up the momentum and dictate to them"; it appeared that moment had arrived. With the score at 76-3 he delivered a remarkable double assault on Shane Warne who was striving to pitch into the early footmarks that had already started to appear outside Lara's off stump. The first of the pair was over-pitched and a good nine inches wide and it was crashed past point with withering power – a poor ball given the treatment. The next ball was almost identical, maybe an inch or two straighter, and this one was swept square to the polar opposite side of the ground. A 180° shift, a nightmare for opposing captain Ricky Ponting. There were still some signs of vulnerability as a decent lbw shout was turned down but Lara's response to the reappearance of McGrath was pure theatre. His first ball was predictably on the spot, pitching on middle and slanting across the left-hander and dangerously Lara found himself on the front foot. But a last-minute adjustment, so indicative of his method, allowed him to stand tall and crash the ball all along the ground through the covers.

When, moments later, at 101-3 the half-century was completed Tony Greig had already seen enough to holler "...that's only the beginning". The momentum had now shifted to such a degree that even the fall of Chanderpaul at 121 was a minor setback as Dwayne Bravo wisely set himself the role of Jimmy Adams – supporting and admiring as his team-mate set about bending the five-man attack to his will. This fifth-wicket partnership saw Lara move into top gear, square driving Lee to the boundary in a manner that reminded Ian Chappell of a mixture of Sobers and Fredericks, before pulling the same bowler to the boundary to complete a memorable century. Shane Warne was quick to recognise an effort of will and talent as he shook Lara's hand before the batsman looked briefly to the sky and mouthed "thank you" to his late father, Bunty.

The final session was a one-man show. With Bravo finally succumbing to MacGill after 95 minutes of resistance and Dwayne Smith following to the same bowler it fell to Denesh Ramdin to support the master who was now in full flow. His first fifty had taken a watchful 92 balls, the next just 52 and the third continued in the same vein. Ponting, with the new ball at his disposal, now brought back his opening bowlers for one last crack and was rewarded with the wicket of Ramdin but at the other end, as Richie Benaud chucklingly observed, the batsman was making the ball look less new as he launched into his supposed nemesis, the fast, short-pitched delivery. Twice Lee was pulled to the leg-side boundary and with the second the double-century was complete and 20,000 people rose to acclaim the achievement. Lara, reflecting on the moment, said "I was ready to bat again and they were still standing and applauding. It's something I will always remember." Two overs later, in the golden evening sunshine, stumps were drawn with the West Indies 352-7 and Lara 202 not out. The crowd had had their money's worth and they knew it.

The press was largely in agreement. Peter English wrote: 'It was not an innings of all-encompassing beauty but it was a fabulous fight back' and Pat Gibson added: 'It was not a work of genius, although genius he has to be, but reward for his dedication to the art of batting.' Both these responses were largely based on the uncertainty of the morning session and the caution of the first half-century. After that Lara scored at almost a run-a-ball, hitting the world's best attack (and a great one by any standards) to all parts with a flair and verve beyond the reach of any of his contemporaries. And all the time he carried the hopes of survival, or even victory, on his shoulders.

On day two, his stay was brief but even during the half hour history was made as Allan Border's record fell and the entire Australian team came forward to congratulate the new champion. His dismissal, 13 runs later, was bizarre – with three wickets still standing he attempted to step away from a good-length ball and smash it through the covers. Even genius can miscalculate and McGrath had his man as the off stump was sent cartwheeling – Lara, by turns bewildered and furious, knew that his 226 was, in all likelihood, not enough.

His suspicions can only have been compounded by the rest of the day's events. Australia galloped to 229-3 by the close, although still 176 adrift. If it hadn't been for the relative strengths of the teams the favourites would still have been the West Indies but with the hosts having now recovered from the first-day mauling there was little doubt which way the punters were leaning. The evening press conferences and following morning's back pages were dominated not by the evenly-balanced Test but the milestone of the world's most prolific Test-match batsman.

On all reasonable reckoning he was now in the twilight of his career and scribes across the world took this golden opportunity to look back at 15 years of sublime batting and the controversies that so often went with it hand-in-hand. In Australia, Allan Border described Lara as a "genuine genius" although rating him as "one of the best three batsmen in the world" was slightly less than giddy praise. Justin Langer, who had been dismissed for 99, was more forthright and witty: "I love watching Lara bat, he's the king…I just wish I could bat like that…If I was Lara I'd have danced down the pitch and whacked it over the top [when on 99] but that's why he's Lara and I'm Langer." The English press got caught up with lazy and inaccurate comparisons with George Best, whose funeral had taken place that day. Drink had effectively destroyed the Irishman's wonderful talent well before his 30th birthday and here was Brian Lara, at 36, playing one of his best ever. But they were both quite small and had a way with the ladies…

However, there was no lack of insightful analysis. Mike Atherton was drawn towards the contrast between the record-breaker and his predecessor:

> 'Border was the epitome of Aussie grit and grind…a man who preferred to camouflage his natural gifts to the demand of team and time…[Lara] is a cricketer whose value has been questioned, whose reputation among team-mates and contemporaries is mixed and whose legacy is, therefore, open to query.'

Like most others, though, Atherton was sure of one thing:

> 'Lara stands for batsmanship at its purest, at its most instinctive. The image of him with his backlift so high…recalls the unfettered batting of a golden age, when attacking instincts dominated and when wristiness and placement mattered more than the size of the muscles and weight of bat.'

Maybe Simon Hughes could have reflected on these words before he opined: 'Lara is not in the league of Sir Vivian Richards.'

Bob Woolmer was entranced not just with the batting craft but also the man: 'He was a lovely bloke to work with, very gentle…an awesome batsman, the best in our era without a shadow of doubt.' Yet there still is and always will be the view of some that Lara somehow damaged cricket in the West Indies despite his achievements with the bat. If he presided over the terminal decline of West Indian cricket it is at least worth bearing in mind that in his debut match he followed Greenidge, Haynes and Richardson to the wicket before taking his place in the slips to Ambrose, Bishop, Marshall and Walsh. His final game, in 2006, was in a vastly inferior team. Had he somehow contributed to this decline or was he the last bastion on which the crumbling edifice somehow weathered storm after storm before being finally torn asunder by forces beyond his control? Trinidadian journalist Vaneisa Baksh expressed the idea that he was caught between two eras:

> 'Lara had been thrown up at this convulsive time in the social order. While his front foot was firmly pointed in the direction of the new, global outlook, his back foot still carried an imprint of the traditional West Indian world…and within this complex role he has often been misunderstood and vilified.'

Back at Adelaide the generosity of the Australians was now at an end with a Test to win. On day three, Mike Hussey's century enabled them to gain a small first-innings lead, and without a major contribution from Lara the West Indies slid to just 204 in their second innings before Matthew Hayden led a comfortable run chase and a seven-wicket win. The result was only what had been expected all along but for two wonderful sessions Brian Lara had stood against the tide of all reason and placed the Australians in the shadows, something he had been doing for over a decade.

A final word from three wise men:

"The scale of his talent was way outside my understanding." – Michael Atherton

"I just wish I could bat like that." – Justin Langer

"He was just in a different world from the likes of me." – Nasser Hussain

West Indies

WW Hinds	c Hayden b Lee	10
DS Smith	c Hayden b Lee	7
RR Sarwan	c Symonds b Lee	16
BC Lara	b McGrath	226
S Chanderpaul*	c †Gilchrist b Symonds	25
DJ Bravo	c Ponting b MacGill	34
DR Smith	c Symonds b MacGill	14
D Ramdin†	lbw b McGrath	27
DBL Powell	lbw b McGrath	14
FH Edwards	c Hayden b Warne	10
CD Collymore	not out	5

Extras (b2, lb5, w1, nb9) **17**
Total (all out; 111.2 overs; 488 mins) **405**

Fall of wickets 1/16 2/19 3/53 4/121 5/237 6/263 7/333 8/381 9/388

Bowling	**O**	**M**	**R**	**W**
GD McGrath	30	3	106	3
B Lee	28	3	111	3
A Symonds	16	5	44	1
SK Warne	19.2	2	77	1
SCG MacGill	18	3	60	2

WW Hinds	st †Gilchrist b Warne	15
DS Smith	c Ponting b Lee	0
RR Sarwan	lbw b Lee	62
DBL Powell	b Warne	2
BC Lara	c Hayden b Warne	17
S Chanderpaul*	c Hodge b Warne	4
DJ Bravo	b Lee	64
DR Smith	lbw b Warne	0
D Ramdin†	c †Gilchrist b Warne	28
FH Edwards	c Warne b Lee	9
CD Collymore	not out	1

Extras (lb2) **2**
Total (all out; 81 overs; 339 mins) **204**

Fall of wickets 1/2 2/60 3/72 4/96 5/96 6/106 7/106 8/160 9/203

Bowling	**O**	**M**	**R**	**W**
GD McGrath	18	8	25	0
B Lee	17	5	46	4
A Symonds	2	0	9	0
SK Warne	33	9	80	6
SCG MacGill	11	2	42	0

Australia

JL Langer	c †Ramdin b Edwards	99
ML Hayden	c Chanderpaul b Bravo	47
RT Ponting*	lbw b Bravo	56
BJ Hodge	lbw b Edwards	18
MEK Hussey	not out	133
A Symonds	b Bravo	9
AC Gilchrist†	c Chanderpaul b Bravo	6
SK Warne	c & b Bravo	0
B Lee	c †Ramdin b Bravo	9
SCG MacGill	b Edwards	22
GD McGrath	b DR Smith	5

Extras (lb7, w2, nb15) **24**
Total (all out; 123.3 overs; 573 mins) **428**

Fall of wickets 1/97 2/2111 3/228 4/238 5/271 6/277 7/277 8/295 9/388

Bowling	**O**	**M**	**R**	**W**
FH Edwards	23	4	114	3
DBL Powell	24	6	80	0
CD Collymore	23	1	59	0
DJ Bravo	27	7	84	6
DR Smith	17.3	3	59	1
WW Hinds	9	1	25	0

JL Langer	c DR Smith b Collymore	20
ML Hayden	not out	87
RT Ponting*	c Sarwan b Collymore	3
BJ Hodge	c DR Smith b Powell	23
MEK Hussey	not out	30

Did not bat A Symonds, AC Gilchrist†, SK Warne, B Lee, SCG MacGill, GD McGrath

Extras (lb3, w1, nb15) **19**
Total (3 wickets; 58 overs; 261 mins) **182**

Fall of wickets 1/51 2/55 3/110

Bowling	**O**	**M**	**R**	**W**
FH Edwards	11	1	52	0
DBL Powell	14	2	40	1
CD Collymore	20	6	51	2
RR Sarwan	12	2	35	0
DR Smith	1	0	1	0

Gordon Greenidge – 226

West Indies v Australia, Bridgetown 19-24 April 1991

12

-Daniel Harris-

Cuthbert Gordon Greenidge. Cuthbert Gordon Greenidge. How could you possibly be called Cuthbert Gordon Greenidge and not be a brilliant bastard? You could not possibly be called Cuthbert Gordon Greenidge and not be a brilliant bastard. It is scientifically, biologically, psychologically impossible to be called Cuthbert Gordon Greenidge and not be a brilliant bastard. Cuthbert Gordon Greenidge was a brilliant, brilliant bastard.

Most viscerally striking was the speed and power of his bat, imparted via a pair of forearms fashioned from elasticated rope, but the apparatus that underpinned them was equally important: dancer's feet, and an eye that could curdle curd. Or put another way, within him coalesced the aspects of timing and technique that define batsmanship. The vast majority of sportsmen are left with little choice as regards how to play, serfs to their talent, but the very best are able to do so as they want, impressing personality upon ability. Greenidge was such a type.

The bastardliness was more complex. Like so many of the best cricketers, sportsmen and anythings, he was cocky, aggressive and could bear a grudge, admired and criticised for the very same characteristics. Some of this was innate, some of it inculcated and some of it learned.

When he was 14, his family left Barbados for England, during a period that saw the island's population reduced by a third. His experience was not an especially happy one, and he returned after resolving to become a cricketer, picked to make his Test debut in 1974 at Bangalore – along with one IVA Richards. The chatter before the match concerned how a rain-affected strip might assist the Indian spinners, but in the event, West Indies won by 267 runs. Greenidge was run out for 93 in the first innings and made 107 in the second.

But the effort that defined him, or at least announced him as more than simply a very good player, came at Lord's in 1984. One-up after the first Test, West Indies were on the back foot in the second, England declaring early on the fifth day to set a victory target of 342. Incredibly, it was reached for the loss of just one wicket and in only 66.1 overs, thanks principally to the controlled violence of Greenidge. Out of form at the time – his average for the tour was just 14.17 – and batting with an injured leg, he was forced to score mainly in boundaries, slaughtering 29 fours and two sixes in his 214 not out. "Every little bit of power you could imagine going into that stroke", marvelled Richie Benaud after one particularly vicious straight drive.

Though West Indies had by then been the best team in the world for a few years, Greenidge's innings ported them into a different domain. Dominating and consistent victories are one thing, seemingly impossible victories something else entirely, and the preserve of the very finest; a self-fulfilling, self-perpetuating prophecy that endures even when in all apparent terms, the ability that first created it has expired.

And few teams have carried similar aura, their strength grounded not just in cricket but in attitude. Genuinely representative of newly independent and confident islands gathered together for nothing else, they enhanced and inspired an identity and pride, their significance extending far beyond simple affiliation to a sports team based on coincidence of residence, and proudly proclaiming a shared history and suffering.

The notion that international competition – the battle between one arbitrary, bordered landmass and another – is not political, is a fatuous notion. But even in that context, cricket is different, its fierceness of a different order to that in almost every other sport. The story of the game is the story of civilisation, its old rivalries based on more than simple you and me, us and them dichotomies, its various antipathies rooted not in sport but actual, real things, a narrative with a genuine moral dimension.

So against England, Greenidge had unleashed the rage of generations. 'All those years of hurt now have to be put in focus', he explained.

> 'My anger came up in the way I played. I felt that to forcefully go at what I was doing, to attack, perhaps was a way of letting out that anger. It wouldn't be right to do that on another human being, although it felt like it at times, but I'm sure gonna take it out on five and a half ounces, so I took it out on the ball.'

And from December 1984 onwards, West Indies were led not by the measured Clive Lloyd, but by Viv Richards, a man who put the ire into fire, the ow into power and the fucking fury into fucking fury. "Some of them really look at you out there like you should be hunted", he said. "But I can tell you, no man is going to hunt me in this day and age. I take up the pursuing first."

And no side was pursued with greater alacrity than Australia. The last of the cricketing nations to disengage with apartheid South Africa and only then following protests against a planned rugby tour, its sporting establishment had also projected intense outrage at the role of Peter Norman in the black power salute given by Tommie Smith and John Carlos at the 1968 Olympics – an event that meant a lot to many in the West Indies team.

But it was personal, too – with Richards and Greenidge, the political always was, but in this instance, specifically so. Touring Australia in 1975-76, the abuse the players had received from the crowd was distressing and formative. 'Being bombarded by comments and behaviour, well, I'd encountered some ignorance before, but this was very different, very very different...it degraded me and downgraded me a great deal', said Greenidge.

The next series between the sides was in 1977-78, and during it, Bobby Simpson, the Australian captain, traversed Richards' pectorals to considerable degree, particularly in his behaviour towards umpires. Then, in later years, and particularly after being appointed coach, he was one of the most outspoken critics of West Indian methods, a carping that came with vocabulary – brutal, wild, dangerous – to which was imputed a racial dimension.

This brought matters to a pitch before the two sides met in 1991, contesting what some were calling the 'World Championship Series'. Before it, Simpson suggested that West Indies' batting was brittle and accused them of intimidating umpires and deliberately slow over-rates – what was termed 'a professional foul' – and so, towards its end, Richards would wade into him in grand style. "Bobby Simpson and other individuals were shouting their mouths off", he told the press. "I never shouted my mouth off. I dismiss anything that Simpson says. He is a moaner and bad loser. He is a very sour sort of guy. Bobby Simpson ain't our cup of tea at all."

But there was plenty that had to happen prior to then, in one of the most eventful contests of all-time. Though West Indies were unbeaten in 10 years, Australia had reason to believe; in the summer of 1989, they had filleted England who'd then travelled to the Caribbean and competed for the first time in a generation. The team was still some way from achieving the implacably confident lunacy that became its hallmark, but nevertheless boasted a collection of bristling, bustling larrikins: men like Allan Border, David Boon, Merv Hughes, Dean Jones, Craig McDermott and the Waughs. And while their unique brand of psychicide also remained in development, it went down exceptionally badly with their hosts. The insults began during the one-day rubber that preceded the Tests, and in Guyana, Mark Waugh directed Desmond Haynes hutchwards with some choice invective following a marginal lbw decision. Then, during the Australian innings, the ball sneaked out of Phil Simmons' hand before he intended, Border stepping down the pitch to whack it for four. This led to the two captains exchanging language at volume, during tea.

Australia took the one-day series 4-1 but it was when the Tests began that things became really serious, the series pulsating with every aspect of spontaneous narrative that makes sport the most compelling of all human inventions, simultaneously buddy movie and biopic, drama and fantasy, epic and documentary.

The first Test in Jamaica, was drawn, Australia irate at a missed an opportunity and also at the rudimentary covers that elongated the various rain delays. Though West Indies never felt in contemplation of defeat, their selectors were concerned, informing Richards of a plan to drop Jeff Dujon, Malcolm Marshall – and Greenidge. "He has been hit on the head" said one, when challenged. "Haven't we all", came back the rejoinder, but it failed to convince. "He is not picking up the ball…He's finished", said another, "He's lost it", agreed a third. But Richards, convinced that it was personal, protected his man – who had passed 50 just once in the previous two years.

So the team for the Guyana Test was unchanged. During the one-day series, a vex crowd had supported the tourists, the country's predominantly East Indian population taking exception to Richards' assertion that his team was an African one. But a clarification meant that things were back to normal by the time the players returned, and a near run-a-minute partnership of 297 between Haynes and Richie Richardson helped West Indies to a first-innings lead in excess of 200, parlayed into a ten-wicket victory. The match was a personal triumph for Richards; Marshall took three wickets in each innings and Dujon a total of seven catches. However, with West Indies requiring just 31 to win, and while Haynes swiped 23 off 27 balls, Greenidge could only finagle five off 21.

But this was not all that happened; of course this was not all that happened. During Australia's second innings, Courtney Walsh – who, playing for Jamaica earlier in the tour, had hit both Mark Waugh and McDermott – bowled Dean Jones, who amongst the fuss, failed to hear the call of no-ball. By which time Carl Hooper had dashed across from gully, uprooted middle stump, and begun a celebration as the square-leg umpire raised a finger, ignorant of the law stipulating that a batsman could not be run out without attempting a run.

West Indies felt not the remotest guilt, convinced that Australia would have done the same, and when Jones was asked as much, he smirked and said that he did not respond to hypothetical questions. He then approached Richards to offer his congratulations, only to be shocked by the stunted nature of the shrift with which he was presented. "After being abused by a guy," Richards later explained, "you don't expect him to come over and say, 'How are you doing? You want a Toohey's?' You don't do things like that. When I draw the sword, I draw the sword. When I draw it, that's it."

The confrontation crystallised the crux of the conflict. For West Indies, respect was absolute, essential, and indivisible; they relied on presence and deed to achieve the required intimidation. "They didn't talk at you, but more across you," said Mark Waugh. "Things like 'Come on Amby, he's your meat. Get him on the step-ladder,' meaning dig in the short balls." Australia, on the other hand, considered respect a fluid notion, largely irrelevant in the course of competition and most likely to take the form of disrespect, the aim distraction by provocation; a life untainted by bigotry facilitated levity and perspective, sport treated simply as sport.

After the Trinidad Test was ruined by rain, the teams moved to Bridgetown, another packed crowd announcing its allegiance in a din of horns and improvised drums. Traditionally where West Indies bowlers were at their most sphincter-looseningly fearsome, Border decided that he required just three frontline quicks, supplemented by his own spin and the Waughs' trundlers, assessing the pitch as one that gave them a decent chance of winning. "Like a good Gabba or Adelaide Oval wicket," he declared, "with predictable bounce and good pace."

But the principal focus of attention was Cuthbert Gordon Greenidge, playing on his home ground, where he had scored just one Test century in 21 innings. He was also just a couple of weeks shy of his 40th birthday, the best known on the island – "Gordon, he over de ropes, man," was reported by the London *Daily Telegraph* as the refrain amongst the locals.

Australia won the toss and elected to field, the 10th team in a row so to do – though the method had delivered victory only for West Indies. But given their line-up, they had no choice, needing the benefit of whatever juice was in the pitch, and they used it well. McDermott made the first incision, tempting Greenidge to hook directly to Bruce Reid at long leg with the score on 17, after which wickets fell constantly.

And – of course – there was additional beef. With the score on 22-3, McDermott swung a ball away from Haynes, who removed his bat from its path – but it caught his shirt on the way through. Behind the stumps, Ian Healy went up for the catch without really meaning it, so Haynes indicated what had happened, Healy explicit in informing him of the extent to which this was not his place. But Haynes was in Barbados, 'my home, in front of my people', which 'made it harder to take and easier to snap back'. Accordingly, he didn't take it and snapped back, theatrically flinging off his helmet and brandishing his bat behind his head, suggesting that they reconvene at close of play in order to perpetrate violence. Healy blew him a kiss, then Boon refused to clear a speck of dirt from his eye prior to the next ball.

The kerfuffle elicited particular kerfuffle because the series was the first between the sides to be transmitted from the islands to a worldwide audience; even as early as 1991, the global pandemic of remote offence-taking had begun its creep. Haynes was dismissed soon afterwards for 28 and West Indies for 149 in just 61.1 overs.

But for any side facing them, there was a downside – and trepidation – that a pitch offering help to its bowlers would do the same for their better ones. In the space of just six overs, Taylor was out lbw after a delivery from Ambrose kept low, then Ambrose broke Border's finger – he would not field in West Indies' second innings – and Jones was also forced to seek medical attention. When Marshall bowled Border with a grass-cutter, the impression was of a pitch misbehaving, and Australia were decimated for 134, their last seven wickets mustering a measly 39 runs.

So it was the second afternoon when West Indies came out to begin their second innings, Greenidge not so much fighting for his place – he didn't have long left, whatever happened

– but for dignity and pride. And he was seriously feeling the pressure. There is perhaps no examination in sport more exacting than opening the batting in Test cricket, certainly none more extensive and probing. The Tour de France might be harder, but is repetitive and principally a suffering competition, most of those involved simply trying to finish. Fighting is more obviously dangerous, but lasts a maximum of 33 minutes, tennis more physically arduous, but without the variety of opponents and frisson of harm. Opening the batting, on the other hand, demands from every faculty, physical and mental, that a sportsman can possibly be forced to employ: speed, skill, strength, bravery, application, instinct, intellect and improvisation.

The first ball of the innings was an obliging one, McDermott straying onto the pads and Greenidge turning it down towards the fence at square-leg. Hughes then garnished the error by galumphing into a misfield, which went down exceptionally well with the exceptionally proximate locals – in particular a dancing man with a long, inflatable banana, able to lean over and wave it about his ears.

Steadily, Greenidge settled in, taking the score to 30 before beating a booming drive through extra-cover off the bowling of Reid. Gradually, he widened his array of strokes, introducing his trademark drives and pulls, the glorious thwack of leather on willow suddenly more frightening than comforting. But though his batting was fuelled by anger, never did it manifest in indulgent, self-defeating explosion, rather a calculating, focused, rolling boil. Consequently, if a ball could be hit, it was annihilated, but if it couldn't, then it wasn't; there was no compulsive flailing. Replete with arrogance, devoid of ego, his shot selection showcased the beautiful side of discrimination.

And he was discriminating hard against Reid, hooking a low bouncer to the boundary – precisely the shot that had got him out in the first innings. But this time he was well on top of the ball, the sign an ominous one: Australia had only three real bowlers and no captain. In the circumstances, they needed all the help that they could get, and appealed confidently when a Hughes inswinger clattered Greenidge on the inside of his front pad, below the knee-roll. But the umpire had seen an inside-edge, and adjudged him not out.

With Steve Waugh already involved, the Australian attack must surely have been feeling its impending destruction, but the manner in which Greenidge raised his fifty ought to have triggered thoughts of a despisèd life. First, a power-tuck to the mid-wicket boundary sent Jones, the team's fastest fielder, thudding against the hoarding in deepest futility, and then the landmark was greeted with the most cursory of bat raises. This was not over, not by a long way.

The hundred partnership came via a deft flick to fine-leg, Greenidge by now in complete control of his skills. This was illustrated in particular by a drive to the cover boundary off Mark Waugh, the apparently dainty execution belied by a resonant knuck and the speed at which the ball disappeared. He finished the day 85 not out, joined in the middle by Malcolm Marshall when Haynes was caught behind for 40.

And Marshall's dismissal early the following morning only brought Richie Richardson to the crease, who quickly unfurled the more relaxed and unburdened sadism of the younger generation. Not a man to drop twice, Australia dropped him twice, and he set about administering due punishment, his timing exquisite and square-drive causing particular devastation.

At the other end, Greenidge accumulated more slowly, determined to take maximum advantage of the form that he'd somehow manufactured. With his score on 93, he hopped to hammer a short one from McDermott straight to Steve Waugh at cover-point, the bowler sufficiently demoralised to consider this a victory, disbursing various verbals. Greenidge, of course, responded, seeming to issue a threat via finger-pointing, McDermott seeming to respond by ironically intimating fear. And the patter continued when Hughes again beat the bat with an inswinger, this time hitting even lower on the pad and with Greenidge even further over in front of the stumps. But again, the appeal was rejected, the two men sarcastically clapping one another after a subsequent ball was met with a perfect forward-defensive shot.

Greenidge then continued as before, reaching his century with an almighty cover-drive off McDermott for another four, and again, despite the jubilation in the crowd, there was neither fist-pumping nor bat-waving; this was not over, not by a long way. Even when Richardson came down the pitch to offer congratulation, leading with a handshake but hankering after a hug, the focus remained, Greenidge turning away to ensure that there would be only a brief touch of gloves.

In quick time the score motored towards 200, an irate McDermott persuaded to bang one in short. Greenidge responded with a one-legged pirouette, but not to play a pull; instead, somehow keeping his bat straight and adding a flourish both overstated and necessary, the ball steamed to the square-leg boundary once again.

At 220-2, Australia's last chance to avert a massacre: the second new ball. An hour later, it was a scuffed, dull mess, their bowlers savaged for 40 in five overs and 85 in 12. The 23 overs between lunch and tea yielded 124 runs.

Running out of options, Reid had a go from around the wicket, clunking in like a human-shaped ironing board. So Greenidge clouted him through extra-cover, exaggerated backlift flowing into a drive and following through into a whipcurl, then swatted the next one, delivered fuller, to long-off for four more. He was seeing it.

And he was also approaching satisfaction, arriving at 150 with a drive taken from outside off stump to long-on, for three. This time the bat was fluttered – now it was a proper innings, and it was he who had compiled it. Then another landmark, West

Indies' 300, achieved by way of straight-drive – "a bit of variety" explained Michael Holding's laconic commentary.

Greenidge was really drubbing it in now, abusing another shot through the covers, before a flagellation through mid-wicket brought up his 200 – he became the third-oldest man to reach the landmark, behind Jack Hobbs and Patsy Hendren. The hint of a smile playing across his moustache, he pointedly pointed towards the pavilion, and the only men who hadn't doubted him. His fourth Test double-century had taken 563 minutes and 402 balls – almost twice as long as his first – and was furnished with 30 fours.

Then, after two more boundaries – one a murderous crack to square-leg – he played across a ball from Hughes, trying to swish to leg from off, and missing when it kept a little low. Finally, he was given out lbw, but given the 226 runs he'd accumulated it seemed more like an act of sarcasm than a genuine dismissal, West Indies' lead now a match-winning 469.

On his way off, Greenidge removed his helmet, looking dapper even in headband and the sweat of more than 11 hours at the crease, pausing to acknowledge all sides of the ground; it was over and he made sure everyone knew it. Throughout his career he batted for the cause, but this one was for him, his highest Test score, in his penultimate Test match, to clinch a series; less dead cat bounce, more resuscitated lion vault. The brilliant bastard.

West Indies

Batsman	Dismissal	Runs
CG Greenidge	c Reid b McDermott	10
DL Haynes	c ME Waugh b Hughes	28
RB Richardson	c Boon b McDermott	1
CL Hooper	c Jones b Hughes	0
IVA Richards*	c Hughes b McDermott	32
AL Logie	c Taylor b Reid	11
PJL Dujon†	c †Healy b Hughes	10
MD Marshall	c Marsh b Reid	17
CEL Ambrose	not out	19
CA Walsh	c ME Waugh b McDermott	10
BP Patterson	c ME Waugh b Hughes	1

Extras (lb3, nb7) 10
Total (all out; 61.1 overs; 279 mins) 149

Fall of wickets 1/17 2/21 3/22 4/72 5/89 6/96 7/103 8/125 9/148

Bowling	O	M	R	W
CJ McDermott	22	6	49	4
BA Reid	21	8	50	2
MG Hughes	16.1	2	44	4
SR Waugh	2	0	3	0

Batsman	Dismissal	Runs
CG Greenidge	lbw b Hughes	226
DL Haynes	c †Healy b ME Waugh	40
MD Marshall	c †Healy b McDermott	15
RB Richardson	lbw b ME Waugh	99
CL Hooper	c †Healy b ME Waugh	57
IVA Richards*	lbw b ME Waugh	25
AL Logie	not out	33
PJL Dujon†	c ME Waugh b McDermott	4
CEL Ambrose	b Reid	2
CA Walsh	c Marsh b Reid	0
BP Patterson	not out	4

Extras (lb19, nb12) 31
Total (9 wckts dec; 162.3 overs; 766 mins) 536

Fall of wickets 1/129 2/153 3/352 4/454 5/470 6/512 7/522 8/525 9/525

Bowling	O	M	R	W
CJ McDermott	37.3	8	130	2
BA Reid	30	4	100	2
MG Hughes	36	6	125	1
SR Waugh	28	6	77	0
ME Waugh	28	6	80	4
DM Jones	3	1	5	0

Australia

Batsman	Dismissal	Runs
MA Taylor	lbw b Ambrose	26
GR Marsh	c Logie b Ambrose	12
DC Boon	c Hooper b Marshall	0
AR Border*	b Marshall	29
DM Jones	lbw b Marshall	22
ME Waugh	not out	20
SR Waugh	c †Dujon b Patterson	2
IA Healy†	c †Dujon b Walsh	2
MG Hughes	c Logie b Walsh	3
CJ McDermott	b Walsh	2
BA Reid	b Walsh	0

Extras (lb2, nb14) 16
Total (all out; 50.1 overs; 257 mins) 134

Fall of wickets 1/24 2/27 3/59 4/95 5/97 6/100 7/106 8/121 9/127

Bowling	O	M	R	W
CEL Ambrose	16	5	36	2
BP Patterson	13	6	22	1
MD Marshall	16	1	60	3
CA Walsh	5.1	1	14	4

Batsman	Dismissal	Runs
GR Marsh	lbw b Ambrose	0
MA Taylor	lbw b Marshall	76
DC Boon	b Ambrose	57
AR Border*	c †Dujon b Ambrose	0
MG Hughes	c †Dujon b Marshall	3
DM Jones	b Hooper	37
ME Waugh	b Hooper	3
SR Waugh	not out	4
IA Healy†	lbw b Marshall	0
CJ McDermott	c sub (RIC Holder) b Walsh	2
BA Reid	b Walsh	0

Extras (b3, lb5, nb18) 26
Total (all out; 87.2 overs; 383 mins) 208

Fall of wickets 1/0 2/111 3/111 4/122 5/190 6/200 7/200 8/200 9/208

Bowling	O	M	R	W
CEL Ambrose	19	7	36	3
BP Patterson	15	3	56	0
CA Walsh	14.2	4	37	2
MD Marshall	17	4	35	3
CL Hooper	19	4	28	2
IVA Richards	3	0	8	0

Neil Harvey – 151*

South Africa v Australia, Durban 20-24 January 1950

-David Frith-

When contributing to a book on cricket heroes long ago I had selection difficulties. Some favourites were English, some Australian. My incontinent plea was to be allowed to write about two players. Permission granted. From that cluster of candidates emerged Ray Lindwall and Neil Harvey.

Now it's time to focus on Harvey again, and on one performance in particular. So many of his Test innings were outstanding. He often triumphed in adversity, on awkward, unprotected pitches against bowlers who knew how to exploit them. His woes against Tony Lock and Jim Laker in 1956 were a bitter exception.

I first set eyes on Robert Neil Harvey on January 8, 1951, my first day at a Test match. The elegant Sydney ground was packed, and Harvey's 39 (bowled by Alec Bedser) was overshadowed by Keith Miller's 96 not out. But the boyish left-hander was to win us youngsters over with 190 in the Sydney Test against South Africa early in 1953 and with Shield centuries, before, to our delight, switching to New South Wales in 1958-59. His quest for a steady job in an era when there were no riches in cricket seemed never-ending.

Neil Harvey was regarded as the world's premier batsman during those years. He made 834 enchanting runs against South Africa in the Australian summer of 1952-53, leaving people wondering if there could ever have been smarter footwork, more pleasing strokeplay, or a better eye – despite the fact that an optometrist later disclosed that his long vision was defective.

There was a further, rather crazy reason why Neil was my dream batsman. In the 1950s, pop music was innocent and melodic. Top among the vocalists who escorted me through my youth was little Guy Mitchell. That plaintive, joyous, carefree voice gave us *Truly Fair* and *My Heart Cries for You*, crystal-clear melodies that lifted and sustained anxious teenagers, exactly as did Neil Harvey's dainty batsmanship. Neil was a study in cream: no commercial logos then (least of all affixed to the white boundary pickets or splattered even more intrusively across the sacred turf), just a clean bat wielded by a young chap with shirt-sleeves rolled high, pads gleaming white, dark hair unencumbered by cap or sunhat (let alone helmet), head slightly tilted as he walked.

Consequently, whenever I watched Harvey play, a Guy Mitchell song would float through my head. And whenever I listened to those 78rpm records at home, they sparked visions of Neil Harvey at the crease. So I've now confessed to a modern readership. And if that portrays the young me as a dreamer, anchored securely in a world of innocence and joy, so be it. Despite all the tensions and crises that life has thrown up, little has changed. I owe a lot to Neil Harvey.

Matters became complicated in the 1960s. I had made it into Paddington's first team. Sydney's district grade clubs fielded past or present Test players in those days. We were to play Gordon at Chatswood Oval. There was a nice link here with Victor Trumper, who had played his early seasons with Paddington – my club now – with home matches at Trumper Park, which was a further cause for young Frith to go weak at the knees whenever he played there, treading the same splintery floorboards of the same old wooden pavilion used by the legendary Victor. But Trumper finished his short life elsewhere: here with Gordon. Charlie Macartney also used to play here, often tonking the bowling onto the railway embankment.

Trumper and Macartney were dead, although I'd had a quick, treasured handshake with the latter in Bert Oldfield's shop just in time. Beyond these ghostly associations there was a pressing reason to lose sleep that Friday night, for tomorrow I would be sharing a cricket field with Neil Harvey! I don't like exclamation marks as a rule, but this one's unavoidable. Playing against Neil Harvey! I'd read Arthur Mailey's poignant essay about playing against his hero, Vic Trumper. If I'd earlier found Mailey's near-hysterical countdown a bit over the top, I didn't think so now. So, God, please don't let it rain.

I'll keep it brief. Harvey back-cut a ball, which I chased. Picking it up near the pickets, I gazed at it. Gosh, this ball had just been stroked by Neil Harvey! Our wicket-keeper was screaming, "Come on, Frithy! Throw the bloody thing in!" I did, shamefaced at the silly delay. Then our off-spinner annoyingly dismissed Neil for 10.

On the second Saturday I got in. *ABC* Radio were experimenting with live broadcasts from grade matches. My old scrapbook shows that I scored 29 in 100 minutes, a dreary effort that may well have been solely responsible for the abandonment of the commentary idea. What must Neil Harvey have thought? What really matters, though, is how my precious innings ended. Harvey bowled a curving off spinner outside leg. I tried to glance it, but that ball was loaded. It swerved, what, two feet? Well, two or three inches anyway. Maybe there's something wrong with me, but I left that field slightly elated.

A few weeks later Neil Harvey was charming 154 off England's attack of Trueman, Statham, Illingworth and Titmus, adding 194 with my former Under-16 captain Norm O'Neill. It was clearly time to abandon all ambition of ever playing Test cricket and concentrate instead on becoming a cricket scribbler.

That encounter with Harvey at Chatswood Oval came 13 years after he had played perhaps the finest and most dramatic of all his Test innings, the one now under review. It was in an age when the images could not be secured in high-definition colour on a television recording for posterity. There are a few brief descriptions in books and magazines, and a short sequence of grey long shots in a newsreel, retrieved for a video history of South African Test cricket. In that programme, made long after Harvey had retired, he was asked if this Durban knock of 151 not out was the best of all his innings (he made 21 hundreds in his 79 Tests). "Yeah, absolutely", he replied.

Neil Harvey had entered Test cricket in 1947-48, against India, scoring 153 in his second Test, at Melbourne, his home ground, when symbolically Don Bradman played his last Test innings in Australia. Neil was only 19 years and 121 days old, becoming the youngest Australian Test centurion. Soon he was in England, where he had to wait until the fourth Test, at Headingley. There he stroked 112 on Ashes debut to keep Australia in the match, shepherded initially by Keith Miller then encouraged by another fellow Melburnian, six-hitting Sam Loxton.

Years later Loxton told me of his paternal feelings towards young Harvey:

> "Harv never got any advice from The Don, and consequently ended up believing that Don didn't totally believe in him. Many years later I asked Don about it. He said he'd only ever thought of making one suggestion: not to step back and cut but to play more safely through square cover with a straight bat. But he refrained from offering this suggestion because he didn't want to deprive hundreds of thousands of spectators of the great pleasure Harvey's shot gave – and of third-man running round and gathering the ball out of the gutter! I passed this on to Harv, and his feet didn't touch the ground for three weeks!"

Next, Australia were in South Africa for the five-Test series of 1949-50. It was to be another emphatic Australian triumph, though not before the high drama at Kingsmead, Durban in the third Test match had been resolved. The tourists had won the first two Tests, Harvey, batting at No.5, making a modest 34 at Ellis Park, Johannesburg (his 'elder brother' Loxton 101, captain Lindsay Hassett 112); then a superb 178 to set up the Cape Town victory. Sixteen days later the teams assembled in Durban to contest what turned out to be one of the most bizarre of matches.

Harvey had already made a neat century at Kingsmead in a preliminary match but this time the circumstances could hardly have been more different. South Africa's solid 311 was built around the tempestuous 40-year-old Eric Rowan's 143 (6½ hours) and 39-year-old skipper Dudley Nourse's 66 in almost four hours. It might have been more, with the home side 240 for 2 after the first day. But overnight rain rendered the pitch highly responsive to spin. South Africa had to bat on, hoping that Australia might be bowled out cheaply enough to allow for a follow-on (200-run deficit). The home side had no desire to bat a second time on this treacherous surface, while Australia, with no wish to bat just yet, wanted Nourse's men to occupy the crease for as long as possible. But even with the field scattered and key catching positions vacant and then refraining from taking the new ball when it was available, there are limits as to how far conspiring bowlers and fieldsmen can go in their subtle efforts to keep their opponents at the crease. Batting became more difficult the longer play went on, and later consensus indicated that South Africa should have declared. This cricket match truly was 'chess on grass'.

The start of that second day had been delayed 45 minutes. Nourse eagerly wore flannels at the pitch inspection. Hassett was pointedly and persuasively still in his civilian suit. After the second inspection, the umpires felt obliged to order a resumption, and the hazards posed by this rain-damaged surface were soon apparent. The hosts lost their remaining eight wickets for 71 runs, notwithstanding two dropped catches.

Arthur Morris (25 in 87 minutes, with one four) and Jack Moroney (10 in an hour) now agonisingly posted 31 for the first wicket in Australia's reply, with alert onlookers urging Nourse to bring on his spinners in place of fast men Cuan McCarthy and John Watkins. Ten wickets then crashed for 44. Hassett juggled the batting order: Harvey (two off 10 balls, caught brilliantly by bowler Hugh Tayfield) was held back to No.9, and Loxton (16) to No.10. It made no difference. On a pitch utterly in favour of South Africa's spinners Norman 'Tufty' Mann (left-arm) and Tayfield (off-spin), Australia were helpless. Mann, bespectacled and so recently an Allied prisoner-of-war on the run in Italy, had lost a little of his control since the 1947 tour of England, but still finished with 3 for 31. Tayfield, slim, square-shouldered and with surly dark-ringed eyes, bagged 7 for 23, sending the innings into free-fall by trapping Ian Johnson, Miller and Hassett all in one over. The ghoulish wondered if absent off-spinner Athol Rowan might have been even deadlier. Laid up with a serious knee injury, Eric Rowan's brother had taken a spectacular 9 for 19 (15 for 68 in the match) for Transvaal in the Australians' match at The Wanderers just over five weeks earlier. It was clear that Hassett's men were vulnerable against spin on responsive pitches.

None of the 17,000 spectators who witnessed this extraordinary Saturday's play would ever forget it. And there was much more drama still to come in this classic tactical battle. Australia's last wicket had fallen neatly at the close of the second day. There was now a Sunday of rest so South Africa's skipper Nourse had plenty of time to decide whether to enforce the follow-on. "A lot of criticism was levelled at him," seamer John Watkins later recalled. "I went with him to the Met Office and he was assured it was going to rain." That's what persuaded Nourse to bat again. "It turned out to be the wrong decision," Watkins reflected, "but it's easy to back the right horse after the race is over."

Hassett's strategy continued to rest on buying time. He wanted South Africa to bat as long as possible. In that oddly deep and earthy voice of his, Australia's whimsical little skipper, for a second time in the match, instructed his bowlers to keep it tight without taking wickets. He wanted South Africa to use up as many hours as possible. Whether the pitch would ease later was a matter for conjecture. Catches were to be missed only with the greatest subtlety.

Notwithstanding Australia's cunning, South Africa made only 99, the last eight wickets crashing for 14 runs. The situation would have been laughable had it not been so tense. Left-armer Bill Johnston took 4 for 39, off-spinner Ian Johnson 5 for 34 with his crooked elbow and brave flight, as the Springboks nervously extended their hefty first-innings lead of 236. Owen Wynne's 29 took 70 minutes, Jack Nel's 20 more than two hours, and Dudley Nourse's 27 lasted just over 90 minutes, his first 10 runs coming in singles. Had the Springbok skipper listened to pre-war player Cyril Vincent, who, from the members' enclosure, had spotted Australia's tactical ploy of just rolling their arms over, he would have closed earlier and got Australia in while the pitch was still very nasty. Hassett even persuaded the umpires to recall Nel after he was run out, saying that he had accidentally impeded the batsman.

This still left Australia needing a seemingly impossible 336 to win on a pockmarked surface. South Africa's first Test victory against Australia for 39 years was there for the taking. And the run-rate remained turgid on this surface made for bowlers: Arthur Morris took 2½ hours to score 44, Jack Moroney 45 minutes for 10, Keith Miller 19 minutes for 10, Lindsay Hassett 43 minutes for 11 as four wickets fell for 95 to spinners Mann and Tayfield. The home side's long-awaited victory was close at hand.

Yet one figure stood out. Neil Harvey, in at 59 for 3, had been batting steadily, elegantly, as if at work on another pitch entirely. Footwork was the key, together with an unusual calmness of demeanour. Years later his skipper, Hassett, reflected on the blossoming of his left-handed fellow Victorian, who had turned 21 earlier in the tour: "It was the first time he'd ever had a drink in his life, and he had a few glasses of champagne, and he reacted the way most people do." On the tour overall:

> "His form was tremendous. Match after match he hit the ball in the middle of the bat. Neil had all the strokes, a good driver, beautiful puller of the ball, never hooked it very high in the air but used to keep the ball down."

Years later Harvey himself recalled that the Kingsmead pitch "was full of divots, ball marks, and was a real turner, and it wasn't just because it was unplayable that we were concerned, it was because they had as good a pair of spinners as any in the game." Someone else wrote colourfully that the pitch looked as if a herd of wildebeest had spent the night on it. Perhaps the young batsman was sustained by memories of the cobblestone lane in the Melbourne industrial suburb of Fitzroy where he learned the game with his five brothers in conditions distinctly alien to batsmen.

Close of play on the third day saw Australia 80 for 3, still wanting a faraway 256 more for victory, Morris 35, Harvey 12, one day of the four remaining. That stand was soon broken on the final morning when Morris fell to Tayfield. Six wickets remained with 241 runs still needed as tour room-mate Sam Loxton joined Harvey. The younger man recalled his cocksure mate barking: "We'll win this match!" Harvey also remembered his own determination to continue to play his natural game: "When we resumed on the final morning we neither played for a draw nor a win. We just treated each ball on its merits." That's often more easily said than done. "Time was the least of our worries," he said, "and I did not forget to hit the bad ball."

Against eager South African expectations, on an oppressively hot and humid day, the Australians gradually turned the match. A catch went down. Nourse tried for a breakthrough with a new ball. Tayfield and Mann had merely looked like taking wickets for just too long. Billy Wade (another ex-PoW) still seemed bemused years later as he recalled the escapes Harvey had against Mann: "Tufty must have morally bowled him half-a-dozen times. The ball just went over the top!" Harvey acknowledged his luck:

> "I can still see Tufty Mann midway through my innings. Perfectly pitched off-break to me. I just sort of prodded at it. As soon as I missed it, I thought: that's going to hit the stumps for sure. Billy Wade was keeping wicket and he must have got as big a shock as I did, and he put his hands up and the ball went for three byes."

The priceless Harvey-Loxton stand lasted 166 minutes and amounted to 135, Loxton having survived a stumping chance at 16 and a catch at 31. But with Loxton now bowled by Mann for 54 (166 minutes), five top wickets had gone. The pitch remained capricious, and 106 runs were still needed as former commando Colin McCool strode to the crease. With Harvey's century now up on the board after he'd placed Tayfield to mid-wicket for two, the pair pressed on for victory. The momentum was back with Australia. With little batting to come, the sixth-wicket pair pressed on to victory as the frustrated South Africans watched, the wily McCool cautioning his young partner against carelessness. Time was just on their side. McCool, unfamiliar with such a damaged pitch as this, later considered his own unbeaten 39 (111 minutes) one of his top innings.

Bareheaded as ever, shirt unbuttoned to the breastbone, Neil Harvey clipped Mann to leg and trotted the two which won an amazing match for Australia with 25 minutes to spare, while the frustrated home players scrambled for souvenir stumps. The young Victorian's unbeaten and chanceless 151, his longest innings to date, had come in 325 minutes, with 14 fours. "I had some good allies", he remarked, with typical self-effacement.

Thus the series was won. He made four centuries all told, and another four in the return rubber in 1952-53. He even married a South African girl. A tree planted at Kingsmead in honour of this monumental innings was felled when the inevitable redevelopment took place. Nonetheless, everyone who had witnessed that matchwinner knew they had been watching a young genius at work, one with the footwork of a Sammy Davis Jr. and the calm temperament of a monk. Guy Mitchell must have been singing his heart out over in New York.

South Africa

Batsman	Dismissal	Runs
EAB Rowan	c Johnston b Miller	143
OE Wynne	b Johnston	18
JD Nel	c & b Johnson	14
AD Nourse*	c †Saggers b Johnston	66
WW Wade†	b Lindwall	24
NBF Mann	b Johnston	9
JE Cheetham	c Hassett b Johnston	4
JC Watkins	b Lindwall	5
HJ Tayfield	run out	15
VI Smith	b Lindwall	1
CN McCarthy	not out	0
Extras (b3, lb7, nb2)		**12**
Total (all out; 109.2 overs)		**311**

Fall of wickets 1/32 2/75 3/242 4/264 5/283 6/289 7/293 8/304 9/308

Bowling	O	M	R	W
RR Lindwall	19	3	47	3
KR Miller	24	5	73	1
CL McCool	13	3	35	0
WA Johnston	31.2	5	75	4
SJE Loxton	6	1	31	0
IWG Johnson	16	5	38	1

Batsman	Dismissal	Runs
EAB Rowan	c †Saggers b Lindwall	4
OE Wynne	b Johnson	29
JD Nel	lbw b Johnston	20
AD Nourse*	c McCool b Johnson	27
WW Wade†	b Johnston	0
JE Cheetham	c Hassett b Johnson	1
JC Watkins	st †Saggers b Johnson	2
HJ Tayfield	b Johnston	3
NBF Mann	lbw b Johnson	0
VI Smith	b Johnston	4
CN McCarthy	not out	2
Extras (b5, lb1, nb1)		**7**
Total (all out; 46.2 overs)		**99**

Fall of wickets 1/9 2/51 3/85 4/85 5/88 6/90 7/93 8/93 9/93

Bowling	O	M	R	W
RR Lindwall	4	1	7	1
KR Miller	7	0	12	0
WA Johnston	18.2	6	39	4
IWG Johnson	17	2	34	5

Australia

Batsman	Dismissal	Runs
AR Morris	c Smith b Tayfield	25
J Moroney	b Tayfield	10
IWG Johnson	lbw b Tayfield	2
KR Miller	b Tayfield	2
AL Hassett*	lbw b Tayfield	2
RA Saggers†	c Cheetham b Mann	2
CL McCool	lbw b Mann	1
RR Lindwall	b Mann	7
RN Harvey	c & b Tayfield	2
SJE Loxton	c Cheetham b Tayfield	16
WA Johnston	not out	2
Extras (b3, lb1)		**4**
Total (all out; 28.4 overs)		**75**

Fall of wickets 1/31 2/35 3/37 4/39 5/42 6/45 7/46 8/53 9/63

Bowling	O	M	R	W
CN McCarthy	6	2	8	0
JC Watkins	4	1	9	0
NBF Mann	10	1	31	3
HJ Tayfield	8.4	1	23	7

Batsman	Dismissal	Runs
AR Morris	hit wicket b Tayfield	44
J Moroney	lbw b Tayfield	10
KR Miller	lbw b Mann	10
AL Hassett*	lbw b Mann	11
RN Harvey	not out	151
SJE Loxton	b Mann	54
CL McCool	not out	39

Did not bat IWG Johnson, RA Saggers†, RR Lindwall, WA Johnston

Extras (b7, lb9, nb1)		**17**
Total (5 wickets; 123.6 overs)		**336**

Fall of wickets 1/14 2/33 3/59 4/95 5/230

Bowling	O	M	R	W
CN McCarthy	12	3	32	0
JC Watkins	6	2	10	0
NBF Mann	51.6	13	101	3
HJ Tayfield	49	5	144	2
VI Smith	5	0	32	0

Herbert Sutcliffe – 161

England v Australia, The Oval 14-18 August 1926

10

-Stephen Chalke-

It was half past five on Monday afternoon when Herbert Sutcliffe's innings began. England had spent a hot and sultry day in the field, their energy sapped as the Australian lower order recovered from 122 for six to 302 all out and a first innings lead of 22 runs. Such was England's frustration that, according to Neville Cardus, their fielding declined visibly during a ninth-wicket stand of 67: 'The returns to the keeper were often inaccurate. I got a sense that we were falling a little out of humour.'

Invigorated by this change of fortune the Australians came down the steps of The Oval pavilion with a purposeful bounce, to be followed by England's opening pair: Jack Hobbs, 43 years old now, playing on his beloved home patch, and his trusty 31-year-old partner from Pudsey in West Yorkshire, the unflappable Herbert Sutcliffe who had held together the first innings with a calm, assured 76. If they could only reach close of play without setback, the disappointments of the day could be put aside. The teams would start the morrow on level terms.

The Ashes were at stake. In the aftermath of the Great War of 1914-18, in three five-match series, Australia had beaten England 5-0, 3-0 and 4-1. Yet now the two teams were playing the final Test of 1926 with the series still locked at 0-0. Test matches in England were three-day affairs and, though the bowlers completed their overs at a brisker rate than now (411 in the three days at Lord's), a mixture of rain and good batting meant that not one of the first four games came close to a conclusion. So as an experiment it was resolved that this Oval Test would be played to its conclusion, however long that took. One or other team would win the Ashes here in south London, and every spectator knew it.

There were 32,000 of them that Monday, standing several deep around the ground, many of them barely able to glimpse the action. Several times the ambulance men fetched fainting girls out of the packed throng while on the grass the boundary rope had inched forward in places. By close of play they were all exhausted – by the heat, by the discomfort and by the sheer tension of the play.

Herbie Collins, the Australian captain, used four bowlers that evening: paceman Jack Gregory and three slower men: leg spinners Arthur Mailey and Clarrie Grimmett and the left armer Charlie Macartney. Gregory was past his best, carrying a leg injury, so mostly that evening Collins attacked the batsmen with his two leg spinners, Mailey cheerfully flighting it high and tempting the false shot, Grimmett miserly with his almost round-arm style. Mailey's deadliest weapon was his googly, Grimmett's the top spinner that scuttled on. Hobbs and Sutcliffe played the two of them judiciously, picking the deliveries to hit and never once lofting the ball into the air. By stumps they had reached 49 for no wicket: Hobbs 28, Sutcliffe 20.

Hobbs and Sutcliffe. Nineteen times before this day they had walked out together at the start of an England innings, and the average of those partnerships stood at a reassuring 102.99. All England went to bed praying that they would continue serenely in the morning, laying the foundations of a winning total.

Hobbs and Sutcliffe. More than any other players in those years they raised the status of the professional cricketer – though in different ways. Hobbs, the master craftsman, had the most placid of temperaments, and he carried himself at all times with a modest decency that was inspiring. The son of a Cambridge college servant, he remained deferential to those born into a higher social station.

Sutcliffe, by contrast, was a self-made man, ambitious and confident, acquiring the vowels of the amateurs and calling them by their Christian names. An orphan brought up by strict Congregationalist aunts, he had started his working life at 13 as an apprentice boot-maker and was rising through cricket – and through a sports outfitting business – to a social status unknown to previous generations of paid cricketers. Indeed, it was his mission to raise the standing of his profession. When he became a senior player in the Yorkshire side he would advise the younger men: "Make sure your manners and bearing are better than those of the amateurs. Remember that you are representing Yorkshire, not just yourself."

"Everything had to be done to the highest standard", his daughter Barbara recalled. "He dressed immaculately, and he didn't like anything out of place. He bred pedigree boxer dogs, and he often sat with them in the evening in his office, doing his books for the shop, all in his beautiful handwriting."

As a batsman he had three great shots: an off drive, a back-foot push behind point and a fearless hook. 'There was method in everything he did', his Yorkshire team-mate Bill Bowes wrote, describing how if there were two men back for the hook he would only take it on when he had 40 on the board. "By that time," he reckoned, "I've so much confidence I think I can miss them both." On such days he could be an electrifying sight. At Scarborough in 1932 he took on the Essex fast men, Ken Farnes and Stan Nichols, and he raced from 100 to 182 in 20 minutes.

He was the master of the quick single. He opened with Derbyshire's Denis Smith against the Indians in a Festival match. 'If he was my regular partner,' Smith said, 'I'd average another 15 runs an innings.'

He was also a batsman with a magnificent defence. In accordance with the lbw laws of the time he would – if the situation required – happily ignore or kick away balls pitched outside his off stump, and he would lean forward with elegance to present a calm and unflinching bat to anything straight.

If ever there was a cricketer for a big occasion, it was Herbert Sutcliffe. In a career that spanned the 21 years between the wars, he scored 50,138 runs at an average of 51.95. But in Tests he averaged 60.73, higher than any other Englishman, and in Ashes Tests his 66.85 is second only to Don Bradman among the major batsmen. Len Hutton thought he had a higher level of concentration than any other player he knew, while to Bradman 'he had the best temperament of any cricketer I ever played with or against.'

When he was out, he would return to the dressing room with not a hair out of place. 'The sort of man who would rather miss a train than run for it', RC Robertson-Glasgow called him. 'After a wash and rub down', Bowes wrote, 'he would dress methodically, then produce a writing case and sit down to ten or fifteen letters.' Always a good team man, he would look up from time to time: "How are we doing?"

He was, in the words of the cricket writer A.A. Thomson, 'a personality as dependable as fallible human nature will allow.'

'He was not born to greatness', Cardus wrote. 'He achieved greatness. His wasn't a triumph of skill only, it was a finer triumph, a triumph of character, application, will-power.'

Character, application, will-power. Never did he need those qualities more than on Tuesday 17 August 1926 – with the Ashes at stake and all England willing him to succeed. The country was still healing the wounds of the General Strike in May. What a boost to morale it would be if England's cricketers could win here at The Oval.

There was no overnight covering of the pitch, just two policemen on duty to prevent the interference of intruders. They were standing out on the square at two in the morning when the sticky air turned dramatically into a violent storm, tropical in its intensity. All across the south London sky there were flashes of lightning, claps of thunder and fierce rain lashing down. The pitch, so placid at close of play, quickly became sodden, lakes of water forming all across the field. Outside the walls of the ground the long queue dissolved in an instant, men running in desperation for whatever shelter they could find.

By the morning, when the players arrived, the puddles had drained away. There were birds on the outfield, feeding on the worms which had come to the surface, and in the air was a misty steam as the water on the field and on the surrounding seats evaporated in the warmth of the day. Against all expectations play began, as scheduled, at 11 o'clock. Percy Chapman the England captain ordered the heavy roller, hoping that, by bringing the moisture to the surface, the pitch would be dead for a time while his openers grew used to the new conditions.

Before play began, the umpire Frank Chester looked into the England dressing room. He had expected an anxious atmosphere, but instead he found Hobbs puffing at his pipe as if he were about to step out for a festival match while Sutcliffe was calmly brushing down his sleek, black hair. "The wicket's a bad 'un" Chester said, but the two batsmen seemed to show no flicker of concern.

Hobbs turned to Sutcliffe as they patted down the pitch at the end of the first over. "Jolly bad luck, that rain", he said. "It's cooked our chances." He repeated the remark to the umpire 'Sailor' Young, who offered no words of comfort. "Yes, it's hard luck", he replied.

With sawdust all around them and the ball biting into the surface, leaving indentations that needed regular flattening down, the two batsmen concentrated solely on survival. Sutcliffe's first run of the morning came after 40 minutes while at one point Hobbs was content to play out eight successive maidens from the medium pace of the off spinner Arthur Richardson, bowling round the wicket with a cluster of fielders in the leg-trap. Chester recalled an early delivery from Mailey to Hobbs that pitched on leg, spat and spun viciously, missing the off stump by a whisker. "We'll not get 70 on this", Sutcliffe whispered to him, and Chester agreed.

It was a timeless Test, and the knowing south London crowd showed their grasp of the game, loving every minute of it. "Steady, now, Jack boy", one man called out when Hobbs broke loose with two boundaries. Then, when Sutcliffe let yet another delivery go past him and an impatient spectator called out, "Don't 'urt the ball, mate", his neighbours were quick to tell him to "put a sock in it." The *Manchester Guardian* had a correspondent nestled among the masses. 'We did not want runs', he reported. 'We longed to see the bowlers worn down: such was the grim spirit of the day.' Meanwhile, in the trees that overlooked the ground opposite the gasworks, a swarm of boys hung like monkeys to the branches. 'They regarded it as a huge spree and roared the changing score to their friends below and to passers-by in the street with happy-go-lucky cheerfulness.'

By 12 o'clock the sun was out and the effect of the heavy roller had worn off. Now, in the 90 minutes till lunch, the pitch was at its most spiteful. 'The Australians were on tiptoe,' Hobbs wrote later, 'and undoubtedly should have got many of us out.' Indeed, the next England batsmen – Frank Woolley, Patsy Hendren, Percy Chapman – were all stroke-makers, much less well-suited to battling it out on such a devilish pitch. One false shot from Hobbs or Sutcliffe and the game would swing decisively towards the visitors.

Perhaps the Australian attack was not at its supreme best – Grimmett still to reach his peak, Mailey too slow and flighty for the surface and the left-armer Charlie Macartney, now primarily a batsman, past his most potent. The real danger lay with Richardson, and some say he was at fault in bowling always a leg-stump line. Yet, in the words of the *Times*, 'the pitch was horrid', and the Australians 'bowled on it each of them as well as he knows how. Nearly every ball cut out a little fid of turf when it pitched.' Through it all Hobbs and Sutcliffe 'remained masters of their fate. Their artistry in manipulation of the bat was consummate, their judgment infallible, their patience inexhaustible.'

The two men gave not a chance, and they were still there at lunch. In two-and-a-half hours, on the stickiest pitch umpire Chester ever saw, they had lifted the total from 49 to 161. Hobbs, the freer of the two, had moved from 28 to 97; Sutcliffe, with his immense self-control, from 20 to just 53.

The players and umpires made their way towards the pavilion, but the two batsmen remained for a minute in the middle, meticulously clearing the little divots of earth and patting down the pitch with their bats. "Well played, Jack", said Sutcliffe. "Well played Herbert", said Hobbs. Three words each, but in that very English way they acknowledged the ordeal of what they had been through. Back in the dressing room, they were still unbuckling their pads when they were summoned to the office to meet the Prince of Wales.

'What Hobbs and Sutcliffe achieved that day', Pelham Warner wrote, 'will be talked of as long as cricket is played. They have made their names immortal in cricket history.' Len Hutton, then a boy of 10, was still writing about it 60 years later: 'If I could be granted one wish, I would be tempted to ask for a rerun of their famous stand. Wilfred Rhodes, who played in the match at the age of 48, used to talk about it with a faraway look in his eyes.'

Yet the job was not done. By the time play resumed the pitch had eased, and the bowlers' run-ups had dried sufficiently to allow Gregory to take the ball. Hobbs soon completed his hundred, and pandemonium broke out. Cheer after cheer – "Hip, hip, hooray" – rent the London air. Then the joyous crowd burst into a rendition of "For he's a jolly good fellow". Within minutes, though, they were clapping again, this time with a heavier heart, as Hobbs made his way back to the pavilion, bowled by Gregory for exactly 100.

The England lead was only 150. It fell to Sutcliffe to ensure that the hard work of the morning would not be in vain. The next batsmen all made contributions but, even with the pitch growing more benign, none proved as durable as Sutcliffe: Woolley 27, Hendren 15, Chapman 19, Greville Stevens 22. As the afternoon wore on, Sutcliffe grew more expansive though his powers of mental application never weakened. By tea he had made a faultless 125. Then as the sun dropped in the late August sky he batted without bother through the final session, reaching the day's last over with 161 to his name. At that point, with England on 375-5, he misread a Mailey googly and was bowled. Many a lesser mortal would have strode off, head held high, proud of his innings. Not Herbert Sutcliffe. Aghast at his momentary lapse, he thumped his bat on the ground in self-disgust.

In the two sessions since lunch he had scored 108 runs, but it was not his scoring strokes that the *Times* correspondent chose to describe in detail. Not the calculated shots to leg, nor the many gentle pushes into off-side gaps. 'What every one who saw it will remember to his dying day was the graceful solidity of his defence, his subordination of self to side, and his almost uncanny wisdom.'

When he came out of the pavilion, he was besieged by well-wishers and autograph hunters. Patiently he stood and talked to them all. Then outside the gates he was mobbed by an even greater crowd. It took four mounted police and a whole posse of constables to clear a path to a waiting car. Then, as the vehicle drove away, it was followed by hundreds of running, cheering admirers. Several of them had to be removed from the car's footboard.

Next morning England took their total to 436. Then, in front of Prime Minister Stanley Baldwin and the King of Iraq, they bowled out Australia for 125, with Wilfred Rhodes – recalled after a five-year absence – taking four wickets.

The vast crowd in front of the pavilion cheered themselves hoarse. "We want Hobbs", they chanted. "We want Sutcliffe." Pelham Warner in the *Cricketer* was full of the significance of the moment: 'Had we been beaten, despondency would have crept over the land. As it is, our cricket will be fortified and refreshed.'

Given the importance of the match, and the difficulty of the pitch, the batting of Hobbs and Sutcliffe in that second innings ranks still as one of the greatest achievements in all Test history. Some regard the innings of Jack Hobbs, always the most popular of cricketers, to be the greater, because he scored more runs in that crucial morning session when almost every ball was full of venom. Men still argue whether it was he or Wally Hammond who is the greatest English batsman ever.

But what of Herbert Sutcliffe, less elegant, less powerful but with an inner steel that was at its very best when the going was toughest? As he said to the editor of the *Cricketer*, "Yes, Mr Warner, I love a dog fight." And that day at The Oval, when all England held its breath, he was the supreme master, batting with calm determination for almost four more hours after his partner's dismissal. Survival in the morning had been against all the odds, yet he achieved so much more, steadfastly guiding the England innings through the afternoon and evening till the advantage was overwhelming.

It was indeed a triumph of character, application and will-power.

England

JB Hobbs	b Mailey	37
H Sutcliffe	b Mailey	76
FE Woolley	b Mailey	18
EH Hendren	b Gregory	8
APF Chapman*	st †Oldfield b Mailey	49
GTS Stevens	c Andrews b Mailey	17
W Rhodes	c †Oldfield b Mailey	28
G Geary	run out	9
MW Tate	b Grimmett	23
H Larwood	c Andrews b Grimmett	0
H Strudwick†	not out	4
Extras (b6, lb5)		**11**
Total (all out; 95.5 overs)		**280**

Fall of wickets 1/53 2/91 3/108 4/189 5/213 6/214 7/231 8/266 9/266

Bowling	**O**	**M**	**R**	**W**
JM Gregory	15	4	31	1
CV Grimmett	33	12	74	2
AA Mailey	33.5	3	138	6
CG Macartney	7	4	16	0
AJ Richardson	7	2	10	0

JB Hobbs	b Gregory	100
H Sutcliffe	b Mailey	161
FE Woolley	lbw b Richardson	27
EH Hendren	c †Oldfield b Grimmett	15
APF Chapman*	b Richardson	19
GTS Stevens	c Mailey b Grimmett	22
W Rhodes	lbw b Grimmett	14
G Geary	c †Oldfield b Gregory	1
MW Tate	not out	33
H Larwood	b Mailey	5
H Strudwick†	c Andrews b Mailey	2
Extras (b19, lb18)		**37**
Total (all out; 182.5 overs)		**436**

Fall of wickets 1/172 2/220 3/277 4/316 5/373 6/375 7/382 8/425 9/430

Bowling	**O**	**M**	**R**	**W**
JM Gregory	18	1	58	2
CV Grimmett	55	17	108	3
AA Mailey	42.5	6	128	3
CG Macartney	26	16	24	0
AJ Richardson	41	21	81	2

Australia

WM Woodfull	b Rhodes	35
W Bardsley	c †Strudwick b Larwood	2
CG Macartney	b Stevens	25
WH Ponsford	run out	2
TJE Andrews	b Larwood	3
HL Collins*	c Stevens b Larwood	61
AJ Richardson	c Geary b Rhodes	16
JM Gregory	c Stevens b Tate	73
WAS Oldfield†	not out	33
CV Grimmett	b Tate	35
AA Mailey	c †Strudwick b Tate	0
Extras (b5, lb12)		**17**
Total (all out; 152.1 overs)		**302**

Fall of wickets 1/9 2/44 3/51 4/59 5/90 6/122 7/229 8/231 9/298

Bowling	**O**	**M**	**R**	**W**
MW Tate	37.1	17	40	3
H Larwood	34	11	82	3
G Geary	27	8	43	0
GTS Stevens	29	3	85	1
W Rhodes	25	15	35	2

WM Woodfull	c Geary b Larwood	0
WH Ponsford	c Larwood b Rhodes	12
CG Macartney	c Geary b Larwood	16
W Bardsley	c Woolley b Rhodes	21
HL Collins*	c Woolley b Rhodes	4
TJE Andrews	c Tate b Larwood	15
JM Gregory	c Sutcliffe b Tate	9
AJ Richardson	b Rhodes	4
WAS Oldfield†	b Stevens	23
CV Grimmett	not out	8
AA Mailey	b Geary	6
Extras (lb7)		**7**
Total (all out; 52.3 overs)		**125**

Fall of wickets 1/1 2/31 3/31 4/35 5/63 6/83 7/83 8/87 9/114

Bowling	**O**	**M**	**R**	**W**
MW Tate	9	4	12	1
H Larwood	14	3	34	3
G Geary	6.3	2	15	1
GTS Stevens	3	1	13	1
W Rhodes	20	9	44	4

Don Bradman – 212

Australia v England, Adelaide 29 January-4 February 1937

-Ric Sissons-

Don Bradman did not play in the 1934-35 domestic season due to illness. In April 1935 Don and his wife Jessie moved to Adelaide. He began work as a stockbroker with Harry Hodgetts and took over as captain of South Australia. He chose not to tour South Africa in 1935-36, instead leading the young South Australian side to their first Sheffield Shield championship in 10 seasons. He finished the season with a batting average of 130.33.

In October 1936 England arrived for a post-bodyline reconciliation tour. Gubby Allen led a party including Les Ames, Charlie Barnett, Ken Farnes, Wally Hammond, Maurice Leyland, Walter Robins, Hedley Verity and Bill Voce but compared to 1932-33 the side was missing Patsy Hendren, Harold Larwood, Eddie Paynter and Herbert Sutcliffe. Australia had lost senior batsmen including Alan Kippax, Bill Ponsford and Bill Woodfull but they still had the experienced Bert Oldfield behind the stumps. As expected, Bradman took over as Australian Test captain. He also became one of the selectors with EA 'Chappie' Dwyer (NSW) and WJ Johnson (Victoria).

The series did not start well for Bradman. Australia lost the first Test in Brisbane by 322 runs. The home side managed only 58 in their second innings. Bradman contributed an un-Bradmanlike 38 and 0. England won the second Test at the Sydney Cricket Ground by an innings and 22 runs. Bradman made a duck in the Australian first innings and 82 in the second innings, but his two consecutive ducks had shocked the Australian public.

No side had come back to win a Test series from two-nil down. After the failures of the first two Tests, doubts were raised about Bradman's batting. Neville Cardus, who was in Australia covering the series for the *Manchester Guardian*, wrote:

> 'England two up and only three to play: Australia will win the rubber only by a remarkable act of regeneration…The turning point arrived today when Bradman got out not by a stroke which he will wish to remember. A brave stand by Sievers and a superb innings by McCabe suggested how easily Australia might have scored enormously had Bradman been Bradman. But Australia must learn not to depend too much on Bradman: he is only human.'

Questions were being raised about the impact of the captaincy on Bradman's batting. Jack Hobbs, covering the tour for the *Star*, was quoted in the *Sydney Morning Herald*:

> 'I suggest Australia would gain strength if Vic Richardson were made captain. That may sound hard on Bradman. I do not imply that because he has lost two tests he is not a good captain. It goes deeper than that. People tell me Don is not playing as well as he did two years ago, and from what I have seen of him I do not think he is. Possibly the cares of captaincy detract from his batting.'

In Richardson and Stan McCabe, Australia had two alternative captains. Richardson had captained the successful touring party in South Africa, while McCabe was captain of New South Wales. However, there was never any doubt that Bradman would retain the captaincy for the third Test. He had the backing of his co-selectors and retained the full confidence of the Australian Board of Control.

The third Test began in Melbourne on New Year's Day 1937. Bradman declared the Australian first innings at 9-200 before England responded by declaring on 9-76 on a difficult wet wicket. Bradman reversed the batting order and on a recovered surface hit 270, batting at seven, in Australia's second innings and the home side won by 365 runs.

The Test ended in 'sensation'. Immediately after the match McCabe, along with fellow team members Bill O'Reilly, Chuck Fleetwood-Smith and Leo O'Brien, was asked to attend a 3pm meeting with the Board of Control Executive. Waiting for the players at the Victorian Cricket Association rooms were Board members Oxlade (NSW), Hodgetts (South Australia), Hutcheon (Queensland) and chairman Dr Robertson (Victoria). Robertson, reading from four pages of foolscap paper, outlined three charges:

- Someone was not 100 per cent loyal to the captain.
- Some players were indulging in too many alcoholic beverages.
- Others were not trying to keep fit.

McCabe interrupted Robertson and asked if the Board was laying formal charges. Robertson said "no" and the meeting ended after 45 minutes. The *Daily Mail* claimed to have the inside story and suggested that the trouble was due to some players thinking that McCabe should replace Bradman as captain.

McCabe asked Bradman if he had anything to do with this 'carpeting', Bradman replied in the negative. The *Canberra Times* thought otherwise: 'The complaints are believed to have been brought under the notice of the Board by Bradman a few days ago.' Throughout his life, Bradman remained steadfast in claiming his innocence. In February 1951, in a letter to fellow selector Dwyer, Bradman wrote:

> 'What about the experience I had when I first captained Australia? I just had to take it on the chin and be blamed by close associates even for the Board's action in putting players on the mat when I was not only innocent, but completely ignorant of what was happening.'

Given the detailed accusations – and if Bradman was not the source – then it must have been a senior player or a selector.

The incident has gone down as one of the most notable examples of religious sectarianism in sport. Four Catholic players called to account before a Board of Protestants and Freemasons, based – some say – on a report from Bradman, the Protestant captain. This was the view promoted by O'Reilly. In *Tiger: 60 Years of Cricket*, O'Reilly wrote that the Catholics were made to feel like an 'insubordinate and disloyal team of slackers and boozers.'

O'Reilly's 'Micks v Masons' view of the world has one problem – Chappie Dwyer. Dwyer, a Test selector from 1930 to 1952, was a devout Catholic. His father had established a well-known Catholic emporium, while his brother was a superior of a Redemptorist monastery. According to the *Catholic Press*, Dwyer regularly visited Catholic schools and young men's clubs with McCabe and O'Reilly. But he also developed a long friendship with Bradman. Writing to Bradman in 1947, Dwyer – referring to O'Reilly – said:

> 'In days gone by I was closely associated with some of these people…I was most irritated and annoyed at the biased and unfair comments that were made about you by fellows who should have been full of gratitude and praise for the splendid job you did for Australia. These people seem to be tainted by an obsession to write you down and I am sure that it became quite obvious to thinking people that a germ of jealousy has almost possessed them.'

It was against this divisive backdrop that the players gathered for the timeless fourth Test in Adelaide. The London *Daily Telegraph* hoped that the Test 'will not be spoiled by the effects of the rumours about players.' Public interest was high. The South Australian Centenary Accommodation Committee was retained to handle requests for rooms from all parts of Australia. At times demand reached 110 calls an hour. The *Adelaide Advertiser* reported that:

> 'City and suburban hotels have done their utmost to cope with the extraordinary demand, and in many cases lounges and balconies, as well as the private rooms of the licensees, have been converted into temporary bedrooms. Guest homes and boarding houses have also co-operated, in addition to many private homes, which have provided beds for visitors.'

Unlike the previous three Tests the outcome was not going to be influenced by rain. Hot, dry conditions were forecast.

Play began at noon on the Friday. Bradman won the toss and Australia batted on a good wicket. By the close the home side was 7-267 thanks to 88 from McCabe. Allen bowled

Bradman for 26. On the second day the Australian tail offered little resistance as Australia was dismissed for 288. Chipperfield remained 57 not out. By stumps England was in a strong position at 2-174, with Barnett on 92 not out.

Sunday was a rest day and Adelaide sweltered. Cardus described the city as an 'oven' and he 'escaped to the hills.' Monday was Australia Foundation Day and a public holiday. Cardus described the scene as he returned to Adelaide: 'We met an endless procession of vehicles leaving the city…all packed with people. I thought they were refugees flying from the horrors of the Test match – women and children first.' The daily attendance dipped below 30,000 for the first time.

England was dismissed for 330 on a bone-dry pitch, a lead of 42. Their remaining eight wickets added only 156 runs as Fleetwood-Smith and O'Reilly each took four wickets. In *Farewell to Cricket*, Bradman wrote that England was, 'frittering away a golden opportunity to establish a big lead.' Cardus had been impressed by the wrist spin of Fleetwood-Smith: 'It was he who disturbed the English confidence by bowling touched with the incalculable properties of genius. Considering the amount of break he exploited, his length was astonishingly good.'

In the first 30 minutes of the Australian second innings, Allen tried four bowlers and just before five o'clock Hammond trapped Jack Fingleton leg before wicket. Keith Rigg was listed to bat at three as he had in the first innings. His name appeared on the board but the crowd's cheering told another story. Bradman had changed the batting order and accepted the responsibility as the side's leading batsman. The *Sydney Morning Herald* wrote: 'Bradman decided that he was the man for the critical position that had arisen and he returned to his old place of number three batsman.'

Bradman knew the destiny of this Test and the series lay in his hands and he batted with restraint. In his first hour at the crease he had scored just 26. He refused to play the hook shot, which had been his downfall in the first innings. When Allen bowled a tempting short ball, Bradman let it pass and just smiled at the England captain. One journalist noted that his timing was much better than in his first innings.

By the close, Bradman and Bill Brown had taken the score to 1-63. Australia had fought back and the Test now hung in the balance. Vic Richardson, reflecting on the day's play, wrote in the *Adelaide Advertiser* on 2 February that: 'The evidence of spin yesterday was a forbidding sign for England, as when its second innings arrives 300 runs, if needed, will be very difficult to obtain against Australia's spin bowlers.'

Tuesday – day four – was a working day but a crowd of 38,334 packed the Adelaide Oval. With Bradman batting, this was the largest daily attendance of the Test. When he was on 32, Brown was caught down the leg side by Ames. McCabe joined Bradman. Denzil Batchelor, writing for the *Sydney Morning Herald*, described Bradman's performance:

> 'There was from the first a leisurely mastery about his every stroke. Before lunch he hardly drove at all, but stroked the ball through the slips with an insinuating touch, and glided it with feathery lightness to fine leg. He had been batting for two hours before his first boundary came, and then it was from a stroke not generally associated with Bradman – an exquisitely performed late cut that somehow sent the ball to the on boundary behind the wicket..'

Allen, desperate for Bradman's wicket, set a field that was considered a first in Test history. The left-handed Verity bowled to Bradman with two silly points and no slips. Batchelor wrote, 'The bold policy succeeded fairly well, or at least it was no worse a failure than any other policy adopted against Bradman.'

Bradman and McCabe added 109 in 92 minutes before McCabe, on 55, hit a full toss from Robins hard to the leg side. The shot was destined to be six until Bob Wyatt took a running, juggling catch. Rigg, batting at five, joined Bradman. Batchelor wrote:

> 'Rigg's innings was a pantomime that might easily have become a tragedy. No able-bodied batsman in history has ever been more adroit at making a perfectly comfortable single into a full-length, five-act drama, fraught with ambition, doubt, eagerness, and a Hamlet-like indecision in quickly recurring order. No one in the English team looked half as likely to bowl or catch Bradman as Rigg looked to run him out.'

However, Bradman remained unperturbed. Batchelor continued

> 'It was not an innings of flaunted aggression. It did not glitter with unforgettable strokes… but the salient impression that Bradman's innings gave, during its six infallible hours, was that it was beyond human power to get him out…it is impossible to expel the suspicion that he will go, not because he must, but because, with an unassailable score on the board, he may.'

Rigg made only seven. Bradman reached his century with a majestic cover drive. This was his first Ashes century in his new home city, his 11th against England and his 17th in all Tests, eclipsing the record previously held by Jack Hobbs.

Australia was 195 ahead when 'baby-faced' 20-year-old Ross Gregory joined Bradman. This was Gregory's first Test and the public's expectations were high. Only a handful of Australian batsmen had been younger than Gregory on debut and they included some illustrious names – Clem Hill, Archie Jackson, Bradman and McCabe.

Bradman reached his 150 with a cover drive off Voce. It had taken him 274 minutes. In his book *The Ross Gregory Story*, David Frith quotes Arthur Mailey as saying this was the greatest innings he had ever seen. To thwart Bradman, Allen came up with a new slower form of leg theory. Verity bowled outside the leg stump with a packed leg-side field. In 13 overs Verity conceded just seven runs. By the close of play, Australia was 4-341 and 299 runs ahead. Bradman was 174 not out having batted for 358 minutes, but to that point had hit only 10 fours.

As day five began, the English camp feared the worst. With Bradman still batting, England was facing a total in excess of 300 on a pitch that was showing signs of wear. On the previous day a few deliveries had kept low. Nearly 22,000 spectators gathered in sultry conditions. Bradman faced Voce and hit a powerful drive to the mid-off fence. Having asserted his authority, he now reverted to building his innings to ensure Australia was in an unbeatable position. Bradman and Gregory added a priceless 135 runs in 175 minutes, before the young Victorian was run out for 50.

Bradman reached his two-hundred after 422 minutes at the crease. According to Alan Eason in *The A-Z of Bradman* this was the longest time Bradman ever took to reach 200 in a first-class innings. This was his seventh double-century against England. Arch-rival Wally Hammond had made only three doubles against Australia to this point.

Denzil Batchelor described the scene in the *Sydney Morning Herald*:

> '[Bradman] was as unruffled and immaculate as ever, scoring steadily from delicate flicks and gentle deflections that looked commonplace, but had the saving grace of being directed to the wide-open spaces. But the robot had a crack in his armour...He pounced upon two half-volleys from Hammond and thrashed them to the long-on and long-off boundaries. The next ball was hit with thunderbolt force to the bowler's left hand, and the impassive, world-despising Hammond unemotionally caught him.'

Bradman had made 212 in 437 minutes with only 14 fours and 99 singles. This was a great exhibition of control and concentration. The *Sydney Morning Herald* reported that although Bradman was tired, his stamina had stood the test but his 'right hand was puffed up as a result of the continual jarring.' Two former great Test batsmen paid Bradman the highest compliments. Jack Hobbs, 'the Master' summed up his performance:

> 'Bradman's was a remarkable innings by an astounding cricketer, and it doubtless decided the issue...It proved that he can play a fighting game with his back to the wall. In the past he has scored hundreds of runs with his own trade-marked hook shot but once or twice this season he has got out with it so he has completely eliminated it except when hitting a 4 off a no-ball...Bradman looked absolutely invincible.'

Charlie Macartney, the 'Governor General', wrote:

> 'Bradman played an innings that Australia needed. He gave nothing away and soundness was the keynote. No bowler could induce him to take a risk, and he never lost sight of his own value for the achievement of victory. He pasted anything loose, and did not lose the value of a no-ball. His restraint and discrimination were remarkable.'

The Australian tail again failed – the last four wickets added just 11 runs. Hammond finished with 5 for 57. Australia had been dismissed for 433, setting England 392 for victory and a chance to win the Ashes.

By the close on the fifth day England was 3-148 requiring another 244 to win. England's hope lay with Walter Hammond who was not out on 39. Jack Hobbs was confident. He had expected Australia to score more runs and feared England would have lost more wickets.

Despite a great finish being in prospect, the smallest crowd of the Test attended on the sixth day. In the first over, Fleetwood-Smith bowled Hammond with an unplayable ball and the fate of the match was sealed. In *On Top Down Under*, Ray Robinson wrote that Fleetwood-Smith strolled over to Bradman and said, "Was that what you wanted, Goldie?" The significance of Hammond's wicket was not lost in the wider community. In the Adelaide City Courts an unofficial 'exhibit' was handed to the Bench. It read, 'Hammond clean bowled second ball by Fleetwood-Smith.' In an odd coincidence, the case being heard involved a man who blamed Bradman for his offensive behaviour. The defendant claimed he became so excited when Bradman was batting that he did not know what he was doing.

England was dismissed for 243. Fleetwood-Smith took 6 for 110 as Australia won by 148 runs. Robins, the last man out, grabbed a stump as a souvenir, but tossed it to Bradman. The press described this as a gracious tribute to Bradman's great individual performance and successful captaincy.

Bradman and Allen were escorted into the Vice-Regal enclosure to meet Sir Winston Dugan, the governor of South Australia and the visiting MCC president, Lord Somers. In his speech to the cheering crowd Allen said, "I want to congratulate Don on his great play. He played a great innings."

With the series now tied at two Tests apiece, the focus moved to the fifth Test in Melbourne on 26 February. Bradman again dominated with 169. Australia won by an innings and 200 runs. Bradman had re-asserted his position, was the best batsman in the world and also ended any speculation about his captaincy. Hammond won the second Test for England but Bradman won the next three for Australia with scores of 270, 212 and 169. In the last three Tests, Bradman batted for a total of just over 20 hours.

During the tour Cardus wrote that, 'England without Hammond could defeat Australia without Bradman.' His speculation was dismissed as pointless conjecture. His view that

Australia, from two-nil down, could only succeed with a 'remarkable act of regeneration' was more realistic. That regeneration was Bradman.

Australia

Batsman	Dismissal	Runs
JHW Fingleton	run out	10
WA Brown	c Allen b Farnes	42
KE Rigg	c †Ames b Farnes	20
DG Bradman*	b Allen	26
SJ McCabe	c Allen b Robins	88
RG Gregory	lbw b Hammond	23
AG Chipperfield	not out	57
WAS Oldfield†	run out	5
WJ O'Reilly	c Leyland b Allen	7
EL McCormick	c †Ames b Hammond	4
LO F-Smith	b Farnes	1
Extras (lb2, nb3)		**5**
Total (all out; 77.6 overs)		**288**

Fall of wickets 1/26 2/72 3/73 4/136 5/206 6/226 7/249 8/271 9/283

Bowling	O	M	R	W
W Voce	12	0	49	0
GOB Allen	16	0	60	2
K Farnes	20.6	1	71	3
WR Hammond	6	0	30	2
H Verity	16	4	47	0
RWV Robins	7	1	26	1

Batsman	Dismissal	Runs
JHW Fingleton	lbw b Hammond	12
WA Brown	c †Ames b Voce	32
DG Bradman*	c & b Hammond	212
SJ McCabe	c Wyatt b Robins	55
KE Rigg	c Hammond b Farnes	7
RG Gregory	run out	50
AG Chipperfield	c †Ames b Hammond	31
WAS Oldfield†	c †Ames b Hammond	1
WJ O'Reilly	c Hammond b Farnes	1
EL McCormick	b Hammond	1
LO F-Smith	not out	4
Extras (b10, lb15, w1, nb1)		**27**
Total (all out; 123.2 overs)		**433**

Fall of wickets 1/21 2/88 3/197 4/237 5/372 6/422 7/426 8/427 9/429

Bowling	O	M	R	W
W Voce	20	2	86	1
GOB Allen	14	1	61	0
K Farnes	24	2	89	2
WR Hammond	15.2	1	57	5
H Verity	37	17	54	0
RWV Robins	6	0	38	1
CJ Barnett	5	1	15	0
M Leyland	2	0	6	0

England

Batsman	Dismissal	Runs
H Verity	c Bradman b O'Reilly	19
CJ Barnett	lbw b F-Smith	129
WR Hammond	c McCormick b O'Reilly	20
M Leyland	c Chipperfield b F-Smith	45
RES Wyatt	c Fingleton b O'Reilly	3
LEG Ames†	b McCormick	52
J Hardstaff jnr	c & b McCormick	20
GOB Allen*	lbw b F-Smith	11
RWV Robins	c †Oldfield b O'Reilly	10
W Voce	c Rigg b F-Smith	8
K Farnes	not out	0
Extras (b6, lb2, w1, nb4)		**13**
Total (all out; 113.4 overs)		**330**

Fall of wickets 1/53 2/108 3/190 4/195 5/259 6/299 7/304 8/318 9/322

Bowling	O	M	R	W
EL McCormick	21	2	81	2
SJ McCabe	9	2	18	0
LO F-Smith	41.4	10	129	4
WJ O'Reilly	30	12	51	4
AG Chipperfield	9	1	24	0
RG Gregory	3	0	14	0

Batsman	Dismissal	Runs
H Verity	b F-Smith	17
CJ Barnett	c Chipperfield b F-Smith	21
J Hardstaff jnr	b O'Reilly	43
WR Hammond	b F-Smith	39
M Leyland	c Chipperfield b F-Smith	32
RES Wyatt	c †Oldfield b McCabe	50
LEG Ames†	lbw b F-Smith	0
GOB Allen*	c Gregory b McCormick	9
RWV Robins	b McCormick	4
W Voce	b F-Smith	1
K Farnes	not out	7
Extras (b12, 1b2, nb 6)		**20**
Total (all out; 74 overs)		**243**

Fall of wickets 1/45 2/50 3/120 4/149 5/190 6/190 7/225 8/231 9/235

Bowling	O	M	R	W
EL McCormick	13	1	43	2
SJ McCabe	5	0	15	1
LO F-Smith	30	1	110	6
WJ O'Reilly	26	8	55	1

Adam Gilchrist – 149*

Australia v Pakistan, Hobart 18-22 November 1999

-Rodney Ulyate-

Would that cricketers had better lines, or at least that their most famous were not also their tritest or most banal. "This thing can be done", said Fred Spofforth in 1882. "We'll get 'em in singles", George Hirst did not say 20 years later. "You guys are history", growled Devon Malcolm in 1994. "You've just dropped the World Cup", Steve Waugh may have crowed in 1999. At least two of these could have been put into the mouth of Arnold Schwarzenegger. A few months after Waugh's apocryphal contribution, Adam Gilchrist strode assertively to the crease and heard the following from Justin Langer: "You never know..."

The remark fits happily into the canon, but it was delivered without conviction or sincerity; nor did its recipient much credit it. "Whatever his words," recalled Gilchrist, "his grin said to me: 'We're gone, but let's just have a crack and see what happens.'" Langer had long since turned to 'thinking about my own position in the side rather than of winning or even drawing the match.' His solipsism is forgivable, and not only because Australia's situation was hopeless. His own form had been desperate, and the media were barking for his head: 'It was almost like being on death row for the week leading up to the Test.' A Pakistani bowler had spoken for many when he sneered at Langer early in his innings, "You wouldn't make our second XI."

It was 17:04 on a fading Saturday evening. The Australians, in quest of 369, were 126 for five. Gilchrist, the last of the recognised batsmen, was in only his second Test match. The tail in the first innings had imparted just seven. With an hour remaining of the fourth day's play, it might be all over by stumps. The bookmakers were offering 9/1 against the home side. 'They were bad odds,' thought Robert Craddock of Sydney's *Daily Telegraph*. 'History suggests they should have been 50/1.'

The target was mountainous. Only twice, in 120 years of Test cricket, had a team chased down more. The Australians had failed only the previous season to score 175 off England; five years ago, in pursuit of 117 against South Africa, they had been choked out for 111. The pitch at the Bellerive Oval was reputed to be one on which teams could chase, but not against the best attack in cricket. Pakistan's bowlers had more than 800 wickets between them: Shoaib Akhtar was the fastest in the terrestrial universe, Wasim Akram the world's finest left-arm seamer, Waqar Younis the *nonpareil* of reverse swing, and Saqlain Mushtaq the first to master the doosra. Even Azhar Mahmood, very much the Ringo of the group, had proven himself baneful, having taken two wickets in two balls earlier in the day. The

Australians had not lost a rubber at home since 1992-93; they were on the very precipice now. With half their wickets gone, they still needed 243.

The fielders crowded the bat, like metal filings drawn to a magnet, as Gilchrist played out a maiden from Saqlain. Despite claims to the contrary in Steve Waugh's published diary, Australia had been unprepared for the doosra in the first innings, in which an eight-over spell generated 6-17. John Buchanan, the Australian coach, had since requested slow-motion footage from *Channel 9*, that they might unpick the mystery of this new-fangled *legerdemain*. Their conclusion was that Saqlain hardly ever spun his off-break; his stock delivery was his wrong 'un. They had decided, therefore, to play him as a leg-spinner, and to negate with their pads the occasional orthodoxy.

Gilchrist applied the tactic well, trying at first just to survive – "but my natural instincts for survival are to play aggressively." It was not long before he brought out the sweep, which surprised the bowler and quickly untuned his rhythm. Gilchrist's confidence billowed. Presently, with might and main, he clubbed a long hop onto the pavilion roof – the first of his 100 Test sixes, two-thirds of which would follow it over mid-wicket. A sinewy drive succeeded a crunching sweep, and Saqlain's bowling went flat. Gilchrist had been among the doosra's victims in the first innings, but he had no difficulty picking it now. Bad light terminated play three overs early, but the momentum had subtly shifted. Gilchrist, going at better than a run a minute, was the first of the Australians to take runs regularly off the spinner. His 45 off 55 balls set the Pakistanis on their heels.

His partnership with Langer was so far worth 62. The latter had hushed his doubters, if not quite put them to silence, with an unbeaten half-century. Langer put up a defiant front at the press conference – it would be "ludicrous" he averred, not to play for the win – but victory was the furthest thing from his mind. With Australia still 181 runs adrift, he reposed his hopes in the weather forecast, with its promise of rain.

The Australian team was lodged in the Grand Chancellor Hotel, overlooking the Hobart docks. Langer took his father out for fish and chips at the harbour, where they were joined by Gilchrist and Steve Waugh. The mood was light, and lightened further on the arrival of a brief shower. Langer even permitted himself a glass of red wine: 'Well, after all, it was my 29th birthday.' He slept that night like a suckling, convinced that the Test had been saved, and that his place in the side was secure.

Gilchrist stayed up watching an Andrew Symonds favourite. ("What's that movie with Jerry Maguire in it called again?"). He told Damien Fleming at its 23:30 conclusion that there were two items on his docket in the event of an Australian triumph: "I will do a little dance like Rod [Tidwell] did, but I won't cry at the press conference like he did."

Langer drew back the curtains the next morning – 'and as the Poms say, it was cracking flags.' The sun shone out of a vacant sky. The forecast had lulled him into complacency:

'Now I knew we had a fight on our hands.' Gilchrist bumped into Bill Brown at breakfast. The old Invincible smiled at him: "We'll need a century from you today." 'Sure', thought Gilchrist. 'No pressure!' When he asked Brown how many *he* had scored at Headingley in 1948, in the record run chase of 404, 'he was a bit dirty. Turns out he was twelfth man.'

Buchanan gave Gilchrist some 15 throw-downs before the start of play, while Langer took 45 minutes of amateur leg spin. Dave Misson, official team fitness guru and unofficial team poet, read out some bad but rousing verses:

> With our backs to the wall,
> Let's throw the wall at the Pakis.
> Embrace the challenge and enjoy the fight,
> We must *all* believe that victory is in our sight.
> Concentrate hard but stay positive out there,
> So at the end of the day, a great victory we can share.

Buchanan, more prosaic, led 'a brief but to-the-point discussion', to which several players contributed. 'We knew it was going to be tough' wrote Waugh. 'The first hour was crucial. We knew they'd come at us hard.'

But they didn't. They opened the day instead with Azhar's docile medium pacers and Saqlain's neutered off spin. 'The Pakistanis played into our hands,' recalled Langer, 'still surprised about their decision' a decade on. There were complicating factors – a diabetic Wasim had been sick all tour, and felt especially dreadful today, and Waqar had rolled an ankle in the popping crease – but there was no reason not to give Shoaib a couple of overs. 'The last thing I expected', wrote Langer, 'were some "sighters" from Azhar Mahmood.'

The field, too, was strangely defensive. Gilchrist and Langer played themselves in quietly: 'We didn't go out and blaze; we tried to wear them down.' The surface was hard and dry, still very good for batting – perhaps better than it had been all match. Gilchrist brought up his fifty with a drive on the up past mid-off for three. When, after 10 overs, Wasim commandeered the new ball, the batsmen were set and had evolved a strategy: they would focus not on the ultimate goal of 369, but on targets small and incremental. Langer set himself 10 runs at a time; for the faster-scoring Gilchrist, it was 10 minutes at a time. Langer exhorted him after each such milestone: "C'mon, another 10 now!"

They made for a contrastive pair. 'Langer might have been in the Dardanelles', ventured Peter Roebuck. 'Gilchrist seemed to think he was on Perth's Cottesloe Beach.' They were 143 runs short at drinks. Gilchrist, on 65, had intuited that 'the Pakistanis might help us by self-destructing.' As he had observed the day before:

> 'Their mood was always unified, one way or the other. They were a real team, if you like. When they were going well, as they were that day, they were exuberant, laughing, talking nonstop, all encouraging each other. But we knew that when they turned, they turned together, and it wouldn't take much before they'd be pointing fingers and gesturing at each other. Towards the end of the day, with our counter-attack, there had been a few promising signs.'

That promise now manifested itself. Their out-cricket, uncommonly vibrant in this match so far, grew ragged as the final morning progressed. Soon bowlers were waving down their captain and complaining about the fielding; they discouraged each other even as they bucked up the batsmen. The main culprit was Saqlain, a ghost of his first-innings self, who began to act up at mid-on. Twice in two balls he forced Gilchrist to pull away as Shoaib charged in. Better behaved on the third attempt, he farcically misfielded, giving Australia another two runs.

Pakistan were still just one major hurdle from victory, however, and Wasim thought he had vaulted it with Australia 132 runs short. There was a wooden, clicking noise as the ball passed Langer's bat on its way through to Moin Khan. It registered at precisely the right moment on the snickometer; there was even a small deflection, visible from the reverse-angle replay. (The reader is directed to *YouTube*.) But home umpire Peter Parker was having none of it. He shook his head, and Wasim was livid: "I can't *believe* you didn't hear it!" "Come *on*!" moaned Moin.

Parker had earlier apologised to Langer for a poor first-innings decision: "A silly thing to do", in the view of his colleague Peter Willey. When the fact was publicised, the suspicion naturally arose that Pakistan had been hard done by. The umpire, it seemed, had attempted to make amends. "I honestly believe I didn't hit it", Langer claimed afterwards. He was lying through his teeth, and he would lie a decade more, attributing the sound, whenever he was asked about it, to "a clicky bat handle." He even kept this up with his father. It is a wonder anyone believed it. 'Truth is,' he admitted 10 years later, when it no longer mattered, 'I absolutely smashed it.'

But Langer's mendacity, and Parker's possible cowardice, is less interesting and salient for our purposes than the question of whether or not Gilchrist, too, was lying: "I didn't hear anything – absolutely nothing." These were his words to a press conference later that day. But many spectators heard it; Roebuck heard it; Langer's own team-mates heard it; even his father heard it. The claim is also crucially at odds with Gilchrist's own memoir, in which he affirms that 'there was a noise, but it was inconclusive.' It is difficult to say what he could mean by this. The bat had been nowhere near either pad or turf; it could only have been leather. As a 'walker' himself, Gilchrist is acclaimed for his probity. Someone ought to ask him about this episode.

A hinge had given way in the Pakistani psyche. Their morale was shattered, their concentration broken, and the air rang with their sledging – both of the batsmen and of each other. Later that over, when Langer edged one past first slip, Wasim was spitting nails. "Come on!" he bellowed. Gilchrist lifted the next ball down to third-man for a brace, then yanked its successor through mid-wicket for four. Wasim stormed and chuntered, his face a tablet of unutterable thoughts. He found he could no longer trust himself to deliver his jumper personally to Parker; instead he tossed it irritably to Ijaz Ahmed, who acted as courier.

Gilchrist scented blood. He grew in stature and hostility, timing the ball sweetly off both front foot and back, and putting Willey in mind of "a brutal Gower". Langer had enjoyed a head start of over two hours, but he was overtaken on 77. Gilchrist hied ahead, pulling and driving with freedom and force. An off-driven four, to a perfectly respectable delivery, brought up the 250. He was scoring now at more than a run a ball, but he was taking no risks; his strokes were impeccably orthodox, apotheoses of timing and placement. Two sizzling drives helped his tally to 85, and the crack of his bat reverberated all over the ground. 'Pakistan will be hearing the sound of Gilchrist's off-drive in their sleep', predicted the *Telegraph*. When an ailing Waqar came on for Wasim, Gilchrist mastered him immediately, pulling his first over for seven more runs.

Gilchrist prided himself, and always would, on never counting his chickens. In his debut Test, a week before, he had reached 81, but 'never once thought that I was closing in on a hundred. It just never entered my mind'. Here, though, on 97, the thought was irresistible: 'What will I do if I get 100? I've seen [Michael] Slater kiss his helmet, and Junior [Mark Waugh] just sort of ignore everyone. What am I going to do?' He tranquillised himself with a reminder of the labours ahead: 'Well, I don't need to do anything. Don't carry on, because we still need another ninety or so to win.'

It came just before lunch, with a crisp straight drive off a sterile Waqar. 'Gilchrist screamed. Then I screamed, and lost the plot for about thirty seconds.' As the ball reached the boundary, he pumped his fists and cried, "Come on!" – flexible expression, that – before saluting the dressing room and embracing his giddy partner. At 110 deliveries, it was the fastest Australian century since Ray Lindwall's 88-baller at the MCG in 1947. (This excludes Richie Benaud's century in 78 minutes in 1955, whose strike-rate was not recorded). His second fifty had run through just 38 deliveries.

Australia went to lunch needing 92 more. As they worked their way through their calamari, chicken wings and spring rolls, 'Justin and I could feel the optimism oozing out of the boys.' The ambience was 'more like that of a football change room. Everyone was pumped and telling us we could win it. They had music playing and even Tugga [Steve Waugh] was agitated, tossing an orange worry ball from hand to hand.' Only now did it occur to Langer that victory was feasible; Gilchrist, on all available evidence, seems to have believed throughout.

The tempo advanced with the resumption. A bowling combo of Shoaib and Saqlain lasted just five bootless overs. Saqlain was otiose, and Shoaib took refuge in bouncers, menacing brainpan and thorax. One pinged Langer flush on the chin:

'It hurt like hell but I just turned and grinned at him. There's a photo of it somewhere. I look crazed, my grin only made worse by a missing tooth I had from an injury early in my career. I always took the plate out when I batted because I couldn't chew gum otherwise. It left a gaping hole in the front of my mouth which made me look like a crim.'

Gilchrist walked down the pitch to offer his congratulations: "Mate, you're crazy." He would never forget the sight. Langer summons this as the moment "I knew we were going to win."

Gilchrist had 107, and the Australians were 79 behind, when he thrust his pads at a drifting, well-pitched doosra. Parker rejected the appeal, and Saqlain, tired and emotional, seemed to have given up. Gilchrist gorged deep on his lobbed half volleys. When Wasim and Azhar took over, the floodgates opened still wider: the pulls were effusive and the off drives fluid. Gilchrist was especially severe on Wasim, whose wounds were salted by twenty *borachios* in the outer. They ragged him and his bowlers with some foul-spoken chants, and the Pakistani captain allowed them to play on his mind; at one point he turned and responded in kind.

Up in the Australian dressing room, the players were chained to their seats. No-one had moved – and Waugh had permitted no-one to move, save at intervals – for three hours now. 'It was a surreal atmosphere,' he recalled, 'particularly as it was like being in a time capsule, in our own room with no outside noise or fresh air coming in. The only sense we had available to us was sight, and it was all good as the target kept tumbling at an increasing rate.' A similar atmosphere prevailed on the Australian mainland, during Question Time in Federal Parliament, where a cricket-tragic prime minister was taking regular updates on the progress of the national team.

Langer went to his century with a paddled single. Gilchrist's had required barely a session; Langer's consumed the better part of a day, but it was 'probably my best Test innings'. His partner marked the occasion with a pair of coruscating boundaries. Fewer than 50 runs now separated the sides, and each scoring shot brought a roar from the Australian change room. Wasim rung the changes, but the batsmen recomposed themselves for each. Langer lost count of the number of times he instructed his partner, "Now, this is an absolutely crucial spell we must get through." They exchanged mutual confidences after every ball, and touched gloves for every boundary; each promised the other that he would not get out before the job was done.

Langer broke his promise a mere five runs short, 'trying to hit Saqlain out of the park. But I wasn't upset – we had won.' The partnership was worth 238: a sixth-wicket record, by 99 runs, for any country against Pakistan, and the third-highest for Australia. Langer raised his bat to a standing ovation. His father hugged him at the gate. 'Personally, it was probably the proudest moment I've had playing for Australia.'

Gilchrist had crossed while the ball was in the air; now he rocked back and cut Saqlain to the fence. As the next ball glided over long-on, he lifted his arms in jubilation. The triumph was consummated. Australia had won by four wickets, with more than a session to spare. When the forecast rain finally arrived, the players were two hours into their celebrations. The scoreboard was preserved for several days, as visitors paid homage to the greatest run chase ever in Australia.

With 149 off 163 balls, including one six and 13 fours, a new star had come into the sky. It was a match-winning innings, but Gilchrist's centuries would almost always be so. Fourteen out of seventeen coincided with victory, only one with defeat. His average had swollen to 118. It was suggested to him at the press conference that he was finding Test cricket easy. "I never said that", came his stern reply. "I never will. I realise how quickly things can turn. I've got to enjoy it but keep my mind on the big picture and be realistic about it, and look to next week, I suppose. After tonight."

Pakistan

Saeed Anwar	c Warne b McGrath	0
M Wasim	c †Gilchrist b Muller	91
Ijaz Ahmed	c Slater b McGrath	6
I-ul-Haq	b Muller	12
Y Youhana	c ME Waugh b Fleming	17
A Mahmood	b Warne	27
Moin Khan†	c McGrath b Muller	1
Wasim Akram*	c †Gilchrist b Warne	29
S Mushtaq	lbw b Warne	3
Waqar Younis	not out	12
Shoaib Akhtar	c †Gilchrist b Fleming	5

Extras (b10, lb6, w3) **19**
Total (all out; 72.5 overs; 283 mins) **222**

Fall of wickets 1/4 2/18 3/71 4/120 5/148 6/153 7/188 8/198 9/217

Bowling	O	M	R	W
GD McGrath	18	8	34	2
DW Fleming	24.5	7	54	2
SA Muller	12	0	68	3
SK Warne	16	6	45	3
GS Blewett	2	1	5	0

Saeed Anwar	b Warne	78
M Wasim	c McGrath b Muller	20
S Mushtaq	lbw b Warne	8
Ijaz Ahmed	c SR Waugh b McGrath	82
I-ul-Haq	c ME Waugh b Warne	118
Y Youhana	c Ponting b Fleming	2
A Mahmood	lbw b Warne	28
Moin Khan†	c †Gilchrist b Fleming	6
Wasim Akram*	c Blewett b Warne	31
Waqar Younis	run out (†Gilchrist)	0
Shoaib Akhtar	not out	5

Extras (lb6, w1, nb7) **14**
Total (all out; 128.5 overs; 521 mins) **392**

Fall of wickets 1/50 2/100 3/122 4/258 5/263 6/320 7/345 8/357 9/358

Bowling	O	M	R	W
GD McGrath	27	8	87	1
DW Fleming	29	5	89	2
SK Warne	45.5	11	110	5
SA Muller	17	3	63	1
SR Waugh	4	1	19	0
ME Waugh	2	0	6	0
RT Ponting	2	1	7	0
GS Blewett	2	0	5	0

Australia

MJ Slater	c Ijaz Ahmed b S Mushtaq	97
GS Blewett	c †M Khan b A Mahmood	35
JL Langer	c M Wasim b S Mushtaq	59
ME Waugh	lbw b Waqar Younis	5
SR Waugh*	c Ijaz Ahmed b W Akram	24
RT Ponting	b Waqar Younis	0
AC Gilchrist†	st †M Khan b S Mushtaq	6
SK Warne	b S Mushtaq	0
DW Fleming	lbw b S Mushtaq	0
GD McGrath	st †M Khan b S Mushtaq	7
SA Muller	not out	0

Extras (b2, lb6, nb5) **13**
Total (all out; 80 overs; 355 mins) **246**

Fall of wickets 1/76 2/191 3/206 4/206 5/213 6/236 7/236 8/236 9/246

Bowling	O	M	R	W
W Akram	20	4	51	1
S Akhtar	17	2	69	0
W Younis	12	1	42	2
S Mushtaq	24	8	46	6
A Mahmood	7	1	30	1

GS Blewett	c †M Khan b A Mahmood	29
MJ Slater	c A Mahmood b S Akhtar	27
JL Langer	c I-ul-Haq b S Mushtaq	127
ME Waugh	lbw b A Mahmood	0
SR Waugh*	c & b S Mushtaq	28
RT Ponting	lbw b Wasim Akram	0
AC Gilchrist†	not out	149
SK Warne	not out	0

Did not bat DW Fleming, GD McGrath, SA Muller

Extras (b1, lb4, nb4) **9**
Total (6 wickets; 113.5 overs; 503 mins) **369**

Fall of wickets 1/39 2/81 3/81 4/125 5/126 6/364

Bowling	O	M	R	W
W Akram	18	1	68	1
W Younis	11	2	38	0
S Akhtar	23	4	85	1
S Mushtaq	44.5	9	130	2
A Mahmood	17	3	43	2

Marcus Trescothick – 180

South Africa v England, Johannesburg 13-17 January 2005

-James Mettyear-

When Marcus Trescothick took guard at the start of England's second innings of the fourth Test at the New Wanderers Stadium, he did so amid muttered disquiet from within the ranks of the travelling press corps. He had failed in the first innings, launching himself at a full delivery from Dale Steyn with his front foot some way from the ball and edging to Mark Boucher for 16. Caught behind: a not unfamiliar mode of dismissal. His form had been patchy throughout the series and what with the Ashes in the coming English summer and his record found wanting against Glenn McGrath and Jason Gillespie in particular, there were calls from some to drop him down the order and so 'protect him from the moving ball'.

It was not for the first time. Even when he was blasting the quickest and best of fast men or the most skilful of spinners with an exhilarating dominance perhaps not seen in an England opener since Colin Milburn briefly flared, there remained among many English cricket followers persistent doubts about Tressie.

It was not that they mistrusted the man. This cricketing son of Somerset with a name as if chiselled from a Cornish tin mine; the apple-cheeked yeoman whose natural affability hid a staunch dependability as sure as his bucket hands in the slips, was a stalwart, plain and simple. Self-effacing, loyal, the archetypal good egg. As Michael Vaughan put it in his 2005 autobiography: 'He is the ultimate team player...just about as dependable a guy as there is in the dressing room'.

No, it was not the man we worried about. At least not then, not before he had told us with such brave candour of his illness. It was not the man. It was the technique. The technique, honed though we knew it to have been, that triggered the unease. The feet were the problem. Despite the honing, they didn't seem to want to move and were thus heretical to the long held orthodoxy that they must. Small wonder the likes of writer and broadcaster Christopher Martin-Jenkins remained ever unconvinced.

But it wasn't just the purists. We all, as England followers, couldn't help but fret in the early stages of a Tresco knock. Even if he'd biffed his way to a quick-fire 30-odd, it could still be akin to watching a man on a tightrope. When the mechanism clicked and the rhythm was right, then the coming together of all the workings – head and body held guardsman still and straight; the reflex to gorge outside off stump held in check; outstanding eye, consummate timing and effortless power – all held him in perfect balance and never looking down, he seemed to glide fearlessly in a bubble of sustained concentration high above the context of the game, of the attack, of the world outside his immediate gaze.

But then, at other times, as in the first innings of this game, as if dulled by doubt, he would prod or lunge, stiff-legged, leaden-footed and then topple and fall. And when he fell, he would plummet, dropping like a stone through all the strata of the game to land without safety net amongst the knowing refrain of pundit and public alike: 'Great eye. Awesome power. Doesn't move his feet. Club cricketer.'

It was a reluctant chorus for the most part, in deference as it was to his palpable decency and in recognition of all the times it went right, but it was there nonetheless. And, it has to be said, even among his most ardent admirers, not without reason. Throughout Trescothick's career, periods of serene dominance had been punctuated by alarming slumps in form. As a youth he had blazed his way into the record books. His diet of sausages and fizzy pop and a resultant frame he himself would later describe as 'on the portly side of chubby', no impediment to his summary dismissal of age group, senior club and junior international attacks. Leaving his comprehensive school with a single GCSE, he joined the Somerset staff in 1992 at just 16 years old. His baptism in the first team came the following year and began with so dismal a run of scores – 1, 3, 6, 28, 0, 4, 0, 0, 7, 2 – that the candle lit as schoolboy prodigy was not just guttering but on the point of being permanently snuffed out.

But then the following first full year in the first team, the runs flowed again. He scored 2,500 of them in all forms of cricket, including 924 at 48.63 in the County Championship. Pretty impressive for an 18-year-old. It was to be a year of plenty, however, that presaged nigh on seven of famine. These were the wilderness years when things fell into place only occasionally, his greatest strength, his unquenchable appetite for tucking into balls outside his off stump, also time and time again his undoing. Unfulfilled early promise drifting toward a premature exit from the higher levels of the game. Club cricketer.

In the winter of 1998-99, in a last ditch effort to turn the tide, he battled the homesickness and travelled to Australia to work with Peter Carlstein, the world-renowned South African batting coach, and play grade cricket. And it was there that he had the epiphany that would bring him back from the edge of likely professional oblivion. He describes the moment in his 2008 autobiography *Coming Back to Me*:

> 'And finally, one bright clear day in Perth…one ball in particular told me I was going to be all right. I saw it leave the bowler's hand, and I recall watching it so closely that the rest of what followed happened in super slow-motion even though it was travelling around mid-80s mph. I saw it pitch about two yards from me and slightly to my off-side and realised I had all the time in the world to make a clear choice whether to play it or not. And in the instant I made my decision to leave it, a small happy bomb went off inside my head. I'd got it. By George, I'd got it.'

And he had. Later that summer, on a fast pitch at Taunton under the discerning gaze of the then Glamorgan coach, Duncan Fletcher and carrying with him the new knowledge that he could leave the ball if he wished, he elected not to and hit the then decidedly quick Jacques Kallis repeatedly out of the ground. He reached 167 with 25 fours and five sixes. The next highest score was 50 and he had caught the future England coach's eye.

Opening his England account with 79 for the one-day side in July 2000 against Zimbabwe, his five-day debut followed the same year in the third Test against the West Indies. He began well, scoring 66 in the first innings and 38 not out to finish with 190 runs at 47.5 in his three games. From that point on, after a lean second series away to Pakistan, Trescothick would remain at the forefront of the Fletcher/Hussain England resurrection that followed the nadir of their home defeat to New Zealand the previous summer. On his first tour, he was asked to join the management committee with an express remit from Nasser Hussain to keep a check on banter drifting into bullying; on the 2002-03 tour to Australia he was appointed vice captain.

By the time of the Johannesburg Test at the start of 2005 he had scored 4,207 test runs at 42.49, including nine centuries. That the first two of these were in losing causes, served as testament to his ability to hold his head still and clear when those around him were losing theirs. Innings of 122 at Galle against Chaminda Vass and Mutiah Muralitharan (no other Englishman made 50) and a second innings 117 against Waqar Younis and Wasim Akram at Manchester (again where only one other batsmen reached 50) gave the lie to C M-J's rather dismissive description of him in the *Times* before the Wanderers Test as one who 'where the ball is moving through the air or off the pitch is fodder for a thorough-bred bowler'.

And yet, even then there had been wild fluctuations in form. Calmly assured highs, followed by, at the time, baffling lows most, but not all, coinciding with time spent away from Taunton. Times when we'd watch him edge to the cordon yet again, turn and with his knock-kneed stride walk swiftly from the crease, his rounder-shouldered form somehow already softening into the lurking tubbiness he'd fought against since youth. In the 18 months before the 2004-05 tour to South Africa, there'd been an unfulfilling home series against the Proteas until the final match at The Oval where, with a game-moulding 219 in the first innings and an unbeaten 69 in the second, he provided the platform for England to draw the series. There was then an autumn away to Bangladesh (202 runs at 68.66) followed by a scratchy pre-Christmas Sri Lanka tour (167 runs at 27.8); then a bleak spring in the Caribbean (166 at 23.71) before a run-rich home summer in 2004 against New Zealand and the West Indies (641 runs at 53.4). The first six innings in South Africa had seen him register oscillating scores of 47, 0, 18, 132, 28, and 0. Not by any means disastrous but enough to put us all a little on edge.

241/Masterly Batting

The first three games of the series had ebbed and flowed with the lurching movement of a spring tide. A confident England, ranked number two in the world and unbeaten in 2004, won the first by seven wickets. They stuttered badly in the first innings of the second and then ultimately failed to drive home their advantage allowing the home side to secure a slightly lucky draw. In the third, they emphatically hit the dirt losing to a resurgent South Africa by 196 runs. Level pegging and two to play.

The first three days of the fourth Test followed the same template. England won the toss and on a Wanderers' pitch of uncharacteristic low bounce, an imperious Andrew Strauss with 147 supported by Robert Key dominated the first two sessions taking the visitors to 227-2 before Key fell for 83. After tea though, a previously sluggish Makhaya Ntini, reinvigorated by an enforced ice bath and the second new ball, took the two late wickets of Strauss and Graham Thorpe just before the close. England stumbled to 263-4 at the end of an ultimately disappointing day.

On the second morning, under lowering skies and with Ntini and Shaun Pollock making the most of damp conditions, the England middle order folded before a grafting Vaughan, struggling with timing and confidence and supported first by the lively Ashley Giles and then a free-hitting Steve Harmison, took the tourists to 411-8 at the end of a day shortened by bad light.

With further rain forecast, England declared overnight only to wake to sunny skies and a growing Wanderers crowd who saw the hosts, let off the hook by woeful English bowling and dropped catches, take their score to 306-6 at stumps on the third day; Herschelle Gibbs unbeaten for a brilliant hundred. At the start of the fourth day, a weary England failed to polish off the hosts who edged past the visitors' total to reach 419.

The tourists began their second innings with just two overs to face before lunch and the rollercoaster game still precariously balanced. With Harmison, Geraint Jones and Giles all carrying injuries, the predicted course was for England to dig in and make the game safe. Losing the match, and with it all chance of winning the series and with that the spectre of embarking on the long-awaited sold-out Ashes summer with wings clipped, meant that pushing for victory was surely freighted with too great a risk. They would have to bat well to secure the draw.

If that was their plan, they couldn't have got off to a worse start with Strauss, England's in-form banker, wafting loosely at Ntini at the start of the second over and falling for a duck. Whichever way they were going to play it, there was much now resting on his opening partner.

Trescothick began quietly, struggling a little with his timing. At the end of the seventh over he had scored just six from 19 balls, allowing Key to take the lead. But then in the eighth, leaning forward, he clipped Ntini off his legs in front of mid-wicket for his first boundary. In the next over, with Pollock attacking him from round the wicket he repeated the stroke, this time waiting a fraction longer and with his head still and body perfectly balanced, the ball eased backward of square and to the rope. The next delivery, Pollock over-compensated and changed his line to further outside off stump to be met with a firm-footed, arms-free lash to the extra-cover boundary. A Tresco trademark. The next ball, just outside off stump was cut hard, a certain four saved by a sprawling Gibbs in the gully. The fifth, again too straight, was picked up from just outside off stump and flicked between mid-wicket and mid-on. This was perhaps the pivot-point over for Trescothick. Fourteen off it, with three fours and each ball played with a controlled intent that made clear Banger was not planning to allow the innings to suffer from a lack of momentum.

He lost Key in the following over to Ntini and at 52-2 a period of retrenchment might have been the order of the day. Rather than a drawing in of the horns, however, what followed was a period of play described even by the lugubrious Bob Willis on commentary as 'scintillating'. Together with Vaughan, who by the end of his first innings had finally played himself into some sort of form, Trescothick put the South African attack to the sword. By the time his skipper fell to Pollock for 54, he had reached 88 off 141 balls with 13 fours and in a partnership of 124 captain and vice captain had taken their side to 175-3 from 47 overs.

This was Trescothick at his stand and deliver best. There were broadsword drives through extra-cover, slashing cuts backward of point as well as brutal pull shots. One of these, to a quick ball from Kallis pitched just short of a length outside off stump with the upper body swivelling swiftly from a rooted base, sent the ball scudding to the mid-wicket fence before the bowler had completed his follow-through. A crunching exemplar of his awesome power and timing. But there were also rapier thrusts: a deft soft-handed dab through gully off Ntini, a leg glance off Pollock and a late cut off Nicky Boje all instances redolent as much of David Gower as the 'left-handed Gooch' Nasser Hussain later dubbed him.

But by the end of the fourth day in a match that often seemed, as *Wisden* editor Mathew Engel put it, 'four-sided', the pendulum had swung yet again. Vaughan's dismissal was followed swiftly by the wickets of Thorpe for one and Andrew Flintoff for seven and it was no surprise when, unbeaten on 101, Trescothick and an out-of-touch Geraint Jones took the offer of the light.

With England closing the truncated day on 197-5, just 189 runs ahead, it was the home side who finished the day in the more buoyant mood. Five quick wickets in the morning and then, with Harmison's calf meaning he was unlikely to bowl and Jimmy Anderson still searching for his radar, a post-lunch run chase was how Boje, South Africa's stand-in captain after Graeme Smith's concussion in practice, saw things at the end of play. England's undefeated centurion viewed it differently insisting that, with the Wanderers pitch prone to unreliable bounce on the final day, an England win was still on the cards. In fact, with a 30 per cent chance of rain signalled by the forecasters, the draw was firm favourite.

The fifth day began badly for the visitors with Jones caught behind off Pollock in the sixth over of the day for 13: England 222-6. Trescothick, mindful of the need to husband the tail, batted carefully at first but then, with Giles as foil, he dispensed with the sword, brought out the bludgeon and proceeded to pulverise the South African attack with a controlled brutality that belied his ever-benign mien. It was heady stuff. When Giles fell for a quick-fire 31 with the score at 272 and Matthew Hoggard was out two runs later, 'Banger' upped the pace still further and put on a further 58 with Harmison whose contribution was just three. Particularly unforgiving of Boje, who he hit for two sixes and three fours in the space of two overs, he was finally out, caught Boucher, bowled Ntini for 180 off 248 balls with 24 fours and four sixes.

It was a masterly innings. In a match that mattered, in the unpredictable conditions of the Highveld summer and on a pitch which though fundamentally solid was never entirely straightforward, it was played out against an attack which held the threat of four bowlers – Ntini, Kallis, Pollock and a young Dale Steyn – who would all take more than 250 Test wickets. It was also chanceless. Indeed, save for an inside edged four from an Ntini delivery that lifted from a length early in his innings, it contained scarcely a false shot. 'Fodder to the thoroughbred bowler'? Hardly.

Throughout the heart of two days of pulsating Test cricket, Trescothick played, as he later described it, as if batting in *The Matrix*: 'I experienced that super slow-motion effect almost from the first ball I faced and…just felt the ball that had not yet been invented that could actually get me out.'

It was the pace of the innings as much as its size that allowed Michael Vaughan to declare on 332 at the fall of Trescothick's wicket and leave South Africa to score 325 in little more than two sessions. From there, despite Smith coming in at number 8 still groggy from his concussion and battling his way to a brave unbeaten 67, an inspirational spell of bowling from Matthew Hoggard with a Test-best spell of 7-61 off 18 overs (including Kallis, caught Trescothick first ball) carried England to an unlikely 77-run triumph.

In the afterglow of Hoggard's heroics, Trescothick's masterpiece was almost forgotten. No matter. For the man Nasser Hussain described as 'almost too nice for the top job', and who always put the team before self, the fact that Hoggard garnered the primary plaudits would have bothered Tressie not a jot.

Unsung or otherwise, however, it was the yeoman with the heart of willow who formed the platform for the victory that, after a rain-affected drawn fifth Test in which 130 overs were lost, proved to have launched his side, first to a series victory and from there perhaps to that unforgettable England-versus-Australia summer. As Geoff Boycott wrote at the time:

> 'Marcus Trescothick played so well...It was his innings that gave Hoggard the opportunity of winning the match. He'll find it difficult to play a better and more important innings in his career.'

Doesn't move his feet? Who cares? Neither did Graeme Pollock. Trescothick would finish the series with 448 runs at 44.80. In April, he would be named one of *Wisden's* Five Cricketers of the Year. By the end of the summer he was an Ashes hero. Not bad for a club cricketer.

England

Batsman	Dismissal	Runs
ME Trescothick	c †Boucher b Steyn	16
AJ Strauss	c Kallis b Pollock	147
RWT Key	c Smith b Ntini	83
MP Vaughan*	not out	82
GP Thorpe	c Dippenaar b Ntini	0
MJ Hoggard	c de Villiers b Ntini	5
A Flintoff	c Smith b Ntini	2
GO Jones†	c Smith b Pollock	2
AF Giles	c Gibbs b Steyn	26
SJ Harmison	not out	30
JM Anderson	did not bat	
Extras (lb13, nb5)		**18**
Total (8 dec; 124 ovrs; 558 mins)		**411**

Fall of wickets 1/45 2/227 3/262 4/263 5/273 6/275 7/278 8/329

Bowling	**O**	**M**	**R**	**W**
SM Pollock	33	12	81	2
M Ntini	34	8	111	4
DW Steyn	21	7	75	2
JH Kallis	22	2	79	0
N Boje	14	2	52	0

Batsman	Dismissal	Runs
ME Trescothick	c †Boucher b Ntini	180
AJ Strauss	c de Villiers b Ntini	0
RWT Key	c Kallis b Ntini	19
MP Vaughan*	c †Boucher b Pollock	54
GP Thorpe	c & bKallis	1
A Flintoff	c †Boucher b Pollock	7
GO Jones†	c de Villiers b Pollock	13
AF Giles	c Gibbs b Kallis	31
MJ Hoggard	c †Boucher b Kallis	0
SJ Harmison	not out	3
JM Anderson	did not bat	
Extras (lb7, w6, nb11)		**24**
Total (9 dec; 81.1 ovrs ; 367 mins)		**332**

Fall of wickets 1/2 2/51 3/175 4/176 5/186 6/222 7/272 8/274 9/332

Bowling	**O**	**M**	**R**	**W**
SM Pollock	19	2	74	3
M Ntini	20.1	2	62	3
JH Kallis	21	5	93	3
DW Steyn	9	0	47	0
N Boje	12	0	49	0

South Africa

Batsman	Dismissal	Runs
GC Smith*	lbw b Hoggard	29
HH Gibbs	c Hoggard b Anderson	161
JA Rudolph	c Giles b Hoggard	4
JH Kallis	b Hoggard	33
HH Dippenaar	c Trescothick b Flintoff	0
AB de Villiers	c Giles b Hoggard	19
MV Boucher†	c Strauss b Anderson	64
SM Pollock	lbw b Hoggard	0
N Boje	run out (Hoggard/ Giles)	48
M Ntini	b Giles	26
DW Steyn	not out	0
Extras (b9, lb11, w6, nb9)		**35**
Total (all out; 118.1 overs; 555 mins)		**419**

Fall of wickets 1/64 2/75 3/138 4/149 5/184 6/304 7/306 8/358 9/399

Bowling	**O**	**M**	**R**	**W**
MJ Hoggard	34	2	144	5
SJ Harmison	12.5	4	25	0
JM Anderson	28	3	117	2
A Flintoff	30.1	8	77	1
AF Giles	8.1	0	25	1
ME Trescothick	5	1	11	0

Batsman	Dismissal	Runs
AB de Villiers	lbw b Hoggard	3
HH Gibbs	lbw b Giles	98
JA Rudolph	b Hoggard	2
JH Kallis	c Trescothick b Hoggard	0
HH Dippenaar	c Giles b Hoggard	14
MV Boucher†	c †Jones b Hoggard	0
N Boje	c & b Hoggard	18
GC Smith*	not out	67
SM Pollock	c †Jones b Flintoff	4
M Ntini	lbw b Flintoff	13
DW Steyn	c †Jones b Hoggard	8
Extras (b2, lb5, w1, nb12)		**20**
Total (all out; 59.3 overs; 271 mins)		**247**

Fall of wickets 1/10 2/18 3/18 4/80 5/86 6/118 7/163 8/172 9/216

Bowling	**O**	**M**	**R**	**W**
MJ Hoggard	18.3	5	61	7
SJ Harmison	14	1	64	0
A Flintoff	16	2	59	2
JM Anderson	6	1	32	0
AF Giles	5	0	24	1

Clem Hill – 188

Australia v England, Melbourne 29 January-2 February 1898

-Sean Ehlers-

The 1894-95 Test series had been the first truly great one with England surrendering a 2-0 lead, only to win a classic fifth Test against the odds, to claim the rubber 3-2. It is said the battle generated such excitement that Queen Victoria requested regular updates. The hero of the series was the extremely popular English captain Andrew Stoddart.

It was no surprise that the organisers of the next Ashes series, to be played in Australia during the summer of 1897-98, again invited the charismatic Stoddart to be the sole selector and captain. He was charged with finding a team with what we now call 'drawing power'. The biggest cricketing star at the time was WG Grace, however, even if he had been available his asking price would have resulted in a loss for the promoters, it being noted he alone would drink enough wine 'to swim a ship'. Stoddart, in a masterstroke of publicity, convinced the exotic Indian prince, Kumar Ranjitsinhji, to make the tour.

It was stated that Ranji's arrival in the Antipodes had created more interest than that of Grace in 1892-93. He proved particularly popular with women and was a regular feature in the social pages of Australian newspapers. The name Ranji was seemingly everywhere in the summer of 1897-98. You could buy 'Ranji' cricket shoes and boots, ginger ale, cricket bats, matchboxes, chairs, brushes and even hair-restorer. A potential embarrassment was averted when the New South Wales government waived the £100 deterrent tax for 'coloured' visitors.

As tours at the time were organised and sponsored privately, the promoters took all the financial risks, so a draw card such as Ranji was the answer to their pecuniary dreams. The organisers, the Melbourne Cricket Club and the Trustees of the Sydney Association Cricket Ground, negotiated directly with those most likely to represent Australia against Stoddart's XI. The home-team players were all offered the same terms except the youngest prospective representative; 20-year-old Clem Hill was asked to accept £50 less than the rest of his countrymen. The promoters justified this because he was single, still residing with his parents and was no certainty to be selected for the first Test.

Hill put to rest any doubts about his selection for the Test matches in the tourists' very first game of the summer at his home ground Adelaide Oval, when he peeled off a faultless double-century. His fine innings, plus the urging of a senior Australian player, saw him belatedly elevated to the same pay scale as the rest of the team.

Ranji, writing in the press about Hill's innings, was quick to highlight his predilection for scoring to the on side and conversely his lack of strokes to the off. This criticism of the home-grown hero and some disparaging remarks the prince made about the Adelaide Oval was to see him barracked when he returned to Adelaide for the third Test, with the crowd christening him with a rhyming epithet "Rum and Whiskey".

Now assured of his place in the Australian team, the left-handed Hill would have to defy history if he was to be successful in the Tests. By the start of the 1897-98 series there had been 53 Test matches played, with a total of 42 centuries registered and not one of those had been scored by a lefty. This would change in the first Test of the series but it was not to be Hill who bucked the trend. Instead it was his fellow left hander and South Australian, Joe Darling, who scored 101 in Australia's second innings. Hill came within a whisker of being the second when he was dismissed for 96. Despite the fine batting of the pair, the home team suffered a crushing defeat, losing by nine wickets, as Ranji proved he was a great batsman and not just an exotic object for admiration or subject for derision. Hill had struggled in the first innings, making only 19, as the English bowlers, having learnt their lesson after his 200 in Adelaide, concentrated on his off stump to cramp his propensity to favour the on side.

Notwithstanding the big loss in the first Test, the signs were there that Australia, with their two left handers, would be more competitive in the remaining games. So it proved, the home team winning the second and third Tests, each by an innings, with the mollydookers dominant. Hill scored two half centuries (58 and 81) and Darling a magnificent 178 in the third Test in Adelaide, during which the two put on 148 together.

Hill, who had enjoyed a consistent series, was yet to reach his maiden Test century and was clearly behind his older team-mate as the best batsman of the summer. This was due to change in the fourth Test, to be played at the MCG. A victory at Melbourne would win back the Ashes, lost in 1893, and give Australia their first-ever win against England in a five-match series.

In the preceding three Tests, the side winning the toss and batting first had won easily on batsmen's wickets. It was odds-on that the captain calling correctly in the fourth Test, in front of an estimated crowd of 19,600, would take first strike. For the first time in a Test match, according to the *Sydney Morning Herald*, the captains tossed in front of the pavilion, with Stoddart using what he hoped would be a lucky florin. The luck was with Harry Trott, the Australian captain, who called heads and duly elected to take first strike on what appeared to be yet another fine pitch. With the temperature registering 107°F in the shade, it was going to be a tough day in the field. As it turned out, the heat hardly relented during the whole match. The enervating conditions inspired Frank Allan, the former Test player who had been labelled the 'Bowler of the Century', to give the Australian team a small bundle of vine leaves to wear under their hats to help keep them cool. These he presented with the dedication, 'Good luck chaps'.

The Australians did not seem to need any more luck than winning the toss on a pitch that was so flat it was thought a spirit level could not find an undulation. Despite there not being a crack in the glossy surface, some of the batsmen believed one end of the wicket contained too much moisture. One or two reporters – based on subsequent events – disparagingly questioned whether the majority of the Australians were at the wicket long enough to express a creditable opinion of the strip.

Whether the pitch assisted the bowlers or not, England made an ideal start as Jack Hearne dismissed Charlie McLeod. Clem Hill strode out to join Joe Darling at 1-1 but hopes that the two would repeat their Adelaide heroics were soon dashed as Tom Richardson, who had been troubled by rheumatism all summer, suddenly returned to the form that had seen him rated the best fast bowler in the world. He removed Darling for 12 and then clean bowled 'Tich' Gregory first ball. Frank Iredale survived the hat-trick but was caught at the wicket off Hearne from the next delivery he faced. Hill, who had moved to 13 in confident style, desperately needed someone to stay with him as Australia collapsed to 4-26.

Next in was Monty Noble, destined to become one of Australia's great allrounders and finest captains, who was involved in his first Test series. He started with a couple of nice drives before tamely returning a soft catch to the bowler, Hearne, whose third wicket sank Australia further into the mire at 5-32. A shocked and subdued crowd now found supportive voice as the Australian captain entered the arena. Harry Trott had been in poor health throughout the summer and would be admitted to Kew Asylum before the end of the year. He was also rumoured to be losing the sight in his right eye and although he was troubled by the bowlers he was desperately trying to support Hill as the lunch break loomed.

Just before the interval the crowd was reduced to a despairing groan as the umpire put up his finger in response to a run-out appeal against Hill as he attempted a sharp single. The crowd's despair turned to relief when it was realised the umpire, Charles Bannerman, was just brushing away a fly. Bannerman, who was the scorer of Test cricket's first century back in 1877, perhaps missed the limelight and was playing to the gallery. A relieved Hill left the field for lunch on 34 out of a score of 5-58, with Trott on seven. The paucity of runs gives an idea of the superiority of the bowlers but the fervent hope of home supporters was that Hill and Trott could combine after the break to bring Australia back into the match.

The recovery was not to be, as three balls after the resumption and without adding to his score, Trott was caught by wicket-keeper Bill Storer, giving Hearne his fourth scalp. At 6-58, and with all the other recognised batsman back in the pavilion, the untroubled 20-year-old was fast running out of partners. The next man in, Hugh Trumble, appeared nonchalant as he approached the wicket. Certainly no mug with the bat, Trumble had, throughout his career, the happy knack of scoring runs when his team most needed them and his calm disposition was just what was required in the crisis. Hill seemed to take heart from Trumble's attitude and started to play more shots and typically he was especially severe on anything pitched near his pads. It was just such a clip off his pads for a boundary that brought up his fifty. Although ungainly as he lost his feet in playing the stroke, Hill was quickly up to acknowledge the applause.

Hill was now into stride, punishing anything short with vicious cuts. To try and slow the scoring Hearne commenced bowling 'off-theory', pitching the ball wide of the off stump with, typically, eight fieldsmen backing his line. The crowd began to jeer at the tactics and although successful to a degree they did not stop Hill bringing up his first Test century by again taking the ball off his pads just before the tea break. His hundred had taken just under three hours. At tea the score was now a more respectable 6-151, with Hill's dominance apparent, his share being 107 and Trumble on a solid 20.

During the break Hill, refreshed from a shower and a change of clothes, had told Trumble as they returned to the field, "I think I shall have a go at them now." Trumble was not impressed with the impetuousness of youth, clasping his young team-mate by the shoulder and replying seriously: "You young devil; you have to stop there. Go along as you have been doing." Contemporary reports suggest Hill did not pay full attention to the advice as, after playing sedately for a few balls, he went after the bowling, especially that of Richardson. He was now playing drives to both sides of the wicket, compelling the Adelaide newspapers to ask whether Ranji still thought his stroke quality lacked polish on the off side.

In desperation, 'Drewy' Stoddart told wicket-keeper Storer to have a bowl and while he removed his pads ice was brought out to the players. But he proved expensive, both batsmen being severe on the part-time bowler and Hill taking the opportunity to hit consecutive boundaries to reach his 150. Just when Stoddart would have considered taking Storer off, as he was leaking six runs an over, he struck; Trumble smashing a long hop to square-leg, only to see the amateur Jack Mason take a 'grand catch' low to the ground. He had made a fine 46, sharing in a partnership of 165 at better than a run-a-minute.

Hill continued to play his strokes and by stumps he had raced to 182 out of 7-275. His score would have been higher had heat fatigue not set in which saw the batsmen walking singles when braces were on offer. Ever the team man, however, Hill ran out his partner's runs right to the end of the day. Early in his innings he had played in the style he had employed all summer, showing a propensity for the leg side with the occasional hard hit cut shot. However, later in his innings he played every conceivable stroke on both sides of the wicket. His performance was faultless with contemporary reports recording he gave no chances and played only two faulty strokes in the whole innings.

He had been severe on Tom Richardson throughout the summer, but he was especially harsh on the great fast bowler in this innings. Hill wrote in 1933 that his valiant opponent came up to him after play saying that: "I seem to have become a fast bowler for your special amusement." Throughout his career he was to show a preference for fast bowling.

As Hill left the field at the end of the first day, he was approached by a photographer and asked to pose for a photo the following rest-day morning. His succinct reply was: "Not if I know it; you can have me when my innings is over." Jack Worrall, the Australian twelfth man, who was covering the Test for the *Referee*, later recorded Hill's comments to yet another photographer's request: "I'll do nothing of the sort. I've had my luck spoilt before this year. When I get out we'll talk about it." The reason for his reluctance was the result of a superstition that had gained credence amongst the Australians. Some players after being not out overnight had then been dismissed early the next day after having their photos taken before the start of play. This had occurred when Hill had failed to add to his 200 for South Australia in the first match against Stoddart's XI. Joe Darling had similarly fallen foul when dismissed without increasing his wonderful 178 in the third Test in Adelaide. This was particularly upsetting as his father and Sir ET Smith, a cricket-loving business mogul, had both promised him £100 if he passed William Murdoch's record Test score of 211.

With some smoke in the air from nearby bushfires on the second day, and despite avoiding the photographers, Hill added just six more, finishing on 188, which included 21 boundaries and a five containing four overthrows. This was to remain his highest score in Ashes Tests. The *Adelaide Observer* gave the following breakdown of his scoring strokes: five runs by pulls, one in the slips, 24 by back cuts, 29 by cuts, 16 to mid-off, 10 by off drives, 31 by on drives, 25 to mid-on, 39 by square-leg strokes, and 8 by leg glances. In total, 80 on the off side and 108 on the on side. The runs scored confirmed the young man who had struggled with his off-side strokes and especially the drive early in the summer, had worked diligently to rectify his limitations and was now being spoken of as one of the best batsmen in the world.

Melbourne Punch was inspired to break into verse after Hill's coruscating innings.

I would like to sing
A little thing
About young Clement Hill,
Whose plucky play
On Saturday
Completely filled the bill.

Tom Horan, writing under the pen name 'Felix', considered Hill's innings as the best ever played by an Australian, surpassing what he had previously thought to be the finest century, the 165 by Charles Bannerman in the first-ever Test. Horan was one of the few who had watched both. The fact that Bannerman was an umpire in this match, lent a nice symmetry to the occasion.

In reply to Australia's 323, with Jack Hearne claiming 6-98, England collapsed for just 174 and, following on, were dismissed for 263. Even this effort, notwithstanding the smoke from the bushfires, was flattering with the Australians dropping five catches, three of which were missed in the slips by the usually reliable Trumble. Storer, who had broken his finger in two places while 'keeping, was forced to play his shots with just one hand on the bat, but still managed to hold on until stumps on the third day, finishing not out 24. With Jack Mason not out 25, England looked to have a chance of setting Australia a tricky target in the last innings. Alas both were dismissed early next morning. Australia, needing only 115 for victory, won comfortably by eight wickets. Hill was somewhat brought back to earth when he was trapped lbw by Tom Hayward for a duck. The young batsman showed his ignorance of the laws, since 'he erroneously maintains that a batsman cannot be given out lbw to a bowler bowling round the wicket,' recorded Worrall in the *Referee*.

The Australian captain Harry Trott's speech at the post-match function was quite brief, stating that Hill had played a great innings but admitting he had not watched very much of it as he was too nervous and stayed in the changing room with wicket-keeper Jim Kelly, not emerging until the 200 had been posted, "Then I went to see 'the boy' bat, and I never saw anything fine (sic) in my life." He said, tongue in cheek, that he could not go into the points of the game as he was writing a book on the series soon. The England captain's speech was extremely gracious; Stoddart made no excuses and praised the Australian team as clearly the better side, but stated he was still proud of his own XI. Ranji summed up the Australian approach to Ashes cricket, even in 1898, when he quipped referring to the bushfires, "Australia was the only country that would set itself alight just to win a Test Match."

The hosts went on to win the fifth Test, when Joe Darling became the first batsman to score three hundreds in a series, with a sublime 160 from as many balls on a wearing pitch. Hill described Joe's innings as the second-best Australian century he ever witnessed – the best being Victor Trumper's 185 in 1903-04. Hill failed in the fifth Test with Tom Richardson extracting some revenge by claiming his wicket in both innings.

So, with the summer over, Clement Hill had announced himself on the international cricketing stage. He would go on to play many more fine innings throughout his 17-year Test career, but he would never again reach the heights of his MCG masterpiece. There should be no surprise in this; few cricketers in the history of the game experience the 'zone' as Hill did at the MCG as a 20-year-old. Perhaps the best cricket writer of the 19th century, Tom Horan, should have the final word: 'Clem Hill's innings on January 29, 1898, will be talked of when the smallest boy who saw it will be white with the snows of time.'

Australia

CE McLeod	b Hearne	1
J Darling	c Hearne b Richardson	12
C Hill	c Stoddart b Hearne	188
SE Gregory	b Richardson	0
FA Iredale	c †Storer b Hearne	0
MA Noble	c & b Hearne	4
GHS Trott*	c †Storer b Hearne	7
H Trumble	c Mason b Storer	46
JJ Kelly†	c †Storer b Briggs	32
E Jones	c Hayward b Hearne	20
WP Howell	not out	9
Extras (b3, w1)		**4**
Total (all out; 101.4 overs)		**323**

Fall of wickets 1/1 2/25 3/25 4/26 5/32 6/58 7/223 8/283 9/303

Bowling	**O**	**M**	**R**	**W**
T Richardson	26	2	102	2
JT Hearne	35.4	13	98	6
TW Hayward	10	4	24	0
J Briggs	17	4	38	1
AE Stoddart	6	1	22	0
W Storer	4	0	24	1
E Wainwright	3	1	11	0

CE McLeod	not out	64
J Darling	c †Druce b Hayward	29
C Hill	lbw b Hayward	0
SE Gregory	not out	21

Did not bat FA Iredale, MA Noble, GHS Trott*, H Trumble, JJ Kelly†, E Jones, WP Howell

Extras (nb1)		**1**
Total (2 wickets; 39.4 overs)		**115**

Fall of wickets 1/50 2/56

Bowling	**O**	**M**	**R**	**W**
JT Hearne	7	3	19	0
TW Hayward	10	4	24	2
J Briggs	6	1	31	0
E Wainwright	9	2	21	0
JR Mason	4	1	10	0
KS Ranjitsinhji	3.4	1	9	0

England (followed-on)

AC MacLaren	b Howell	8
E Wainwright	c Howell b Trott	6
KS Ranjitsinhji	c Iredale b Trumble	24
TW Hayward	c Gregory b Noble	22
NF Druce	lbw b Jones	24
W Storer†	c & b Trumble	2
JR Mason	b Jones	30
AE Stoddart*	c Darling b Jones	17
J Briggs	not out	21
JT Hearne	c Trott b Jones	0
T Richardson	b Trott	20
Extras		**0**
Total (all out; 61.1 overs)		**174**

Fall of wickets 1/14 2/16 3/60 4/60 5/67 6/103 7/121 8/148 9/148

Bowling	**O**	**M**	**R**	**W**
WP Howell	16	7	34	1
GHS Trott	11.1	1	33	2
MA Noble	7	1	21	1
H Trumble	15	4	30	2
E Jones	12	2	56	4

J Briggs	c Darling b Howell	23
E Wainwright	c McLeod b Jones	2
AC MacLaren	c Iredale b Trumble	45
KS Ranjitsinhji	b Noble	55
TW Hayward	c & b Trumble	25
AE Stoddart*	b Jones	25
NF Druce	c Howell b Trott	16
JR Mason	b Howell	26
W Storer†	c Darling b McLeod	26
JT Hearne	not out	4
T Richardson	c Trumble b McLeod	2
Extras (b1, lb11, w1, nb1)		**14**
Total (all out; 114.2 overs)		**263**

Fall of wickets 1/7 2/63 3/94 4/147 5/157 6/192 7/211 8/259 9/259

Bowling	**O**	**M**	**R**	**W**
WP Howell	30	12	58	2
GHS Trott	12	2	39	1
MA Noble	16	6	31	1
H Trumble	23	6	40	2
E Jones	25	7	70	2
CE McLeod	8.2	4	11	2

Mark Butcher – 173*

England v Australia, Leeds 16-20 August 2001

5

-Mark Butcher, 23.04.2013-

"The moment I think I treasure the most is after I hit the final shot through point off Shane Warne – we ran three and running the third, the winning run, as I ran past Usi [Usman Afzaal] and towards Shane he [Warne] stuck up a high-five to me and I high-fived him on the way past. We clap hands together and I turn around, arms aloft, and I look a bit like 'What the hell just happened there?' That was a really lovely moment."

"When I got picked in '97 it was on the back of averaging 50 in the Championship the year before and similarly on an England A tour of Australia. England were getting the run-around in Zimbabwe and various places and there was a lot of clamour for change. It would have been fine but as is the way I really struggled at the beginning of '97 except for making a hundred in the freezing cold in a Champions versus MCC game. That pretty much nailed me on as a starter in that Ashes series. Obviously I was very excited, it was all I'd ever wanted to do but I wasn't playing very well, simple as that. I should have got a hundred at Lord's but they were a great side and it was a difficult summer.

"[After the West Indies tour of 1997-98] I'd played 10 Tests, made a couple of fifties and generally struggled, but that summer was completely different. I'd had a really good build up, came back from the West Indies and knew there was plenty of work to be done if I was going to make this a regular thing and I really got my head down and changed some technical things. The beginning of '98 was fantastic, all the rhythm was back. The first Test [against South Africa] was at Edgbaston and Athers [Mike Atherton] and I put on 180-odd which was a record at the time and I just felt really good. That was the first time I'd played the way I knew I could play in a Test match and I felt in control of what was going on. Then I went back to play for Surrey and snick, broke my thumb and missed two Tests. Then I should have made a hundred at Trent Bridge. Then Headingley, the maiden hundred. It was a little bit like what happened three years later – everything seemed to hit the middle of the bat. In terms of feeling like I'd arrived that series was it. I was really very pleased, the celebrations after the series confirm that!

"One of my main attributes was that the opposition didn't particularly bother me – it didn't matter who it was, for me it was all internal, how I was moving and how I was feeling, not whether it was some bloke out of the University side or Curtly Ambrose. If I didn't feel good about my game the Uni bloke had every chance of getting me out. But all the while there were some bad habits creeping into my game that, because of confidence being high and form being good, I was able to overcome and still score runs.

"Then we fly off to Australia, pretty confident having beaten South Africa. We had some good players but there was always the feeling that theirs were slightly better, particularly because they had the two weapons that nobody around could match. But we went out there confident we could make a good fist of the series.

"[After the first Test and a century] I couldn't hit it off the square. I ended up with 10 innings averaging 25 which is pretty much the story. Rather disappointed. I went back and worked my nuts off technique wise (fitness as well) – it's World Cup year. I was really looking forward to the summer. I made 260 against Leicester, who were reigning champions, at Grace Road, played as well as I ever have done and I was full of confidence. A couple of low scores against New Zealand [in the first Test] then two shit innings at Lord's and Nasser [Hussain] breaks his finger so I captain the side at Old Trafford. I got the feeling this wasn't a popular call within the dressing room but that didn't bother me. What did bother me was the fact that we had completely the wrong side. I said: 'Old Trafford has a history of reverse swinging plus the forecast is awful and you've got to give me a third seam option.' I suggested Craig White to which they said 'No, deal with it.' We were fucked before we'd even started. They get 500, I get nicked off for not many. The last day was washed out and we drew – what I'll never forget was being left to do the press conference on my own and then I get dropped for the next Test. I was spewing; very, very unhappy. We lost the Test and the series and ended up bottom of the Test rankings. That was English cricket in a nutshell, disappearing up its own backside at every turn. Something had to give, Nasser knew it and thankfully Duncan Fletcher came on the scene. Nasser's a guy who's not going to do it unless it's done properly and he had an ally.

"During that summer my marriage went completely south so that had a massive effect mentally, not really being able to concentrate or prioritise the cricket side of things and then we went to South Africa with pretty much an experimental side. Nasser and Duncan took a few players people had made a lot of noise about, it was a real mish-mash and I turn out to be one of the senior players but in no fit state mentally to play and at one stage I begged Nasser to let me go home. I was in a right state, drinking heavily and the problems at home were magnified by my not being there and cricket was the least important thing. Nass said: 'I need you to stay', so I stayed. If it had been 10 years later my request probably would have been granted but it was a massive life lesson. It could and should have ended my Test career.

"Athers was still in the side, as were Alec [Stewart] and Nasser so there was a group of senior players and then the addition of Trescothick and Vaughan who seemed to take to Test cricket like ducks to water. So you look at it from the outside – they're winning Test series, there's a relationship between captain and coach and everything seems to be heading in the right direction and it looks as though you're getting further and further away from ever doing it again and to be perfectly honest I don't think I really cared. I was desperately unhappy in my personal life, cricket seemed like a massive chore and slightly pointless. At one point I was playing second XI cricket but by the end of the summer [2000] I found a little bit of fun and enjoyment.

"It was in the winter, I was sleeping in a friend's spare room and doing a bit of work for *Sky* watching England in Pakistan and Sri Lanka – slight twinges of jealousy in terms of seeing them having such a good time. Then in mid-January I called my old man [Surrey second XI coach Alan Butcher] and said I need some help. I said: 'I've no idea what I'm doing, do what you like and I'll listen and try to do it.' I remember him having a grin on his face and he said: 'Ah good, I've been wanting to do this for ages.' We did at least three one-on-one sessions every week from January to mid-March. He tried to put me in the most neutral position he could. He said: 'With your eye you can hit the ball anywhere you want but the way you are doing everything means your brain thinks you can hit the ball over there but physically you can't.' I look back at the South Africa series [1998] and wince, 'how did you score any runs doing it like that?' So we're in the Ken Barrington centre at The Oval – long, long sessions with tennis balls and a bowling machine at 100mph until I get to the point where I feel unrecognisable as a player, feel my options are so much more open, my movements more fluid and something that will feel much easier to replicate under pressure.

"I was having fun and cricket was the only thing I had left. I'm not even considering I'll be involved in the Ashes – there are six or seven in front of me. All I want to do is score as many runs as possible for Surrey. I'm in a good place, enjoying life and, as the Ashes starts to creep closer, so people start getting injured. There was a Benson and Hedges semi-final on TV against Notts, I made 90-something and played really nicely; Ramps [Mark Ramprakash] gets injured, Vaughan's injured, Thorpe's gone in the back so suddenly they're looking around thinking, 'we haven't got a number three, we need some experience' and the next thing I know I get a phone call saying get yourself up to Edgbaston. So that's it, I'm back in the team. God knows how. But I've made a resolution: I'm going to enjoy it. Don't know how long it'll last, don't know how I'll play, I'm just going to go out and have as much fun as I can.

"The only time I can vividly remember being nervous was the first innings of that Test. I came out through the gate and suddenly my arms just went to jelly. I was absolutely terrified walking out to the middle. I took guard facing Jason Gillespie and he bowled me this quick yorker-thing which somehow missed off stump and I thought 'bloody hell' – I've never felt so scared in my life and then it [the nerves] went and I played alright.

"We lose the Test – get hammered – all in all it's been a great comeback for me. Four wickets, 80-odd runs – the rest of the team's played like shit! Because I didn't think I'd actually be there I had none of the build-up, none of the hype and it didn't feel like it was my place to care. It wasn't an obsession or I tried not to let it be, I'd been in that position before and nothing any good ever came from it. I'm massively competitive but it's only a game.

"Second Test – I absolutely loved Lord's Test matches – another great occasion playing against Australia, what could be better? Feeling more confident and determined to play as well as I can and enjoy it as much as I can. We dropped about six or seven catches and second innings, as usual, we're batting to save the Test. I'm in total control, we're losing wickets at the other end – I played really, really well. Gillespie had made some comment along the lines of 'I've thrown everything I had at this bloke and he's still there' – that was nice, reinforced what I already felt. I was walking pretty tall. So we move on to Trent Bridge. Turning this round was going to take something, all I can do is play as well as I can. Nightmare, that's it. Ashes finished, eleven days. Eleven days.

"Back then it was pretty much get your big, tall heavy seamers at Headingley. I was lucky to play in that Test – there was a bit of an incident in Nottingham where a member of the public had seen me out having a drink around midnight on the Friday. I was already out but it gets put in the newspapers and I'm actually dropped. They have a meeting; Duncan and Nasser, Atherton might have been involved somehow, one misdemeanour too many and Dave Fulton was going to be picked. The story goes that Nasser on his way back to Chelmsford is running through it and it's not sitting right and he phones Athers and Stewart and they're both like 'Are you sure? He's the only bloke who's scored a run so far.' So Nasser phones Duncan and says: 'I'm not happy with this, if the word hasn't gone out yet I want him in the side.' I didn't know any of this till after the Test.

"Glenn McGrath's famous 5-0 prediction hadn't happened since he'd started making it in '97, though they had seen nothing from us to indicate that this wouldn't be the year. They knocked us over reasonably cheaply in the first innings for a change, so we'd given them a lead of 140-odd. I played well, ran myself out – hit the ball back up the pitch, gone past the stumps at the other end and I just set off. It would've been fine had the fielder not been Brett Lee. Haven't missed a ball, everything's hit the middle of the bat, just felt great. The technical stuff I'd gone through was now bedded in, I just felt in really good control, the footwork was fantastic.

"Ponting comes out, blazes it to all parts. Absolutely sensational innings and they've just put hours of time back into the game and then it rained. A session or more disappeared, they declare and stick us back in. They would have been out of sight, potentially another 140 runs on top. It made our job of perhaps saving the Test that much easier.

"We were 8-0 overnight and I remember doing an interview – Mark Nicholas said: 'What do you think your chances are?' I said: 'Well, all it takes is for one of us to get a hundred, they're not out of sight by any means.' I didn't think Gilchrist had made a mistake – perhaps with hindsight there was a bit of hubris in it but why the hell would England even get close? You can't tell me Steve Waugh wouldn't have done the same thing, he was in the dressing room. I had a couple of beers in the hotel and went to bed early just thinking 'you're playing well, who knows?' I had quite a feeling of expectation, we've got a chance of doing something ridiculous.

"Athers gets an unplayable one so I get up. There's two ways you can go out, you can go back inside the pavilion downstairs and out but I thought 'sod it, I'll walk down through the crowd'. I got to the middle and I remember it being complete carnage. McGrath may have hit me in the face early on and Tres [Marcus Trescothick] pushed forward to one off Gillespie, it went straight over his head, over Gilchrist and two bounces, four byes. I'm walking down the pitch tapping away, I said: 'You alright?' He said: 'Yeah, yeah, I'm fine' and I'm pissing myself laughing. Tres ends up chopping one to gully and Nass comes out and he's got a black humour anyway and is pretty much cup half-empty but somehow we make it through to lunch. It had brightened up a little bit and we played OK without a massive amount of alarms. So get to lunch on 118-2 and I thought, 'Jeez, you've broken the back of this'.

"We pretty much dominated the lunch-to-tea session. McGrath started up the hill and unusually for him he bowled me a couple of shortish wide ones and I absolutely smoked them through cover and played a couple of paddle-pull shots. I just had the feeling I had to get him off his length a bit so I was getting unbelievably deep in my crease and we got him out of the attack in a really short time. That meant that Brett Lee was going to bowl more in the session than he might have done and he always went for a few anyway and Warnie wasn't getting anything to happen so we had our best session of the series. The rate didn't matter because we'd made so many runs in the first session; it was simply 'don't make a mistake'. Nasser was great at keeping me focused and we batted well together because he was always very tense and I was the opposite and together it worked. He lost the ball – he smashed Gillespie into where the cherry-picker was up in the garden at Kirkstall Lane End. Losing the ball was significant because the one they got to replace it didn't seem to do as much as the previous one. They started to make little mistakes but they had no doubt they only needed to 'open up an end' and they would go through us which was a good thing to keep you focused.

"I remember Ramps coming in [just before tea at 214-3] and he hit his first ball like an absolute shell through mid-off – 'Wow, that's good'. That's great you're not worrying about your partner, that's as good a start as you're going to make. At tea I just sat on the rim of one of the baths with my shirt off and just had a cup of coffee and a cigarette – couldn't eat. Then you're thinking 'we have to win this' but I think in run chases that's often the point where you mess it up, that's where the pressure starts to come in. I'd been concentrating so hard and well, having that absolute crystal-clear, totally unwavering concentration. Eyes feeling like lasers, so in the moment of what you are doing. Why I couldn't re-create that more often I don't know. The thought going through my head was 'if you don't get out we've won the game'. They were on the back foot now, becoming less certain in terms of getting a wicket and their chat. I'd gone from picking off the odd bad ball to if there's anything off line I'm hitting that for four too. It's like everything is in slow motion, everything coming down the pitch seems exactly where I want it to be – it was like you had enough time to make a decision twice. Brilliant……f-a-n-t-a-a-a-s-t-i-c.

"I desperately wanted to take the stumps off. I don't think I ever hit anything where it shouldn't have gone – that would be by definition of keeping true to my tea-time word. I didn't try and do anything outrageous. On the way off, every single one of them came up and shook my hand. You can afford to be magnanimous when you're as good as they were. 'But that wasn't meant to happen, how have I ended up doing that?' I've never doubted I was good enough to do that but maybe the major mental flaw I had was that I wasn't obsessed enough to make it happen regularly. Making numbers of runs wasn't something I ever went after. I loved the idea of playing beautifully more than anything else. The reason I managed to play as many Tests as I did was that I learnt you're not going to play that beautifully very often so I was able to chisel out ugly runs and because the team needed me to. Ambition, not overriding ability!"

Australia

MJ Slater	lbw b Caddick	21
ML Hayden	lbw b Caddick	15
RT Ponting	c †Stewart b Tudor	144
ME Waugh	c Ramprakash b Caddick	72
DR Martyn	c †Stewart b Gough	118
SM Katich	b Gough	15
AC Gilchrist*†	c Trescothick b Gough	19
SK Warne	c †Stewart b Gough	0
B Lee	c Ramprakash b Mullally	0
JN Gillespie	c Atherton b Gough	5
GD McGrath	not out	8
Extras (b5, lb15, w1, nb9)		**30**
Total (all out; 100.1 overs; 449 mins)		**447**

Fall of wickets 1/39 2/42 3/263 4/288 5/355 6/396 7/412 8/422 9/438

Bowling	**O**	**M**	**R**	**W**
D Gough	25.1	4	103	5
AR Caddick	29	4	143	3
AD Mullally	23	8	65	1
AJ Tudor	18	1	97	1
MA Butcher	1	0	7	0
MR Ramprakash	4	0	12	0

ML Hayden	c †Stewart b Mullally	**35**
MJ Slater	b Gough	**16**
RT Ponting	lbw b Gough	**72**
ME Waugh	not out	**24**
DR Martyn	lbw b Caddick	**6**
SM Katich	not out	**0**

Did not bat AC Gilchrist*†, SK Warne, B Lee, JN Gillespie, GD McGrath

Extras (b5, lb7, nb11)		**23**
Total (4 wkts dec; 39.3 overs; 182 mins)		**176**

Fall of wickets 1/25 2/129 3/141 4/171

Bowling	**O**	**M**	**R**	**W**
D Gough	17	3	68	2
AR Caddick	11	2	45	1
AJ Tudor	4	1	17	0
AD Mullally	7.3	2	34	1

England

MA Atherton	c †Gilchrist b McGrath	22
ME Trescothick	c †Gilchrist b McGrath	37
MA Butcher	run out	47
N Hussain*	lbw b McGrath	46
MR Ramprakash	c †Gilchrist b Lee	40
U Afzaal	c Warne b McGrath	14
AJ Stewart†	not out	76
AJ Tudor	c †Gilchrist b McGrath	2
AR Caddick	c †Gilchrist b Lee	5
D Gough	c Slater b McGrath	8
AD Mullally	c Katich b McGrath	0
Extras (b2, lb3, nb7)		**12**
Total (all out; 94.2 overs; 428 mins)		**309**

Fall of wickets 1/50 2/67 3/158 4/158 5/174 6/252 7/267 8/289 9/299

Bowling	**O**	**M**	**R**	**W**
GD McGrath	30.2	9	76	7
JN Gillespie	26	6	76	0
B Lee	22	3	103	2
SK Warne	16	2	49	0

MA Atherton	c †Gilchrist b McGrath	8
ME Trescothick	c Hayden b Gillespie	10
MA Butcher	not out	173
N Hussain*	c †Gilchrist b Gillespie	55
MR Ramprakash	c Waugh b Warne	32
U Afzaal	not out	4

Did not bat AJ Stewart†, AJ Tudor, AR Caddick, D Gough, AD Mullally

Extras (b14, lb16, nb3)		**33**
Total (4 wickets; 73.2 overs; 329 mins)		**315**

Fall of wickets 1/8 2/33 3/214 4/289

Bowling	**O**	**M**	**R**	**W**
GD McGrath	16	3	61	1
JN Gillespie	22	4	94	2
SK Warne	18.2	3	58	1
B Lee	16	4	65	0
ME Waugh	1	0	7	0

Kevin Pietersen – 186

India v England, Mumbai Wankhede 23-26 November 2012

-James Cory-Wright-

DOOF! A full-blooded cover drive first ball up. Thirty thousand voices roar their approval as the scuffed cherry scuds over the rope at 60 mph. Then a deft cut, as sharp as the batsman's number two crew cut. – four behind square. Harbhajan groans. Down the wicket to the next one. **BIFF!** Slapped over mid-wicket – inches from being a six. The wild crowd jump and holler and cheer in a hot wave of sound. Then another. **SMACK!** Back foot, carved clean through the covers. Four. He's up and running alright. **BOFF!** Then a hop and a skip, neat feet forward and drives with sweet timing wide of mid-off. Six of his first nine scoring shots are fours. He's got to his fifty in 63 balls.

A little blue-helmeted figure in the middle of a vast dusty amphitheatre raising his bat handle, gripped down near the splice acknowledging each cricket-crazed corner of the Wankhede stadium in turn. Loving it. And they love him. The tall South African who does it all for his adopted England. Record breaker. Innovator. The Decimator. They love the way he tears it up in the IPL and now on the biggest stage of all. Big shots, new shots. They love his swagger. His dominion. They love KP. 110%. KP. Legend. And that's just his fifty.

It's quite amazing how things go. England and Pietersen had come into this match under enormous pressure, having been walloped in the first Test by nine wickets; a match in which he had failed miserably with scores of 17 and two, out both times to the 26-year-old left-arm spinner Pragyan Ojha. This cricketing ignominy had merely added to the off-field pressure Pietersen was already under *vis a vis* the little matter of his 'reintegration'.

Rewind to the previous summer when it appeared that his entire international career seemed destined to unravel under the weight of bad, not to say foolish, decisions. Firstly there was the announcement of his retirement from certain forms of the game, a 'decision' that seemed to place Pietersen above his team and country. But, as he said at the time: "It's tough being me." This was followed by ill-considered back-tracking and half-hearted pangs of conscience resulting in the shambles of a *YouTube* statement. Who told him this was a good idea? Then there were derogatory text messages about some of his team-mates to some of his mates in the South African team. In the understated argot of all sportsmen, Pietersen commented at the time: "To say I am gutted is an understatement." Not for him the eloquent response of England fast-bowling legend and poet John Augustine Snow who, back in 1969, on being dropped for disciplinary reasons, had penned *On Being Dropped* which put it all in perspective with the closing lines: 'So come on, who's king of the castle/

now I'm the dirty rascal/standing/on a still summer's day/eye watching swallows/insect-chasing way'.

For less poetic and more pragmatic reasons, by November 2012 everyone had kissed and made up in good time for the tricky tour to the subcontinent under new England captain Alastair Cook. But with one condition: that Pietersen demonstrate his 'reintegration'. The only real way back would be by dint of his batting prowess and weight of runs. Never knowingly one to help his own cause, this process did not, for example, extend to staying in the same part of the hotel as the rest of the squad, enabling the *Daily Mail* to tittle-tattle:

> '...although the five-star Tower accommodation is good enough for everyone else, including Mumbai's greatest, Sachin Tendulkar, KP has paid for an upgrade for himself and wife Jessica to the even more luxurious Palace rooms that were refurbished to their former glory after the terrorist attack in 2008.'

But at least on the pitch things are looking up. Back to the action. After tea on day two, with a chanceless fifty under his belt, the 6' 4" KP is getting into his not insignificant stride; in this case a neat angled shot off pace bowler Zaheer Khan for his ninth four to bring up the 100 partnership with Captain Cook who is on 84 not out. England 171-2, in reply to India's first innings 327 and both players perhaps heading towards equalling the England Test record of 22 centuries.

However, despite the inclination to the positive, if either of these two had been dismissed at this point in the proceedings, on a strip turning as wickedly as this one, then the Indian total would have looked daunting. After all, Monty Panesar and Graham Swann had taken nine Indian wickets the day before leaving Mahendra Singh Dhoni perhaps ruing his request for a turner from day one. But you could see the logic, especially in the case of England's danger man, Kevin Pietersen, whose vulnerability to left-arm spin was his Achilles heel and maybe the key to the series. And it was precisely this weakness that had been exposed in the first Test – clean bowled twice by left-arm spinner Ojha which meant that, coming into the Mumbai Test, Pietersen had fallen an unlikely 25 times to this variety in Tests. Rarely has a cricketer attracted so much psychoanalysis or, for that matter, barely disguised equivocation: 'Kevin Pietersen's paranoia of left-arm spinners is destroying him,' ran the Vic Marks headline in the *Guardian*. 'Do not believe him if KP says he does not have a thing about left-arm spinners,' he opined, 'Pietersen does not believe that at the start of his innings in a Test he can survive against a good left-arm spinner on a slow-turning track by playing in orthodox fashion.'

And here in the Sheshrao Krushnarao Wankhede Stadium was a spinner's paradise as Pietersen himself testified: "It's spinning, bouncing, from straight, from off-straight." On

39, he received one from Ojha described by *Cricinfo* thus: 'Jeepers! That's unplayable. Leaps off a good length and spits past Pietersen's outside edge as he comes forward. Pietersen even has to lurch his head out of the line…KP takes a moment to compose himself.' Next ball: 'Pietersen…gets well forward…which isn't easy to do when one has just spat past the face.'

But right from the start of his innings it was clear to see he had put things right. He led with judicious defence mixed with knowing which balls to leave before easing onto the front foot with real intent and aggression – taking the attack to the opposition. "I didn't trust my defence in Ahmedabad…and as a batter if you don't trust your defence as much, you try too many things and you try and force the issue." And so, as many great players had done before him, Kevin Pietersen had gone back to basics with the help of England's batting coach, the grizzled Graham Gooch.

And now it was paying off with both he and Alastair Cook batting through to stumps on the second day, displaying exemplary discipline and technique because that was exactly what the pitch, the bowlers (nearly 900 Test wickets between them) and England's situation in the match required of them. Cook progressing with the calm of a man with destiny on his side to an unbeaten 87 and a determined Pietersen exorcising his ghosts on 62 not out and England 178-2 at close of play.

Day three. Forty degrees of heat. Ravichandran Ashwin with his carom ball and Ojha resume hostilities. KP to face. Last ball of the over. Ojha invites the drive and beats the bat with one that turns and bounces away. "Note to self. This pitch means business." Next over, Cook takes a single. Then it's Ashwin to KP. **SWISH!** Swept for four. A single takes KP on to strike next over. Ojha to bowl. KP swings. Thick edge. Two runs wide of gully. Next ball Ojha retaliates at 93 kph. The pace is quickening all round. KP up to 73, Cook on 90. A botched run-out of Cook reminds us that the Indian fielding is below par but essentially this is all about the pressure being exerted by these two great batsmen.

Apart from his run-rate, what's really making it work is KP's offensive-defensive cricket where even the shots that find fielders, mid-off, point, or cover, they're back-foot punches, firm drives and forward defence with an open face of the bat – pushing the fielders, testing the nerve of the bowlers, looking for the angles. And great patience too, then **BANG!** Last ball of a near maiden from Ojha, he's straight down the wicket swinging his arms and smacking a big one straight over mid-on for four. The next ball he faces from Ojha will also be despatched for four. As Shane Warne has it, 'Pietersen can destroy you in a session...he is like Lara in that he strikes boundaries in clusters.' More like clusterlets in this match and it helps explain how this innings was becoming a truly great one and one that exemplifies KP's stature as a batsman.

A Pietersen Big Innings makes for wonderful TV highlights; strong, assertive defence, a dazzling array of sure-footed shot-making, finely-executed sweeps, cuts, big lofted drives, switch hits, scoops and hoofs. Clustered, relentless and climbing bigger and bigger; and yes there would be big slog-sweep sixes to follow. And such is it that when it's all put together it builds into an innings that's bigger than the batsman himself, an innings that transcends the individual, and begins to shape the match itself. And crucially here, he is never alone. With England on 219-2 there's the little matter of Alastair Cook's record-equalling 22nd Test hundred gracefully achieved with a fine, driven boundary and graciously acknowledged with all the pride and pleasure one would expect in a 27-year-old cricketer at the top of his game with plenty more to come.

But enough of the captain, back to KP. The batting genius is up to 97 and facing Harbhajan who tosses it up on leg. KP closes the face enough to reverse sweep and guides it past slip. Four! Now 101 not out. As Australian rockers *AC/DC* put it "For those about to rock, we salute you." No fancy celebrations this time. No grand gesture. A patient raise of the arms. Hugs Cook. Takes the tip of his bat close to his helmet grille. Aaah Excalibur. No grand gesture? Nothing for the televised audience of millions?

This is the age of the tweet, of kevinpietersen.com. KP, T20 cricket commodity auctioned to the Delhi Daredevils. England 236-2. KP resumes. He's clicking through the gears now, taking the game away from India as he does so. The shots are getting bigger, the sweep of his bat more deadly and synchronised and he's reading the bowlers, moving his feet to pick the gaps. He sees the three men on the leg-side boundary and goes against Ashwin's spin with a full bat. **THWACK!** Fired away over mid-on for a big six. Then he leaves a few that turn sharply. However, in his 18 overs bowled so far, Harbhajan has yet to complete a maiden, Pietersen is reading all Ashwin's variations and as for the left-arm spinner Ojha, KP has not finished with him yet! This is payback time.

It couldn't go on for ever and finally Cook departed to a beauty from Ashwin, edged to wicket-keeper Dhoni for 122 with England on 274-3. He and Pietersen had steered England to within 53 runs of India's total in their stand of 206, the highest third-wicket stand ever in India and this on a pitch where wickets could fall in a hurry. As if to advertise the danger, Jonny Bairstow was soon out, caught off the bowling of Ojha for nine, heralding lunch on the third day with Pietersen unbeaten on 138.

He returns for the afternoon session with new partner Samit Patel. This would prove to be the most destructive session of his batting masterclass. The first few overs from Ojha and Zaheer see KP patient and circumspect as he allows his lunch to digest, then suddenly it's **BAM!** The ball a little short from Ojha and cracked off the toe of the bat past point. Then **KERRANG!** A great lolloping slog-sweep six into the crowd who are off their seats and cheering wildly as KP acknowledges his next landmark, equalling the most 150s for England alongside Len Hutton and Walter Hammond.

Now KP seems to be getting larger than life; it's going all Roy Lichtenstein. He is the comic book hero. The jutting square jaw, the GI Joe haircut, the sap white-toothed sportsman grin. The slightly robotic straight-backed running, 3D computer-game style and the mannered salute – bat aloft to a distant British public, saved from defeat and humiliation. He's here to help in his own modest way. Order restored.

Back to business – another six off Ojha, a massive maximum swatted over extra-cover. **KERPOW!** Then mere mortal Samit Patel gets out. Matt Prior in. England 357-5. First ball of Ojha's next over, **SLAP!** KP slog-sweeps him for another six into the stands followed by a top-edged paddle-sweep for four. Those mini-clusters sure taste sweet. KP 180 not out. England have a first-innings lead of 41. Then suddenly it's over. Ojha gets his man. KP chases a ball spinning outside off, gets a thin edge, Dhoni pouches and he marches off, bat under his arm, job done – "So I went and did a lot of hard work as I always do and luckily it paid off."

Scyld Berry for the *Daily Telegraph* was less prosaic:

> "What he did with his bat in this Test match was nothing short of genius. It was virtually free of flaw for a start. He edged his main adversary, the left-arm spinner Pragyan Ojha, through gully early on Sunday morning, after he had resumed on 62. Thereafter he rose and soared, above and beyond the capacity of any other mortals in this match. His innings, secondly, was composed in extreme conditions that were far too demanding for most batsmen, including some of the best players of this era."

Pietersen's dismissal was the beginning of the end (or the end of the beginning) for England as their last five wickets fell for only 31 runs. But the lead of 86 was the platform for Panesar and Swann's demolition of India's second innings with only two players making double figures and the spin twins sharing all the wickets. With just 57 needed, England won by 10 wickets. The whole momentum of the series had changed in three sessions – India were rattled and England went into the next Test with their tails up and duly won by seven wickets. A drawn fourth Test meant England took the series 2-1; only David Gower's 1984-85 vintage had previously come from a Test down to win a series in India and the home team had been outplayed in all departments, the most striking being spin.

So how great was Pietersen's innings in the great scheme of things? After he was out on day three, the pundits rushed to rate it his best ever but the man himself would not be drawn into agreeing with them until, tellingly, after the game was won. Only then did he finally admit it came "top". So even a player with as big an ego as Pietersen, a quintessentially modern sportsman acutely aware of his image and his standing in the game, even he recognised that the true 'greatness' of his personal contribution was enormously enhanced by the collective result if not defined by it. And there's no doubt this innings directly contributed not only to winning this Test but, such was its dominance and flair on a testing wicket, that it set the tone for England to go on to one of their greatest achievements ever in winning the series in India.

Having said that, this was not one of those great solitary innings against all the odds, the quality of the Indian attack was not vintage, though still good enough to account for the rest of the England team for 98 runs while Pietersen and Cook amassed 308 runs for the team. And there's the crux of it. Pietersen was, for the most part, not alone in his great endeavour and a huge amount of credit has to go to Alastair Cook – he had played Adams to Lara or Dravid to Laxman. But this can't detract from one of the greatest Test-match batting displays as a spectacle, a feast set before the most passionate, cricket-obsessed nation on the planet. Who could not marvel at the bravura shot-making on a par with Viv Richards or Virender Sehwag at their brutal best, or admire his discipline and technique on a genuinely challenging pitch from first ball to last like a Glenn Turner or Hanif Mohammad. And even the most partisan home crowd could not fail to celebrate his reduction of bowlers to spectators at their own disembowelment, of fielders left diving after a ball that either cut between them with surgical precision or flew over their heads into the stands.

And as for the man himself: "I never know what is going to happen tomorrow. I don't take myself that seriously. I do everything on a day-by-day basis. What will be, will be. I live my life by the day", he says. So are we to believe that Pietersen is some *doppelganger* of Albert Camus' existential anti-hero in *L'Etranger*, a latter-day Meursault whose lack of remorse or guilt confounds the judge at his trial?

Certainly the questionable sincerity of his reintegration or any of the other regrets he may, or may not have had, about incidents in his career, such as being stripped of the England captaincy, put him in the existential frame; not to mention the insularity, and maybe even guilt, of his English paymasters and the press corps (less so the paying public) that also cast him in the role of perpetual outsider. But to be truly existential, Pietersen would need to exist in a godless universe and this is simply not the case. Cricket is full of gods! And perhaps deep down, despite his showbiz lifestyle, love of publicity, the website, tweeting, texting and tattoos – all the trappings of the thoroughly modern sportsman, perhaps what Kevin Pietersen has to say about himself, tells us that rather than being remembered for what he isn't, 'one of the greatest cricketers of all time', he'd actually settle for being described for what he truly is: 'A hell of a great cricketer'.

India

G Gambhir	lbw b Anderson	4
V Sehwag	b Panesar	30
CA Pujara	st †Prior b Swann	135
SR Tendulkar	b Panesar	8
V Kohli	c Compton b Panesar	19
Yuvraj Singh	b Swann	0
MS Dhoni*†	c Swann b Panesar	29
R Ashwin	lbw b Panesar	68
H Singh	lbw b Swann	21
Z Khan	c Bairstow b Swann	11
PP Ojha	not out	0
Extras (lb1, nb1)		**2**
Total (all out; 115.1 overs; 462 mins)		**327**

Fall of wickets 1/4 2/52 3/60 4/118 5/119 6/169 7/280 8/315 9/316

Bowling	**O**	**M**	**R**	**W**
JM Anderson	18	3	61	1
SCJ Broad	12	1	60	0
MS Panesar	47	12	129	5
GP Swann	34.1	7	70	4
SR Patel	4	1	6	0

G Gambhir	lbw b Swann	65
V Sehwag	c Swann b Panesar	9
CA Pujara	c Bairstow b Swann	6
SR Tendulkar	lbw b Panesar	8
V Kohli	c sub (JE Root) b Swann	7
Yuvraj Singh	c Bairstow b Panesar	8
MS Dhoni*†	c Trott b Panesar	6
R Ashwin	c Patel b Panesar	11
H Singh	c Trott b Swann	6
Z Khan	c †Prior b Panesar	1
PP Ojha	not out	6
Extras (b6, lb3)		**9**
Total (all out; 44.1 overs; 183 mins)		**142**

Fall of wickets 1/30 2/37 3/52 4/65 5/78 6/92 7/110 8/128 9/131

Bowling	**O**	**M**	**R**	**W**
JM Anderson	4	1	9	0
MS Panesar	22	3	81	6
GP Swann	18.1	6	43	4

England

AN Cook*	c †Dhoni b Ashwin	122
NRD Compton	c Sehwag b Ojha	29
IJL Trott	lbw b Ojha	0
KP Pietersen	c †Dhoni b Ojha	186
JM Bairstow	c Gambhir b Ojha	9
SR Patel	c Kohli b Ojha	26
MJ Prior†	run out (†Dhoni/Kohli)	21
SCJ Broad	c Pujara b H Singh	6
GP Swann	not out	1
JM Anderson	lbw b H Singh	2
MS Panesar	c Khan b Ashwin	4
Extras (b4, lb2, w1)		**7**
Total (all out; 121.3 overs; 482 mins)		**413**

Fall of wickets 1/66 2/68 3/274 4/298 5/357 6/382 7/406 8/406 9/408

Bowling	**O**	**M**	**R**	**W**
R Ashwin	42.3	6	145	2
PP Ojha	40	6	143	5
Z Khan	15	4	37	0
H Singh	21	1	74	2
Yuvraj Singh	3	0	8	0

AN Cook*	not out	18
NRD Compton	not out	30

Did not bat IJL Trott, KP Pietersen, JM Bairstow, SR Patel, MJ Prior†, SCJ Broad, GP Swann, MS Panesar, JM Anderson

Extras (b8, lb2)		**10**
Total (0 wickets; 9.4 overs; 31 mins)		**58**

Bowling	**O**	**M**	**R**	**W**
R Ashwin	3.4	0	22	0
PP Ojha	4	0	16	0
H Singh	2	0	10	0

Graeme Smith – 154*

England v South Africa, Birmingham 30 July-2 August 2008

-Rob Smyth-

Never judge a day by its cover. On 2 August 2008, just after 5am, Graeme Smith awoke feeling dreadful. His back was extremely sore, his tennis elbow was worse, and he was being tormented by thoughts that South Africa had blown it in England yet again. The personification of an up-and-at-'em attitude could barely drag himself from bed; he missed breakfast before joining the team for their journey to Edgbaston. It turned out to be the defining day of Smith's career. His immense 154 not out – described by *Wisden* as 'one of the all-time captain's innings' – was a miracle of will and power that gave South Africa their first series victory in England for 43 years and exorcised an army of ghosts. The fact it was Edgbaston, where South Africa suffered their greatest heartache in the World Cup semi-final against Australia in 1999, did not do any harm either.

South Africa's relationship with the 50-over World Cup is one of sport's tragically doomed love stories; until 2008, their relationship with touring England had a touch of Heathcliff and Cathy as well. The three series since their return from isolation followed soul-crushingly familiar patterns. Each time they stomped all over England to take the lead, only to fail wretchedly at the last. On each tour they lost the final Test. In 1994 and 2003 they drew the series; in 1998 they were beaten. They should have won all three. To err once might be considered unfortunate; to do so three times had everyone reaching for the ch-word.

This was the almost overbearing context in which Smith considered South Africa's prospects on that Saturday morning. He should not even have been playing. He spent much of the build-up either in hospital or on the physio's bench suffering from back spasms so severe that he couldn't even go the toilet properly. On the morning of the game he pretty much failed a fitness test but played anyway. In his book, *A Captain's Diary*, Smith estimates he was 70 to 75 per cent fit.

South Africa, deservedly 1-0 up in the series with two to play after thrashing England at Headingley, took control by dismissing England for 231. At 226-4 in reply, they had fingers on the Basil D'Oliveira Trophy. Then Andrew Flintoff memorably yorked Jacques Kallis in the gloaming at the end of day two, and the contest began to turn. South Africa were dismissed for 314. England finished the third day on 297-6, a dangerous lead of 214 on a wearing pitch, after a raucous 94 from Kevin Pietersen and a career-saving century from Paul Collingwood.

What troubled Smith as much as England's lead was the speed at which they had accumulated it. South Africa's watchwords – discipline, patience, control – had gone out the window as a seam attack missing the injured Dale Steyn lost their heads. Instead of bowling dry, they leaked runs. 'We finished the day emotionally drained and very tired', wrote Smith.

'I was still struggling with my back, but my tennis elbow was even worse. I can cope with pain…but this was something I hadn't experienced before.' The mental strain was just as great. 'It was driving me mad. I wanted the series so much. I was feeling pretty drained. I had room service, watched some arbitrary movie and tried to chill out as much as possible and get some rest.'

He didn't get nearly enough. 'I felt exhausted and wasn't looking forward to the day', he said of his feelings when he woke on the Saturday morning. 'We had played so poorly the day before that I was still wincing from the memory.' Not that anybody would have known. When Smith finally dragged himself from bed, he applied his game-face before joining the rest of the team. With the flick of an internal switch he became the omnipotent leader his team so depended on. 'I obviously came across as bullet-proof. But my insides were eating themselves alive.' The great captains have always been pretty good actors.

Smith would soon have the chance to write his own script. When England were eventually dismissed just before lunch for 363, South Africa were left with a target of 281 – a record score to win at Edgbaston, and the highest in a match between these sides for over a century. Big fourth-innings chases are not quite the Everest they once were – South Africa would chase over 400 against Australia at Perth later in the year – but these were extraordinary circumstances. It could have been a *Krypton Factor* endurance test: try going about your usual work while carrying tonnes of psychological baggage. South Africa knew that, with just over five sessions remaining and the weather good, this was it: they would either win the series or blow an almighty opportunity. If it had gone to 1-1 ahead of the final Test, the strain would surely have been too great for South Africa to win at The Oval.

In the five overs before lunch Smith struggled badly, particularly against Jimmy Anderson, at that stage a dangerous but erratic bowler. It seems ridiculous now, but in 2008 Anderson was regularly discussed in terms of Good Jimmy and Bad Jimmy. With the captaincy concerns still draining out of his brain, Smith was beaten as often as not in Anderson's two overs, responding only with one impressive punch down the ground for four. He decided to sit alone at lunch to compose himself and gather his thoughts. He had no solids for lunch, just an energy sachet and a meal replacement drink.

It worked. Smith felt better immediately after the break and dealt far more comfortably with the rest of Anderson's new-ball spell. With an unfit Ryan Sidebottom offering little threat, England turned to Flintoff and Monty Panesar, who was getting spiteful turn out of the rough to the left-hander. Smith and his opening partner Neil McKenzie proceeded fairly comfortably to 65 when an unsighted McKenzie offered no shot to a Flintoff yorker and was lbw.

It was the start of a farcical period in which a number of Flintoff's deliveries were not seen by South Africa's batsmen because of a sightscreen problem, with his release point lost in a couple of sliding doors just above screen level. It was only an issue with very full deliveries, only from Flintoff and almost exclusively to the right-handers. Nasser Hussain's suggestion that it had something to do with snap of Flintoff's wrist at the point of delivery was the most persuasive explanation.

Hashim Amla went soon after, lbw to Panesar for six. It was a decision that would have been overturned with DRS, as the ball was bouncing over the stumps. The new system was being trialled in the simultaneous Test series between Sri Lanka and India. In England the umpire's word was final. Amla was out and South Africa were 78-2.

After the McKenzie dismissal, Smith took 19 consecutive deliveries from Flintoff so that the right-handers would not be exposed. Flintoff, playing his second Test after an 18-month absence, was at his most messianic and bowled a famous spell to Kallis in the first innings. It was Saturday afternoon, it was Edgbaston and a formidable opponent was chasing a target in the 280s to go 2-0 up – just as they had in 2005 when Flintoff, in the space of one over, changed from an ordinary human being into SuperFred. A raucous crowd, consumed with the cult of Freddie, expected something similar three years on. It wasn't quite a World XI at one end and Ilford seconds at the other – as Graham Gooch famously said of the New Zealand side containing Richard Hadlee in 1986 – but it did feel like there were two separate games going on: when Flintoff was bowling and when he was not. With the window adding to his already abundant threat, there was a danger South Africa would drown in testosterone.

Smith's vigil almost saw Flintoff out of the attack. But with Kallis on strike at the end of Panesar's over, Flintoff was given one last burst, the eighth over of his spell. It worked. Kallis, again unsighted, ducked into a thigh-high full toss and was lbw to Flintoff. He swished his bat furiously, almost knocking over the stumps, and walked off swearing at either the umpires, Dame Fortune or both. One of South Africa's most important Tests in decades was turning into a farce.

It would have been easy – understandable even – if Smith accepted that some things weren't meant to be, that fate had found yet another perverse way to stop South Africa winning in England. It would have been easy to let the mental tiredness take hold – even more so when Ashwell Prince nicked Anderson behind to leave South Africa 93-4, still 188 from victory. Instead the problem with the windows provided an even bigger window into Smith's soul and his indecent strength of character. He did not so much cope with the pressure as ignore it. 'I was feeling very little emotion, strangely enough', he said.

> 'I was concentrating hard on staying calm and focused, thinking about my batting and what I needed to do. It obviously wasn't a very calm environment, but it was a simple case of logic. If I wasn't calm, we lost the Test match. I needed to be calm, therefore I was.'

He reached his fifty from 86 balls, and at tea South Africa were 111-4. For the first part of the innings he looked ahead only in 10-run segments. When South Africa reached 120-4, he says in *A Captain's Diary*, he started to consider the bigger picture. By then he was so sure he would see the innings through and score between 50 and 60 per cent of the runs that he started to halve the necessary target. In many men this would be a dangerous conceit; with Smith it was a simple case of logic.

By now he was engaged in a fascinating battle with Panesar, who was spitting the ball viciously out of the rough. Most only had eyes for Flintoff but Smith perceived a far greater danger. Panesar was at his most hyperactive, appealing for something unspecified almost every delivery. 'It was obvious he was the biggest threat', said Smith. He played Panesar more respectfully than the seamers, and with a simple plan: to get outside off stump and take lbw out of the equation. Twenty-two of his 31 scoring strokes off Panesar were to leg. Those works to leg off Panesar defined his innings almost as much as the belting drives through mid-off and thumping pulls that accounted for more than half of his 17 boundaries.

Those boundaries dried up for a time, with Smith hitting none in an 18-over spell that also included the most difficult period of his innings. On 74 he padded up to a wickedly spinning delivery from Panesar and survived a huge lbw shout. Hawkeye suggested it would have hit the stumps although, given the level of guesswork involved, Aleem Dar's decision was an understandable one. Four overs later Smith should have been run out. He called the striker, AB de Villiers, through for a tight leg bye when the ball dropped on the leg side. Had wicket-keeper Tim Ambrose's throw hit the stumps, or had it been claimed by Ian Bell, Smith would have been gone for 79.

In Panesar's next over there was a very gentle inquiry – if that – for a catch down the leg side. Dar had no real appeal to answer, yet replays showed it had clearly hit the glove. Panesar was the only man who might have seen it, with all the other England fielders behind the bat and unsighted. But having appealed for everything all day, he went quiet. Smith survived. In a long essay about this innings in *A Captain's Diary*, Smith does not even mention this chance, as if the personal omerta of not walking extends beyond the field of play.

Smith, flustered for the only time in his innings apart from that pre-lunch spell, slog-swept the next ball towards deep mid-wicket, where Andrew Strauss was so close to taking the catch as he dived forward that many of the crowd thought they had finally seen the mighty oak felled. A split-second later Strauss's body language betrayed the fact it had bounced fractionally short.

A drinks break a few moments later certainly helped Smith. England's over-rate didn't; an hour into the evening session there were still 31 overs remaining, extending a day that had, for Smith, begun almost 12 hours ago. Yet he seemed to find a second wind and began to again bat with formidable authority. He was surely further empowered by seeing off another six-over spell from Flintoff, who had now bowled 14 in little over three hours. At that stage Smith had faced more than two-thirds of the deliveries of Flintoff. Even if he thought Panesar was the biggest threat, it was a textbook example of his selflessness.

He lost AB de Villiers with the score at 171, caught at slip off Panesar. South Africa needed 110, with Smith and his grizzled lieutenant Mark Boucher at the crease and an unusually long tail to follow. At least he had a partner he trusted implicitly, who would be stimulated rather than cowed by the challenge, and who – having toured England in 1998 and 2003 – knew precisely what it meant. Smith said the first 30-40 minutes of his partnership with Boucher were 'as much tension as I have ever experienced'.

In that spell came the fleeting relief of reaching a century from 177 balls. Smith's celebration was notable only for how muted it was. Not that anyone doubted it, but he made it doubly clear that business was unfinished. He knew the worth of the innings would be decided by the next two hours, not the previous three. At first he and Boucher were content to survive, with 12 runs from their first seven overs together. But with every dot ball the momentum shifted almost imperceptibly until they sensed a slight England weariness.

England only had a four-man attack; Sidebottom was at half ratpower and Panesar's will had been broken by Smith. South Africa ran with the mood, and what started as an exploratory counter-attack soon became a brazen assault on a tiring attack. Smith asked Boucher if he wanted him to take Flintoff; Boucher said no and the pair tucked in to some weary bowling. The tactic was also designed to reduce the potential time the tailend might have against the second new ball. They could not have planned it better: the winning runs eventually came off the final ball of the 80th over.

The umpire Steve Davis checked the light meter at 198-5. There was only one side who wanted to go off. South Africa had scored 21 from the last three overs and England were assuming the mercy position. The partnership was a mini masterpiece of game management and controlled aggression. Smith hadn't just silenced the crowd; he'd sent them home. Edgbaston, drunken and boisterous only an hour before, was now quiet and emptying, tedious partisan concerns overriding the chance to see the completion of one of the great innings. By now Smith looked as if he could go all night. He outlasted England both physically and mentally. It was not necessarily that he wanted it more, but he and South Africa certainly *needed* it more. With 24 runs needed, he claimed the extra half-hour. Soon after he brought up his 150 from 237 balls. The third fifty had taken only 60 deliveries.

Smith's next scoring stroke was the most cathartic of his career. He pulled his old friend Pietersen for four to move to 154 and seal South Africa's first series victory in England since the pre-isolation days of Graeme Pollock and Eddie Barlow. His team charged on to the field to embrace a man who was both peer and hero. Smith faced 246 balls, hitting 17 fours. He had withstood tennis elbow, a bad back, a dodgy sightscreen, the force of Flintoff's personality, the rough outside his off stump, a lack of solids, a 47-over session and 45 years of history. He left pieces of his soul all over the Edgbaston wicket. If great and legend are the most abused words in sport, then epic is not far behind. Even the most pedantic, curmudgeonly patriot in England would concur this was an epic innings. Perhaps the biggest compliment you can pay Smith is that the scale and manner of that innings were not remotely surprising. It is the innings he was born to play.

On a personal level, Smith upgraded the archetypal captain's innings for the 21st century. It had all the over-my-dead-body qualities associated with the genre, but its purpose was victory rather than the avoidance of defeat, and he scored at a 21st-century strike-rate of 63. In some ways this was the completion of an almost Shakespearean character arc. He lost his way after the spectacular start to his captaincy career in England in 2003. He went two-and-a-half years without a Test century between 2005 and 2007 and was often criticised for immaturity or boorishness and embarrassingly misplaced machismo. He did not make the *Wisden Almanack* list of the world's 40 best players in 2006 and 2007. In 2008, still aged only 27, he matured into the spiritual heir to Steve Waugh he had promised to be on the previous tour of England.

Smith scored 277 at Edgbaston on that tour. This innings trumped it comfortably. It is one cricket's fascinations that 154 can be greater than 277, 153 greater than 375 and 154 greater than 333. Everybody knew instinctively that this was an innings Smith would never top. Just as you can't put the genie back in the bottle, so you can't put the monkey back on the back.

It is the second-highest innings by a captain in a successful fourth-innings run chase, behind Don Bradman's 173 not out at Headingley in 1948. Captains are supposed to set the tone but Smith knows it's even more important to set the tone in a different sense – to cement the final judgement of a match. He is a rough-track bully, addicted to tough runs.

The opportunity to play this kind of innings is what gets Smith going, and he is the only man in history to score 1,000 Test runs in successful fourth-innings chases. That includes four centuries. Only one other captain – Ricky Ponting – has managed even two. Smith is arguably cricket's greatest triumph of substance over style, a man who can will his way to

Test hundreds. And, while this was one of his better-looking innings – there was plenty going on in the V – it is remembered for its significance rather than its aesthetics.

Smith bent a match, a series and even history to his granite will. Thereafter South Africa's series in England would be discussed in entirely different terms. Instead of wondering if South Africa would ever win, focus turned to whether Smith would see off another England captain. Michael Vaughan resigned the day after Smith's 154, following Nasser Hussain's decision to quit in 2003. And four years later, Smith's team prompted the retirement of Andrew Strauss as well.

It is easy to forget, in view of England's lost years under Peter Moores, just how much victory meant, both to South Africa in 2008 and India a year earlier. Smith described it as the 'first massive stepping stone' of a team who went on to become irrefutably the world's best. In some ways it was also their final frontier, not because of what they achieved so much as what they had been through to achieve it. South Africa won in Australia for the first time later that year, a far greater feat but one that, following heavy beatings in 2001-02 and 2005-06, came out of nowhere rather than at the end of a long journey. The win in England was not just for his current team-mates: it was for Hansie Cronje, Kepler Wessels, Allan Donald, Shaun Pollock, Gary Kirsten and the others who had been denied in 1994, 1998 and 2003.

After the match Smith returned to the dressing room to drink with his team-mates. 'Jeez it was a really special feeling.' For a consummate team man, these are the moments that take up a lease in the memory bank. Amid the dressing-room celebrations, McKenzie and Boucher made Smith 'down a beer or two in a compromised position for having *die groot balles* to bat through to the end'. The team eventually went back to the Radisson Hotel to continue their celebrations. At around 11pm, Smith realised he had not eaten all day, and slipped out to eat alone at a Lebanese cafe near the hotel. He says that, as he sat fiddling with a plastic knife and fork and a paper plate, the scale of the achievement sank in for the first time.

The team shambled to bed in the small hours. The following morning Smith was ripped from his sleep – not by nerves this time but by a fire alarm, which kept the players out on the street for 45 minutes. His back and his elbow hurt; he had a pulsating hangover. Graeme Smith awoke feeling dreadful. It was the most beautiful pain of his life.

England

First innings

AJ Strauss	hit wicket b Nel	20
ANCook	c Kallis b Nel	76
MP Vaughan*	c †Boucher b Nel	0
KP Pietersen	c Prince b Kallis	4
IR Bell	c †Boucher b Ntini	50
PD Coll'wood	c Smith b Kallis	4
A Flintoff	not out	36
TR Ambrose†	b Kallis	22
RJ Sidebottom	c †Boucher b Ntini	2
JM Anderson	run out (Prince)	1
MS Panesar	run out (Amla/†Boucher)	1
Extras (b1, lb7, w2, nb5)		**15**
Total (all out; 77 overs; 334 mins)		**231**

Fall of wickets 1/68 2/68 3/74 4/136 5/158 6/173 7/212 8/215 9/230

Bowling	**O**	**M**	**R**	**W**
M Morkel	15	2	50	0
M Ntini	19	5	70	2
A Nel	17	7	47	3
JH Kallis	15	5	31	3
PL Harris	11	1	25	0

Second innings

AJ Strauss	c Kallis b Morkel	25
ANCook	c †Boucher b Ntini	9
MP Vaughan*	c Amla b Nel	17
KP Pietersen	c de Villiers b Harris	94
IR Bell	c †Boucher b Ntini	20
PD Coll'wood	c †Boucher b Morkel	135
A Flintoff	c Amla b Harris	2
TR Ambrose†	b Morkel	19
RJ Sidebottom	c Amla b Morkel	22
JM Anderson	b Kallis	1
MS Panesar	not out	0
Extras (b8, lb2, w6, nb3)		**19**
Total (all out; 98.2 overs; 432 mins)		**363**

Fall of wickets 1/15 2/39 3/70 4/104 5/219 6/221 7/297 8/362 9/363

Bowling	**O**	**M**	**R**	**W**
M Morkel	19.2	1	97	4
A Nel	20	3	79	1
M Ntini	18	4	58	2
JHKallis	20	5	59	1
PLHarris	21	3	60	2

South Africa

First innings

ND McKenzie	lbw b Flintoff	72
GC Smith*	c Strauss b Flintoff	7
PL Harris	c Cook b Sidebottom	19
HM Amla	c & b Anderson	9
JH Kallis	b Flintoff	64
AG Prince	c †Ambrose b Sidebottom	39
AB de Villiers	c Sidebottom b Flintoff	5
MV Boucher†	c Vaughan b Anderson	40
M Morkel	lbw b Anderson	18
A Nel	b Sidebottom	0
M Ntini	not out	0
Extras (lb35, nb6)		**41**
Total (all out; 90.2 overs; 408 mins)		**314**

Fall of wickets 1/17 2/94 3/117 4/135 5/226 6/238 7/264 8/293 9/298

Bowling	**O**	**M**	**R**	**W**
RJ Sidebottom	25	9	81	3
JM Anderson	26.2	6	72	3
A Flintoff	30	8	89	4
PD Coll'wood	2	0	12	0
MS Panesar	7	0	25	0

Second innings

GC Smith*	not out	154
ND McKenzie	lbw b Flintoff	22
HM Amla	lbw b Panesar	6
JH Kallis	lbw b Flintoff	5
AG Prince	c †Ambrose b Anderson	2
AB de Villiers	c Coll'wood b Panesar	27
MV Boucher†	not out	45

Did not bat
M Morkel, PL Harris, A Nel, M Ntini

Extras (b10, lb8, w2, nb2)		**22**
Total (5 wickets; 80 overs; 341 mins)		**283**

Fall of wickets 1/65 2/78 3/83 4/93 5/171

Bowling	**O**	**M**	**R**	**W**
RJ Sidebottom	10	1	26	0
JM Anderson	13	0	60	1
MS Panesar	33	3	91	2
A Flintoff	20	5	72	2
KP Pietersen	4	0	16	0

Brian Lara – 153*

West Indies v Australia, Bridgetown 26-30 March 1999

-Patrick Ferriday-

Great Test matches come in all shapes and sizes, from the thrilling nail-biter to the overwhelming expression of superiority, the awe-inspiring comeback, the triumph of the team ethic or the one-man show. It is just part of the five-day maze that it exposes so many blind alleys and false dawns before the final path is cut and the identity of the victor can be revealed late into the afternoon in the last of the 15 sessions. Of course, the vast majority of Tests have none of these epic ingredients and many hundreds have been destined to result in anodyne draws before the second day is out, but it is precisely the rarity of the grandstand finish that makes it so precious and memorable.

The two ties are etched into the memory of any cricket lover, those rarest of jewels taking place at Brisbane in 1960 and Chennai in 1986. Up to the end of 2012, only nine Tests had been won by a margin of less than eight runs with just the one minimum, when, in 1993, Courtney Walsh broke a heroic 10th-wicket stand of 40 between Tim May and Craig McDermott with just two runs required for victory. Then there is the narrowest of wins for the side batting last. Just 12 have been decided by this margin in 135 years of Test cricket and of those, five have featured centuries in the fourth innings. Gilbert Jessop, Lindsay Hassett and Mahela Jayawardene all departed before victory was achieved which leaves just two centurions who shepherded their teams to victory by the skin of their collective teeth – Inzamam-ul-Haq against Bangladesh in 2003 and Brian Lara against Australia in 1999.

Inzamam had pedigree in this situation, having shared a 10th-wicket partnership of 57 with Mushtaq Ahmed to defeat Australia at Karachi in 1994. This time the bowling was considerably less fearsome and quite frankly Pakistan were in a mess of their own making having rested two leading players on the back of losing three others to injury. Three debutants were picked and one, 17-year-old Yasir Ali, was making his first-class debut in this dead rubber. And it was this very Ali who came to the wicket at the death after Inzamam had run out Umar Gul. He survived four balls, scored a run and Inzy completed the victory; marvellous drama and a great tale but a very different situation to that faced by Brian Lara at Bridgetown's Kensington Oval in March 1999.

This was the third of four Tests that would decide the destiny of the Frank Worrell Trophy and the score was 1-1. After a catastrophic capitulation in the first match, the West Indies had come out fighting at Kingston and Brian Lara's epic 213 had levelled the series and, even more importantly, given his side and his islands renewed belief in their ability to beat the best in the world. But surely this was but a thrilling blip? Only Lara, Jimmy Adams, Courtney Walsh and Curtly Ambrose could be placed in the upper echelons of Test cricket and arrayed against them was the batting of the Waughs, Justin Langer, Matt Elliott, Ricky Ponting and Michael Slater with bowling to match led by Shane Warne and Glenn McGrath.

Even amidst the euphoria of the Kingston victory, Lara had remained calm and reminded anyone who cared to listen that the Australians would be determined to avenge this defeat. They had retired to Antigua to lick their wounds and hand out a comfortable drubbing to the West Indies A team – Langer and Elliott hitting centuries and Ricky Ponting doing enough to replace the injured Greg Blewett in the team for the Bridgetown Test. McGrath and Jason Gillespie were rested in preparation for a renewed assault on Brian Lara – would his fallibility against short, quick bowling be exposed this time? For the home side the huge positive was that Carl Hooper scored a century and would vault straight back into the national side – a fifth genuine Test cricketer.

26 March

Steve Waugh won the toss and, on a wicket expected to have customary early life but likely to turn later, he had no hesitation in batting and his openers duly took their punishment in the morning before the middle order cashed in later in the day. A lunch score of 78-3 could be considered an even session; against top-class fast bowling with a new ball on a rock-hard wicket the loss of only three wickets was no mean feat, at the very least no terminal damage had been inflicted. For the home side there was plenty of encouragement in removing Slater, Elliott and Mark Waugh in a session, two more quick wickets and they would be into the tail.

The afternoon brought one slow wicket as Langer fell to Hooper for 51. Youngster Ponting joined his captain who was already mid-battle with his old adversary Curtly Ambrose. This pair had history from Waugh's defiant 200 at Kingston four years earlier when Ambrose had peppered him with bouncers and verbals; Waugh was even less likely to back down now that he was captain and at tea the worm was turning with the score at 195-4 and both batsmen set.

The final session was a disaster for the West Indies. Thirty-six overs, no wickets and 127 runs. Steve Waugh well into three figures and Ponting grinding his way carefully towards what would be only his third century in 23 Tests. A stumps score of 322-4 meant it had been Australia's day.

27 March

The second morning brought more of the same even for such great bowlers as Walsh and Ambrose. The second new ball delivered precisely no reward as Waugh and Ponting continued to rub collective Caribbean noses in the dirt. The addition of just 70 runs from 29 overs was equal testimony to the efforts of the West Indian attack and the importance attached to the passage of play by their opponents.

For no obvious reason the afternoon ushered in a new slant and the West Indies either fought their way back into the game or slipped through a door carelessly left unlocked, depending on your viewpoint. No sooner had Ricky Ponting reached his century than he departed for 104 in over six hours of studied concentration. In the next over Ian Healy was out first ball and then spinner Nehemiah Perry, having dismissed one centurion took out another just one run before he became a double-centurion. One more wicket before tea and suddenly Australia were only 446-8 having been 425-4. This was a collapse of sorts and certainly a far cry from the orders of Doctor Steve Waugh who would certainly have prescribed a score of 600 to inoculate his side from the danger of defeat.

The evening session sent the game back the other way. Just 28 balls were required to finish the Australians on 490 but this left almost a full session for a full probing of the soft underbelly of the West Indian batting. Adrian Griffith was run out in the first over by Ponting and then the bowlers went to work. Dave Joseph resisted for over an hour before falling to McGrath who then trapped nightwatchman Pedro Collins first ball for a duck. This brought Brian Lara to the wicket for some overs he would happily have avoided – little to gain and plenty to lose. Within 25 minutes he was gone, caught behind off Gillespie for eight. The fact that Hooper and Sherwin Campbell successfully negotiated the final four overs was little consolation now that the talisman and batting genius was out and the West Indies were still 410 behind.

28 March

The only men that might turn the game around both departed to slip catches in the first hour and without Hooper and Adams it was left to opener Sherwin Campbell and wicket-keeper Ridley Jacobs to protect the tail. For once the West Indians produced unsung heroes and the pair took their side to 151-6 at lunch. The first and only realistic target was surely to avoid the follow-on but the required 290 runs was still only just visible on the horizon.

Undaunted, the pair battled all afternoon against the best that the Australians could throw at them. Shortly before tea they were parted when Jacobs fell to a sign of Australian desperation, the bowling of Ricky Ponting. But by now just 39 were needed and Campbell had completed a battling century under huge pressure and hauled his side out of the fire, the trick now was to jump out of the frying pan as well and this was pulled off by some sound late batting by Perry, Ambrose and Walsh. A first-innings deficit of 161 could have been much worse and the West Indies were at least still in the game. The last eight overs that evening put them further into it as batsmen-turned-bowlers, Walsh and Ambrose, removed Elliott and Langer.

29 March

With just the whiff of a chance the West Indies were a team transformed on the fourth morning and the Australians were steamrollered by a superb team effort led, once again, by Walsh and Ambrose. The largely luckless Ambrose took care of nightwatchman Gillespie and Walsh trapped Mark Waugh lbw while Campbell ran out Slater with a superb direct hit from third-man. Then Collins bowled Steve Waugh soon after he had signalled his intent by launching Perry into the stands over mid-wicket for six. At 73-6 the lead was still 234 but this was no longer a rout and was beginning to look like a contest.

A sudden downpour took the players off the field but did nothing to revive the visitors' fortunes as Courtney Walsh, with 5-39, picked off the tail and they were dismissed for a meagre 146. The upside was that they now had more than four sessions to dismiss the West Indies who in turn needed 308 to win – a total that had only ever been reached in victory 13 times in Test history and certainly never against a better bowling side.

With plenty of time to play with, the priority for openers Campbell and Griffith had to be to stay put, tire the bowlers and take the shine off the ball with runs being almost an added bonus, and they took this strategy to heart. Surely if they could see their team through to the close then it was even-money the pair on the final day? Thirty-three overs of solid resistance took their side to 72 before Glenn McGrath finally achieved the breakthrough and trapped the first-innings centurion lbw. Half an hour later they had lost all the hard-won ground as Dave Joseph and perennial nightwatchman Collins both fell lbw and here was Brian Lara again, just where he didn't want to be, coming in on the fag-end of the day with his team's hopes resting on his shoulders. Six overs of cautious defence later and Griffith and Lara were back in the pavilion to ponder the next day. Seven wickets standing and 223 runs to win.

30 March

The final day could hardly have started worse for the home side as the resolute opener Adrian Griffith fell to Gillespie without adding to his overnight 35. Actually it could have been much much worse but Lara stood firm in the face of the inevitable opening salvo that was laced with short balls. To compound the early misery, the one man capable of matching Lara, Carl Hooper, lasted just 17 minutes before touching one off Gillespie who was now looking a match winner in waiting. Again it was the turn of the great straight man, Jimmy Adams, to come and join his captain. He had kept Lara company during his match-changing 213 at Kingston only two weeks before and, with the pressure even greater now,

Adams was not found wanting as, again, it was not only his occupation of the other crease but also his calming influence that enabled his younger partner to thrive. Lara had spoken of 'allowing the bowlers their hour' and this was his plan if only someone could stay long enough to allow *him* that luxury. As Adams settled in, it became apparent that the main danger might well be the bustling energy of Gillespie although McGrath was his usual niggardly self. Of the spinners, there was no doubt that Warne was not at his best after struggling with injury although even at 80 per cent he would be a match for most batsmen. Could Stuart MacGill prove to be the key figure? With that possibility in mind, Lara went for one aggressive burst. Having narrowly survived a leg-before shout when not playing a shot, he responded by twice skipping down the pitch to flick MacGill through the leg side for four and immediately the bat-pad fielder was withdrawn. A miscued on drive off a full toss was followed by a fine sweep and 14 had come from the over.

But there was no great hurry and Lara was a model of restraint all morning with the exception of that burst of tactical aggression; just the rare errant delivery was given the full treatment from the towering backlift. When lunchtime came the West Indies had moved on to 161 without further loss and Brian Lara was a mere 44 after batting for more than 36 overs. Speed was not the crucial issue at this point with 147 needed in two sessions.

The first hour after lunch proved to be similar to the hour before in respect of lack of wickets but now Lara was taking the attack to the opposition and the runs were coming more freely from the old and, by now, soft ball. Intent was signalled as Warne was put into the Greenidge and Haynes stand for a massive six and then the next, not dissimilar, ball was cut as late as could be, for four. The bowler's face betrayed his disbelief. In 20 overs 77 runs were scored and only 18 from the bat of Adams. Best of all, the new ball had been successfully negotiated, helped by the fact that Gillespie had left the field for treatment for back spasms forcing Steve Waugh to partner Glenn McGrath. Waugh may not have been the ideal new-ball bowler but his shortcomings revealed a batsman now in total control – a guided cut between two gullies was followed by a cuttable long hop that was belted past mid-on. "Set a field to that if you can", it shouted.

The tension had been high enough but now it reached a new level and the commentary box was infected. A short ball from McGrath failed to get up and struck a ducking Lara on the back of the helmet barely above stump height and as the batsmen ran one extra Lara chose, unwisely, to take issue with the bowler, who, seizing the chance, was quick to respond. Umpire Eddie Nicholls was asked to intercede by Lara but it was the soothing arm-around-the-shoulder of Jimmy Adams that brought some calm – "This is what Test cricket is all about" exploded commentator Tony Cozier, his customary mellifluous tones now raked by excitement and anxiety. Minutes later, another short-pitched delivery from the same bowler was thrashed through mid-wicket – "You could not want it better, as a battle, as a contest." Echoing Cozier's words came David Hookes: "If this doesn't get the hairs up on the back of your neck, nothing will...outstanding Test match cricket." Michael Holding whispered in response, "He has to settle down." Another minor altercation between batsman and bowler followed before tactical drinks appeared from the pavilion and Jimmy Adams was allowed to lay Lara on a metaphorical calming-couch.

After the resumption, Gillespie tore into the fray with a couple of wonderful balls slanted across the left hander but then, when he over-pitched, he was spanked through the covers with no hint of justice for the overall quality of his bowling. At 230-5 a shimmy down the pitch and a boundary wide of mid-on brought up the century. It had been a tale of contrasts – the first 50 taking 118 balls and the second just 51. If Lara had given the bowlers 'their hour' in the morning he was getting it back with interest now and when Warne failed to hold a very difficult return catch it seemed as if the impossible might just be happening. But then, as if inspired by the sole responsibility, McGrath broke through not once but three times. Adams was squared up and bowled as if he'd only just come to the wicket and then 20 minutes later two beauties brought successful lbw appeals in successive balls and saw the back of Jacobs and Perry. With four overs till tea and 60 runs still needed it was now Brian Lara, Curtly Ambrose and Courtney Walsh versus Australia. Just six runs were added in those four overs but Ambrose had stood firm and consigned the Kensington Oval crowd to a diet of nerves and nails for the next 20 minutes.

The final session had the feeling of a dream at the time and, even now the *YouTube* highlights are thrillingly tense in the way that Paul Greengrass' *United 93* loses nothing in the outcome being anchored in public knowledge. The odd couple re-emerged to roars of encouragement and the flinty stare of Steve Waugh and his less-than-merry men. With Jason Gillespie now revived, the attack was back at full strength and the ball just 20 overs old – surely enough shine and bounce to take out the tailenders before Lara could steer his side to victory? But, straining every sinew, the Australians couldn't budge the big man and what's more he began to add to the total off the limited amount of balls he was required to face – fewer than one-third of all those delivered during his stay. His square drive at 276 went to the boundary but Lara was apparently still unconvinced of his partner's staying power and renewed the attack. A glorious drive off Warne was followed by an ugly and ungainly one-day heave at McGrath in the next over. This was in turn followed by a superb bouncer from round the wicket which struck the batsman on the helmet. At 291-8 Ambrose poked a ball between the gullies for four and the target was down to 13 with McGrath on his knees at the injustice of it all.

Then at 301-8, and just seven needed, the pivotal moment arrived. One more mighty effort from Gillespie saw the ball spear across Lara, take the edge and head straight for Shane Warne at first slip. Wicket-keeper Healy, already labouring with sore calf muscles, forgot himself, dived to his left and grounded the winning chance. Next ball, clearly disturbed by what had almost transpired, Lara took a single and left Ambrose to face four balls. Trying to emulate his earlier steer through the gully he put it straight into the hands of Elliott. Drama heaped upon drama and with six to win and last man in it could scarcely be closer.

Down the steps came Courtney Walsh, apparently cool as a cucumber, adjusting his eyes to the light – bowling legend and batting leg-end with three balls of Gillespie's over to face. He survived, as any true West Indian knew he would, and an extra brought the target down to five with McGrath to bowl to Lara. So close, but still the best quick bowler in the world to overcome. A two from the first ball followed by three dot balls and then an unaccountable wide. The fifth ball was pulled to long-leg, Lara scampered the first but, wisely, Walsh was having nothing to do with a run-out now. The scores were level with one ball to face. All the fielders in, McGrath versus Walsh. Tie anyone?

The plan was something half-hittable outside off stump and with this in mind the cover region was left almost unattended. Dreams of glory and lack of skill would do the rest but Courtney was not for tempting even when McGrath hit the perfect spot with the perfect gimmee ball. The most extravagant of all leaves left the captain to deliver the *coup de grace*. "It's never over till that lady sings and the whole crowd is on its feet" were the words drifting from the commentary box above the cacophony. Gillespie was not about to serve it up on a platter but a decent ball was hammered through the covers and the deed was done; cue mayhem. And all that with a hairline fracture of the arm that only came to public notice later.

A quick grab of a stump and a run to the pavilion and within minutes the plaudits were pouring in and out down the overloaded Barbadian telephone and satellite network. And who could blame those reporters, most days consigned to digging deep to find a glimmer of gold in the deepest Test-match gloom and here was a glittering bounty just waiting to be polished.

The *Barbados Daily Nation* opted for a religious note: 'From the cruel crucifixion, to the renowned resurrection, to the astonishing ascension' with the London *Times* slightly more restrained, 'It surpassed everything that even he has done...one of the truly great innings in cricket history.' This was no slow-burner, everyone knew exactly what they had seen – the best of batting in the best of Test matches. Steve Waugh, frightening during but generous after, was in no doubt it was the best match he'd ever played in, while Michael Slater later reflected that "we sat in the dressing room and were stunned by what we had just witnessed". Clive Lloyd, team manager and not one for hyperbole, said:

> "It is the stuff of genius. You dream of watching innings like those. I did not think you could

> see better than his double hundred in Jamaica, but this was the crowning glory. To bat like that with guys of lesser stature, to nurse them along and win a Test match in the way he did, proves how great he is. I will remember this for the rest of my life."

Back in Australia, Malcolm Knox in the *Sydney Morning Herald* was dumbfounded but realistic: "This gut-twisting, eyeball-popping match was a laboratory of emotion. Words cannot do justice to it." True enough.

Australia

MJ Slater	c Lara b Ambrose	23
MTG Elliott	c †Jacobs b Walsh	9
JL Langer	b Hooper	51
ME Waugh	b Ambrose	0
SR Waugh*	lbw b Perry	199
RT Ponting	c Hooper b Perry	104
IA Healy†	lbw b Walsh	0
SK Warne	c Lara b Perry	13
JN Gillespie	not out	23
SCG MacGill	run out (Ambrose)	17
GD McGrath	c Joseph b Hooper	3
Extras (b4, lb10, nb34)		**48**
Total (all out; 153.4 overs; 648 mins)		**490**

Fall of wickets 1/31 2/36 3/36 4/144 5/425 6/427 7/429 8/446 9/483

Bowling	**O**	**M**	**R**	**W**
CEL Ambrose	31.3	7	93	2
CA Walsh	38	8	121	2
NO Perry	33	5	102	3
PT Collins	35.3	7	110	0
CL Hooper	15.4	4	50	2

MTG Elliott	c †Jacobs b Walsh	0
MJ Slater	run out (Campbell)	26
JL Langer	lbw b Ambrose	1
JN Gillespie	b Ambrose	14
ME Waugh	lbw b Walsh	3
SR Waugh*	b Collins	11
RT Ponting	c Griffith b Walsh	22
IA Healy†	c †Jacobs b Collins	3
SK Warne	lbw b Walsh	32
SCG MacGill	c Campbell b Walsh	1
GD McGrath	not out	8
Extras (lb5, w1, nb19)		**25**
Total (all out; 50.1 overs; 251 mins)		**146**

Fall of wickets 1/0 2/12 3/35 4/46 5/48 6/73 7/81 8/134 9/137

Bowling	**O**	**M**	**R**	**W**
CA Walsh	17.1	3	39	5
CEL Ambrose	20	2	60	2
PT Collins	9	0	31	2
NO Perry	4	0	11	0

West Indies

SL Campbell	c SR Waugh b Gillespie	105
AFG Griffith	run out (Ponting)	0
DRE Joseph	lbw b McGrath	26
PT Collins	lbw b McGrath	0
BC Lara*	c †Healy b Gillespie	8
CL Hooper	c Warne b McGrath	25
JC Adams	c M Waugh b McGrath	0
RD Jacobs†	c ME Waugh b Ponting	68
NO Perry	lbw b Gillespie	24
CEL Ambrose	not out	28
CA Walsh	c Slater b Warne	12
Extras (b10, lb3, nb20)		**33**
Total (all out; 103.5 overs; 440 mins)		**329**

Fall of wickets 1/1 2/50 3/50 4/64 5/98 6/98 7/251 8/265 9/291

Bowling	**O**	**M**	**R**	**W**
GD McGrath	33	5	128	4
JN Gillespie	28	14	48	3
SK Warne	15.5	2	70	1
SCG MacGill	20	5	47	0
RT Ponting	4	1	12	1
ME Waugh	3	0	11	0

SL Campbell	lbw b McGrath	33
AFG Griffith	lbw b Gillespie	35
DRE Joseph	lbw b MacGill	1
PT Collins	lbw b McGrath	0
BC Lara*	not out	153
CL Hooper	c †Healy b Gillespie	6
JC Adams	b McGrath	38
RD Jacobs†	lbw b McGrath	5
NO Perry	lbw b McGrath	0
CEL Ambrose	c Elliott b Gillespie	12
CA Walsh	not out	0
Extras (b8, lb13, w2, nb5)		**28**
Total (9 wickets; 120.1 overs; 525 mins)		**311**

Fall of wickets 1/72 2/77 3/78 4/91 5/105 6/238 7/248 8/248 9/302

Bowling	**O**	**M**	**R**	**W**
GD McGrath	44	13	92	5
JN Gillespie	26.1	8	62	3
SK Warne	24	4	69	0
SCG MacGill	21	6	48	1
ME Waugh	5	0	19	0

Graham Gooch – 154*

England v West Indies, Leeds 6-10 June 1991

-Derek Pringle-

John Woodcock, the esteemed cricket correspondent of the *Times*, called it 'the finest innings by an England captain since the Second World War.' *Wisden Almanack* reckoned it was as 'fine a captain's innings as there has ever been' and that 'no praise was too lavish.' True to form, Graham Gooch, the man who played the innings considered here to be the greatest in Test history, was more prosaic in his assessment. Stroking his stubbled chin, Gooch recalled that it was the only time he had been offered the light against the West Indies' fast bowlers and turned it down. "It was a rare event to get on top of that pace attack but I wasn't going to let them have a breather while we were in front", he said, eyes brightening at the memory of his seven-and-a-half hour unbeaten 154 that is both his and Test cricket's magnum opus.

Gooch played countless great innings for England and Essex but this one stands so proud that even this disarmingly modest man believes it to be his finest. "In the context of the game and the opposition it was my best innings", he said recently when interviewed for this piece.

> "With their four fast bowlers we were under the cosh for long periods, something we had been ever since I started playing Test cricket against the West Indies in the late 1970s. I'd seen batsmen I admired like Geoff Boycott and Dennis Amiss battle hard against the West Indies with little to show for it. We had waited a very long time to beat them on home soil, which made that innings all the more satisfying for me both as a batsman and a captain."

The West Indies' fast bowlers of the 1980s and '90s bestrode world cricket like colossi, their strike power ensuring their team's pre-eminent position during that era. Their phenomenal record between June 1980 and April 1995, of 20 Test series won, nine drawn and none lost, was achieved on the back of aggressive batting and a bowling attack few opponents were able to dominate long enough to fashion a winning position. In that period they lost the odd match but never a series though Gooch's England team, away in 1990 and home in 1991, ran them closer than most.

The Test match at Headingley was one they lost but only because of Gooch's monumental achievement in England's second innings where he carried his bat, something only Len Hutton had managed previously for England in a home Test. Three other Englishmen had achieved the feat including Geoffrey Boycott, Gooch's one-time partner, but none had contributed such a high proportion of the side's total, Gooch's 154 being a whopping 61.11 per cent. Indeed, out of England's second innings total of 252, only two other batsmen, Mark Ramprakash and myself, reached double figures.

Many innings accorded legendary status have freakish tendencies played on the back of adrenalin rushes or extraordinary alignments of the senses, but not this one. Gooch's monolithic effort was a concrete slab of intractability, requiring deep reserves of concentration and more watchful defence than cavalier attack, though nonetheless compelling for it.

One of the first players to work hard on his fitness outside the normal demands of practice and nets, Gooch believed that good physical health improved his concentration. For him, this enabled his batting in two ways. Firstly, it allowed him to minimise the errors crucial to long innings and secondly, it meant he was ready to pounce on the few bad balls bowled by the West Indies' bowlers.

"There were not many four balls floating around against them in those days,", said Gooch recently.

> "I had noticed how Sunil Gavaskar never seemed to miss out on a bad ball when it came his way, so I worked on making sure I did the same. The best way to describe it is that I learnt to shut out all the white noise that comes with big sporting events and just learnt to focus on the bowler. Just me and him, a ball at a time – ready for six leaves outside off stump or six scoring shots should the opportunity arise."

The West Indies' attack at Headingley comprised Malcolm Marshall, Curtly Ambrose, Courtney Walsh and Patrick Patterson, a formidable quartet in a long line of superb, athletic fast bowlers stretching back to the mid-1970s when Andy Roberts led their deployment of pace as an intimidatory force.

The main trident for that first Test, Marshall, Ambrose and Walsh, are now recognised as three of the finest fast bowlers in history while Patterson was, during his pomp, one of the quickest. Indeed Patterson, a strapping Jamaican, had made his Test debut against England in front of his home crowd at Sabina Park in 1986, on a fast pitch with uneven bounce. Gooch faced him wearing his usual grille-free helmet, claiming it to be the only time in his career, due to the unpredictable nature of the surface and the sheer speed generated by Patterson, where he might get struck in the face and not to be able to do anything about it.

Reputation wise, Patterson was the weak link in that quartet but one thing they all had in common was the belief that few sides could withstand them if they bowled anywhere close to potential. In addition to that self-belief, all four had good experience of English conditions – Marshall with Hampshire, Ambrose with Northamptonshire, Walsh with Gloucestershire and Patterson with Lancashire. Combined, though, they had a quality and collective menace that hindered the digestion of breakfast for those about to face them.

Having played his first internationals against the West Indies in 1976 (three one-day matches), Gooch had battled their fast bowlers on many occasions. Most who faced them struggled for success but Gooch averaged just over 41 against them with four hundreds, prior to Headingley. As someone whose batting stance was upright, with bat held aloft rather than tapped by the feet, Gooch was always more comfortable when the ball was thigh level and above rather than at his shins – in other words where the Ambroses and Walshes tended to bowl it as opposed to the Terry Aldermans.

The conditions at Headingley compounded the theory. Keith Boyce, the Yorkshire CCC groundsman, pronounced it the best Test pitch he had produced though as Gooch said at the time: "He says that every year." The reality, given the Test took place in early June, was of a slow surface that offered regular seam movement under the slate-grey cloud which, with rain never far away, clung to the ground for most of the match. These were conditions that demanded vigilance and more front-foot play than back, which was not Gooch's forte. Add to that the fact that his Test average at the ground was a less than eye-catching 20 to that point, and the portents for a big score were not promising.

Where Gooch did score was in knowing what to expect. Playing high quality fast bowling requires courage and that is generated entirely from the mind. Skill and the ability to pick up the ball help but without bravery they rarely reveal themselves when the bowling reaches the 90mph mark. Gooch had all three though when people used to ask him why he seemed so adept at facing fast bowling he was typically modest: "Nobody likes facing it – it's just that some are better at playing it than others."

With helmets, gloves and armguards still fallible compared to today's gear, any engagement with the West Indies was more gladiatorial than bucolic, the romantic image of cricket. Eyeing a young England team with three debutants, Graeme Hick, Mark Ramprakash and Steve Watkin and missing Ian Botham (injured with a pulled hamstring) and David Gower (not showing enough form in county cricket), Vivian Richards, the West Indies captain, was quick to probe for brittleness, something he began at the toss.

Having won it, Richards did not tell Gooch immediately what he might do. Instead, about 15 minutes before the start of play, he popped his head around the dressing-room door, and informed England and their skipper that they could have first knock. That right has been changed with Law 12.5 now stating: 'As soon as the toss is completed, the captain of the side winning the toss shall notify the opposing captain and the umpires of his decision to bat or to field. Once notified, the decision cannot be changed.' Back then the delayed decision kept England's batsmen on tenterhooks and Mike Atherton recalls sitting there unsure whether to focus his nervous energy on facing the new ball or trying to catch it at slip. As Richards knew only too well, while the reality of facing his bowlers was always daunting, not knowing when you might do so created even bigger demons.

There was also the added drama for Gooch, as captain, of Chris Lewis pulling out just before the toss with a migraine, something the allrounder had done before. That meant a debut for Watkin, Lewis' equivalent as a bowler but a rank tailender with the bat – a change that placed even greater pressure on the top order to perform.

England had failed to reach 200 in two of their previous four innings against the West Indies and they failed again in their first innings after making 198. Robin Smith top-scored with 54 while Gooch made 34, falling to his old nemesis Malcolm Marshall. The innings did, however, provide useful pointers to how runs might be eked out the next time around and also how England might best bowl at their opponents.

When the West Indies batted, the discipline required to counter accurate seam bowling on a responsive surface was not much in evidence and they missed the experience of Gordon Greenidge who had retired a few months earlier. With conditions forcing batsmen to adapt, only the best prospered as Richards proved when he top-scored with 73, though even he needed a life which he got when Allan Lamb dropped him at first slip just before close of play on the first evening.

With Philip DeFreitas taking 4-34 in a fine display of seam bowling and with the unexpected bonus of two run-outs, one a brilliant piece of athletic fielding by Ramprakash, England took an unexpected first innings lead of 25 runs.

Reasoning that any target over 200 would be challenging for the West Indies, providing the pitch stayed in character, Gooch gave a short dressing-room address. With time not really an issue he stressed that wickets should be sold dear. There was even talk of running byes to Jeffrey Dujon, the West Indies wicket-keeper, whenever he was forced to make a diving stop, so far back was he standing to Ambrose and Patterson. But otherwise the mantra was: "Don't give it away."

The new ball, taken by Ambrose and Patterson, was also crucial. See it off with minimal damage and 200 would be almost a formality. Ambrose, with his towering arm had other plans though and in an awesome display of accurate fast bowling whipped out Atherton, Hick and Lamb, the latter for a first-ball duck, to leave England reeling on 38-3.

For the first few days of the match, the weather had been chilly and miserable with Saturday reported as being the coldest day's Test cricket for 26 years. With Gooch wearing both a tee-shirt, as an undervest, and a long-sleeve sweater to keep out the brisk nor'easter while he batted, one of the theories being expounded was that Marshall and co. could not get warm enough to operate at full tilt. But if there was any substance to it, Ambrose managed to scotch it in the second innings when he managed to raise the temperature of the match single-handedly.

Watching the wickets tumble, and with it England's chances of setting the West Indies a competitive target, Gooch could easily have been panicked into chancing his arm before he ran out of partners. Instead, he did not waver from his plan of lengthy occupation, placing his faith in someone staying with him long enough to see it to fruition.

His first ally was the 21-year-old Ramprakash, a precocious batting talent with an emphasis on craft. He had scored 27 in the first innings and fielded brilliantly, taking a superb catch and running out Richie Richardson with a direct hit. Feeling you have contributed to the team cause does wonders for self-belief and he kept Gooch company for the next 142 minutes of rain-interrupted play to add 78 vital runs for the fourth wicket.

"I just hung in there but Goochy was a revelation in the way that he played on a tricky pitch against those fast bowlers", said Ramprakash, who made 27 for the second time in the match.

> "The way he was fighting and gutsing it out, playing and missing then producing a thundering pull for four, showed me how important it was to try to put away the bad ball. The pressure was intense despite the three interruptions we had for rain. During those breaks I remember Goochie putting his helmet down in the dressing-room, almost reverentially, and then sitting back with his eyes shut, drained from the concentration."

Their stand galvanised the dressing-room. Against an attack of that eminence a ball with your name on it was likely to be produced at any time, but there was the growing feeling that Gooch was in control and just needed support. Unhappily, for England and their fans, Ramprakash's dismissal was immediately followed by that of Robin Smith, top-scorer in the first innings, for a first-ball duck to Ambrose. Jack Russell fell soon afterwards to leave England 124-6, the lanky Antiguan having taken all six wickets to fall.

At that point I joined the fray and remember Gooch simplifying things for me during our chats between overs. "Don't look beyond the end of the over. Leave anything you can and play only that which you have to. And keep going", was the encouragement he delivered, and repeated like a stuck record, in that high, keening monotone of his.

Having played with Gooch at Essex for 14 years I was already full of admiration for him. But it swelled that day and the next, the first time Test cricket had been played on a Sunday, as we compiled our 98-run stand – him with authority and the odd play and miss, me through grim defence, a lot of luck and the odd stroke into a gap.

One factor that Gooch admitted to spurring him on was the captaincy. "It is the greatest honour being asked to lead your country", he once told me. "The flag, the sweater, the cap, it has always turned me on to play for them. Being in charge took it to another level, which brought out the best in me as a batsman."

He was at the limits of that excellence here, though that is how he liked it. Robin Smith once told me that the thing he most admired about Gooch was that the tougher the challenge the more he seemed to relish it. On a technical matter, Smith also pointed out how Gooch never followed the ball when it seamed or became even slightly agitated when it beat his bat, which was just as well given the amount of playing and missing batsmen on both sides had to endure during this match.

It is important to remind people that Gooch's innings was no carve and clout fest of the kind Ian Botham had so thrillingly delivered against Australia on the same ground a decade earlier. Then, England looked down and out only to be revived by one of sport's biggest extroverts chancing his arm albeit with great verve. Although Gooch's determination to succeed was as great as Botham's, the latter only ever saw an upside. Gooch, though, was an introvert who viewed situations from two angles – pitfall and opportunity. England had not beaten the West Indies in a home Test since 1969 (also at Headingley) and were not expected to win this one before the start, though the expectation of an upset rose with every minute Gooch remained at the crease. To that end it was a grim-faced and pragmatic innings that drew more on self-control than flashes of inspiration, though it possessed a noble majesty all of its own. Grinding out each run meant one more for their opponents to make, something Gooch took as his template until he ran out of partners.

Later, when time had afforded some perspective, Gooch said that he doubted that he had timed eight shots perfectly in seven-and-a-half hours, which showed just how well he must have battled despondency as well as the bowling. "There were", he later admitted, "not many red blotches near the sweet spot of my bat." The innings was so nearly stillborn too, with Gooch almost holing out to his first ball after a miscued drive off Patterson. Had Marshall, who was fielding at mid-off at the time, been two yards closer or less keen on preserving a tight hamstring, then Test cricket's greatest batting feat might never have been.

Marshall was not at his very best with the ball in the second innings but his presence still acted as extra motivation for Gooch who rated him more highly than any other he had faced during his long career. "It gave me something extra facing Malcolm given my respect for him as a bowler", he admitted. "Like a little side bet."

There was another moment, before he had reached his hundred, when the West Indies felt they had got him caught behind after Walsh had cut him in half with one that jagged back sharply off the seam. Certainly, bowler, wicket-keeper and the slips all felt the ball had taken Gooch's inside edge but the umpire, Dicky Bird, remained unmoved. "I like the umpire to make the decision, but I'm certain I didn't get a touch." The West Indies were less convinced and several players did not applaud when he reached his hundred.

Below form or not, it was Marshall that made the breakthrough, having me caught behind after 142 minutes and although the last three batsmen only managed seven runs between them the score rose from 222 to 252, adding an invaluable 30 runs to the target. The last man, Devon Malcolm, faced only 11 balls in his half-hour stay before finally succumbing and leaving his captain unconquered on 154.

As captain, Gooch could not dwell on his incredible achievement despite Robin Marlar having described its value as 'beyond rubies' in the *Sunday Times*. Requiring 278 to win, the West Indies still needed to be bowled out a second time.

Nothing can ever be taken for granted in a team that contains batsmen like Richards, Richardson and Desmond Haynes, but buoyed by the discipline of Gooch's innings, England's seam bowlers, led once more by another four-wicket haul from DeFreitas, niggled away to dismiss them for 162 to record a famous 115-run victory.

In a rare moment of largesse, the Test and County Cricket Board offered England's triumphant players the opportunity to stay another night in the team hotel to celebrate the win. Back then, county cricket was given equal priority and Gooch headed home to see his family and prepare for Essex's semi-final against Worcestershire in the Benson and Hedges Cup scheduled less than 36 hours later. For those who stayed to sample the delights of Leeds on a Monday night (very limited in 1991), the toasts were few. One was to a rare win over the best cricket team of the era, the other to an extraordinary Test match innings which only now is getting the recognition it deserves as the finest ever played.

England

Batsman	Dismissal	Runs
GA Gooch*	c †Dujon b Marshall	34
MA Atherton	b Patterson	2
GA Hick	c †Dujon b Walsh	6
AJ Lamb	c Hooper b Marshall	11
MR Ramprakash	c Hooper b Marshall	27
RA Smith	run out	54
RC Russell†	lbw b Patterson	5
DR Pringle	c Logie b Patterson	16
PAJ DeFreitas	c Simmons b Ambrose	15
SL Watkin	b Ambrose	2
DE Malcolm	not out	5
Extras (lb5, w2, nb14)		**21**
Total (all out; 79.2 overs)		**198**

Fall of wickets 1/13 2/45 3/45 4/64 5/129 6/149 7/154 8/177 9/181

Bowling	O	M	R	W
CEL Ambrose	26	8	49	2
BP Patterson	26.2	8	67	3
CA Walsh	14	7	31	1
MD Marshall	13	4	46	3

Batsman	Dismissal	Runs
GA Gooch*	not out	154
MA Atherton	c †Dujon b Ambrose	6
GA Hick	b Ambrose	6
AJ Lamb	c Hooper b Ambrose	0
MR Ramprakash	c †Dujon b Ambrose	27
RA Smith	lbw b Ambrose	0
RC Russell†	c †Dujon b Ambrose	4
DR Pringle	c †Dujon b Marshall	27
PAJ DeFreitas	lbw b Walsh	3
SL Watkin	c Hooper b Marshall	0
DE Malcolm	b Marshall	4
Extras (b4, lb9, w1, nb7)		**21**
Total (all out; 106 overs)		**252**

Fall of wickets 1/22 2/38 3/38 4/116 5/116 6/124 7/222 8/236 9/238

Bowling	O	M	R	W
CEL Ambrose	28	6	52	6
BP Patterson	15	1	52	0
MD Marshall	25	4	58	3
CA Walsh	30	5	61	1
CL Hooper	4	1	11	0
IVA Richards	4	1	5	0

West Indies

Batsman	Dismissal	Runs
PV Simmons	c Ramprakash b DeFreitas	38
DL Haynes	c †Russell b Watkin	7
RB Richardson	run out	29
CL Hooper	run out	0
IVA Richards*	c Lamb b Pringle	73
AL Logie	c Lamb b DeFreitas	6
PJL Dujon†	c Ramprakash b Watkin	6
MD Marshall	c Hick b Pringle	0
CEL Ambrose	c Hick b DeFreitas	0
CA Walsh	c Gooch b DeFreitas	3
BP Patterson	not out	5
Extras (lb1, nb5)		**6**
Total (all out; 54.1 overs)		**173**

Fall of wickets 1/36 2/54 3/58 4/102 5/139 6/156 7/160 8/165 9/167

Bowling	O	M	R	W
DE Malcolm	14	0	69	0
PAJ DeFreitas	17.1	5	34	4
SL Watkin	14	2	55	2
DR Pringle	9	3	14	2

Batsman	Dismissal	Runs
PV Simmons	b DeFreitas	0
DL Haynes	c Smith b Pringle	19
RB Richardson	c Lamb b DeFreitas	68
CL Hooper	c Lamb b Watkin	5
IVA Richards*	c Gooch b Watkin	3
AL Logie	c Gooch b Watkin	3
PJL Dujon†	lbw b DeFreitas	33
MD Marshall	lbw b Pringle	1
CEL Ambrose	c Pringle b DeFreitas	14
CA Walsh	c Atherton b Malcolm	9
BP Patterson	not out	0
Extras (lb1, nb6)		**7**
Total (all out; 56.4 overs)		**162**

Fall of wickets 1/0 2/61 3/77 4/85 5/88 6/136 7/137 8/139 9/162

Bowling	O	M	R	W
DE Malcolm	6.4	0	26	1
PAJ DeFreitas	21	4	59	4
SL Watkin	7	0	38	3
DR Pringle	22	6	38	2

Statistical Summary

Countries

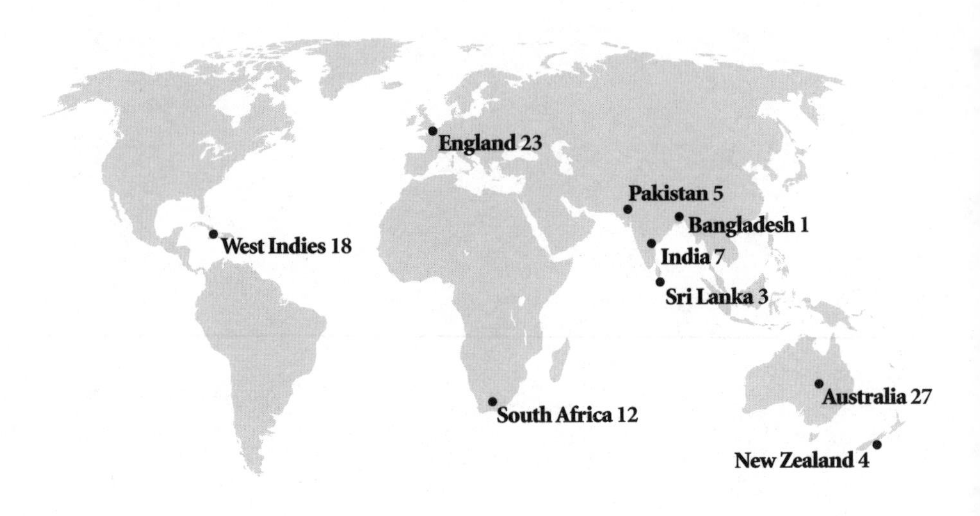

Batting Positions

1 – 23
2 – 16
3 – 13
4 – 20
5 – 15
6 – 5
7 – 6
8 – 1
9 – 1

Innings

1st 39
2nd 26
3rd 23
4th 12

Two in a Match

Sobers & Milburn
Walters & Redpath
Anwar & Mahmood
Kallis & Kallis

Eras of Equal Test Matches Played

1877-1952 – 18
1952-1971 – 12
1971-1985 – 20
1985-1997 – 12
1997-2004 – 18
2004-2012 – 20

Players With More Than One Innings

Bradman 5
Lara 5
Gooch 4
Greenidge 4
Pietersen 3
Sehwag 3
Anwar 2
Botham 2
Butcher 2
Harvey 2
Kallis 2
Richards 2
Sobers 2
Sutcliffe 2
Walters 2
Waugh S 2
Chappell G 2
Clarke 2
Edgar 2

Top/Bottom in Categories

Speed – Jessop 76=/Edgar 46= , Hutton 86
Percentage – Slater 27/Dev 82=
Size – Bradman 60/Kirsten 21, Greenidge 44, Hughes 45
Match Impact – Lara 2/Pietersen 40
Series Impact – Sutcliffe 10/Ashraful 58, Lara 59, Butcher 5, Jessop 76=
Chances – Multiple/Jessop 76=
Conditions – Walters 17=/Amla 62=
Attack – Hughes 45/Sutcliffe 48
Intangibles – Lara 2, Sobers 42/Multiple
Compatibility – Multiple/Multiple

Grounds

Melbourne 10
Lord's 8
Leeds 7
Sydney 7
Auckland 6
Kingston 5
The Oval 4
Adelaide 4
Durban 4
Cape Town 3
Kolkata 3
Christchurch 3
Chennai 3
Bridgetown 2
Faisalabad 2
Birmingham 2
Galle 2
Mumbai Wankhede 2
Perth 2
Nottingham 2
Johannesburg Old W 2
Manchester 2
Port Elizabeth 2
Hobart
Johannesburg New W
Mumbai Brabourne
Karachi
Chittagong
Centurion
Brisbane
Georgetown
Wellington
Delhi
Kandy
Bangalore
Port of Spain

Authors – Innings 100-26

100. Sachin Tendulkar – *Dave Wilson*
99. Ricky Ponting – *Rodney Ulyate*
98. Kumar Sangakkara – *Dave Wilson*
97. Dudley Nourse – *Sean Ehlers*
96. Stan McCabe – *Martin Chandler*
95. Walter Hammond – *Rodney Ulyate*
94. Kamran Akmal – *Martin Chandler*
93. Graham Gooch – *David Taylor*
92. Azhar Mahmood – *Patrick Ferriday*
91. Greg Chappell – *Sean Ehlers*
90. Frank Worrell – *Martin Chandler*
89. Chris Gayle – *Rodney Ulyate*
88. David Boon – *Martin Chandler*
87. Graeme Pollock – *Martin Chandler*
86. Len Hutton – *Patrick Ferriday*
85. Bob Barber – *Patrick Ferriday*
82=. Viv Richards – *Dave Wilson*
82=. Kapil Dev – *Gareth Bland*
82=. Bruce Edgar – *Patrick Ferriday*
81. Michael Clarke – *David Mutton*
80. Warwick Armstrong – *Patrick Ferriday*
78=. Darryl Cullinan – *Patrick Ferriday*
78=. Damien Martyn – *Sean Ehlers*
76=. Colin Milburn – *Dave Wilson*
76=. Gilbert Jessop – *Dave Wilson*
75. Percy Sherwell – *Patrick Ferriday*
74. Don Bradman – *Rodney Ulyate*
73. Sunil Gavaskar – *Andy Baynton-Power*
72. Seymour Nurse – *Patrick Ferriday*
71. Jacques Kallis – *Patrick Ferriday*
70. Greg Chappell – *Sean Ehlers*
69. Glenn Turner – *Martin Chandler*
68. Brian Lara – *Dave Wilson*
67. Saeed Anwar – *Patrick Ferriday*
66. Herschelle Gibbs – *Rodney Ulyate*
65. Graham Gooch – *Dave Wilson*
64. Alan Steel – *Sean Ehlers*
62=. Steve Waugh – *James Mettyear*
62=. Hashim Amla – *David Mutton*
61. Kevin Pietersen – *James Mettyear*
60. Don Bradman – *Sean Ehlers*
59. Brian Lara – *Dave Wilson*
58. Mohammad Ashraful – *Dave Wilson*
57. Sanath Jayasuriya – *Andy Baynton-Power*
56. Graham Gooch – *Martin Chandler*
55. Mark Butcher – *Martin Chandler*
54. Roy Fredericks – *Sean Ehlers*
53. Virender Sehwag – *Dave Wilson*
52. Ian Redpath – *Gareth Bland*
51. Younis Khan – *Gareth Bland*
50. Ian Botham – *Martin Chandler*
49. Don Bradman – *David Taylor*
48. Herbert Sutcliffe – *Sean Ehlers*
46=. Bruce Edgar – *Patrick Ferriday*
46=. Kumar Sangakarra – *Andy Baynton-Power*
45. Kim Hughes – *Sean Ehlers*
44. Gordon Greenidge – *Rodney Ulyate*
43. Jack Brown – *Martin Chandler*
42. Garry Sobers – *Dave Wilson*
41. Lance Klusener – *James Mettyear*
40. Kevin Pietersen – *Dave Wilson*
39. Colin McDonald – *Dave Wilson*
38. Steve Waugh – *Martin Chandler*
37. Clive Lloyd – *Patrick Ferriday*
36. Saeed Anwar – *Patrick Ferriday*
35. Ian Smith – *Dave Wilson*
34. VVS Laxman – *Dave Wilson*
33. Gordon Greenidge – *Dave Wilson*
32. Don Bradman – *Sean Ehlers*
31. Viv Richards – *Martin Chandler*
30. Ian Botham – *James Mettyear*
29. Garry Sobers – *Sean Ehlers*
28. Gordon Greenidge – *Rodney Ulyate*
27. Michael Slater – *Dave Wilson*
26. Mark Waugh – *Sean Ehlers*